GOOD NIGHT, SLEEP TIGHT

The Sleep Lady®'s
Gentle Guide to Helping Your Child
Go to Sleep, Stay Asleep,
and Wake Up Happy

KIM WEST
WITH JOANNE KENEN

cds books

NEW YORK

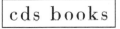

The anecdotes included in this book are based on the real experiences of individuals and families. In all cases, names and identifying characteristics have been changed to protect the privacy of individuals.

The information and advice presented in this book have been reviewed by a qualified pediatrician. It should not, however, substitute for the advice of your family doctor or other trained health care professionals. You are advised to consult with health care professionals with regard to all matters that may require medical attention or diagnosis and to check with a physician before administering or undertaking any course of treatment.

Copyright © 2006 by Kim West and Joanne Kenen

Published by CDS Books

Cataloging-in-Publication data for this book is available from the Library of Congress.

ISBN 13: 978-1-59315-356-4
ISBN 10: 1-59315-356-2

CDS books are available at special discounts for bulk purchases in the U.S. by corporations, institutions, and other organizations. For more information, please contact the Special Markets Department at the Perseus Books Group, 11 Cambridge Center, Cambridge, MA 02142, or call (800) 255-1514 or (617) 252-5298, or email special.markets@perseusbooks.com.

06 07 08 / 10 9 8 7 6 5 4 3 2 1

This book is dedicated to Denise Drake, who helped me expand my vision of my work and encouraged me years ago to become The Sleep Lady.

—KIM WEST

To Ken, Zach, and Ilan, who make my dreams sweet.

—JOANNE KENEN

ACKNOWLEDGMENTS

I want to thank Joanne Kenen for the thousands of hours she put into this book, for hearing and conveying my voice, and for believing in The Sleep Lady program. I couldn't have done this without her expertise, encouragement, and commitment.

Each of the families who have laughed, cried, and celebrated their struggles and progress with me is central to this book. Thank you for letting me into your lives and for allowing me to learn along with you.

My entire family has offered me extraordinary support, endless encouragement, and a willing ear to listen—even when they were tired of hearing about sleep. A special thank-you to my wonderful daughters, who were my first teachers of the gift of sleep and continue to teach me new things to this day.

Finally, thank you to my agent, Gail Ross, and to David Wilk and all of the CDS team who believe in me and my message. Thank you to our editor, Mary Bahr, for her endless patience, time, and enthusiasm for this book.

—KIM WEST

ACKNOWLEDGMENTS

I would like to thank Kim West for sharing her "Sleep Lady" secrets and including me in this book project. In addition, my friends and colleagues—including Deborah Zabarenko, Michael Arkus, Nancy Zuckerbrod, and my mother, Regina Kenen—read and helped me improve sections of this manuscript, as did our editor, Mary Bahr. Sylvia Stein and Andrew Nibley were also great sounding boards. My husband, Ken, and my sons, Zach and Ilan, graciously endured having a book-writing mom in the house. Finally, I want to thank the dozens of moms and dads who found time in their busy lives to share their stories and insights with me. We changed their names to protect privacy, but I hope I remained true to their voices and experiences, and that through them, other parents and children will find their own path to good nights.

—JOANNE KENEN

CONTENTS

FOREWORD

MY FAVORITE PART OF THE TITLE to Kim West and Joanne Kenen's book *Good Night, Sleep Tight: The Sleep Lady's Gentle Guide to Helping Your Child Go to Sleep, Stay Asleep, and Wake Up Happy* is the word *gentle*. The book is gently worded, gentle on the reader's heart, and gentle to implement. For all the parents who have lost countless hours of sleep trying the tough love approach of letting the baby cry it out, this book comes as a wonderful, informative reprieve.

My own son, who is now eighteen years old, had colic as a baby. I nursed him to sleep, and either my husband or I held him all the time. During the first several years of his life I wondered what I was doing wrong. Dr. Richard Ferber had just written *Solve Your Child's Sleep Problems* and I was persuaded to try his cry-it-out approach. My son cried so long and hard the first night that he lost his voice. After a week, he did sleep better but I was wracked with guilt. I wish I had been able to use Kim West's approach back then.

I have been in private pediatric practice for eighteen years, during which time I have noticed that the pace of daily life for most parents has dramatically increased. Not coincidentally, I have seen a marked rise in sleep difficulties in babies and children as the pressures of their parents' busy schedules impact their routine. While there are many books on this issue, most of them take a very firm cry-it-out approach that, in my experience, leaves parents emotionally exhausted and filled with guilt. I have been looking for a definitive how-to book on sleep that I can recommend without reservation. *Good Night, Sleep Tight* is that book—one that will serve as a manual to both parents and medical practitioners.

Good Night, Sleep Tight addresses a wide range of sleep issues for children through age five. Each age-specific chapter provides guidelines for creating a schedule and implementing change, but also invites the parents to tailor the program for their child and their lifestyle. Real-life examples from families helped by Kim West illustrate the program's practical steps and offer encouragement to the reader. And, unlike most authors of books on sleep, Kim West and Joanne Kenen are mothers who share not only their professional expertise but their personal experiences as well.

As a community pediatrician, I give advice about feeding, development, safety, immunization, and behavioral issues at each checkup. Many of the concerns parents want to discuss stem from their child's need for sleep. A parent recently came in with a ten-month-old who was teething, and up all night for nights on end. The mother was fearful that her baby was in severe pain. After a full exam, it was clear that the infant needed a regular sleep schedule. I discussed Kim West's approach and explained why many of the crying spells were related to sleep deprivation. She was relieved to learn how to effectively soothe her baby and delighted to discover that the cry-it-out approach was not her only option. I have sent many families to see Kim West in her private practice and am looking forward to recommending this book to many more.

—FAITH A. HACKETT, M.D.
Fellow of the American Academy of Pediatrics
Courtesy Staff Physician, Johns Hopkins Hospital
Staff Physician, Anne Arundel Medical Center

Part One

INTRODUCTION
Meet the Sleep Lady

OF ALL THE QUESTIONS NEW PARENTS FACE, none is more common than "Does he sleep?" If the baby sleeps well, the answer all too often is "Yes, he's a good baby." By implication, those who don't sleep are bad babies. The mother and father, already overwhelmed by exhaustion, must also deal with feelings that they are failing their first test as parents.

Of course, the millions of babies who don't initially sleep through the night are not moral failures. They are just new little people who have not yet learned to put themselves to sleep. *Learn* is the key word. We all know that the need for sleep is biological but we don't always realize that the ability to sleep is a learned skill. All children can learn it. All parents can teach them. But like everything else in life, some just need a little more help than others.

I'm Kim West, also known as the Sleep Lady, and I have spent a decade providing help to hundreds of weary and bleary families. I won't promise you no tears but I do aim for fewer tears, and I never tell you to just shut the door and let your baby bawl alone in the dark. My gentler method depends on step-by-step changes in bedtime, napping, and overnight routines so that your child can develop sleep independence, go to sleep on his or her own, and sleep more soundly and longer while feeling confident that Mom and Dad will be nearby and responsive. A well-rested baby is usually an easier, less cranky baby. A well-rested mom or dad (in case it feels like it's been so long that you can't remember) is an easier, less cranky parent, able to show the child more joy and love, and less of the irritability and frustration that's inevitable when they are up with him ten times a night.

About ten years ago, my husband, Bill, and I moved to the Annapolis, Maryland, area where I later opened a general therapy practice as a clinical social worker. At the time I had no particular interest or expertise in childhood sleep. But I did have a personal stake in the topic. I need a fair amount of good, solid, uninterrupted sleep myself, and as Bill and I began to think about having children, I began to worry. I saw my friends start families and lose sleep. I saw the rings under their eyes, heard the strain in their voices, witnessed the brittle irritation with their spouses. Sometimes it seemed like their only topic of conversation was what a bad night they'd just had, and I could discern a growing sense of guilt and anxiety on their part. Convinced that there had to be a better way, I began to research everything available to me about the physiology and psychology of pediatric sleep. I began to interweave what I was learning about sleep cycles, arousal states, and the physical need for sleep with what I already knew about child development and behavioral psychology, especially the need for parental consistency as we try to teach and mold our children's behaviors.

When my own two daughters were born, neither were "angel babies" who just drifted off into peaceful slumber. The second one, in particular, was fussy and had reflux, putting my theories to the test. Still, I had Carleigh sleeping for an eight-hour stretch at night by eight weeks, Gretchen at ten weeks— and, yes, I breastfed both of them. Gradually, I began helping my friends to teach their babies and toddlers to sleep, and then friends of friends. Word spread, and soon I had a growing number of sleepy parents with sleepless babies knocking on my door.

Given how common sleep problems are—up to one in four children under age five—finding practical help is surprisingly difficult. The field of sleep medicine has grown in recent years, but specialists are still relatively few and far between. Not all sleep clinics treat very young children, or they only accept pediatric cases involving breathing disorders such as apnea. You do need to rule out any medical conditions that hamper sleep. Talk to your pediatrician about your baby's sleep problems and feeding patterns, and be sure to mention any digestive difficulties, allergies, noisy breathing, or snoring. But most childhood sleep problems are behavioral, not physical, and some pediatricians receive amazingly little training about sleep, often only an hour or two during their residency. You may find that even caring and competent doctors might not have much to offer regarding behavioral sleep problems. That leaves many parents with the mistaken notion that they have no alternative to enduring sleep deprivation indefinitely, that they just have to wait and hope that the child somehow, someday, outgrows it on his or her own.

To the extent that you do get advice, whether from doctors or well-meaning friends or relatives, it usually falls into one of two categories. On one hand are the variants of "crying it out." On the other are the "attachment theorists" who promote co-sleeping and nursing on demand well past the early months of infancy. Either of those approaches is fine—*if* they feel right for you and right for your kids. They aren't fine if they don't feel right, if they strain your marriage, if they don't fit into your adult needs—or if they don't help your child learn to put himself to sleep and stay asleep.

The most common advice is to let your children cry it out, an approach popularized since the mid-1980s by Dr. Richard Ferber, the famed Boston Children's Hospital sleep expert. Simply put, "Ferberizing" means leaving a baby to cry, but having a parent go in to briefly check on the child at regular but less and less frequent intervals. The theory is that if a child can learn to fall asleep on his own, without being rocked, nursed, stroked, or serenaded, he will be able to go back to sleep on his own during the frequent but brief awakenings that everyone experiences, awakenings that a good sleeper doesn't even remember by morning. An even starker method, promoted by Dr. Marc Weissbluth of Northwestern University's Feinberg School of Medicine and known as *extinction*, has the child cry it out as long as it takes without Ferber's frequent parental checks. Research has shown that, while neither approach works all the time, both do have respectable success rates—if parents can turn off their ears and heartstrings long enough to tolerate the screams. Anecdotally, I know that many families who use Ferber or Weissbluth may find it improves their children's sleep—but they absolutely dread the process. (In one case the husband was the enforcer, letting the kids cry at bedtime while the more tender-hearted wife drove around in fierce New England snowstorms until she knew it was safe to come home.)

My Sleep Lady approach is a gentler alternative for families who emotionally or philosophically resist letting their babies cry it out; for families who tried Ferber and it didn't work; and for families who let their child cry it out when she was three or four months old but found it didn't help later. I have also worked with families who believe in co-sleeping but find that their children aren't really sleeping all that well, even nestled snugly with Mom and Dad. And I've helped guide many families who did co-sleep for a few months or a few years but now want the family bed to revert to a marital one.

Much of my work is with babies aged six to eighteen months whose pediatricians agree should be able to sleep through the night. I also run Right Start workshops for pregnant couples or families with newborns, including many couples whose first child had sleep problems and who want less of an ordeal with the second. But if your child is older, don't worry, it's not too late to improve her sleep, although it may take a little longer to break habits that are more deeply ingrained. I have helped numerous toddlers, many sets of twins, and more than a smattering of school-age children. This book contains age-specific advice for the first five years, and I'll give you a glimpse into the sleep challenges ahead in the school years. Even if your child is basically a sound sleeper, you might turn to this book periodically as she enters new developmental stages requiring some minor sleep adjustments. You might need advice, for instance, on how to help her consolidate two naps into one, or on when to move her from the crib to a bed. A child may need a little sleep help as he copes with big changes in life, like the start of preschool, Mom's return to work, or the birth of a baby brother or sister.

A WORD ABOUT ATTACHMENT PARENTING

Because so many of the families I work with tell me they have been influenced by *attachment parenting* or *attachment theory*, it's worth spending a moment discussing this child-rearing trend and thinking about how best to define and achieve a *secure attachment*. I too believe in promoting secure attachment between parents and children; it's a cornerstone of emotional health. But parents, particularly inexperienced new parents, often misconstrue what a secure attachment means, and how we should encourage it in our children. I also think some of the popular child-rearing and parenting books, even if they have some insights and useful nuggets on how to be loving and effective parents, add to the confusion, particularly regarding co-sleeping and how much we should rely on nursing to soothe our babies. Instead of teaching confident parenting, I find they often promote even more insecurity, second-guessing, and guilt.

Attachment theory is not new. Mary D. S. Ainsworth, a psychologist who conducted pioneering research on infant attachment in the 1950s, coined the term *secure base*. More recently John Bowlby—the famed child psychiatrist and author of the classic works *Attachment*, *Separation*, and *Loss* who collaborated with Ainsworth and built on her work—restated the parents' role in forming a secure attachment. He says the parents must be "available, ready to respond when called upon to encourage and perhaps assist, but to intervene actively only when clearly necessary" (*A Secure Base: Parent-Child Attachment and Healthy Human Development* [1988, Basic Books]). He even likens parents to military commanders who know when their expeditionary force, the child, is ready to go out and fulfill its mission, knowing it can return to a secure military base (the parents). We may not want to think of our infants as little combatants, but the analogy is useful. We want them to venture out on their own. We don't want them to stray so far that they get lost or panicked or are at risk in any way, but we do want them to crawl, toddle, or stride away from us to try out a new toy at playgroup, or to chase a butterfly in the park. We don't have to go get the new toy for them; we don't have to force them to be curious. We want them to feel confident in going forth, knowing they can return to us, the secure parental base.

My friend and colleague Peter Grube, a psychiatric social worker who does play and talk therapy with children, likes to give this example of a child at a mall.

> *Mom, Dad, and a four-year-old are shopping. Spotting something that sparks his curiosity, the child moves away from the parents, looking back after every few steps to ensure that the parents are still near. After each peek back, the child becomes a little bolder and explores more. Then a crowd of shoppers gets between the child and the parents, and the interesting environment now feels like a dangerous one for the youngster (although the parents, for safety's sake, always keep the child in their sight). The child cries and runs to Mom and Dad. The parents pick up the child. The child feels safe again. After a few minutes with Mom and Dad, the child wants down. He feels adventurous again. The child begins to slowly wander away again, investigating and exploring. This is what a healthy attachment looks like—the child feels secure, knowing that the parents will protect him and keep him safe. Securely attached children want to explore their world. Parents encourage and allow this exploration while still being there to protect and keep their children safe.*

In *A Secure Base*, Bowlby cites studies that found that nursery schoolers "who are most stable emotionally and making the most of their opportunities are those who have parents who, whilst always encouraging their children's autonomy, are nonetheless available and responsive when called upon." In other words, we don't want to tie our children to us, nor do we want to cut them loose. We want to strike that balance between security and support, confidence and freedom. We need to let our children learn to deal with emotions such as frustration, excitement, and anger, and with behaviors such as sleep, to self-regulate. We can't do this all for them, any more than a coach can get out on the field and play for his team.

Families I work with like that coaching analogy. A coach teaches, directs, and supports the players but he doesn't play the game for them, make the goal for them, swim faster for them. Even when the team loses, the coach can give strategies for doing better next time but he still can't play the game for them. It's the same with sleep. We can help our children learn how to fall asleep, but we can't keep doing so much of it for them, not beyond the newborn stage. When they have trouble sleeping, we can empathize, we can reassure, we can guide, we can support—and like the coach we can help them acquire the skills to do it better next time. But then we have to let them do it themselves.

Though some of the writers who have popularized attachment theory may disagree, I think my own sleep coaching methods conform to Bowlby's ideal. My system promotes a secure attachment, a secure base. Aside from those first three months or so when our newborns do need us to create the magic of sleep, we aren't taking over their sleep indefinitely. I advocate letting them explore how to sleep for themselves, but I do not advocate letting them do it all on their own, or just shutting a door and letting them yell and scream. We need to be, in Bowlby's words, "available and responsive," helping them, comforting them, coaching them, reinforcing their confidence that we are right there and that we love them.

Parents also tell me that they are hesitant about providing structure and direction; they are nervous about enforcing rules, or confronting negative behaviors. I often hear a parent say—and I know Grube and other colleagues hear it too—"I don't want my child to feel bad about himself" or "I don't want to crush her spirit" or "I don't want my child to not like me." As Grube noted to me, "Parents want to be loving, but unfortunately the term *loving* is often interpreted as meaning no boundaries for the child or parent." Countless studies tell us that our children do need structure, consistency, and clear boundaries, at bedtime and during the day. Setting limits does not mean that we don't give our children some choices or autonomy. It means giving age-appropriate choices within healthy boundaries. For instance, you might let a young child decide which pajamas he wants to wear to bed, or choose which dolls she wants tucked in with her at night. But you should not let her decide whether to brush her teeth, or what time to go to bed. Alternatively, some

parents go to the other extreme, never letting their children make any decisions for themselves for fear they might make a wrong choice and experience
frustration.

UNDERSTANDING TEARS

Parents often tell me they can't stand hearing their child cry, that they fear
crying will scar a child, or cause emotional damage. I don't like forlorn hysterical babies any more than you do, and I certainly couldn't have let my own
babies wail in the dark. But there is no such thing as a tear-free childhood.
The Sleep Lady system is designed to *minimize frustration and maximize reassurance*. By being present, by offering physical and verbal caresses and reassurances, we reduce the stress on ourselves and on our children, but we won't
eliminate every single tear. However, it's easier for us as parents to tolerate the
tears if we understand that they are a form of communication, and think about
what our children are trying to tell us through their cries.

Through my Sleep Lady system, you will learn when and how to put your
child to bed when he is still awake—drowsy but still awake. That's where the
tears come in. His cries are his way of saying, "Why did you put me down
awake? I don't know how to go to sleep. You're supposed to put me to sleep. I
am tired! What are you doing? Why have you changed things? This is frustrating and *I don't like it one little bit!*" This is where you have to remember
that you are the coach, not the player. You are giving love and support and
comfort and reassurance—being that secure base. But you aren't fixing, rescuing, or doing it all for him. You aren't erasing every scrap of frustration (even if
your heart aches to) at the price of his learning and sleeping. And once you
give him that safe and secure space from which to learn, from which to
explore, sleep isn't all that different from venturing out at that playgroup or
chasing that butterfly. Watch your baby. You will see him work through that
frustration. You will see him discover what helps him go to sleep, what feels
good, what is soothing. You will see him learn to suck his thumb, or rock his
body, or rub a soft blanket against his cheek. Once children gain confidence,
when they know they own this skill, going to sleep isn't so hard anymore, it
isn't so mysterious. And there's no longer a need to cry. By teaching your child
to sleep, you have not damaged him emotionally. You have helped him grow.

*"We thought we were bad parents if he was crying," said Megan,
whose son, Bruce, you will meet in the chapter on nine- to twelve-month-
olds. "We thought crying made him feel alone and abandoned; we thought*

crying was torturing him. But we learned that we were hurting him by not letting him sleep. Sleep was so important to his growth and development. You have to keep telling yourself that over and over again. He needs to sleep; what you are doing is right."

☺ ☺ ☺

Tess, who vividly recalled her own childhood fears and who had slept in her parents' bed until she was eight, was almost phobic about letting Jason cry, even when she was bone-tired and emotionally drained after being up all night with a ten-month-old who nursed every hour or two, and spending all day in the hospital helping her mom get through chemotherapy. When Tess finally decided she was going to have to tolerate some tears, she handed Jason over to her husband, Ron, and went to a hotel. "I told a friend of mine I was convinced I was going to ruin Jason; she told me she knew a lot of messed up people, but she didn't think it was because they had cried when they were ten months old," Tess recalled with a laugh. The next morning, Tess approached her front door with her own tears flowing, convinced that she was going to find emotional wreckage within. Instead, Jason and Ron were happily playing on the living room floor. Jason had done some crying, and he would cry for two more nights—but only two more nights. He was learning to give himself and his parents some badly needed sleep.

Parents often ask me how long their child will cry. The answer is usually a lot less then you expect. However, older toddlers and preschoolers may cry more than young babies simply because their problematic sleep patterns are more ingrained. Exceptionally aware and alert babies, like Ari in Chapter 4, might cry a bit more than other children because they have a harder time shutting out the world so they can sleep. Children whose parents have been inconsistent about sleep may also cry more as you begin sleep coaching. But throughout this book, you will be able to see how more consistent parenting makes life easier both for ourselves and our children.

YOUR CHILD'S SLEEP SUCCESS

When I work with a family, I explore their values, lifestyles, and approach to parenting as I develop an individual sleep plan. I never suggest anything that would make anyone feel like a horrible parent, nor do I believe in miracle cures. Changing sleep patterns can take time, and it definitely takes consistency. Most families solve their bedtime problems within two weeks, even if napping, early rising, and occasional night wakenings take a little longer. Some of the families you will meet in this book experienced extremely rapid improvement. But more often I've chosen to include hard cases, families who faced challenges and setbacks because I wanted this book to illustrate as many scenarios and solutions as possible. Don't be discouraged if it goes slowly, especially if your child is older and has been sleeping poorly for a long time. (My co-author Joanne Kenen's son fell into that second category. A smart little guy who was able to stay remarkably cheerful on far too little sleep, Ilan was actually a difficult case, but with time, patience, and consistency he reached the point where he would go to bed and declare, "I sleep great.")

You will see progress quickly, but give it a few weeks to consolidate the gains, to see the old patterns fade away. Sometimes you'll accomplish 90 percent of your goals in a matter of days, meaning your life should be much more bearable. But it can then take longer for you to get that last 10 percent in place. Be patient and remember that learning a skill—whether sleeping, walking, handling a fork, or using the potty—takes time. Disruptions of routines, including illness, moving, travel, or a parent away on business, can also cause temporary setbacks. If you stick to the routine, your child should absorb those minor shocks and get back to his normal schedule in a reasonable period of time. Eventually, his sleep skills will be so secure that he can take them anywhere— on vacation, to his grandparents' house, later to slumber parties, summer camp, and even off to college.

Before you turn to the chapter on your child's age group, please read the next two chapters where I outline my methods and review a few simple essentials about sleep science that will help you understand and interpret your child's natural rhythms. My system works, and it can work for you. May you enjoy many peaceful nights of sleep ahead!

THE SLEEP LADY SYSTEM

As a loving and responsible parent, I believe we have five essential obligations to our children. We need to take care of their emotional health and their physical health. We need to give them good nutrition and a good education. And we need to make sure they know how to sleep. It's that simple and it's that important.

The Sleep Lady system gives you a framework for understanding your child's sleep and provides tools for modifying her sleep behavior. I give a lot of age-specific and problem-specific advice throughout the book. In this chapter I am going to tell you about features of sleep shaping that apply to most age groups. I always tell parents I need three things from them: patience, a united front, and consistency. We'll address all three of these in this chapter, particularly consistency, a cornerstone of behavioral psychology. I will also give you some practical tips, like installing room-darkening shades if your child wakes up with the sun, or a white noise machine if you have, for instance, a very loud dog. Always, I will encourage you to mix the knowledge you gain with your own parental insights and instincts to develop sleep-enhancing solutions for your children and yourself.

THE SLEEP LADY SHUFFLE

In the first months of life, we concentrate on soothing techniques and establishing some basic rhythms to help babies learn to sleep. From about six months on, a central aspect of my program is the Sleep Lady Shuffle. Think of it as a kind of weaning for sleep. The Shuffle varies subtly from one age to the next, and I'll walk you through it with a lot more detail in the age chapters. To give the child a consistent response, we use the Shuffle at bedtime, for middle-of-the-night wakenings, and, in many cases, for naps too. But briefly the Shuffle goes something like this: you, or your spouse or partner, are going to start out seated by your child's crib or bed, where you can easily comfort and reassure her. Every three days, you are going to move a little farther away, across the room, to the doorway, right out in the hall, but you will still be able to soothe her. Sometimes I advise parents to sleep on a mattress or sleeping bag in the baby's room for a few nights, as a reassuring prelude. Sometimes if a baby is responding very quickly to the changes, I have the parent move through the Shuffle more rapidly. Finally you will be able to leave her alone for five minutes at a time so she can sleep on her own. This sounds like a huge leap for you, but it's not so huge for her. You've given her nearly two weeks of preparation. As you have soothed her less, she's learned to soothe herself more, sucking a finger, twirling her hair, nestling into her blanket, or snuggling up to a teddy bear. You have slowly and gently moved away at bedtime and during the night, while letting her build confidence that you are still nearby and responsive. She has learned "Mommy is there for me even though I can't see her." "Daddy is nearby and loves me." She will be ready to sleep on her own, if you let her. In all probability you will still face some tears during the Shuffle, but generally much less than the hours parents commonly report in the crying-it-out and extinction methods. And usually you are close by and comforting her when she does cry, which is far less stressful for the parents.

PATIENCE

You might be very tired the first few nights you embark on this program because in the short run you might get even less sleep. That's because as you modify your baby's sleep behavior, you are going to have to give up some of the middle-of-the-night crutches known as *negative associations* that may get her back to sleep in the short run but won't prevent her from popping up again in an hour. She may resist the change. The behavior may even get worse before it gets better as she adjusts to new routines, to new positive associations. Try to find some time to nap, or try to get to bed a little earlier than usual. Each morning, give yourself a pep talk and a reminder that it is worth it, that soon you all will be sleeping through the payoff.

A unique aspect of my private practice that parents find extremely helpful is frequent morning telephone calls. We speak every morning for the first five days, and then about every other day for the next two or three weeks. These intensive calls are part fine-tuning and part pep talk. They help a lot during those first draining days when it can be hard to keep perspective, to be patient and consistent, particularly if you've already gone months or years without a decent night's sleep.

As you aren't going to have me on the phone, find a sympathetic soul, a buddy to talk to each morning. A spouse who is also familiar with the Sleep Lady approach. Another mom who has been through it all. Another sleep-starved parent who can be a partner as you go through the program together, critiquing, cheerleading, and supporting one another. You may find that every mom in your playgroup wants to take part! The point of these morning calls is to rehash the previous night, talk about what adjustments you need to make, whether it was great or whether you caved and did something you probably shouldn't have. Parents tell me they feel more accountable and stay on track when they have to report to someone every morning. They also like having someone to commiserate with during the hard parts, and someone with whom to celebrate each bit of progress. You can also share experiences on my community message board at www.sleeplady.com.

UNITED FRONT

Before you decide exactly where you want to go with your child's sleep, take a good look at where you are. Get both parents involved, and, where relevant, other caretakers and grandparents. Parents need to talk about their goals, and make sure they agree. For instance, if Mom wants the child to sleep in the family bed, and Dad wants the baby in his crib, it is just not going to work. Similarly, if a mom's head is telling her that Junior should be in his crib, but her heart still yearns to have that sweet-smelling head of baby curls snuggled up next to her chin at night, it's a problem. Think it through. Talk it through. Discuss how much crying each of you can tolerate, and what your parenting styles are regarding limit-setting and consistency. Think about your child's temperament, history, and ability to self-regulate. What soothes him? What does he do to soothe himself? How can that be incorporated into his bedtime routine? You can't cleanly separate sleep from everything else in life in terms of parenting. If you make a plan and the mom or dad can't follow through together, it won't work and it's unfair to your child.

 CONSISTENCY

One of the most damaging things we can do as parents, whether we are dealing with sleep or other aspects of child rearing, is to be inconsistent. Psychologists call it intermittent reinforcement, and it means that sometimes you give in, and sometimes you don't, giving such a mixed message that a child, particularly a baby or toddler, can't make any sense of it. He can't figure out what behavior he must change and what behavior will be rewarded if he screams, whines, or wheedles enough. *Inconsistently reinforced behavior is the hardest type to modify or extinguish. It takes the longest to change, and it often provokes even more of the tears we are trying to avoid.* This is particularly true if the child is more than a year old. Sometimes it is okay for us as parents to bend rules, make exceptions, give treats. We all do it. But breaking rules hither and thither, responding in different ways all the time is counterproductive, and that's doubly true for sleep.

The obvious example, the one we've all seen and most of us will experience, is the toddler in the supermarket checkout line demanding candy. Usually Mom (or Dad) says no, and the kid stops whining fast—or reasonably fast. But one day, for whatever reason, Mom gives in. Maybe she's tired. Maybe he's making a bigger scene than usual and Mom just wants to spare the other hundred sets of eardrums in the store. Whatever the reason, he smells blood—or at least he smells chocolate. The next time they are in the store, when he asks for candy and Mom says no, he's not going to stop whining. He knows that she gave in once, if he makes enough of a fuss, she may give in again. And he won't really understand if she doesn't. He'll be asking himself, quite legitimately, "How come I can't have the candy now if I had it yesterday? What can I do to get my way?" He's going to try everything he can think of, and it's not going to be pretty.

Now, if it's that hard to deal with lollipops with a well-rested child in a nice bright supermarket, think about how painfully difficult it is to deal with a tired child in the middle of the night who doesn't know how to sleep. Consistency is absolutely crucial. *If you aren't consistent, you aren't just making it harder for yourself. You are making it harder for your child.* If you are trying to move a child out of your bed and into a crib, you need to keep him in the crib every night, not most nights. If you are trying to stop pacing up and down the hallway with him from 3:00 to 4:00 a.m., you need to resist the urge to pace every night, not most nights. He can't understand why you bring him in your bed on Tuesday but you let him scream for ninety minutes on Thursday, or why you won't take him to your bed at 1:00 but are too wiped out to resist at 4:00. *Babies can't tell time!* He's going to cry, his way of saying, "Hey, what's going on here? It's late and I'm tired and I need to go back to sleep and why can't I get into your bed now when you let me yesterday?" The best way to minimize, and then eliminate, the bedtime tears is to have a consistent plan. Decide on a response to his awakenings and then stick with it. You'll get some tears at first but remember, you don't have to turn your back on those tears. Soothe him, help him, show and tell him that you love him and the tears will stop. Children actually crave that consistency; it reassures them, helps them feel safe and sound. It is the key to success.

> *Ellen, the mother of two, knew that it wasn't going to be easy to follow the Sleep Lady advice in the middle of the night. She was soft-hearted and didn't like tears—and she was just so very, very, very tired. Sometimes it was so tempting to just give in and let James have one more bottle or let him snuggle in her bed. But Ellen knew she had to be consistent or she was going to be exhausted for the long haul—and her kids would end up with more of the tears of exhaustion, frustration, and confusion that she had hoped to avoid. Since I couldn't be there by her side cheering her on all night, she did the next best thing. She made herself cue cards and taped them by the crib. Here's what she wrote:*
>
> *1. Good sleep is good for the whole family. All deserve it and all benefit from it. We will be better parents, partners, friends, workers with enough sleep.*
>
> *2. Good sleep habits are learned. I as a good parent must teach them to my children.*
>
> *3. Husband and wife can sleep together. Their healthy relationship is very important to family life. A happy marriage helps kids be happy.*
>
> *4. My child will grow and develop better with good sleep.*

CO-SLEEPING

Numerous studies and surveys have shown that co-sleeping is on the rise, partly because more women are breastfeeding and many nursing mothers find it much easier, particularly during the first few months, to have the baby right alongside them. Some families make a conscious decision to co-sleep, either for the first few months or for several years. Others just sort of end up with the baby in bed as the path of least resistance. I devote a whole chapter to co-sleeping, and I really encourage you to think it through before the baby is born, or at least in the first few months. Ask yourself where you want your child sleeping at age two, or four, or six. Think about changes in your lifestyle—another baby, a new partner if you are a single parent—that could alter the composition of the family bed or the dynamic of the family. If you want your child to be in her own bed by age two, I strongly recommend you begin the transition much, much earlier. How many two-year-olds willingly abandon Mom and Dad's bed to start sleeping alone in her own room? Since birth she has been under the impression that your bed *is* her bed!

If the family bed is the right choice for you emotionally and philosophically, if it's the right match for your personal parenting style, I am not going to demand that you stop it. If you like the idea of co-sleeping, but everybody is tired all the time—if it's all "co-" and no "sleep"—I would ask you to think it through once more. If you want to stop, Chapter 10 will guide you. If you want to continue, the chapter will show you how a co-sleeping child can still learn how to put herself to sleep, letting everyone have more restful nights in your shared bed.

GETTING STARTED

Now that you've learned a little more about my approach, let's talk about some of the nuts and bolts.

Choose the Right Time

Choose a time to start sleep coaching when you can expect about three weeks without any disruptions or major changes, including travel, moving, or having a new baby. If something unexpected occurs once you're in midprogram, such as illness, do the best you can to stick with it. Some families try to make these transitions during the summer or during the winter holiday season because the adults won't have to juggle so many work responsibilities. That often works well, but be very careful to keep the child's schedule consistent even if yours is not. For instance, don't introduce a nice, sensible 7:30 bedtime the very week you plan to let her stay up until 10:00 with grandparents on Christmas Eve or are going to have a horde of entertaining young cousins camping out in your basement over the Fourth of July. *When you do pick a night to start sleep shaping, make sure the child gets a good nap that day—even if you have to bend my napping rules.* You don't want to embark on my program with an overtired baby.

Keep a Log

Keep a log for a week or two as you familiarize yourself with this book. Note when and where your child goes to sleep, naps, wakes, nurses, eats, etc. Some parents find it easiest to keep the log right next to the baby's bed so they can groggily scribble notes even at 3:00 a.m. Having a record in writing, instead of relying on scrambled mental notes in your sleep-deprived brain, will help illuminate your child's patterns and your own responses. Jot down the timing and frequency of night awakenings. Pay attention to how you get him back to sleep: whether you rock him, nurse him, sing to him, rub his back, or take him into your bed. These are called *negative associations* or *sleep crutches,* not because they are bad behaviors in and of themselves but because they are behaviors so closely linked in the child's mind with slumber that he cannot drift off without them. Compare your child's daily schedule with the typical routine I suggest in the chapter corresponding to his age.

Once you start my program, continue your log. Keep it simple and easy; you don't have to add extra chores and complications to your already hectic life. Tracking his sleep patterns will help you better read the cues he sends when he is tired, and to know when to seize a sleep opportunity before that lethal second wind of infant or toddler energy kicks in. The log will help you detect what situations or circumstances throw your child off so you can figure out how to avoid them or compensate for them in the future. The log will also help you see much more vividly those little steps of progress that might not be so clear to you from day to day—or night to night.

"I took a lot of notes. I looked at it like a prescription. This is the routine. This is what I have to do. I had to just try to stick to it as strictly as I could," said Linda, whose experiences with daughter Amy you will read about in the chapter on nine- to twelve-month-olds. Adele, whom you will read about in the chapter on thirteen- to eighteen-month-olds,

found that keeping a rather detailed log helped her stick to the program, although she had tried and failed a half-dozen other sleep systems before. "I would look at my log and spend all day telling myself over and over this is what I had to do at three a.m. If I had thought about it only before I went to bed, I would never have remembered in the middle of the night. You have to coach yourself."

Routines

When I talk about routines, I don't mean rigid, inflexible worship of the schedule gods. I mean a degree of predictability and stability, which study after study has shown that children need. I will give you detailed suggestions of what an age-appropriate daily structure should look like for a newborn, an infant, a toddler, and a preschooler. If you are wildly off, start adjusting. Eleven p.m. is just not a suitable bedtime for a baby or even a school-age child, and 6:00 p.m. is not a wise time for a nap. Although I usually recommend making these adjustments gradually, thirty minutes or so at a time, sometimes with a child under age three you can make the changes quite quickly if you learn to recognize his natural patterns. For instance, if your twenty-month-old is used to going to bed at 10:00, but you can see he is drowsy at 7:30, you don't need to spend days gradually adjusting. Just put him to bed at 7:30 and make sure you do so again the next night and the night after that.

Bedtime

All children need a comforting and predictable bedtime routine, and they need it from early infancy right up through the school years. A few quiet activities like books, songs, or prayers help the baby throw that switch in his brain from "alert" to "sleepy." My bedtime motto is "Bore Them!" It's not the time for tickling, wrestling, pillow fights, scary stories, or anything else that stimulates him or makes him fight sleep. I also encourage attachment to a "lovey," a favorite stuffed animal or blanket that he can use to comfort himself when he sleeps. The whole tone of bedtime should be calm and reassuring as you prepare him to separate from you all night.

If your child hates some aspect of bedtime, get that part over with first. For instance, if she can't stand having her pajama top pulled over her head, do it right after her bath, not after you've nursed her, read three books, sung two songs, and gotten her all snug and cozy. If she can't stand brushing her teeth, even if you spent seven dollars on a purple and pink vibrating enchanted mermaid toothbrush, brush them as soon as you get her upstairs, not when she's drowsily saying her prayers. The point of your bedtime routine is to calm your child, not to get all those stubborn little baby juices flowing.

Drowsy but Awake

Often in this book I will instruct you to put your baby down to sleep when he is "drowsy but awake" so he can learn to do that last part of falling asleep on his own. If you have trouble visualizing what "drowsy but awake" means, imagine a scale of one to ten, one being wide awake and ten being deep sleep. You want to put the baby down at about seven or eight. He should be quite sleepy but awake enough to know that he is going into the crib. *Similarly, if he falls asleep too quickly, in less than five minutes or so, he was probably too drowsy; put him to bed when he is a tad more alert the next night.* If he's still waking up a lot at night, you may need to put him to sleep a little more awake, so he gets better at resettling himself when he stirs at night. Even when you put him down at the right point on the drowsiness scale, he might wake up a bit and protest and fuss as you lay him down. Don't worry—but don't get him out and start the whole routine over again. Instead, stay nearby and use Sleep Lady tricks to comfort and reassure him, and he will learn to transition from drowsiness to sleep.

If your child just doesn't get drowsy, if he's really good at fighting sleep to keep you close by and engaged, you will have to put him into his crib or bed anyway. But make sure you have an appropriate bedtime and an appropriate evening routine to help prep his mind and body for sleep. We will talk about that a lot in each age chapter. Once he's in bed, use your repertoire of soothing techniques to help him transition to sleep.

If you rock, swing, or walk your baby to sleep, you may want to try cutting it down ten minutes at a time. You want to reach the point where he is very calm and drowsy but not sound asleep. Watch your baby to see how he responds and adjust the timing accordingly. If you were nursing to sleep—by far the most common pattern I see with newborns and infants—shorten the last nursing before bedtime, and pay close attention to the baby. When he stops sucking energetically and swallowing, and instead is suckling gently, a sort of fluttering motion on your breast (or bottle), he is past the "drowsy" target. In fact, if you look, you'll see his eyes are probably closed.

(Try nursing with a dim light on. It will help you monitor his behavior and see where he is on that drowsiness scale. The dim light will also help lessen that association in his mind between nursing and falling asleep after the first few months.)

Unlatch him, put him down, and try to catch him a little earlier the next time. If he wakes up as you are unlatching him and still seems hungry, giving you that look that says, "Hey, I didn't mean to fall asleep on the job," then give him one more chance. Help him latch back on or give him the bottle. If he starts eating, fine, let him finish. But if he just goes back to that fluttery suckling, you've been duped! He isn't hungry, he just wants to suckle himself to sleep. Unlatch him, burp him, give him a kiss, and put him to bed.

If this seems daunting, don't worry! I give you lots of advice throughout the book on how to eliminate these sleep crutches without enduring too many tears, or causing your child too much frustration. "Drowsy but awake" becomes less important as children get older. With toddlers and preschoolers, the calming bedtime routine of songs and stories prepares them for slumber.

Some Other Helpful Hints

- Most sleep problems are behavioral, not medical, but check with your pediatrician to rule out any physical causes or undetected disease. Make sure medications, including over-the-counter remedies, aren't disturbing her sleep.

- Install room-darkening shades if your child wakes up very early or has trouble napping.

- Leave a dim night-light on. (A few kids I've worked with did better in total darkness but not many; you'll probably be able to figure it out quickly.)

- Consider using a white noise machine or a fan if you live in a particularly noisy home. Children learn to sleep through routine household sounds but some places are just really loud, and some kids are really sensitive. Go ahead and block the noise from heavy traffic, rumbling trucks, nearby construction, barking dogs, noisy neighbors, or siblings and the like. Some families like to use lullabies to mask sounds, but I prefer playing lullabies during the bedtime routine, not while he's falling asleep, so he doesn't get so accustomed to the music that he needs you to come in and press Rewind five times a night.

- If you will worry less—and sleep better yourself—when you can hear *and* see your baby stir at night, you may want to buy a video monitor.

That way you won't be tempted to rush in and wake your baby even more just as she is learning to self-soothe herself back to sleep, and you may find that you fall back to sleep more easily yourself if you don't get up and walk (or run!) around. On the monitor, you'll see that she's all right—and know if there's a problem that really does require your presence.

- If you aren't ready or willing to take the pacifier away from your child, consider restricting pacifiers to bed and nap times. Pacifier issues vary with the age, so I'll talk about them more throughout the book. But if you don't want to get rid of the pacifier altogether and she's able to grip and maneuver it, consider leaving several strewn around the crib so she can find one herself, instead of demanding that you come in over and over again to retrieve and replug it. When she's older and out of the crib, put a few in a basket on the bedside table and teach her how to find them herself.

- You might be astonished to learn how many babies and toddlers have televisions in their bedrooms. I recommend against this. TV is a common sleep crutch for adults; it's why companies manufacture sets with timers. Watching television puts the brain into a light trance, similar to the first stages of sleep. You want this to occur in a crib or bed, without the television as a sleep crutch. Also, as children get older, they learn to put the television on themselves, and if it's in their room, it becomes harder for you to monitor what they are watching, and when they are watching it.

- To the extent possible, work with nannies, babysitters, and child care centers to develop consistent, or at least not wildly incompatible, sleep rules and schedules. But if your otherwise warm, loving, and reliable nanny can't handle any aspect of sleep coaching, particularly nap training, which can be hard, do your best to work around her and improvise where you have to. For instance, focus on nights and weekend naps if you can't get the nanny to do weekday naps. Ditto for day care centers, which may or may not have the flexibility to work with you. Quality day care is too hard to find to risk losing it. (For more details on how to negotiate napping with a day care center, see Day Care Nap Obstacles on page 313.)

- If your child has a particularly rough night, don't stop the sleep training, keep going. But you may need to let him nap more for a day so he doesn't get impossibly overtired and make the next night even more of a challenge. Provide the extra nap time within the sample timelines I give in each of the age chapters. Let's say that your eight month old has been up since 5 a.m. On a normal day, he would start his nap at around 9 a.m., but on this day, he'll be too tired to stay awake until 9. Don't force it, let him nap at 8—but don't throw his schedule completely out of whack by letting him nap at 6:30. If he takes a third little nap in late afternoon, that's fine. Or if he sleeps a half hour longer than usual for a nap, that's fine too. Similarly, if your preschooler normally naps from 1 p.m. to 3 p.m, it's OK to let him sleep until 4 if he needs it after a rough night or too early morning—but don't let him snooze all the way until dinner. Another way of handling a temporary sleep deficit is to put the child to bed a little earlier than usual for a few nights. In short, watch your child, trust yourself, and make some common sense adjustments, but keep them within the basic framework of an age-appropriate schedule.

- If your child gets soaking wet at night, or goes through an occasional phase when he gets soaked, use a larger-size diaper with an insert or find extra-absorbent overnight diapers. Not all stores carry the overnight varieties anymore, but if you look around you will find them. Diaper inserts or "doublers," are an extra pad that you can stick in the diaper and use overnight, or when the child is sick. They can be very handy when you are taking a long car or plane trip as well. If you are a good quick-change artist, you might be able to remove the soaked diaper quickly while he is in a deep sleep. Try to do this without taking him out of his crib or bed.

- Some children dirty their diaper just as you put them to bed at night or naptime—and some parents become convinced that it's intentional, that the child knows you will pick him up and get him out of the crib. Obviously you need to change the child, but do it as quietly as you can, in light as dim as possible. If you can manage it, change him in the bed or crib. Then hand him his lovey and return to your Shuffle position. If this happens at nap time, view it as a too-short nap and follow the nap-training advice in the appropriate age chapter. If it happens at 5:00 a.m., follow the advice for early risers. Children often find it difficult to go back to sleep after a thirty-minute nap and then a diaper change, or after a 5:00 a.m. diaper change. You may see some crying here, but stay consistent and reassuring. If you have completed the Shuffle and you feel your child needs a little more reassurance than normal to go back to sleep after his diaper change, then it is okay to sit closer that night if you feel it will help. On the following night return to your usual routine.

· A lot of parents worry that if they let their babies cry too long, they will vomit, particularly if the child has or had reflux. This may be the case if you leave the child to cry on his own, but it seldom happens when the parent remains in the room and practices my gentler, more gradual method. To alleviate this problem, avoid feeding him right before sleep.

Some young children, even babies, vomit intentionally because they know the parent will take them out of their crib and fuss over them. If you see your child trying to make himself gag (and they can do this without using fingers), firmly say "No!" but immediately follow up with soothing reassurance. If he does throw up, try to keep the cleanup as quick as possible, and engage with him as little as possible. Use wipes or a diaper or a washcloth, if you can, rather than getting him completely up for a bath. Don't turn the lights on, if you can help it. Some parents leave an extra sheet on the floor to use for cleanup so they can just roll it up and toss it in the hamper. Then reassure your child back to sleep. Remember, you don't want to give the message that if he throws up he will get out of the crib and not have to go to sleep.

Obviously, this doesn't apply to a child who is sick. In that case, you need to comfort him and follow your doctor's timetable for giving him fluids.

· Children need morning rituals just as much as they need bedtime rituals. These rituals help reinforce their understanding of wakeup time versus sleep time. Do a *"dramatic wake-up."* Throw open the blinds, switch on the lights, sing some cheery good-morning songs, and start the day. A lot of families like having morning be "Daddy playtime," especially for fathers who come home on the late side from work and get little or no evening time with their child. Dads also tend to like to play games that are very active, maybe a little rambunctious, and it's far preferable to play helicopter or rocket ship in the morning than right before bed.

THE SLEEP LADY SYSTEM · 25

- I will often remind you to avoid picking up or snuggling your baby at certain times of night, or after the first night of the Shuffle (although I do believe in lots of soothing and physical affection). If your child is crying very hard, go ahead and pick him up briefly to reassure him, but don't let him fall asleep in your arms. The no-snuggles edict does not apply to a child who is sick, or who has had a nightmare or fright. Just try not to do so much snuggling that he will expect it even when he is feeling better. In general, I'd rather have you sleep in a makeshift bed next to a sick child than to allow him in your bed if you've just ended co-sleeping. But I know lots of parents who do bend this rule. Just make sure to get back to your usual routine as soon as possible.

- If you are working on stopping or reducing breastfeeding at night, it's often best to put the father in charge of that aspect of sleep training. If the baby sees Mom, he will naturally hope and expect to be nursed, and he's going to be even more upset when those hopes are dashed by Mom. Also, Dad may or may not have a better tear tolerance than Mom, but he definitely can't cave in, lift his shirt, and nurse.

- Both parents should be able to put the child to bed. They don't have to have absolutely identical routines but they need to be similar, and they need to have similar responses to tantrums, stalling tactics, and the like. It's generally a good idea to have one parent in charge at each bedtime when you are doing sleep training. In other words, if you are on night five of the Sleep Lady Shuffle, and Dad is sitting in a chair halfway across the room at bedtime or for a night wakening, Mom shouldn't switch places with Dad after ten minutes. This just stimulates and confuses the child. It's also often a good idea to have one person "on duty" per night for middle-of-the-night wakenings. Some couples do, however, trade off because of their own sleep needs and body rhythms, Mom taking say midnight to 3 a.m. and Dad taking 3 to 6 a.m.

- Occasionally in my practice I've found that unusually alert, bright and aware children tend to have a little more trouble learning to sleep. These children often reach their physical milestones, like walking, on the early side, and they tend to have slightly disturbed sleep. Temperamentally, they may be the kind of children who know what they want and when they want it, and are willing to hold out until they get it. That's a great quality in an adult but it can be a little daunting to parent such a determined little person. Make sure you don't fall into the trap of thinking that an alert child needs less sleep than average. He needs just as much sleep as any other baby—maybe even a little more than average—but he has a harder time shutting out the world in order to get to sleep. Room darkening shades are essential for these babies and children; sound screens can help for naps. Be extremely vigilant about watching their sleep windows. These children tend to be less flexible sleepers for several years, so they can be extra sensitive to disruptions of routine or travel. My suggestions in Chapter 14: Routine Busters can help.

· If you anticipate needing the crib for a new baby, make the older child's transition to a bed *at least* two months before or four months after the birth to avoid feelings of displacement. Better yet, if your toddler or preschooler is not ready to give up the crib, don't push it. Borrow a crib for the new baby, or buy a secondhand one until he is ready. I address bed readiness in Chapters 8 and 9 (for one and a half to two and a half years old, and two and a half to five years old) and I talk more about sleep-related adjustments to a new sibling in Chapter 14: Routine Busters.

THE SLEEP LADY SYSTEM WORKS

One reason I believe so strongly in my approach is that I've seen it work over and over and over again. I can't tell you how many times I've had parents tell me that their child was impossible, that I wouldn't be able to help them, only to hear them declare a few weeks later that I had wrought a miracle: the baby was sleeping. In some cases, particularly with older children, a brief night wakening might persist for a while but if you stick to it, he'll eventually drop that one too. Occasionally your child might regress, either because his routine has been thrown off or he's entering a new developmental stage or he's just having a few "off" days. Don't despair. You will now have the tools to get him back on a good sleep schedule.

Nicole's Story

When people ask me for a real-life example of how this works, I often think of Nicole. When Cory and Alan consulted me Nicole was eleven months old and still getting up once or twice every night to nurse. Although she took two ninety-minute naps, her schedule was *unpredictable, as was her morning wake-up time. Earlier Nicole had had several health problems—reflux and dairy sensitivity, frequent ear infections—and Cory and Alan were not willing to let her cry too much at night. "She was crying from pain, not behavior," Cory said. "Letting her cry that way just wasn't in me." By the time I met the family, Nicole's doctors had corrected or controlled her physical ailments. But her discomfort had left its mark. It had robbed her of the chance to learn to self-soothe and fall asleep on her own. Months later, the whole family was still paying the price. Cory later confided that when she logged on to my website, she literally burst into tears, so relieved that help was at hand. She recalled feeling that "I just can't function like this anymore, I'm going to lose my mind."*

While Nicole was very little, she had slept in her parents' bed. "We enjoyed that," her mother said. "I was nursing and it was easy for me to have her there." This was particularly true after Cory went back to her accounting job part-time when Nicole was three months old. At six or seven months, they moved her into a crib in her own room, but it wasn't easy to get her to sleep and she still ended up in their bed a lot.

Even before they started working with me, Alan and Cory did have the beginnings of a good bedtime routine. At around 7:15, they would put on a classical CD and Cory would nurse. They would put the baby into her crib with a pacifier and Kitty the bear, her lovey. Sometimes she would drift off quickly, if a parent stayed in the room. But often she would need a few sessions of back rubbing. When they—intermittently—tried leaving her alone for ten minutes to see if she could fall asleep without them, she would scream and scream. Either Alan or Cory would return to her, rub her back, and sit by her side until she slept. Even then, she used to rouse herself the minute she heard one of the floorboards squeak as her parents tried to leave. "I used to wish I could fly," Cory recalled thinking as she tried to tiptoe out. Once they finally got her to sleep, it didn't last long. Sometime between 11:30 p.m. and 1:30 a.m. she awoke wanting to nurse. Occasionally they tried to break her of the habit but they never stuck to it (intermittent reinforcement!) and as far as Nicole was concerned, nursing was a nonnegotiable demand. After a few minutes, one of the sleepy parents would surrender, bringing her into their bed, where Cory would nurse and they would all try to sleep. "It was the path of least resistance," Cory said.

When I met Cory and Alan, we agreed on a few immediate changes. Cory nursed Nicole a half hour before bedtime, not right at the bedtime, to blur her association between nursing and sleep. They put a night-light in her room and gave her more time to wind down in her room before they put her in her crib. And they would talk to her about their expectations. "We would have a conversation. 'Now it's time for bed. We're putting on your night-light. We're pulling down the shades.' They understand a lot more than you think they do, and we got her to sleep at night without a whole lot of crying," Cory said. They began the Shuffle but never got past the first step. Nicole began falling asleep and staying asleep on her own almost immediately.

Though thrilled with the quick bedtime progress, Cory and Alan were apprehensive about her nighttime awakenings. That too went more smoothly than any of us anticipated. In the past when they'd tried to stop nighttime nursing, Alan would let her fall asleep in his arms. But no matter how delicately he handled his "little package," she woke up the instant he put her down. With my help, he learned how to soothe her while she stayed in the crib. He responded as soon as he heard her stir, trying to reach her before she was sitting up and moving much in her crib. He tried to soothe her back to sleep, without picking her up or bringing her to their bed. Instead, he rubbed her back sporadically and whispered to her just as he did at bedtime. The first three nights were rough, but by the fourth night there was peace and quiet. Nicole had gotten the message and quickly decided that if she wasn't going to get nursed in the middle of the night, she wasn't going to bother getting up anymore. "It's amazing how quickly it went. She almost knew we were trying to do something that was helpful to her," Alan said. "We had been artificially doing things she needed to learn on her own. But she was really ready for us to stop it." She needed her parents to change their behaviors so she could learn to change hers.

As Nicole matured, her bedtime routine changed. She listens to more bedtime stories, and now she puts both Kitty and her baby doll to bed before her parents put her to bed. But by setting rules and sticking to them, Cory and Alan have kept bedtime a warm and cozy time, not a tug-of-war. They have also remained vigilant about keeping her bedtime steady, even on weekends. "We work ourselves around her bedtime," Cory said. "We don't work her bedtime around ourselves."

Looking back, Cory realized how anxious they had been about Nicole's bedtime, and how they may have transmitted that anxiety to their daughter, making it even harder for her to sleep. "We used to think, 'Oh no, it's bedtime.'" Now Cory and Alan listen to Nicole murmur herself to sleep, look at each other, and say, "Oh my goodness, she's asleep. It's that simple."

2
SLEEP BASICS

SLEEP IS A VITAL ACTIVITY. When we are asleep, we don't shut off. Our body and brain are hard at work. Sleep enables a child to produce growth hormones, build the immune system, and work on memory storage, organization, and retention—the foundations for learning. Good sleep lets children get through the day without melting down.

Keep this essential concept in mind—so crucial but often misunderstood by parents: *sleep begets sleep*. The phrase was coined by Dr. Marc Weissbluth of Northwestern's Feinberg School of Medicine, and the author of *Healthy Sleep Habits, Happy Child.* It means that well-rested children find it easier to sleep and stay well rested. I know, I know. This sounds counterintuitive. Stop and think about your own child. Have you ever put him to bed very late, say at 10:00 p.m., and assumed he would just sleep late in the morning to compensate—but instead he woke up at 5:15 a.m.? Overtired children have trouble falling asleep, and staying asleep. They have more nap difficulties, more bedtime resistance, more night awakenings, and more early risings. Sleep deprivation becomes a self-perpetuating cycle of exhaustion, for you and your child.

To follow the Sleep Lady method, you don't need to understand all the complex physiology of sleep, but it does help to have a grounding in the basics. I want you to know just enough for you to problem solve, now and as your child faces new sleep challenges and demands as he grows older. We are also going to learn how to recognize your child's sleep window, when he is emotionally, chronologically, and physically ripe for sleep.

SLEEP LEARNING

In the early weeks and months, before children learn to soothe themselves, we do need to actively step in and soothe our children to sleep. The problem occurs when they get a little older and we don't phase ourselves out of the picture. We continue to intervene so much—rocking, singing, nursing, walking, snuggling, cooing, back-rubbing, tummy-circling—that we don't give them the space they need to fall asleep themselves. A major theme of my book is how to help children soothe themselves, starting with how to calm a newborn and going right up to helping a five-year-old recover from a nightmare. It helps to remember that an adult typically requires fifteen to twenty minutes to fall asleep. If you put your head on the pillow and are "out" instantaneously, you are probably sleep deprived. Children also need those fifteen to twenty minutes—but we as parents are often too anxious about their falling asleep to give them the gift of a quarter-hour. We try to "rescue" them and put them to sleep, before they get a chance to discover what they find comforting themselves. Then they become dependent on us to rock them, hold them, nurse them, snuggle them. There's a whole list of these *negative associations*, behaviors that aren't negative in and of themselves but become negative because they can't sleep unless we do it for them. I call them sleep crutches. In fact, some babies need more and more of this assistance. Nursing twenty minutes doesn't work anymore, they need forty minutes; and then not even forty minutes works anymore, and we panic and introduce new sleep crutches, new patterns, new associations. But if you give your baby the freedom to learn, he will find his own soothing rituals, and that ability to self-soothe over time also promotes confidence and security. Babies find all kinds of safe things to suck, twirl, rub—corners of blankets, legs of stuffed animals, even their own hair or ears. (Ear-pulling may be a sign of an ear infection, but some babies just think ears are cool.) Some rock themselves, lift their legs up and down, even lightly bang their head against the crib bumper. When they get older, they may murmur or even sing to themselves.

PHYSICAL BASICS

Sleep Cycles

I'm going to give you a little bit of information about sleep cycles, sometimes called *sleep architecture*. I'm going to keep it brief and simple, and not overload you with science. But it helps to understand the basics.

Sleep is divided into two basic types, REM (rapid eye movement, also known as dream sleep) and non-REM. REM sleep is active sleep, and it's also a lighter sleep. It's the sleep in which we dream and organize our memories. During REM we have limp limbs, irregular breathing, twitching, and rapid eye movement.

Non-REM has several stages of its own. They are called *light sleep*, *true sleep*, and *deep sleep*. As we pass through these non-REM stages, we move from a gentle drowsiness to that state of deep, deep, deep sleep where, if awakened, we feel groggy and a little disoriented. During non-REM sleep our breath is slow and regular. Our muscles are a little tense, not as floppy.

Children also have both non-REM and REM cycles, although their sleep cycles differ from adults'. For the first four months, their sleep, particularly daytime napping, is not very organized neurologically. About half of their sleep is light, REM sleep, when they are quite active and easily aroused. For a newborn, that's about eight hours of REM sleep and eight hours of non-REM sleep a day. At around four months, REM sleep begins to slowly drop off, and by age two a child's sleep cycles more closely resemble those of an adult. REM comprises about 20–25 percent of adult sleep, or about two hours a night.

Parents need to understand that nobody sleeps through the night. We all go through these sleep cycles, and as we switch from one phase to another, the change in our brain activity often wakes us up a little bit. This is called a *partial arousal.* Everyone experiences it. Sometimes we are more awake than other times. For instance, about every 90 to 110 minutes (fifty minutes for infants), while we are still in a fairly light sleep, we have a partial arousal. But we don't wake up completely. We may mumble or roll over, for example. But every three to four hours, we experience a partial wakening that is a little more pronounced. Maybe we notice that our pillow is on the floor, or we want a sip of water, or need to adjust the blanket. Usually we get right back to sleep and scarcely remember the awakening in the morning. But that's because we know how to get ourselves back to sleep. Babies don't—until we teach them.

When babies experience these partial arousals, they may cry out, thrash around, become startled. If they have negative sleep associations or sleep crutches, if they need us to get them back to sleep, the partial arousal will become a complete arousal. They are basically saying to themselves, "Hey, I'm sort of awake and I'm in my crib, I'm tired and I don't know how to go back to sleep without Mom nursing me or Dad walking me up and down the hallway, or someone helping me find my pacifier. So now I'm going to do the only thing I can do. I'm going to cry." You know the rest. They cry and you rush in and nurse them, rock them, walk them, put on the lullaby tape, perform whatever parental tricks you have taught them are indispensable to their sleep. And you may have to do it several times each night. Once we help our children give up these associations, they can sleep through the night. They will still have the partial awakenings, but they will no longer need to let you in on it. They can open their eyes for a second, recognize that they are safe in their own room—and reach out for their favorite stuffed animal, their thumb, their special blankie, whatever they use to soothe themselves. They can get themselves back to sleep. The partial arousal stays partial.

Clocks and Windows

We all have a circadian rhythm, an internal clock that tells us when to be awake and when to be asleep. Falling asleep when our body clock is set to "wake" is challenging, as is staying alert when our clock says "sleep." Sleep is not as restorative—meaning we don't feel as rested—when we sleep off our clock or when our clock is on a "wake" mode. For example, people who sleep all day and work the graveyard shift, from midnight to 8:00 a.m., often don't get quality sleep because they are not in sync with their internal clocks. Or, for a two-year-old, a nap from 1:00 to 3:00 in the afternoon feels better than a nap from 4:00 to 6:00 in the evening. The clock is mostly set by light, although social cues such as noise and temperature can affect it too. This is one reason that I recommend room-darkening shades for children, particularly those who wake up very early or who have trouble napping.

As adults, we know how to compensate, at least in part, when our circadian clock is upset. If we have to go to sleep one night well before our usual bedtime, to catch a plane or attend an unusually early meeting, we know how to prepare ourselves, to cue our brains to sleep at the unaccustomed hour. We try a hot bath, a good book, a relaxation tape, or maybe just a mental image of a warm palm-fringed beach. Babies don't know all those tricks. They need us to protect their sleep by paying attention to the clock—both the external time and the baby's internal rhythm.

To keep ourselves "ticking" well and protect our sleep, we should regulate our sleep. We sleep better, and we feel better, if we go to sleep at about the same time each night, and wake up at the same time each morning. (This becomes really important when you have teenagers who want to sleep until noon on weekends but have to wake up at 6:00 a.m. on school days to make it to first period! Dr. Robert Stickgold, a psychiatrist and sleep expert at Harvard Medical School, says college kids who starve themselves of sleep during the week and gorge themselves on the weekend suffer from "sleep bulimia.") We can vary our routine on weekends, but only by an hour. Babies are even more sensitive, especially if they are already overtired. A well-rested child can handle variations in a sleep schedule better than an overtired child. We all know they need routines and predictability for their emotional well-being, for that sense of order and security in their new world. But they also need routines to keep their internal clocks correctly "wound," and to cue their brains to start preparing for sleep by secreting melatonin. Production of melatonin, a hormone that promotes sleep by relaxing our muscles and making us drowsy, begins at about three months. Secretion levels are linked to darkness, another aspect of our circadian rhythm.

If you miss your child's "sleep window," that natural time to sleep, his body won't be pumping out calming melatonin. Precisely the opposite will occur. His adrenal glands will send out a rush of cortisol, a stress-related hormone that will overstimulate your baby, make him "wired" and create a second wind. To him, it probably feels like you slipped a double shot of espresso into his bottle. He will be more agitated, more difficult to console, more likely to need a lot more of your time and energy to help him wind down again and get to sleep. So if, by natural rhythm and habit, he is ready for sleep at 7:00 but you keep him up until 8:00, he is going to have a hard time getting to sleep. And even after he does get to sleep—often with a lot more tears and resistance than normal—the cortisol and overtiredness team up to make it harder for him to stay asleep. He is more likely to wake up at night, and to wake up too early in the morning before he is truly rested. This cycle can then lead to poor naps the next day, which will lead to an overtired baby at bedtime, which leads to poor nighttime sleep. We've all seen this pattern in our children at some time—I know I've seen it in mine, and they are good sleepers. Our task is to correct this cycle before it becomes a self-perpetuating downward spiral.

Recognizing your child's sleep windows so that you can get him down before the cortisol rush is key. You'll meet a lot of real-life parents in this book, and many share their own children's signals. Some cues are common and simple—rubbing eyes, yawning, becoming less active, maybe a little listless. Other cues are subtle. One mother described her son as a "spaghetti boy" who gets all limp and loose when he's ready for bed. It takes a little practice to spot the signs because not all kids are the same. For instance, most babies who rub their eyes are saying, "Mom, put me to bed right now or you'll regret it." But a few of those eye-rubbers are saying, "Fooled you, Mom! I needed to nap a half hour ago and you didn't notice and now I'm starting a second wind and if you think it's going to be hard to get me in my crib to nap now, just wait until 3 a.m." If you have trouble detecting your child's signals, keep one eye on him and another on the clock. Try going into a quiet, dimly lit room and engaging in a very gentle activity when you think nap time or bedtime is approaching. The signs may then appear.

> *At two, my co-author's son Ilan would rub his eyes and ask for his special songs when he got sleepy, even if he was proclaiming loudly that he didn't want to go to bed. From monitoring the eye rubbing and his general activity level, Joanne would usually know whether to speed up or slow down the bedtime routine to calibrate exactly when his head should hit the pillow. But some nights, he was able to mask his tiredness. If he began leaping up and down, shouting gleefully, "I jump on bed like monkey, Mommy," she knew she had miscalculated and that window was slamming shut.*

Quality and Quantity

When it comes to sleep, parents sound like they all hail from the dream-world equivalent of Lake Wobegon. Everybody thinks his or her child needs less sleep than average. Wrong. Sleep needs do vary somewhat but the natural variations are a whole lot less than most parents think. These babies may be *getting* less sleep than average but they *need* a lot more than they are getting. Remember, sleep begets sleep. To help you accurately gauge your child's needs, I provide average sleep requirements at the start of each age-related chapter. One telltale sign—if your child always falls asleep in the car, she's probably not getting enough sleep.

Children need to get the right amount of sleep and they need to get the right kind of sleep. Quality counts along with quantity. Good sleep should be largely uninterrupted. If your child is getting up a lot, she isn't getting all the sound sleep she needs. As we've all experienced on nights when we slept poorly, fragmented sleep or interrupted sleep just does not make us feel as rested and refreshed as uninterrupted sleep.

After a newborn's first six to eight weeks, good sleep also means sleep in a crib, bed, or bassinet—not in a car, stroller, or swing. Motion lulls us to sleep, but it also keeps us in a lighter, more fragmented sleep; our brains never reach the level of full restorative sleep if we're moving. Sure your baby will occasionally fall asleep in a car. But make it the exception, not the rule, and even if you occasionally resort to using the car to get him to fall asleep, don't keep driving around. Either transfer him back to his crib as soon as possible, or park and sit in or next to the car so he can sleep without movement. I know one mom who brought her laptop and a pile of blankets into the car. Another would park in the driveway and if the weather was nice, she would leave the car door open and weed the flowerbeds that had otherwise been neglected since the birth of her first child.

Quality sleep also means sleep that is not interrupted by medical conditions such as asthma, allergies, obstructive sleep apnea, reflux, or other disorders. See Chapter 13, Medical Problems, and of course consult your pediatrician.

THE RIGHT START FOR NEWBORNS
AND INFANTS

WHEN OUR DOCTORS AND NURSES HAND us our brand-new babies in the hospital, they make sure we know how to hold them, nurse them, swaddle them, diaper them, and swab that umbilical cord. But they seldom say a word about how to put our babies to sleep, or even help us define realistic expectations about sleep. They don't tell us that sleep is a learned skill, that we have to teach our babies to develop healthy sleep habits. In fact, we may get precisely the opposite advice. They may sympathetically cluck about how exhausted we will be during the first few months, about how it's normal to feel overwhelmed. But it doesn't really have to be that way—at least not for too long. Of course a newborn is a lot of work, and you won't get eight hours of uninterrupted sleep. But there's a difference between being tired, even very tired, for six or eight or even twelve weeks—and being so drained and besieged month after month after month that you can barely function, let alone coo at your own son or daughter, or be civil to your spouse.

In this chapter, I will help you get your baby off to the right start. If you follow the Sleep Lady's Eight Rules of Infant Slumber your baby will have an easier time learning to sleep and will sleep longer. If you learn nothing from me except those eight steps, your life will be simpler. You will learn over the next few years that babies and children go through numerous different sleep stages—learning to sleep through the night, changing nap schedules, separation anxiety, and the like—and laying a good foundation will help your baby and your entire family travel down those developmental paths. I will describe some tricks to help your baby learn to self-soothe so he doesn't need you to spend all night every night rocking, walking, nursing, bouncing, or plugging in pacifiers.

THE FIRST TWO WEEKS

Before we get started, I want to offer a few reassuring words about the very beginning. Don't worry about schedules and rules during the first two weeks—and don't beat yourself up if you make a mistake, because there aren't any mistakes to be made. Just focus on healing and recovering from delivery, establishing your milk supply and learning how to breastfeed, and, most delightfully, getting to know your new baby. Accept as much help as you can get from family and friends, and grab as much sleep as you can whenever you can. Don't worry about the dirty dishes, or that linen closet you tore apart during your "nesting" moments but never had a chance to reassemble before you went into labor. None of that is important.

Your baby will probably sleep most of the time at the beginning, but she won't sleep very deeply. Newborn sleep is not well-organized neurologically, which means it's a very light slumber. Hold her, rock her, swing her, do what feels right and comfortable for the first ten to fourteen days. Then, at the start of the third week, gradually start applying the Sleep Lady slumber rules, and establishing patterns. You aren't seeking a huge, dramatic transition. Just start weaving these routines and patterns into your baby's life. Keep your expectations realistic. This is a process. You won't see enormous overnight changes in her sleep patterns in week three but you will be laying the groundwork for improvement in the coming weeks and months.

THE SLEEP LADY'S EIGHT RULES OF INFANT SLUMBER

1. Create a flexible feeding and sleeping routine.

2. Encourage soothing techniques other than nursing.

3. Offer a pacifier for soothing and sucking, but not as a sleep crutch.

4. Sometimes feed your baby when he wakes up after a nap—not just when you are trying to get him to sleep.

5. Put him down drowsy but awake at least once every twenty-four hours.

6. Introduce one bottle a day—*even if you are committed to breast feeding, as I was with my own children*—by the second or third week.

7. Create a sleep-friendly environment.

8. Carefully think through the whole question of co-sleeping and the family bed.

We'll talk much more about this later, but if you commit to the family bed past the first three months, remember that you may be making a commitment that could last for three, five, sometimes even six or seven years.

SLEEP LADY SLUMBER RULE #1: CREATE A FLEXIBLE FEEDING AND SLEEP ROUTINE.

Lots of parents in our generation cringe at the word *routine*, but by routine, I don't mean a rigid minute-by-minute regimen. I mean a commonsense framework with time mapped out for eating, napping, sleeping, playing, or awake time—a framework that you can adapt as you grow more adept at reading your baby's signals and cues. Even very young babies like predictability. They find it calming; they sleep better, and they are more capable of soothing themselves. Many new parents fear a routine eliminates their freedom. To the contrary, you will find that a flexible routine enhances your freedom. You can't do whatever you want whenever you want, but you will be able to better plan your day. You'll know when you can get out of the house, run errands, meet a friend for coffee, or walk off that baby fat. And you can invite the grandparents over when your baby is going to be at his cooing adorable best, not his tired and crankiest worst.

A routine makes parenting easier. If your baby is crying, a routine helps you figure out what he wants. You can ask yourself, "How long has he been awake? When did he last eat?" If you know by his schedule that he is well fed and well rested, you can then go through a list of questions to figure out what's bugging him. Is it too hot or cold? Are his clothes scratchy? Is his diaper soaked? Is he sick? Is he overstimulated? Does he need to be in a quieter environment—dimmer lights, less noise, fewer people? (A darker, quieter room often helps with those late-afternoon fussy periods.) If you have a completely unstructured haphazard day, you won't be able to answer the basic questions about whether he is hungry or tired because you won't know. The lack of a routine makes it harder for you to interpret what he is trying to tell you and respond to his needs. As you work on developing a routine, keep a simple log. Jot down when he eats, and for how long. The same for sleep. Don't obsess over it; your life doesn't need any more complications with a newborn in the house. But it will help you to detect his natural patterns and establish your own.

> *Carol and Daniel had had a terrible time with their first child, Joshua, and worked with me when he was about fifteen months old. With Deborah, their second child, they tried to build on what they had learned the hard way. "I tried to think more about having a schedule—not a rigid schedule but a schedule. That way if she cried, I would be able to ask myself, 'Is she hungry?' and know that she wasn't, that she ate just an hour ago," Carol recalled. "It wasn't just that she was an easier, mellower baby, she wasn't so colicky. It was also that I more easily recognized the signs of tiredness. And I think I created some of Joshua's sleep problems myself. If Joshua cried, I would give it about one second before I grabbed him and fed him. With Deborah, my instinct is still to rescue her but I have more awareness; I know that I can let her try to get to sleep on her own."*

A routine means a modified approach to feeding on demand. Sure you should feed on demand the first few weeks, and I certainly believe in feeding a baby when he is hungry. The problem is, we as new parents often don't really understand when they are hungry. We think every cry is a hunger cry, and we end up feeding them and feeding them and feeding them, turning ourselves into human pacifiers, or as one mother who nursed her four-month-old three times a night called herself, "the boobie lady."

I have worked with hundreds of youngsters with behavioral sleep disorders and by far the most common problem is that they never learned to fall asleep without a breast or bottle in their mouth. At the beginning, when we are nursing novices, it's very hard to tell how much they are ingesting—whether they are eating or just sucking, and whether they really want to be eating or they are eating simply because we placed them at our breast. And we as new mothers and fathers worry and worry and worry so much about whether they are eating enough and growing enough, whether we are producing enough milk, whether we need to supplement. When in doubt, we feed. If you are having these concerns, a visit to the doctor for a quick weight check can address those questions. It is also wise to arm yourself with knowledge about how often babies genuinely need to eat. Yes, your newborn may have to eat every two to two and a half hours. If you are routinely nursing your baby more frequently, you need to stop and think about why. Is it his hunger, or your reflex? What else could he need? Dr. William Sammons, in *The Self-Calmed Baby: Teach your infant to calm itself—and curb crying, fussing, and sleeplessness* (1991, St. Martin's Press), has a great bit of advice: "We use feeding to help our baby go to sleep thinking that satisfying hunger accomplishes this when it is sucking, body contact, warmth and body motion, and the parents' attempt to calm the environment" that help our babies go to sleep. We're going to learn several techniques, other than the breast, for soothing babies. Keep in touch with your pediatrician about your infant's growth and your dietary concerns (particularly if your child was premature, is not gaining weight, or has other health issues that could require a more frequent feeding schedule). In the next chapter, I'll give you a month-by-month breakdown of feeding and sleep patterns that will help you create a schedule that's right for you and your child.

Remember that nursing has stages, and that too can affect sleep. During the first ten to fifteen minutes, the baby gets the *foremilk*, which is higher in lactose. Next comes the *hindmilk*, sometimes called the *cream*. The fattier hindmilk balances out that high lactose and it also makes babies feel drowsy. But babies who feed more than every two hours often nurse for just a few minutes at a time. That means they are probably getting too much lactose, and not enough cream, missing out on the components that enhance drowsiness. The disproportionate amount of lactose can make them gassy and fussy—and you may respond by nursing them even more, aggravating the problem. Try to help your baby take a complete feeding, at least twelve to fifteen minutes on one breast (or about twenty-five to thirty minutes for both breasts) so he can get to the hindmilk. (As they get a little older they become more efficient at eating so they will get to the hindmilk faster.) In between feedings, if he wants to suck, try offering a pacifier. Also, although some people say it's an old wives' tale, many nursing moms I have worked with swear that if they eliminate caffeine—coffee, tea, sodas, chocolate—and cut back on dairy products their infants are less fussy and sleep better. If you do remove certain foods from your diet, don't expect to see a difference a half hour later. Give it two or three weeks for the change to have a sustained impact on your child.

SLEEP LADY SLUMBER RULE #2:
ENCOURAGE SOOTHING TECHNIQUES
OTHER THAN NURSING.

If you give babies a chance, they will develop a host of ways to soothe themselves, but in the first few months they do need our help. Our challenge is to find soothing techniques other than nonstop nursing, which becomes a problem if the child always needs to nurse to get to sleep. Dr. Harvey Karp's helpful book, *The Happiest Baby on the Block: The New Way to Calm Crying and Help Your Newborn Baby Sleep Longer* (2003, Bantam), recommends the "Five S's,"—swaddling, side holding, "sh-sh-sh," swinging, and sucking—to get the baby through the first few months, sometimes called the *fourth trimester.*

SWADDLING · The pressure of swaddling, similar to what babies felt in utero, comforts babies and lengthens their sleep. Wrap him snugly in a receiving blanket, making sure his ears and toes are not too hot. For the first three months, they usually like having their arms inside the blanket. At about twelve to sixteen weeks, start leaving the arms out. Experiment a little. Your baby might want his arms out a little earlier; you'll be able to tell. I swaddled my own daughters tightly, with their arms at their sides or across their chest during that fussy evening period in the first six to eight weeks. For bed, I tended to wrap lighter around the arms so that they could move a little bit. Sometimes babies like being swaddled and then placed near the corner of the crib. It makes them feel a little less lost in that big crib. When they get a little older, some babies learn how to scooch themselves over to the corner of their crib and sort of snuggle themselves in. You can also tightly roll some baby blankets and place them along his side, from his chest to his feet, to make him feel more snuggled. Make sure you don't put the blankets close to his face. Ask a nurse to show you how to swaddle your baby in the hospital, and I strongly recommend that you take a newborn-baby care class at your local hospital to go over the basics before you give birth.

SIDES · Babies should sleep on their back to reduce the risk of sudden infant death syndrome (SIDS), but not all of them like it. It's not a position they experienced in utero and it may trigger their *Moro,* or *falling reflex.* They don't have to be on their back when they are awake, or when you are holding them. Many find it comforting to be on their side, particularly their left side. You can hold him on his side in your arms or on your lap, swaddled if you like, and make a gentle, rhythmic **"sh-sh"** noise to remind him of your heartbeat in utero. Swing or sway your body a little for comfort. Holding him on his side helps with that fussy evening period or with colicky babies who cry more than average—which believe it or not is three hours a day.

The American Academy of Pediatricians, in 2005, advised against side sleeping for young babies because of the risk of sudden infant death syndrome. If you think your baby is more comfortable on his side, do not make a change without discussing side-sleeping safety with your pediatrician. She may strongly recommend against it at this age, or she might suggest that you buy a sleep wedge to position the baby safely on his side. Make sure you understand how to use the wedge so that he stays on his side and doesn't land in the more hazardous on-the-stomach sleeping position. (Not all pediatricians trust those wedges, and the AAP says they have not been rigorously tested.) When he gets old enough to sleep safely on his stomach or side, usually when he can roll over in both directions, you may find that he suddenly begins to sleep more soundly if that position is naturally more comfortable for him.

SWING · Gently rocking and swinging our babies is so instinctive that I scarcely have to mention it, but it does calm newborns. It's also fine to let your baby nap in a swing during the day for the first two months. After that, he'll still like being in the swing, and you can use it for fun and comfort but don't use it as a bed substitute. To gently ease out of the swing-sleep habit, go ahead and put him in the swing at his customary speed, then slow it down in a moment. Stop it when he's asleep. At about two months, start to move him into his crib for his morning nap. Start his pre-nap routine in his room, and swing him a bit in your arms if it helps the transition. Then put him in the crib. Stay by him; pat, stroke, or gently rock his body, if that helps him, until he drifts off to sleep. He should make the adjustment in a few days. Start this with one nap a day, usually the morning, and add the second nap whenever you think he's ready, usually within a week or two.

SLEEP LADY SLUMBER RULE #3: USE A PACIFIER FOR SOOTHING, NOT SLEEPING.

The final *S* is the **sucking** reflex. Babies do need to suck, especially during the first few weeks; I gave my own daughters pacifiers. But after the first month, let him suck to get calm, but not to get to sleep. Get him used to falling asleep without something in his mouth, whether it's a pacifier, a bottle, or your nipple. Put him down drowsy but awake. If he fusses, pat him, rock him a bit, and sit by his side and murmur "sh-sh." You can pick him up briefly to calm him, but avoid giving him the pacifier or your breast at the first whimper. From about six weeks, it's extremely important that you are consistent about this at bedtime and for at least one nap. Conquer any lingering temptation to nurse or use a pacifier to get him to sleep, or else you will be getting up multiple times a night far into the future to plug in a pacifier or comfort-feed a baby who really isn't hungry. He may fuss a bit if you break the sleep-suck cycle at four or eight weeks—but it's going to be a lot harder later on.

I started breaking that cycle with the pacifier when my oldest daughter was just three weeks old. She was happily sucking on it when my sister-in-law phoned and told me about the crises she faced if she dared venture out of the house without her kids' pacis. I rushed right into Carleigh's bedroom and took it out of her mouth for bedtime. She was so tired she didn't even cry, but she did cry at bedtime briefly for the next several nights, so I used other soothing techniques. She usually cried for only seven or eight minutes, and she never went more than fifteen minutes. After that, I gave her the "binkie" for comfort during the day and in the car, but I didn't let her fall asleep for the night with the pacifier in her mouth. When she got a little older, she began to suck her thumb to self-soothe. Lots of children outgrow thumbsucking on their own, but Carleigh didn't. At age five, we found the perfect behavioral modification technique, although it meant we had to adopt her kindergarten class hamster! I'll describe that adventure in the chapter on ages two and a half to five.

If your baby spits out the pacifier, don't automatically replug it! If you keep plugging up his mouth all the time, you may be hampering his early attempt to communicate with you, as well as your ability to differentiate his cries. Sometimes he will want the pacifier back—and he'll let you know it. But if you don't assume it's the pacifier he wants, you may realize he's trying to tell you something else. You'll be surprised how many times babies spit out the pacifier, parents stick it in, babies spit it out, the parents stick it back in, never stopping to think that maybe the baby is spitting it out for a reason. If, after the first few months, he's taking the pacifier more than you would like, try other soothing techniques and reduce stimulation to lessen the need for sucking. Also, pacifiers don't help very gassy babies because they tend to swallow more air as they suck it.

Lots of babies, like Carleigh, suck their thumb or fingers, even their whole hand. Don't worry about it. It's a perfectly good way of self-soothing and satisfying that instinct to suck. Some parents prefer it. Unlike a pacifier, you can't lose a thumb, you don't have to worry about it falling on the floor, and you can't forget to bring it along in the diaper bag!

SLEEP LADY SLUMBER RULE #4:
FEED YOUR BABY UPON WAKING.

Most mothers breast or bottle feed at bedtime for many months. A nice long nursing, including the hindmilk, does tend to encourage sleep—which is exactly what you want at bedtime. But you want to avoid too strong an association between nursing and sleep because it will cause problems later. So some of the time, nurse when he is getting up, not only when he is going to sleep. This comes naturally when he wakes up in the morning, but try to get in the habit of nursing *after* naps, not *before* naps, at least once or twice a day. Most moms find it's easiest to do this first thing in the morning, and at the first morning nap. It doesn't work as well in the late afternoon or early evening when they are tired and fussy and nursing can help them calm down and get ready for bed.

SLEEP LADY SLUMBER RULE #5:
PUT YOUR BABY DOWN DROWSY BUT
AWAKE AT LEAST ONCE A DAY.

This dovetails nicely with Rule 4 about nursing after napping. In the first weeks, we usually do nurse our babies to sleep at bedtime and when they get up hungry during the night. But once he is about four weeks old, get in the habit of putting him down drowsy but awake at least once in each twenty-four-hour period. He doesn't have to be wide awake, but he shouldn't be out cold from being fed, rocked, or swung each time he goes to sleep. He may fuss a little but give it a moment or two. Don't pick him up again at the first squeak; let him surprise you. The easiest time to do this is usually the morning nap. At around six weeks, try this at bedtime too. Sometimes he will fall asleep nursing, and then of course you shouldn't wake him. What you want to aim for is nursing him until he has had enough to eat and is getting drowsy. Then unlatch him gently before he falls fully asleep. It may take a little practice but you'll figure it out within a few days, and if it doesn't work one night, just try again the next. (See page 20 for more help with "drowsy but awake.")

SLEEP LADY SLUMBER RULE #6:
OFFER YOUR BABY ONE BOTTLE PER DAY.

No matter how committed you are to nursing for the long haul—and I breastfed both of my daughters—introduce a bottle once a day by the second or third week. It's up to you and your doctor whether you use pumped milk or formula, but get him used to a bottle early. It's a commonsense preparation for unforeseen circumstances, be it a huge traffic jam that prevents you from getting home by nursing time or an emergency appendectomy. Although some babies adapt easily to a bottle later, others will refuse the bottle once they differentiate between breast and bottle. Since you have no way of knowing how your baby will respond six months from now, do yourself and him a favor and familiarize him with the bottle now. Some couples also like to use occasional bottles so Dad can share in the feeding, both to give Mom a little break and to have some nice daddy-baby bonding time. My husband and I did that at the 10:00 p.m. feeding. I would pump and Bill would bottle feed, either fresh milk or stored breast milk that I had pumped earlier. Sometimes we used formula, because I wanted the peace of mind of knowing my girls could take formula if they ever needed it. Because formula does take longer to digest, some parents find that a bottle of formula at bedtime lets the baby sleep for at least one slightly longer stretch before he wakes up hungry again. It doesn't work for everybody, but go ahead and try it if you want and your doctor approves.

Some families fear that if they give a baby a bottle, he will then reject the breast. This form of nipple confusion is actually a lot less common than people think, and it tends to be more of an issue if you give a bottle at the very beginning, before he has learned to latch on to the breast and before you have learned to nurse. One bottle a day after nursing has been established for a few weeks shouldn't be a problem.

SLEEP LADY SLUMBER RULE #7: CREATE A SLEEP-FRIENDLY ENVIRONMENT.

I strongly believe that the baby's environment affects his sleep. I like room-darkening shades and calm, soothing colors in the baby's bedroom. I don't like bright or stimulating mobiles in the crib. Let him enjoy the mobile somewhere else, where he spends awake time. At bedtime, the message to the brain is "Slow down," not "Stay up and watch your mobile spin." I also want the crib to be a place for sleep and maybe for a few minutes of quiet play right after waking as he gets a little older. It's not a place to park the baby while you wash dishes, nor is it a place to punish a baby or pen him in when he begins to scoot and crawl.

WHITE NOISE AND MUSIC · White noise machines, fans, or sound screens can be useful during the first two months, or even longer during nap time if you live in a particularly loud area. Babies who are extremely alert also do well with white noise, because it helps them shut the world out. Those very alert babies also may need to be nursed in a dim, quiet environment because they are easily distracted. I have found that a white noise machine or a fan is more effective than music in screening out sounds, but many parents understandably prefer lullabies, and that's fine. By around two to three months, take care to use the music to set the mood. If you let music become a sleep crutch, you'll spend the night running in to turn it on each time he stirs. Play music as he gets ready for bed but don't keep it running as he is falling asleep, and don't keep putting it back on during the night when he wakes up. Let it wind down at bedtime, or turn it off or turn the volume down very, very low. When it goes off, it goes off. That's it.

Moms worry a lot about whether to turn the phone off during nap time. Do whatever makes sense for you. My own approach was to turn the upstairs phone off, which was near the girls' rooms, but leave it on downstairs. That way I could still hear it but the noise would be muted for them.

> *Cheryl and Gary's four-month-old son, Ari, was, as Cheryl put it, "hyperalert." "He's always exploring; he's a distractible, active kid." To help him tune out the world enough to sleep, they created a pre-nap routine that was quite similar to his bedtime ritual, just a bit shorter. They started downstairs, where they spent ten minutes watching a quiet video. Then they'd go upstairs and read to him in his room. After that they'd say good night to various objects in his room—the mirror, Noah's ark, etc. Cheryl would then put on the lullaby CD, lay him in his crib, say "Night-night," and walk out of the room.*

MOTION SLEEP · Motion sleep can trip up parents. Up until about eight weeks, babies are very portable. They can sleep wherever you put them—car seats, strollers, swings, bouncy chairs, noisy cafes, the mall, at your best friend's house when her three kids are all bouncing off the playroom walls. But even though they can do this, it doesn't mean they should. It's okay some of the time, but try to have them nap in a nice quiet crib or bassinet most of the time. Also, nobody ever tells us that they shouldn't nap on the go forever—so we keep doing it, particularly letting them sleep in cars. Motion sleep keeps the brain in a light sleep, and as babies mature, they need deeper sleep as well. Think about it. When you doze off in a car, do you feel as refreshed as if you had slept in a bed? The same is true for your baby, especially after the first eight to twelve weeks. Getting him out of the car and into the crib may mean that you will be more housebound for a few weeks—not forever—until your baby develops more predictable nap patterns. If you go stir crazy, get a sitter for a few hours a week, make a deal with your spouse so you can get some time off, invite your mom to visit for a week, or find a friend to do some co-op babysitting with. Again, you don't have to go overboard with rigidity here. Sure he'll fall asleep in the swing, stroller, or car seat once in a while. Don't worry about it. Just don't make it a habit, and if he does fall asleep in the car seat now and then, remove it from the car and put it in his bedroom or at least in another quiet, sleep-conducive place. (If your baby has reflux, your pediatrician might recommend that he does sleep or at least doze in the car seat to help him digest. See Chapter 13, Medical Problems, for more help with babies who have reflux.)

> *At five months, Lydia was still on the same schedule—or nonschedule—she had as a newborn. Nina and Lydia were often on the go, feeding on the run, grabbing a nap in a car seat or stroller. But Lydia didn't eat well, and she didn't nap well. Nina learned that Lydia needed more structure and less stimulation. She needed to nap in her own home, in a quiet place, with no lights, no noise, no distractions. "She became more aware of her surroundings; she couldn't just nurse anywhere, sleep anywhere," Nina said. "I realized I needed to be home for naps."*

BEDTIME ROUTINE · Developing a bedtime routine early, by about six weeks, is absolutely essential. It will be very simple at first. You'll probably start with a warm bath, then move into his dimly lit room. Maybe you'll do a few minutes of infant massage (take a class!). Nurse him or maybe let Dad give him a bottle. Swaddle him, snuggle or rock him on your lap a little, and then lay him in his crib or bassinet. You'll add little games and stories and other rituals of your own as he gets older. But you'll always need a bedtime routine. Predictable routines not only soothe babies, they cue the brain to slow down and get ready for sleep, just like a good book can help an adult to wind down. If an infant is tired but doesn't get to sleep, he gets a cortisol rush, which then makes it even harder for him go to sleep—a downward spiral.

SLEEP LADY SLUMBER RULE #8: CAREFULLY THINK THROUGH THE WHOLE QUESTION OF CO-SLEEPING AND THE FAMILY BED.

The family bed is such a touchy and complicated subject that I've devoted a chapter to the topic. By family bed, I don't mean keeping the baby near you for two or three months. That's another option, a perfectly acceptable one that I'll talk about in a moment. I mean a multiyear commitment to having the parents and children sleep in the bed together every night. As you evaluate whether that's right for you, and whether it will be right for you in two, four, or six years, please read Chapter 10, Co-sleeping and the Family Bed.

Many couples choose short-term co-sleeping to keep the baby with them for the first few months for bonding, nursing convenience, and parental anxiety control. That's fine, but make sure you know all the co-sleeping safety rules. (I review them in Chapter 10, and you should talk to your pediatrician.) I recommend he makes the transition to the crib in his own room at about three months, when an established, predictable pre-sleep routine becomes so essential. It's a little harder after that, and much harder a year or two later. Some parents keep the baby with them for a few months, and then sleep on a spare bed or mattress in the baby's room for a few days or weeks when they move him to the crib. Either is fine; just make sure you have a plan for getting yourself out of the room, because he'll get more accustomed to it than you realize. If you want the baby close by but don't want him to be actually in your bed, there are various "co-sleepers" available and I'm sure more will come on the market between the time I write this and the time you read it! Among them are bassinets that attach to your bed like a sidecar so the baby is next to you, but in his own space.

If you have the baby in his own crib or bassinet but in your bedroom, the same basic guidelines apply. Make the switch to his own room (or a shared room with a sibling) at about three months. If you want to sleep in his room with him for a few days while he gets used to the new environment (and you get used to having him out of your sight), that's fine but don't do it forever. If you are anxious, and we all are, get a baby monitor.

Some parents start to co-sleep but find that, for them, it's uncomfortable, distracting, or noisy. Don't feel guilty. You need your sleep as much as he needs his, so put the baby in his own room if that's the best solution. I know my own kids made a huge racket at night. As a new mom I was very surprised by all the grunts and squeaks that came out of those little tiny throats at midnight.

If you need a little help with this transition, particularly after the first two or three months, read Chapter 4, Newborn to Five Months.

If you co-sleep, short term or indefinitely, have the baby nap in his crib or bassinet. You don't want to teach him that he must always be curled up against you to sleep. That becomes untenable if you have to take care of another child, leave him occasionally with a sitter, or even need to take a shower while he's napping! Napping in the crib helps him acquire that valuable skill: learning how to put himself to sleep. Once he gets a little older and more mobile, it's also safer to leave him napping alone in the crib than in your bed where he can fall out. Besides, you want his room to be a familiar and comfortable place, not a foreign planet.

REACTIVE CO-SLEEPING

Okay, I've told you what's fine. Time to talk about what's not so hot. Many families end up doing what's called *reactive co-sleeping*. That means the baby starts out the night in his bassinet or crib, but ends up in the parents' bed because that's the only way they can get him back to sleep. Or they wanted to co-sleep for three months and here it is month four or five and they haven't figured out how to stop it. The child does not learn to sleep on his own, and the pattern can last years, to everyone's dissatisfaction. I do not believe it's a good route to good sleep—and, if you read more about the family bed, you'll find that proponents of co-sleeping do not consider reactive co-sleeping an ideal option either. Either use the family bed or the crib; don't mix them up. If you follow my Sleep Lady Slumber Rules you'll find alternative ways of getting your baby back to sleep without bringing him into bed with you, and of getting him to sleep through the night so the problem doesn't arise.

Part Two

NEWBORN TO FIVE MONTHS

Please take a few minutes to read the first three chapters of my book, which give an overview of my system and include some helpful hints that apply to all age groups. It won't take long and you'll have much better results.

☼ ☼ ☼

PARENTS OFTEN WONDER HOW EARLY they can start shaping children's sleep. I say, the sooner the better. Naturally, we are very gentle at first, just nudging them to start distinguishing between day and night, light and dark. Later, we'll start teaching them to fall asleep with less assistance from us, to sleep longer intervals at night, to lengthen their naps. I break this advice down month by month, but of course that's an estimate. Phases overlap, and changes unfold over days and weeks, not overnight. A baby eating every two hours at thirty days is not likely to jump to every three hours on the thirty-first day just because he arbitrarily crosses that "one month old" threshold. But this is a useful guideline. Please keep in mind that my feeding advice is for healthy full-term babies. Preemies will catch up but you may have to supplement and feed more frequently until they reach their adjusted birth-age weight. Then, with your doctor's approval, follow these timelines. If your baby is not gaining weight as expected or has other health problems, please consult your pediatrician about feeding.

Many parents are ambivalent about sleep training in these first six months. On one hand, the moms and dads want to sleep, and know that their babies need to sleep too. On the other hand, infants fuss and cry enough as it is. They wonder why they should endure any more tears or force the child to shed them. In fact, there are a lot fewer tears than you would imagine. In these first few months, we shape sleep ever so gently, and I'll encourage you to do plenty of soothing, holding, and snuggling.

> *Nina, who worked on her daughter's sleep habits at five months, found attachment-parenting practices very attractive, and she was loath to let Lydia cry or to be apart from her very much. But her baby fussed and cried anyway, and the sleep portion of attachment parenting just didn't work for her family. As Nina gently modified her parenting style to introduce more structure and independence, she was thrilled to discover that Lydia thrived. The baby who used to be so tired, who fussed even when riding in her stroller, now smiled all the time, slept all night—and hardly ever cried.*

✿ ✿ ✿

> *After four months of dealing with an overtired baby who had reflux, Tracy reluctantly decided to address Lucas's sleep problems. She knew that postponing the inevitable wasn't going to make the situation any easier. "Many of my friends were embarrassed to admit that their kids still aren't sleeping now that they are two or three years old," said Tracy. "When friends confessed that to me, it really helped me. I knew that my husband and I couldn't live that way. I couldn't function. I needed to sleep. I didn't want to be so tired that I couldn't enjoy my baby."*

HOW INFANTS SLEEP

"Sleeping like a baby," as the saying goes, is not all that it's cracked up to be. Newborns sleep a lot, about fifteen to eighteen hours a day, but their sleep is not organized, not well developed. For the first four months, about half their sleep is REM (rapid eye movement) sleep, the most active kind of sleep. That means they are sleeping lightly, and are more easily aroused than an older child or an adult who spends much less time in REM. Young babies also cycle between the two sleep states, REM and non-REM, much more than adults or even older children do. Each time they switch, they have a *partial awakening*. For us as adults, a partial awakening may only last a few seconds, and we may scarcely remember it in the morning. But that brief moment of semi-awakeness can startle babies, and make them wake up even more. They then cry—and we rush in and frantically try all sorts of things to rescue them from their tears.

I strongly believe in responding to a child's cry, both for his sake and for our own peace of mind. As parents, we need to make sure that they are okay, that they haven't spit up or gotten tangled in something, that their diaper hasn't leaked, that sort of thing. But we shouldn't overdo it. We need to strike a balance between comforting our children and allowing them to learn to comfort themselves. That's an essential component of sleep shaping. If we rescue them by creating a sleep crutch, by teaching them that they must always be held, rocked, nursed, or have a pacifier in their mouth to get back to sleep, they will never learn how to get themselves back to sleep after partial arousals, never learn how to sleep through the night.

FEEDING

As we trace infant development month to month in this chapter, we'll talk a lot about how often babies need to eat—versus how often you think they might need to eat! Remember that when you do feed your baby at night, keep the lights off and don't interact much. Feed him, burp him, give him a few hugs, and then put him right back in his bassinet, crib, wherever he began the night. It isn't playtime and it isn't time for musical beds. If he wakes up between feeding times, make sure he's truly awake before you run in and wake him even more. Sometimes they stir during a partial awakening, make a few strange baby noises, and then go right back to sleep.

> *"With Holly, our first child, with one whimper we'd jolt out of bed and rush into her room," said Marianne, who had three children in three years and became quite a skillful sleep coach out of necessity. "We learned that making noise doesn't mean they are awake. When Holly made a noise, we were actually waking her up by barging in."*

If he's definitely awake, go in and stroke him, pat his back, sh-sh him, swaddle him, or use other soothing techniques to get him back to sleep. Don't overdo it, either. Maybe all he really needs is to be swaddled and put back down. Sit right by his crib until he dozes off if you think it makes him—or you—feel better. Follow this advice not just in the first month but until he outgrows night feedings.

I know there's a lot to absorb in this chapter and following all this advice isn't easy, especially when you are tired and overwhelmed by all the emotional, logistical, and marital changes that accompany parenthood. Some moms who consulted me for sleep problems with their first child vowed to do everything differently with the second child—and ended up calling me sheepishly a few months later to help them undo all the things they failed to do differently!

"My first child was adopted and we didn't get him until he was six months old," said Ellen, the mom who wrote those cue cards I shared with you in Chapter 1. "My second child, Vanessa, was my biological child. I had her from birth, and I had big ambitions of starting good habits with her from the beginning. After all, I was a veteran! But she was so strong-willed and she had horrible reflux and I didn't even try. We both fell over into bed together and I nursed her every two hours." The reflux subsided at six months, and Ellen finally called me at eight months. The good news is that we got her little girl into her crib and off all that nursing in just three nights. Looking back, Ellen realized she could have spared her whole family a lot of sleepless nights if she had not let herself get so overwhelmed and been more consistent.

Lisa had a different experience. Her son, Teddy, had many sleep difficulties that we addressed when he was about seven months old. But when her daughter, Brittany, was born, Lisa began shaping her sleep from the start. She paid more attention to when she nursed, worked on putting her down drowsy but awake, and was careful not to hold her to sleep all the time. And she didn't panic quite so much if the baby cried sometimes. Her consistency, and her more confident parenting, paid off and Brittany slept very well from early on. You'll read more about her experience at the end of this chapter. But whether you are more like Ellen or Lisa, the important thing is this—don't beat yourself up over things you could have done differently. Just focus on making it better from now on.

THE FIRST MONTH (0–4 WEEKS)

For the first week, babies typically sleep a total of sixteen to eighteen hours, about half during the night and half spread out over four daytime naps. By the end of the first month, they sleep an average of fifteen and a half to seventeen hours total, about eight and a half to ten hours at night and six to seven hours during the day spread over three or four naps. They will still wake up two or three times at night for feedings but should go back to sleep quickly.

Even during these first few weeks, your baby is beginning to pick up on your cues and feelings and to realize that he can affect the world around him. He will recognize the scent of your breast milk, will prefer soft sensations to coarse ones, and like to be handled very gently. Abrupt or rough moves can frighten or startle him. Although he won't fully distinguish day from night for six to eight weeks, he will develop this ability faster if you expose him to light now. You don't want to shock him with bright, glaring lights in his eyes, but you can open the blinds when he gets up in the morning, keep him in brighter rooms when he's awake and in dimmer ones when he is going to sleep. Be careful not to overstimulate him, either by letting him stay up too long without a nap or exposing him to too much noise or activity. Sometimes more is less—you could inadvertently stimulate when you are trying to soothe. If you spend thirty minutes trying to soothe a newborn and he's still fussing, try swaddling him and putting him down in a dimly-lit room. He may then calm down on his own. When newborns have had too much stimulation, they may *habituate*. That means they go into a state that looks like sleep but is actually just a way of shutting everything out. It's a form of self-soothing they use up until about six to eight weeks, when they begin to develop other ways of coping with stimulation. It's sometimes hard for parents to distinguish dozing from habituating. A sleeping baby tends to wake up alert and responsive. After habituating, a baby is not so alert; in fact he may be fussy and irritable. You want to avoid a lot of habituation because if he shuts down during the day, chances are he will be up a lot more during the night. Newborns need a certain amount of tranquility when they are awake, and if they can't get that peaceful awake time during the day, they will seek it out at night.

> *I remember taking my first daughter, Carleigh, to a wedding when she was five weeks old. Much to my distress, she cried much more than usual during the ceremony when of course I most wanted her to be quiet—and then she appeared to sleep through the very loud reception, complete with Greek music and dancing. But then she stayed up and cried all night long. Much later, as I learned more about infant sleep, I remembered that wedding. I realized Carleigh had responded to overstimulation at the ceremony with tears, and then habituated during the reception to protect herself from even more sensory overload. She was then so overtired and out of kilter by nighttime, she cried. By the time my second child was born, I was more protective of her sleep and knew better than to take her to a Greek wedding!*

Babies in the first month need to eat every two to two and a half hours. Try not to feed her more often than that. I don't mean you should be absolutely rigid. Two hours is a goal, not a straightjacket. If she's really sobbing, and you already tried other soothing techniques, then feed her, particularly if you're getting pretty close to the two-hour mark. But if you feed her more frequently, pay close attention to her response. If she stops sucking after just a few minutes or she dozes off quickly on the breast, that's your clue that she wasn't really hungry. Review the Sleep Lady's Eight Rules of Infant Slumber beginning on page 38 if you find yourself always nursing, and are too quick to offer the breast as her main means of comfort. The one time when it may be a good idea to feed a little more frequently—but not constantly—is late afternoon/early evening. We call this *cluster feeding*, and it helps in that hungry, fussy, overstimulated-and-getting-tired part of the day. I am talking roughly 3:00 p.m. to 7:00 p.m. here.

You've heard the expression "Never wake a sleeping baby," but I disagree. The Sleep Lady version is "Never wake a sleeping newborn at night—but get him up and feed him after three hours during the day." At night, be grateful for every minute of sleep he gets past two hours. If he needs to eat, he'll let you know. During the day, he should sleep two, sometimes three hours at a time. But you can't let him stay awake too long either. Again the limit is about two hours. He may look alert, he may seem fine, but as countless mothers have learned the hard way, the reality is if we wait until they don't look fine anymore we're too late. They will be overstimulated, overtired, and all that cortisol now rushing through their bloodstream will make it hard to get them to sleep. Similarly, plan his last feeding and bedtime to coincide with your bedtime, sometime between 10:00 p.m. and 11:00 p.m. (His bedtime will be earlier in a few months.) Keep him awake for the two hours before that bedtime. Lots of babies stay up easily during those two hours, and it can become a nice family time, particularly a good time for Dad to be with the baby if Mom has had him all day. Other newborns have trouble staying awake until 10:00. If your baby is tired, fussy, and unable to feed well at 10:00, then move the bedtime to an earlier time. It may take a little trial and error to find the right time but watch for her sleep cues; they will tell you more than the clock. Usually an adjustment of just an hour or a half-hour does the trick, but I've worked with a handful of newborns whose natural sleep window was as early as 8:00 p.m.

A consistent bedtime and some rudimentary bedtime rules, even at this tender age, are important. It's how we start to regulate sleep. These first few weeks he may well need you to hold, rock, or nurse him to sleep in your arms but at least once a day, try to use those tools only to the point of drowsiness, not until he's fully asleep. Then very gently lower him into his crib, swaddled, and let him finish falling asleep. If you find yourself tensing up at the thought that he might cry, take a few deep, calming breaths before you put him down. If he does cry, you'll be right there to comfort him. At this early age, you can pick him up to soothe him again if you need to; just try not to let him fall asleep in your arms all the time.

Napping isn't very predictable these first few weeks, but the first morning nap is a good time to practice the basic rules, including the drowsy-but-awake routine. The morning nap usually starts only an hour or two after he wakes up. Many new parents don't realize he has to go back to sleep so quickly, but if he gets overstimulated the first thing in the morning, you are going to have trouble all day. If he nursed shortly after waking up, as most babies do, he won't need to nurse again before napping. Use your other soothing techniques (see page 42). Even if you are co-sleeping in these early weeks, have him nap in his crib or bassinet. You don't want him to need to sleep curled up next to you all the time; it will make napping harder in the coming months.

Remember to take care of yourself and sleep whenever you can.

THE SECOND MONTH (4–8 WEEKS)

Babies sleep on average fifteen and a half to seventeen hours total, eight and a half to ten hours at night and six to seven hours during the day, spread over three or four naps. Some will now wake only once a night to be fed, although others will still need two overnight feedings for a few more weeks.

Hallmarks of the second month are those adorable first smiles—and intense fussiness, particularly in late afternoon and early evening. At four to eight weeks, babies are too old to *habituate*, to just shut down and shut out stimulation. But they have not yet mastered self-calming techniques. In this section, I will give you some tips on how to get through these difficult fussy weeks, and some advice on how to start helping your baby take the first steps toward sleeping longer and deeper. Always remember to use your whole repertoire of soothing techniques, not just the bottle or breast.

At this point, the maturing brain starts organizing nighttime sleep, and babies sleep up to four hours at a time. By seven or eight weeks, many sleep six or even eight hours at a stretch. During the second month, your efforts to help him distinguish light and dark will start to bear fruit as he begins to recognize day and night and establish his natural circadian rhythms, his body clock. Don't wake him to feed him at night; encourage those longer stretches of sleep. During the day you still want to wake him after three hours so he keeps his best sleep for later. Aim to keep him awake from about 8:00 p.m. to 10:00 p.m. so he can have a final feeding around 10:00 and then go to bed. He should then be able to sleep until about 2:00 a.m., wake to eat briefly, and then sleep again until about 6:00. (A common and acceptable variation is an 11:00 p.m. final feeding, a 3:00 a.m. middle-of-the-night feeding, and a

7:00 a.m. morning feeding.) Although babies get up between 6:00 a.m. and 7:00 a.m., they will nap again within the next two hours. Remember to get yourself to bed as early as you can.

By six to eight weeks, start being more conscious of sleep habits and patterns. Focus on bedtime, when you cue the brain to fall asleep. Help him fall asleep without always needing something in his mouth, be it a bottle, breast, or pacifier. (Don't worry about this in the middle of the night. If he falls asleep while nursing at 2:00 a.m., just return him to his bed and get back to sleep yourself.) You may already be working on drowsy-but-awake for the morning nap. Now start concentrating on it at the 10:00 p.m. feeding too. You want him to be sleepy after he eats but not out so cold that he can't finish the task of falling asleep on his own. Make sure that he's been adequately burped. Swaddle him if he likes it (most two-month-olds do, but over the course of this month he may want his arms wrapped less tightly or left outside the blanket). Lower him gently into his crib with his feet slightly lower than his head so as not to set off his reflexive fear of falling.

If he does cry, you don't have to leave a tiny baby alone in the dark. I couldn't have done that with my babies when they were this little. Sit by his side, pat him, and quietly "sh-sh" him. It's very tempting to pick him up, but try to resist. Do go ahead and hold him, though, if he does begin to cry so intensely that he won't be able to wind himself down. Put him down again when he's calm—but don't wait until he's fully asleep. Avoid picking him up and putting him down repeatedly, as some baby books recommend. That often stimulates babies and makes it even harder for them to go to sleep. You'll use these calming techniques at bedtime, at some nap times, and definitely when he awakens at night when it is not time to nurse.

The brain takes longer to sort out daytime sleep, so napping will remain fairly disorganized this month. He will take three or four naps—don't worry about whether it's three or four, and don't worry about minor day-to-day variations (although you don't want total chaos). New parents often underestimate how frequently babies require sleep. If he stays awake more than two hours at a time, he will become overstimulated as well as overtired, and it will be harder for him to nap. That means that if he wakes up at 7:00 a.m., he should be napping by 9:00. To help him get ready to nap, place him in a quiet environment a half hour or so before you want him to fall asleep (i.e., if he's going to nap at 9:00 a.m., start setting the stage at 8:30). That might mean nursing, it might mean walking him a bit, or holding him while you sing him a song. By the end of this month, around week eight, phase out motion-sleep in cars, swings, and the like and get him napping in a crib or bassinet. Many naps will still be short, just forty-five minutes or so, but gradually some of the naps should last an hour or more. If he usually wakes after only about thirty minutes, try to stretch out some of these catnaps by keeping him in his crib and soothing him back to sleep, comforting him the way you do at bedtime. It won't always work but give it ten minutes or so, and try again the next day. It's usually easier to work on this in the morning than in the afternoon. Even at this young age, some babies act on their growing recognition of their parents by trying to resist sleep. They want to stay awake and hang out with you, a pattern that may intensify as they go through peaks of separation anxiety in the coming months.

As babies sleep longer, they eat a little less frequently if they are healthy and growing well. At four weeks, it's about every two and a half hours, and by eight weeks or nine weeks it's closer to every three hours. That's about five or six times a day. Some will only wake up once at night; some will still need to eat two or three times, although it usually tapers off by the end of this month and certainly in the third month. If you find yourself nursing more frequently, particularly at night, stop and ask yourself whether he is really hungry, when he last ate, whether you should be offering comfort other than a breast. During this month, usually from six weeks on, they begin to differentiate their cries and that helps us figure out what's bothering them and how to fix it. There's a "change my diaper" cry. There's a "pick me up and hold me" cry. There's a "Mom, I'm ready for bed now," cry, a "hey, Mom, I'm six weeks old and I want something interesting to shake and touch" cry, a "give me back my pacifier right now" cry, and there is, of course, a hunger cry. Don't treat all cries as hunger cries.

> "With Holly, I always thought that crying meant hunger. So it was cry, feed, cry, feed. It was food first, then try something else," said Marianne, that mother of three whom you will meet again in Chapter 11, on twins and siblings. "By the time I got to Ally, my third, it was try everything else before I tried food." Instead of automatically nursing Dean and Ally, she'd walk them, rock them, pat them, rub their backs, being careful not to do it so constantly that it would become a sleep crutch.

When she wakes up at night and doesn't need to nurse, don't nurse. It's really that simple. You'll have to resist giving her that extra feeding a few nights in a row, but then she should start sleeping through that spell. If you are inconsistent, if you refuse to give her an extra feeding one night but succumb the next night, the intermittent reinforcement will make the problem more persistent, and it will be more difficult for both you and your child to change it.

At about four weeks, many babies enter that superfussy period. It isn't a whole lot of fun. Late afternoon/early evening is a hard time for parents too. We're pretty worn out after taking care of a little baby all day; we're trying to get some dinner on the table and summon up at least a shred of energy to converse with the spouse arriving home from work. Perhaps we are taking care of other small children who are tired and hungry themselves at this time of day, or older children who see absolutely no point in doing their math homework before watching TV. It helps to remember that the superfussies are a phase, not a life sentence. The fussiness peaks at about six weeks, and wanes by about twelve weeks.

Just do the best you can to get through this stage. Give the baby regular naps and avoid overstimulation. Cut back on socializing and having visitors in the early afternoon. Meet friends and relatives earlier in the day (or hire a babysitter or enlist a friend or relative for an hour or so once in a while so you can get out). Feed her in a quiet, dim room, without the distractions of televisions, ringing telephones, or conversations. Do the best you can to keep older siblings away from the baby at this time of day. If possible, enlist Dad's help and convince him that instead of playing the action-packed games that fathers often favor, he should be soother-in-chief. Fathers tend to arrive home just as the baby hits her fussy peak, between 6:00 p.m. and 7:00 p.m. It creates a discouraging and difficult dynamic. I remember my husband was totally convinced that our first daughter detested him because he'd walk in the door, arms outstretched, and she'd greet him with a howl. Sometimes she'd fuss and scream for an hour in the early evening and Bill learned how to be a very soothing dad, swaddling her, holding her, walking her until she finally got calm. Good thing, too, because our second one fussed even more, doing an outstanding job of disproving the myth that it's easier with your second child!

THE THIRD MONTH (8–12 WEEKS)

Babies this age on average need fifteen hours of sleep, ten at night and five spread out over three daytime naps. Many babies can sleep six to eight hours at a stretch before needing a night feeding. By the end of the month, most should sleep eight hours uninterrupted.

During the third month, babies make lots of progress and you should get more rest. The fussiness ebbs by the end of this month. They are awake more during the day, asleep more at night, and beginning to find their own natural sleep-wake rhythms. Your job will be to adjust and mold that rhythm into a flexible schedule, but her brain and body clock will lay the groundwork for you. Around the third month, babies start producing melatonin, a hormone that relaxes the muscles and promotes drowsiness. Linked to light and darkness, melatonin secretions rise in the evening. By regulating your baby's sleep, encouraging her to maximize her nighttime sleep, you are helping to establish good hormonal rhythms, which will in turn further improve her sleep. I know that regulating sleep still sounds daunting at this age, because your days probably still seem pretty blurry. But actually, you have been building up to this step since birth by limiting daytime sleep, maximizing exposure to daylight, and promoting longer nighttime sleep. You have been helping her brain to learn how to act during the day and what to do at night.

Some babies can now stay awake three hours at a stretch during the day, if they are well rested. This isn't an iron-clad rule so watch carefully and put her down if she starts looking or acting tired. Don't wait too long because if you let her get overtired, she'll have more trouble sleeping and get fussier. Add more structure to her naps. Babies are less portable now for day sleep; they need a quiet and familiar environment without a lot of light, noise, and distractions. They also need a deeper sleep than their brains allow if they are in motion. Get her out of the habit of napping in car seats, strollers, and the like and get her home and into her crib or bassinet. At around twelve weeks, the morning nap should fall into place, lasting about one to one and a half hours. A few weeks later, the stubborn afternoon nap takes on a more dependable shape as well. She will probably take a brief third nap in the late afternoon, forty-five minutes to an hour depending on the quality and quantity of earlier naps. You can be a little more flexible about this third nap than the other two; don't worry if she falls asleep in a car or stroller.

Bedtime should now look like bedtime, and it should be the same time every night, give or take fifteen minutes. Sure, she might just conk out on you at 8:00 one night when you had been planning to put her down at 9:00, but you don't want a completely scattered schedule: a 7:00 bedtime one night and 11:00 the next. You should have a bedtime routine—a very simple one, bath, pajamas, maybe some infant massage, listen to a song or start to look at a simple picture book—that you will build on as she gets older. Nurse or bottle feed her, swaddle her if she still likes it, though a bit more loosely than you used to, and put her down drowsy but awake. If she knows how to put herself to sleep at bedtime, it will be easier for her to start learning to put herself back to sleep in the middle of the night without a round of "comfort nursing."

At this age, babies still need five or six feedings a day, about every three hours, but they don't need to eat as much at night. The sixth feeding is the bedtime feeding. That may still be at 10:00 p.m. or 11:00 p.m. at the beginning of this month, but gradually you will move it earlier, to about 8:00 p.m. You'll know she's ready for the earlier bedtime either when she can sleep eight hours at a stretch overnight, or when you see that she is fading earlier. Watch for sleepy cues, such as yawning, rubbing her eyes, or crankiness. There is some natural variation to how long babies in this age range can sleep at night without a feeding—anything from six to ten hours is normal. Some babies will sleep all the way through the night, and others will semi-rouse themselves for one very brisk and businesslike nursing. They'll only get half awake, they'll eat, and they'll go right back to sleep. Your goal this month should be to lengthen their nighttime sleep, working toward that eight to ten hours of uninterrupted sleep. I breastfed both of my children but I got them both sleeping through the night at this age. At eight weeks, Carleigh slept from around 9:00 p.m. or 10:00 p.m. until 7:00 a.m., and Gretchen at ten weeks slept from 10:00 p.m. to 6:00 a.m.

If your baby is waking up to eat much more frequently, and you've ruled out any health factors, then you should begin gently helping her to change that pattern. Whether you are breast or bottle feeding, make sure that she's eating well during the day, which means she'll have less incentive to eat at night. Be careful to give her full feedings, including both foremilk and hindmilk (see page 41) if you're nursing. Try not to let her graze or snack all day, and try not to feed her more than every three hours (except one additional time during the late-afternoon cluster feeding to avoid that fussiness). Feed her in a quiet place with few distractions so she'll concentrate on her meal, not her environment.

In the evening you will feed her before bed, probably at around 8:00. You will feed her in the morning, at about 6:00. And you will feed her once, and only once, in between. You have two choices as to how you approach this. You can wake her to give her a *dream feed*, at about 10:00 p.m. or 11:00 p.m., before you go to sleep. Keep the lights off, rouse her as little as possible, feed her and put her back to bed. Or you can wait for her to wake up on her own, as long as it's after 10:00 p.m. Whichever system you choose, stick to it; don't go back and forth. If she wakes up more than that, and she well may the first few nights, use other calming and soothing techniques to help her get back to sleep. If she cries a bit, just sit by her and reassure her, but don't feed her. If necessary, pick her up, but put her down when she's calm so she falls asleep in her bed, not your arms. Try not to pick her up and put her down over and over again. If you are clear and consistent, they usually stop waking up for those other feedings within just a few nights.

If you have been co-sleeping but want to switch her into her own bed, or if you have had her in a bassinet but want to transfer her to a full crib, the end of the third month is the ideal time. Put her in the crib for daytime naps first, if she isn't there already. Give her about a week of napping in the crib to get used to it, then move her to the crib at night. Be consistent. If you want her in her crib, you have to keep her there all night, every night. Soothe her, stroke her, do what you need to comfort her, but don't just surrender and bring her back to your bed because you fear it's the only way you can get her to sleep. It's not.

Parents switching an infant out of their bed sometimes worry that she is going to feel little and lost in that great big crib. I'm not sure whether the baby feels that way or the parents are projecting, but here's a trick to make a little nest within the crib. Roll up one or more baby blankets or towels to make a U and place them under the tightly fitted sheet, so they can't get loose and harm the baby. (One mom I know also fastened them with ponytail holders to make the rolls tighter.) Put the baby in the crib, with her feet toward the bottom of the U. (Review the exact placement with your doctor so there's no suffocation or SIDS risk.) Some babies do well with sleep positioners that hold them in place and make them feel more snug. Again, talk to your doctor to make sure it's safe and suitable for your baby. (The U also works for reflux babies, a problem we'll talk more about in Chapter 13, Medical Problems.)

Dean, the second of Marianne's children, had reflux and often slept in a car seat. Marianne didn't know quite how to get him in a bed. "He slept fine but my concern was how do I get an upright baby flat into a crib. I had so many questions that my doctor couldn't answer. Kim taught me how to make that U and to elevate the mattress, so Dean felt snuggled and was still a little tilted to help with the reflux. We did that at night. In the day, I left him in the car seat for a while longer, but I put the car seat in the crib so he would get used to being there."

THE FOURTH AND FIFTH MONTHS

At four months babies should be able to sleep about eight hours at night without a feeding, and by five months they go for about ten or eleven hours. They sleep four to five hours during the day, spread out over three naps.

I get a lot of calls from parents of twelve- to sixteen-week-olds. Lots of moms go back to work around then and they are frantic about juggling work and family when they are getting only a few hours of sleep—and frequently interrupted sleep at that. Also, many parents expect babies to start sleeping better after three months—only they think it just sort of happens magically and they get an unpleasant shock. Luckily, this is an excellent time, often the ideal time, to step in and coach a baby to sleep better. Bad sleep habits are not yet deeply ingrained, and the baby is experiencing physical and developmental changes, including an increased ability to soothe herself, that are very conducive to a more predictable food, sleep, and awake schedule.

Developmental Changes

The fourth and fifth months are a time of transition. Colic and fussiness subside. Babies are more awake and more active. They experience an exciting burst of cognitive awareness, becoming more aware of sights and sounds, and beginning to understand *object permanence*, realizing that people and things exist even when they are out of the baby's view. That's one reason they love hiding games and peek-a-boo, a great new element in the bedtime routine. Along with this greater cognizance of new and old, here and there, familiar and unfamiliar, comes a bout of separation anxiety. When she wakes up at night, she may not be searching for a feeding anymore so much as a brief bit of reassurance that Mom and Dad are right where they are supposed to be.

Neurologically, the character of the baby's sleep is evolving too. Over the fourth and fifth months, melatonin secretion rises and non-REM sleep increases, meaning she sleeps more deeply than she did as a newborn. But the non-REM also means that when she does have a partial arousal every three to four hours, it's more distinct, and she feels more awake. She may need a quick reassurance from you as she adjusts to this change, but she doesn't need a feeding. Some babies may cry out but quiet themselves by the time you reach the bedroom door, so you should tiptoe away before you wake her more. Others get more upset and disorganized and still need your help to calm down. Help her, but don't overdo it. Don't do so much patting or stroking or singing that she can't get to sleep without it. You want to comfort her, not create a new sleep crutch.

As your child's sleep becomes more organized, you can also start reading her tiredness clues. That means keeping one eye on the clock and the other eye on your baby. Is she active or is she yawning? Is she rubbing her eyes? Starting to nod off? These are all sleep signals. Pay attention, because it's a lot better for her to go to bed, whether it's nap time or bedtime, when she's getting tired than waiting until she's overtired. Cynthia's mom, Jayne, found that keeping a detailed sleep log helped her learn to recognize her four-month-old daughter's cues and rhythms, to see when her "sleep window" was open. "She'd yawn, rub her eyes, and start spacing out. I learned that by the second yawn, I'd better get her to bed for nap time."

Babies this age are also very sensitive to changes in routine. An unusually stimulating day, when you have lots of visitors or are out and about in new places, can disrupt her night sleep. That will inevitably happen once in a while. Just take extra care the next day that she gets plenty of naps and has a little extra quiet time so you don't get into that vicious cycle of exhaustion leading to more sleeplessness leading to more exhaustion.

Bedtime

Because four- and five-month-olds are more alert, they need an evening routine that helps them switch mental gears, unwind, and get ready for bed. Bedtime should be between 8:00 p.m. and 9:00 p.m., although you will shift that earlier to between 7:00 p.m. and 8:00 p.m. during the fifth or sixth months as daytime naps decrease and he sleeps longer at night uninterrupted. Remember to get him down drowsy but awake—it's increasingly important at this age. Some babies fuss and cry when you put them into the crib, some just nod off. If yours cries, sit by his crib, pat him, "sh-sh" him, give him the reassurance he needs, but also give him some space to calm down and fall asleep on his own. Be his coach, not his crutch.

If he consistently falls asleep during that last pre-bedtime feeding, pay attention. He's telling you that he needs an earlier bedtime, so move it up fifteen or twenty minutes at a time until you find the right moment for him. That way he can finish nursing or taking his bottle and get into bed drowsy but awake. Even if his bedtime is right, he may still occasionally fall asleep at the breast—or he may use the breast (or bottle) to put himself to sleep, thwarting your efforts to put him to bed drowsy. Remember if his eyes are rolling back and he's suckling but not swallowing, unlatch him and put him down before he's completely conked out. Sometimes the unlatching will wake him up and he will want to latch right back on, almost as if he's saying, "Sorry! I didn't mean to fall asleep on the job. I'm still hungry!" In that case, go ahead and give him one more opportunity to finish. Help him stay awake by stroking his head or rubbing his palms, feet, or back. If he just reverts to suckling again, and isn't taking in any more milk, assume he's done eating and is now trying to nurse himself to sleep. Unlatch him, burp him, swaddle him, and get him into the crib quickly.

> *At about five months, when Nina and Mitch also tackled Lydia's eating and napping patterns, they made a big effort to establish a calm and consistent evening routine. They kept the lights low and the television off. After a ten-minute bath, they moved into Lydia's bedroom, and slathered lots of diaper cream on her so they wouldn't worry about disruptive diaper changes at night to prevent rashes. They dressed her in a "sleep sack," which kept her warm and cozy and freed them from worrying about dangerous or tangled bedding. They played a few quiet games, shunning any toys with "crazy lights or noises" at bedtime. Nina then sat with her in a chair and read the same three little books that Lydia already recognized as part of her bedtime ritual. If Nina saw Lydia's sleep signals—yawning, eye rubbing, or diving toward Nina's chest—she sped up the bedtime process. She nursed Lydia but made sure to unlatch her and put her down drowsy but awake.*

Around the fifth month, babies start to test how their actions can affect the world around them. They want to probe their powers, and your limits. You may see it at bedtime. One favorite experiment for these budding Einsteins seems to be "If I cry, can I make Mommy come to my crib?" Respond and show her that yes, you'll come to check on her. But once you've reassured her, don't linger at her bedside too long.

Feeding

At four or five months, babies still need to eat frequently, at least five times a day, every three to four hours. (By five months, work on stretching it closer to four hours.) Occasionally, perhaps during a growth spurt, he may have to nurse every two to three hours. That's okay but add the extra feedings during the day, not at night. *Cluster feeding,* meaning more frequent feedings in the late afternoon/early evening, may help calm him, enhance his evening sleep, and also reassure you at night that he is getting enough food. With his new alertness and eagerness to take in his surroundings, he may become more distractible while he eats. If so, try to feed him in a quiet, dimly lit place so that he can concentrate, with only a few breaks to look at Mom and smile.

The conventional wisdom on starting solids has shifted several times over the years but these days most pediatricians introduce rice cereal or a similar food at six months. Some babies do well on solids earlier—discuss it with your pediatrician, but I think of this as a dietary issue, not a sleep solution. (If you try solids earlier, and it doesn't go smoothly, just put it off for another month or so with your pediatrician's approval. It should be a pretty natural transition when the baby is ready.) Some parents introduce rice cereal early and give it at bedtime to make a baby sleep longer. After watching scores of families try this without significant success, I have my doubts. I think solids help those relatively few babies who still wake up repeatedly because they are truly hungry at night. That problem is better addressed by making sure they eat more during daytime. In those cases, a little cereal *during the day*, with your doctor's permission, might help shift the feeding clock. But if he is waking up because he has not yet developed good sleep habits, if he needs a bottle, breast, or pacifier to get through those partial arousals, or if he knows that at the first sound of his cry you will hustle him off into your bed, offering your child a few spoonfuls of cereal probably isn't going to solve the problem. You need to address the poor sleep habits themselves.

At four months, your child should be able to sleep about eight hours at night without a feeding. At five months, he should be able to go for ten. The more adept he is at putting himself to sleep, and back to sleep at night, the easier it is for him to give up nighttime feeding. He may even do it without any help from you. If he's getting up once to eat now, semi-rousing himself for one brisk and businesslike meal and then getting right back to sleep, I would leave it alone, as long as he is pretty good at getting himself to sleep and back to sleep. He'll probably outgrow that last feeding soon, or you'll be able to gently train him out of it in another month or two. (Until he does outgrow it, you might want to have Mom nurse some nights and Dad can give a bottle the other nights so you get a little more rest yourselves.)

But if he's getting up frequently at night to eat, it's time to tackle it. You want to get him down to one feeding at night, with the goal of stretching out the time he can go without the breast or bottle to eight and then ten hours.

Often it's the parent as much or more than the child who holds on to excess middle-of-the-night feedings, not quite convinced that the child won't starve. It's an understandable reaction because that's what you have been doing since his birth, and it's hard to feel certain that he just doesn't need them anymore. Talk to your doctor to get reassurance. A food and sleep log can help you see more clearly when he's hungry, when he's nursing for comfort, and how long he can actually go without any food. Resist the urge to nurse at every cry—and pay attention to how your baby behaves. If he cries and you rush in, and he nurses for three minutes and then falls asleep, he clearly isn't hungry. He's using the breast as a sleep crutch, simply because he is used to it.

I'm going to give you several options for cutting back nighttime feedings, similar to the suggestions I made for three-month-olds. Whatever tactic you choose, stick to it. Don't bounce back and forth between systems and schedules. Make sure your doctor agrees that your child is growing well enough, and is healthy enough to have only one overnight feeding.

1. You can give a *dream feed.* That means you rouse him just enough to eat at about 10:00 p.m. or 11:00 p.m., at least two hours after he fell asleep, and just before you go to sleep yourself. Don't feed him again until at least 6:00 the next morning. I have a slight preference for the dream feed at this age because the timing is more consistent, the parent controls the wake-up time, and the baby can work on long, unbroken stretches of sleep at night. I think it's also easier for the parents because it's simpler. You don't have to make any timing decisions in the middle of the night when you are groggy and more likely to second guess yourself or feed when you hadn't intended to—more intermittent reinforcement. In another month or two, you'll probably find it pretty easy to eliminate the dream feed as well, or he may just start skipping it on his own.

2. You can feed him once when he wakes up as long as it's at least two hours since he fell asleep. In other words, if he goes to bed at 8:00 p.m. but wakes up at 9:00, put him back to bed without feeding him and wait for him to wake up another hour or two later. If he goes to bed at 8:00 and wakes up at 10:00 or 11:00, go ahead and feed him. Lots of families are comfortable with this, but it's child-directed, not parent-directed, which means there can be a little built-in inconsistency. One night he'll get fed at 10:00, another night at midnight; he won't always be lengthening that interval.

3. You can "go for the stretch." This is a slight variation on choice number two, but in that option you were counting two hours from bedtime. In this version, you count back from wake-up time, stretching the interval between her last feeding and her wakening. The interval should be based on the longest your child has ever slept without food overnight, even if she only did it once. If she went without food for six hours, you *know* she is physically capable of going for six hours; you

don't have to stay up half the night yourself worrying about whether you are starving her. Determine your stretch based on that time frame, and subtract it from her wake-up time. For instance, if she has gone six hours, and she usually wakes up at 6:00 a.m., then you will feed her when she wakes up around midnight but not again later. If she wakes up at 7:00 a.m., subtract six hours and you can feed her when she wakes up around 1:00 a.m. (You can be a little flexible the first couple of nights, a half hour or so in one direction or another because she may not wake up at midnight on the dot. But don't give too much wiggle room.) When you are ready, add another half hour to the stretch, to six and a half and so on. Your goal is ten hours by five months.

As you'll see in a moment, some families modify these systems based on their child's own wake rhythms and their own comfort zone. The important thing is feeding only once, and doing it consistently.

Whatever option you choose, he may wake up when it's not feeding time for several nights. Sit by his crib and use your comforting tools to get him back to sleep. You may have some tears for a couple of nights, but keep calming him, keep making him feel better; just don't keep feeding him. Usually it only takes a few nights at this age for them to stop waking up.

Let's meet three families who took different approaches to nighttime feeding. Cheryl and Gary took the most radical approach. They had started and stopped several sleep programs already in Ari's four months, and felt they had already confused their son. They decided that the best way for their family to proceed was to cut out nighttime nursing altogether. Nina and Mitch used a modified version of the *go for the stretch* system, counting from bedtime instead of wake-up time. Katherine and Mickey started out with go-for-the-stretch but after a few nights, realized they could stretch Maude even longer than they had planned and she gave up nighttime feeding completely quite quickly.

Ari

> "I'm a therapist, and I'd read all the books, and here I was exhausted, at my wits' end, nursing Ari three times a night—I was the boobie lady," said Cheryl. When Ari was four months old, Cheryl and Gary decided to stop the nighttime nursing completely. Their pediatrician agreed Ari would be fine going ten hours without nursing. In her professional capacity, Cheryl knew a great deal about child development and tears but

as a very hormonal, very emotional new mom (her own description), she couldn't deal with it, so her husband took over the night shift. Gary needed to spell out ahead of time precisely what to do and say when Ari woke up—a script of intervention. "He needed to know what words to say, when to say 'hush, hush,' how long to sit in the rocking chair, how many minutes to pat Ari. Then he could carry it out," Cheryl said. Perhaps because this couple had already started and stopped and started and stopped several other sleep systems, Ari did not respond as quickly as many four-month-olds. Still, in less than two weeks, he was on a very good eating and napping schedule and almost always sleeping through the night.

Lydia

To get five-month-old Lydia to sleep, Nina and Mitch took her into their bed, nursed every one and a half to two hours, rocked her, held her, and walked her—and often that only worked if Lydia could hear running water in the background!

"She was a motion junkie, a nursing junkie, and a white noise junkie. I had to do this tummy-to-tummy rocking motion to get her to sleep in the bathroom with the water on," said Nina, who on really tough nights had to tummy-rock and nurse simultaneously.

Nina knew that Lydia was perfectly healthy and a good size for her age, and that she didn't need to eat that often. Knowing was one thing. Doing something about it was much harder. When Nina asked the pediatricians in her group practice, each gave her totally different advice, none of it terribly useful.

One of the first things I had Nina do was to pay strict attention to how Lydia behaved when she woke up at night. Nina immediately noticed that the baby calmed down as soon as Nina picked her up. Lydia didn't actually need to nurse; her mother's arm or shoulder were reassurance enough. That knowledge made it easier for Nina and Mitch to proceed. Nina remembered that Lydia had once gone six hours without nursing. If she had done it once, her parents knew she could do it again, and they finally got everyone in the pediatrics practice, including the nurse-on-demand lactation consultant, to agree that six hours was a reasonable goal. They didn't count back from 6:00 a.m. as in the usual go-for-the-stretch option. They knew that she almost always woke up at 2:00 a.m., which was six hours after her bedtime. They decided to feed her at 2:00 a.m. and only at 2:00 a.m.

When Lydia cried—and she did wake up on and off and cry the first few nights—Mitch went in to soothe her back to sleep. Once six hours had elapsed since the last feeding, Nina nursed. But she put her back into her crib instead of taking her into the family bed.

Maude

Kathleen and Mickey had endured the poor sleep patterns of their first child, Sean, until at nine months they used Dr. Marc Weissbluth's cry-it-out program. It worked, but the flood of tears made everyone tense and miserable. With Maude, their second child, they wanted earlier and gentler intervention. Kathleen was going back to work and didn't know how she could function while caring for a four-month-old who "did not sleep at all," and a two-and-a-half-year-old who got up at 5:00 a.m. (I also helped the family with Sean's early rising, a common difficulty I discuss in my chapters on older children.)

Although Kathleen and Mickey had tried to stop co-sleeping with Maude after the first few months, the baby seldom slept in her crib for more than an hour or so. She would get up to nurse, and then mother and baby would end up sleeping—or not sleeping—in the spare bed in the baby's room. Kathleen had nursed Sean until nineteen months and was committed to long-term nursing for Maude as well. She knew she had to stop all the nighttime nursing, but was afraid that would make her milk dry up completely. Her doctor convinced her that she could limit nursing without stopping it altogether, and guided her through a nursing/pumping schedule to help her body make the transition.

Kathleen and Mickey decided to use the go-for-the-stretch option. They planned to start with a six-hour interval, and then gradually move to eight. That would mean feeding Maude at midnight, and then not again until 6:00 a.m. As a two-time parent, Kathleen had learned that some tears "aren't going to scar them for life. They aren't going to remember this when they are thirty and blame you." Still the first two nights weren't easy. Emotionally, Mickey and Kathleen both found it far easier to deal with Maude's initial forty-minute crying jag (knowing a parent was nearby) than they had with Sean's far more intense screaming (listening from afar). On the third night, Maude didn't cry—and she didn't wake up at midnight to be fed either; she slept all the way to dawn! Kathleen and Mickey decided to pick up on her cue, and not feed her at night at all anymore. It wasn't always consistent after that. Some nights she slept, some nights she woke up, sometimes she went right back to bed, sometimes she fussed a little, but nothing like that first difficult night. As she had hoped, Kathleen was able to nurse Maude for quite some time to come, only now she nursed in the morning and evening, pumped during the day—and slept at night.

Lots of babies at this age make it almost but not quite through until morning. They get up at about 5:00 a.m. to nurse, and then go back to sleep until 8:00 or so. Phase out that 5:00 a.m. feeding (especially if you fed him earlier in the night). It's a hard time of day to cope, and you might have a few unpleasant days with some tears. But at this age, it's seldom more than a few days. If you let these 5:00 a.m. mess calls continue, early rising becomes an extremely stubborn habit to change and it can cause you grief for the next several years. If he protests when he doesn't get fed at 5:00, remember, you don't have to leave him alone to cry. You can stay with him and soothe him. Once the clock strikes 6:00, if he's still fussing, go ahead and feed him. (If he's fallen asleep, wait until he gets up on his own to feed him.) Be consistent—that's incredibly important when dealing with early risers. Some babies will be up for good at 6:00, others will eat and fall asleep again. If yours gets up at 6:00, leave it alone for a bit while he adjusts to missing that 5:00 a.m. feeding. Then, try keeping him in his crib until 6:15, then 6:30, etc. in fifteen-minute intervals. Keep doing this until he gets to a point where he won't sleep later—or until you reach 7:00 or 7:30, which is a good time for a baby this age to start his day.

Napping

Gone are the days when a thirty-minute catnap would suffice. At four and five months, napping is all about length and predictability. Remember to watch both the clock and your baby's own behavior to know when it's time to put him down. You want to catch him when he's getting tired. Not after he's just fallen off the sleepiness cliff.

At this point, it's usually best if your baby naps in his crib. If you haven't gotten your child out of the car seat, swing, or stroller for naps, do so right now. He is just too old for it; the motion will hamper his ability to get the deeper, more restorative sleep he now needs. If you are committed to the family bed for the long haul, I would still recommend that he nap in his crib now. Some, although not all, moms who co-sleep find they have to lie down with the child at nap time once or twice a day for three or four years. That can become quite limiting, especially if you go back to work or have a second child. Plus, you can leave him alone in the crib safely. Letting a baby nap in the family bed without close supervision creates safety worries as they get older and more mobile.

Nina had taken Lydia everywhere with her, not realizing that Lydia at five months didn't have the same needs as Lydia at five weeks. She was no longer able to get enough rest in strollers and car seats with all that motion, all those distractions. "I changed my life pretty dramatically; we started having a regular bedtime and coming home for naps." For three weeks she was quite housebound. But once she got Lydia on a schedule—or rather, once Lydia got Nina on a schedule—Nina found that the predictability actually enhanced her ability to meet friends or run errands. She knew when she could come and go and still have a happy and rested baby.

Try not to nurse your child to sleep at any naps now. That's easier now that the feedings are further apart and you can plan the naps around them. For instance, a baby can wake up at 7:00 a.m., nurse, nap at 9:00 and not need another nursing until he wakes at 10:30. Feeding him when he's up and alert, instead of ready to go to bed, helps weaken that food-sleep association and reinforces the message that he can get to sleep and stay asleep without a breast or bottle.

Tracy and Drew, whose struggle with Lucas's reflux you can read about in Chapter 13, Medical Problems, found that keeping a log greatly assisted them in detecting his emerging natural daytime sleep rhythms. Since his nap training was slow and difficult, the log also helped them discern the little bits of progress that made it easier to persevere. Tracy had nursed on demand but now structured Lucas's feedings, knowing he would nap longer if he wasn't eating all the time. "I tried to be much more conscious about making sure that he was fed before going down for a nap, and to be very conscious of the gaps between feedings. When I was enforcing the nap rules, I didn't have to worry that he was awake because he was hungry; I knew when he ate." Tracy found it too hard to do full-fledged nap training twice a day plus deal with Lucas's evening problems, so they initially focused on nights and the afternoon nap. The morning nap they tried to stretch for forty-five minutes and left it at that. As he got more unbroken sleep at night and slept later in the morning, the sleep dominos all fell into place. He now slept until 7:00 or 7:30, which meant he was able to stay up a little later before the morning nap. Then, because the morning nap ran later, he wasn't so exhausted by the time his afternoon nap rolled around. That helped him sleep longer in the afternoon, further reinforcing the improving nighttime sleep, which then bolstered the next day's naps and so forth.

Ideally, four- and five-month-old babies should nap for ninety minutes or longer, morning and afternoon. A third late-afternoon nap can be shorter. He may well stir after ten minutes, and again after twenty to thirty minutes, predictable times for a partial awakening from a nap. Don't rush in and get him out of the crib at the first peep. See if he can get himself back to sleep, or if he's getting louder and fussier, try to help him get back to sleep. Go to him before he reaches that full-fledged screaming mode, which will wake him even more. Rub his back or "sh-sh" him or use another comforting technique and see if that will coax him back to sleep. You'll probably have to experiment a bit to see what type of comforting is effective at this time of day. Some babies will fall asleep again if you leave them alone, and get more awake if you try to soothe them. Others will want you in their room but won't want you to touch them. Be patient and give him at least twenty to thirty minutes to resettle himself. He may well reward you with another forty-five minutes' sleep. Phase out your intervention at the partial awakening as he becomes more skilled at resettling himself. Don't let him get dependent on your patting or stroking him to sleep. Once his body clock adjusts to a longer nap, he should gradually learn how to get through that partial awakening on his own and not need your assistance.

Cheryl and Gary used to have the CD player going while four-month-old Ari napped. Naturally the music stopped after forty-five minutes, just around the time his brain was doing its partial awakening anyway. That did it. "I had the monitor on and I'd hear the music go off, and he would stir and I would buzz right into his room all happy and 'rescue' him—I'd wake him up! I learned not to go in, and he'd just stir and go back to sleep. He'd sort of talk to himself—la, la, la, la—and fall asleep," his mother said.

Nap training can be frustrating, but stick to it. Most families see progress in a week or two at this age, but you aren't alone (or incompetent) if it takes longer. If you put it off, if you don't help him learn to take adequately long naps at predictable times, it's going to be much harder to train him later.

Brittany's Story

Lisa and Ted's first child was a poor sleeper until I worked with them when Teddy was about seven months old. Brittany, their second child, was a much easier sleeper. Lisa initially attributed this to Brittany's temperament, saying she was a cheerful, happy child. Actually, Brittany had her fussy moments, and she also had reflux, which often disrupts sleep. Her mom just knew how to deal with it better; she had learned from her experience with Teddy. Lisa followed the Sleep Lady's Infant Slumber Rules and gently taught Brittany to sleep without trauma to mother or child.

"With Teddy, I hadn't realized how important sleep was, or understood how much sleep a baby needed. I figured, when he's tired, he'll sleep!" she recalled. With Brittany, Lisa was much more careful to protect her child's sleep.

For the first ten weeks, Brittany slept in a Pack 'n Play in her parents' room at night, where nursing was convenient. She either napped there or in a cradle in the family room. Lisa did not pay much heed to my rule about a quiet, sleep-friendly nap environment. With a three-and-a-half-year-old boy on the loose, she figured that was a lost cause. "We couldn't tiptoe around with a boy in the house. I did the laundry, let the phone ring, visitors came over." But Lisa let Brittany nap when she needed to nap, even if it meant disappointing a visitor who wanted to see her with her eyes open.

Despite her laissez-faire attitude about noise, Lisa imposed some gentle discipline and structure from the start. She did not nurse Brittany to sleep, or routinely hold her to sleep at nap time. "I did it once in a while. Who can resist holding a sweet, sleeping baby?" Instead, she worked on "drowsy but awake," particularly at nap time. She had carted Teddy around everywhere in a fairly haphazard way but with Brittany, she didn't take her out too much until she was old enough to have a nap schedule. Then they were able to get out and about in Brittany's awake time, but avoid napping in car seats and strollers all the time. The *unavoidable exception was the mornings they had to drop Teddy off at preschool, just as Brittany was supposed to nap. If she fell asleep in the car, Lisa transferred her out of the car seat and into her crib. She usually woke up briefly, long enough to figure out where she was, but then she generally fell asleep again. Lisa let her cry briefly or soothed her back to sleep.*

Like most infants, Brittany experienced a fussy period and the second month was the worst. Not only that, Brittany fussed in the early evening—just as Lisa and Ted were trying to get big brother Teddy into bed! Lisa usually nursed Brittany then to help her calm down but she didn't nurse her fully to sleep. Sometimes on very fussy evenings she would hold Brittany to sleep but that was okay because she didn't do it all the time. It never became a sleep crutch because Lisa made sure to put her down drowsy but awake at other times. By the end of the second month, the fussies subsided. At eight weeks, Brittany was sleeping six hours before she woke to nurse. Then she would go back to sleep quite easily.

Lisa had learned with Teddy the importance of getting a child to bed tired, not overtired, so she watched for Brittany's sleep window clues. Initially it was quite simple. Newborn Brittany sensibly yawned when she was ready for a nap. Later on, she would still yawn as we all do, but it was no longer a reliable sign that she was ready for bed. Instead, Lisa noticed that Brittany sucked her thumb when she was tired or hungry, and seldom sucked when she wasn't. Because Lisa had her scheduled pretty well by then, a quick glance at the clock usually told Lisa whether the baby was hungry or tired. As Brittany was quite even-tempered after she got through that fussy stage, Lisa also knew that if she was cranky and teary she probably needed to go to bed.

Once Brittany was ready for bed, she was really ready. Lisa had a good bedtime routine for Teddy and she tried to follow a very similar one for Brittany—bath, diaper change and pajamas, book, prayer, lights out, and then a final song with a parent sitting near the crib in the dark. Then Lisa or Ted would leave, shutting the door behind them, and the baby would fall asleep. But sometimes Brittany was so sleepy that Lisa couldn't get past the diaper change! "She'd start to cry as I was changing her. She wouldn't even let me sit down to read, she'd just lean toward her crib as we passed it. So we didn't always follow the whole bedtime routine. When she wanted to sleep, it was best to just put her to bed!" In cases like this I would suspect that this baby needed to go to bed a little earlier, that her parents were skating awfully close to missing the sleep window and facing the dreaded second wind. But with Brittany, her mother correctly intuited that it was just the way she was. Some kids go from zero to sixty. Brittany went from sixty to zero.

By the time Brittany was fourteen weeks old, she was sleeping from 6:45 p.m. until 5:30 a.m., when Lisa was so engorged that she woke her to nurse. Then she went back to bed until 7:45. Over the next month or so, Lisa stopped that early-morning feeding and Brittany just slept. If she got up early and stirred out of habit, Lisa and Ted learned to just let her be. After a brief moment of fussing she would fall asleep again on her own. By five months, she was sleeping twelve hours a night, from 7:00 p.m. to 7:00 a.m.

"I used to think the difference was that Teddy was 'difficult,' and Brittany was 'easy.' But now I sometimes do question whether part of Teddy's 'difficult' babyhood was just that he never got enough sleep!" Lisa said. "I took all of Kim's great advice to heart and I know it made a difference in Brittany. In me too. I felt much more confident in scheduling sleep for my baby—and I know it was needed."

SIX TO EIGHT MONTHS

Please take a few minutes to read the first three chapters of my book, which give an overview of my system and include some helpful hints that apply to all age groups. It won't take long and you'll have much better results.

❍ ❍ ❍

AT THIS AGE, BABIES NEED an average of eleven hours of uninterrupted nighttime sleep and three and a half hours of daytime naps spread over two to three naps.

From six through eight months, babies become more mobile. They roll over, sit up, maybe even stand holding on to something. Many scoot or crawl, and the first teeth come in. Most babies sleep through the night fairly regularly but if yours doesn't, it is still quite easy to get them on track. You may also find that at six or seven months, a baby who had been a good sleeper starts having difficulties. As she experiences her first wave of separation anxiety, she may resist being left in her crib at night, or may start waking up more often to see you.

This chapter will help you promote nighttime security, develop a sleep-friendly schedule, and introduce appropriate wind-down activities at night. As your baby grows, bedtime can be fun as you begin to share quiet songs and games and create family rituals. But first you may have to break some patterns. If your baby is used to being rocked, walked, nursed, or stroked to sleep, or to get back to sleep in the middle of the night, you will need to help her discard those sleep crutches, sometimes called negative associations. If she's spent the first few months sleeping in unconventional places, like swings or car seats, you need to get her into the crib. As you make changes you may have to tolerate some tears—but you don't have to let her cry endlessly or alone. Sit by her as she cries, stroke her head or pat her back a little; whisper soothing words. Her tears are her way of saying she is tired and frustrated, or wary of this change. But if you let her, she will learn to cope, adapt, and soothe herself to sleep—and it won't take as long as you fear.

Many, if not most, sleep problems at this age involve associations between sleeping and eating. I'll give tips on how to weaken that link. For instance, it's fine to nurse your baby when she wakes up in the morning or from a nap. But you may want to create a gap between nursing and going to sleep. You certainly don't want her falling asleep at the breast, or with a bottle in her mouth, both because it interferes with sleep independence and because it's terrible for those little teeth that are going to come bursting out any day. You should also start setting recognizable mealtimes, so your baby is not eating all day, an incentive to get up to snack all night. Babies respond well to structured daytime meals. One mom told me that she felt like "a dairy bar that was open 24/7." But when she established "regular business hours" her child cut back on snacking, ate better meals, and slept longer.

You will meet several families in this chapter whose stories may sound like your own. Erin and Teddy both had erratic schedules and inadequate naps. Erin also needed to be walked and walked and walked to sleep every night. Anita was a good napper but she woke up wanting to nurse at night, out of habit, not out of hunger. Adam had several health problems early in life but even when he got better, he still woke up every forty-five minutes or so and efforts to calm him only woke him up more. Each of their parents followed my advice—but with enough freedom to match their family's needs and their infant's emerging personality. Some could tolerate tears at night, others couldn't bear more than a minute or two. They all found the right mix. So will you.

 DEVELOPMENTAL CHANGES

Separation Anxiety

Separation anxiety has its first peak at this age and it increases when babies are overtired. At bedtime, he may fight sleep in order to engage with you and be with you. He may also wake up more often wanting to see you. The gentle techniques I use throughout this book, including attachment to a lovey and helping your child learn to self-soothe, will ease his anxiety. Rarely if ever will you leave him alone to cry in the dark, and never for more than a few minutes. When he wakes up at night, you won't put a pillow over your head and hope the crying stops. You will respond immediately. He will learn that the people he loves are close at hand and watching over him.

Loveys

A *lovey*, a special stuffed animal or blanket, sometimes called a *transitional object*, can be a useful tool to ease separation anxiety and weaken other sleep-disrupting nighttime habits. If your child is not already attached to a lovey, help him forge that bond. A lovey helps the baby cope with nighttime separation, making him feel safe and sound when you are not with him. If he has not yet shown a preference, pick a lovey for him, although he might select a different one when he gets a little older. Usually a nice soft stuffed animal or baby blanket will do, but pay attention to his emerging preferences. For instance, if he's a hair twirler, look for a blanket with a fringe or a stuffed animal with a similar feature, like a Beanie Baby Jellyfish with tentacles. If he likes to rub and massage things, try a small, thick blanket. Six-month-old Erin's parents, Corinna and Jeremy, just used a cloth diaper because she had already grown so accustomed to burrowing into it on their shoulders. The lovey should be small, soft, and safe—nothing that could choke or smother an infant and nothing that he could later use as a launching pad to climb out of the crib. Run any concerns by your pediatrician. Your life may be easier if you find something easy to clean or wash (when in doubt, try putting it inside a tied-up pillow case and washing it in a gentle cycle). Some parents buy two loveys in case one gets lost or left at Grandma's house but, be warned, babies are smarter than they appear! They discern slight differences in touch or scent and will not always accept a substitute.

Encourage the bond by wedging the lovey between you and your baby when you nurse or bottle feed him. Tuck it in his arms, or next to him for naps, bedtime, and when he wakes up during the night. You may want to "wear" the lovey for a few hours inside your own shirt, to impart more of that comforting and familiar scent of Mom. Play with the lovey, especially but not exclusively at bedtime. Incorporate it in peek-a-boo, or have the lovey blow kisses or wave bye-bye to baby.

Some children don't get attached at this age, particularly if they have another sleep crutch, such as nursing, but give it some time. If he doesn't bond, try again every now and then as he gets older. Anita, for instance, rejected the blankie her parents offered her as a baby but when she became a toddler, she adopted "Lamby." Teddy similarly spurned every plush toy he was offered but then cheerfully bonded to two plastic teethers when he was about thirteen months old, happily gripping one in each hand at bedtime.

New Mobility

Babies' increased mobility at this age can cause some new bedtime (or nap time) problems. Sometimes they roll themselves over on one side—but can't roll themselves back. Try not to interfere. Make sure she gets lots of daytime tummy time, maybe on a fun, patterned play mat, to practice these movements. (If you are worried that she can roll onto her tummy but can't yet return herself to the safer back-sleeping position, talk to your doctor about whether you need to gently "flip" her over or whether she has enough control over her neck and head movements to protect herself from SIDS while she develops her rolling skills.) Similarly, babies learn to sit up or stand by holding on to the crib before they learn to lie back down. Give them some time to practice during the day; they will figure it out. It may not be very graceful, but they'll manage and the more you let them, the quicker they will learn on their own. Leaving her in place may mean she'll fall asleep sitting up and just plop over, but don't worry. She won't hurt herself, and once asleep she will wriggle herself into a comfortable position. If you must intervene, do it *once* at what I call the "magic moment." In other words, if your baby is sitting up, help her lie down once at a moment when you think that she'll go down and stay down. If she pops right back up again, don't lay her down. That way you can avoid a prolonged sit up/lie down struggle—which the parent rarely wins.

CREATING A SCHEDULE
Sample schedule:

7:00 to 7:30 a.m. Wake-up.
Upon waking, nurse/bottle feed and solids
(consult your pediatrician about introduction of solid foods).

9:00 or 9:30 a.m. Morning nap, 1.5 to 2 hours.
Upon waking, nursing/bottle and solids.

12:30 or 1:00 p.m. Afternoon nap, 1.5 to 2 hours.
Upon waking, nurse/bottle.

3:30–4:00 p.m. (depends on previous nap time)
Optional third nap, about 45 minutes to an hour.

5:00 or 5:30 p.m. Nurse/bottle feed and solids.

6:00–6:30 p.m. Start bath/bedtime preparations,
which may include an additional bottle or nursing.

7:00–7:30 p.m. Asleep.

When I ask new parents about their baby's schedule, some look as perplexed as if I had posed a problem in quantum mechanics. The prospect of developing a routine should not be so terrifying. A good schedule can transform a tired and fussy baby into a rested and contented one. I don't recommend completely rigid schedules, but I do recommend devoting a few weeks to really focusing on your child's sleep. That means building your other tasks, errands, and activities around sleep, naps, and baby meals, not squeezing the sleep, naps, and baby meals in haphazardly between all the other things you have to do. Nap training, in particular, can be time consuming for a few weeks. Later on you'll have more flexibility—and when everyone is rested, it will be easier to plan, and enjoy, a family outing or a stroller walk with Grandma. But don't overdo the flexibility. Just as we adults need basic structure in order to feel good and function well, *babies need predictability too.* Your baby will not be at her best if her morning naps are at 8:30 one day, and 11:30 the next, or if she goes to bed at 7:00 one night and at 11:30 on another. The trick is to get your child on the right schedule; try to stick to it pretty regularly but know how to read her cues and modify it a little when appropriate. Some days she'll sleep a little more, some a little less, just like you do (and you don't even have growth spurts). When travel, illness, or special events force you to deviate, get back on schedule as soon as possible. Schedule variations are much easier for a child who is well rested than for a tired baby whose life is always in chaos.

Corinna and Jeremy had a very erratic schedule for Erin until she was six months old. She catnapped thirty to forty minutes a few times a day, instead of taking two good solid naps, and her mom said she looked "almost as sleepy after a nap as before one." At night, they had to walk and walk and walk her to get her to sleep—so much that her dad got tennis elbow from carting her around. With my help, we tackled the walking problem (more on that later) and Corinna set regular nap times, regular mealtimes, and a regular bedtime. At the beginning, she stuck close to home and worked her life around the schedule, but once it fell into place she had a little more flexibility. Erin began eating and sleeping better, and Jeremy, who had a long commute and a late workday, adjusted his routine so that if he didn't get home in time to enjoy Erin in the evening, they got great daddy-daughter time in the morning.

◌ ◌ ◌

Teddy was another baby transformed by remarkably few tweaks to his routine. He was waking up too early, napping too briefly, and nursing more frequently, not less, as he grew older, possibly in part because of some separation anxiety when he was about seven to eight months old. He was cranky, and fell asleep as soon as he got into a car—all the classic signs, Ted and Lisa later realized, of an overtired child. Lisa became more consistent about his schedule and lengthened the intervals between nursing. She also modified his nap times by a half hour or forty-five minutes. She began putting him down at 9:00 a.m., instead of 9:45, for the morning nap and at 1:00 p.m., not 1:45, for the afternoon nap. "Those forty-five minutes made the biggest difference in the world," Lisa said. "I had been trying to keep him up too long. I was missing his sleep window and he would be so overtired by the time I tried to put him down that he couldn't sleep." He began eating better, sleeping better, and generally looking much more pleased with life. As his napping improved, he slept better at night, and his parents were able to teach him to sleep through until 6:30 or 7:00 a.m. instead of getting up for a sunrise snack every day.

There is no "right" schedule for all babies, but the sample at the start of this section is a good framework. Some variation is inevitable; a baby who naps for ninety minutes starting at 9:00 a.m. is not going to be on the same clock as one who naps for two hours starting at 9:30. But the starting point, 7:00 or 7:30 a.m., and the end point, 7:00 or 7:30 p.m., should be about the same. Some babies do seem to have internal alarm clocks that go off at 6:00 a.m., so you may have to shift the schedule, particularly morning naps, a little earlier to accommodate. (More on "early birds" later in this chapter.) If she's in child care or with a sitter part of the day, make your home schedule conform as much as possible to the child-care feeding and nap times, as long as that routine is a sensible one. Consistency counts.

Okay. That's the scheduling ideal. Let's walk through it in more detail.

WAKE-UP · When you are ready to start your baby's day, turn on the lights, open the blinds, and say "Good morning." In the Sleep Lady lexicon, I call it *dramatic wake-up time.* You want her to learn to distinguish between daytime awakenings and nighttime awakenings, between daytime feedings and evening ones.

NURSE OR BOTTLE FEED · Nurse when she wakes up, and play for a while. Then get yourself some breakfast and feed her solids if your doctor has recommended them. This is her introduction to breakfast.

MORNING NAP · About an hour and a half to two hours after she wakes up, it's time for bed again. Usually the morning nap starts at around 9:00 or 9:30, a little sooner for early risers. Remember, that's when she should be asleep, not getting ready to sleep. The nap should last one and a half to two hours. A common error is starting the nap at 10:00 or 10:30. That's usually too late—and her fussing and grouching is her way of telling you it's too late. Look for sleepy cues to tell you when she's getting ready. She may rub her eyes, yawn, become less active, or get fussy. Some babies make special little "put to me bed now" noises that an attentive parent can learn to interpret. If you don't detect any tired cues, try taking your baby into a quieter room. If she's in a kitchen, playroom, or some other place full of activity and stimulation, she may mask her sleepy signals. Try not to feed her right before you put her down.

> *Heidi recalled how eight-month-old Kevin would get all loose and limp when he got tired. She called him "spaghetti boy." "If you hold him, he's like Jell-O," she laughed. "It's definitely a tired sign." Corinna and Jeremy's daughter, Erin, would rub her eyes and ears, and make a strange little noise that her mother learned meant "Get me to bed right now or you'll regret it!"*

AWAKE TIME AND LUNCH · Plan to have two to three hours of awake time between the end of morning nap and the start of the afternoon one. This is a nice time to play, take a walk, or run some errands, and of course have lunch (nurse or bottle feed, plus midday solids on the advice of your doctor). If your agenda requires driving, try doing it at the beginning of this awake window, not the end. If she's more alert, there's less chance of her dozing off in the car and throwing off her nap schedule for the rest of the day, or of getting so used to napping in the car (not as restful as sleeping in a crib) that she won't nap in a crib. Some babies will want to have a bottle and eat lunch soon after the morning nap; some can wait. It's up to you but don't wait so long that you run into the afternoon nap. You want to build that separation between nursing and going to sleep.

AFTERNOON NAP · No more than three hours should elapse between the end of the morning nap and the start of the afternoon one. Usually that means between 12:30 and 1:30. Watch both the clock and your baby; she'll signal when she needs to go down. Remember to leave her a little time to unwind, to get ready to sleep. It doesn't have to take as long as the evening bedtime rituals but it serves the same goal. Pull down the shade, then look at a short book or sing a song or two. Give her a few kisses, maybe a little rocking, and put her in the crib. Ideally this nap should last one and a half to two hours.

SNACK · When she wakes, she gets a snack—nursing or another bottle.

OPTIONAL LATE-AFTERNOON NAP · Some babies take a brief third nap, forty-five minutes to an hour, in the late afternoon. If your baby is a poor napper and her two main daily naps are an hour or less apiece, then this little third nap is mandatory. Without it, she'll be running on vapors. For everyone else, it's optional. Don't worry if your baby skips this nap; most give it up themselves by nine months. And although I usually avoid motion sleep, it's okay if she dozes off for this little nap in the car on her way home. Eliminate the third nap if she sleeps so late, 5:00 or 5:30, that she has a hard time getting to sleep at bedtime. If she naps until 6:00, you'll have a hard time getting her to sleep at 7:00. She needs at least two hours between the end of this mini-nap and bedtime.

DINNER · Dinner, another nursing, and the third solids (if advised by your pediatrician) should be at around 5:00. Again, there's a little variation depending on her afternoon nap, but don't let it get too late. Unless you have no choice for work and/or child-care reasons, don't postpone dinner until both parents are home. All that wonderful advice about how families should eat more meals together does not apply to infants! In fact, some couples find that if they get the baby fed and to bed early, they may actually have time to sit down at the dinner table themselves and have a real conversation.

BEDTIME · Bedtime should be at 7:00 or 7:30. I define bedtime as when she's in her crib, not when you are running the bath, putting on pj's, or reading stories. Don't rush it. You need time to get her ready for bed, and she needs time to get herself ready to sleep. At this age, you should usually allow twenty to thirty minutes, plus whatever time you need for bathing and pajamas. Enjoyable bedtime activities include gentle massage, ten minutes or so of quiet music, or looking at short, simple picture books. Peek-a-boo and other calm and gentle games are a big hit. She may enjoy funny little caresses, like having you kiss your finger and then touch it to her nose. Include the lovey in any bedtime games. Have the lovey caress the baby's nose, too, or let it play peek-a-boo. If your baby is used to bedtime music, keep it soft and quiet. Use music to set the mood and cue the brain for sleep, but turn it off before she gets into her crib, or soon after if it's on a timer. You don't want her so accustomed to lullabies that she can't get to sleep or get herself back to sleep without them. If you've been playing music until after she falls asleep, slowly ease it out. Put her in her crib with the music playing very softly. Try to turn it off before she's fully asleep, and if the tape runs out, don't restart it. The same for toys with music and lights: start bedtime with them on if that's what she is used to, but phase them out before she is fully asleep.

BEDTIME FEEDING · It's okay to nurse or give her a bottle right before bed as long as she doesn't depend on it to nurse herself to sleep and you aren't nursing her to sleep when she wakes up at night. If she does depend on nursing, and that's a very common pattern at this age, try to make the final nursing earlier in the bedtime routine, say, before a song or story. (More on nighttime nursers in a minute.) Try not to let her fall asleep sucking; put her down drowsy but awake. Some moms find it easier to create that separation by no longer nursing in the baby's room. Or if you do want to stay in the baby's room, try nursing with a dim light on and turn it off when you want to signal it's crib time. Some families also create some separation in the baby's mind by having Mom nurse but then hand off the baby to Dad, who gives some kisses and then puts her in her crib.

The goal of getting her down drowsy but awake is crucial. (See page 20.) If your baby has trouble with it, focus your energy first on getting it right at bedtime. It's not less important at 2:00 a.m., but it's a lot easier for us as parents to follow through when we are not half asleep ourselves and anxious about who else is being woken and when we'll all get back to sleep. Once you get it right at bedtime, it will be easier to carry this out at other times.

THE SLEEP LADY SHUFFLE

My Sleep Lady Shuffle is a gentle behavioral modification technique that lets you be a comforting presence as your child learns to put himself to sleep in his crib. You are going to start out right by his side, and over a period of about two weeks you will gradually move farther away until you will be able to leave the room. Often, nighttime wakenings will start to taper off because of the combination of a more structured, consistent daytime routine and this newly acquired ability to fall asleep. When he wakes up at night during the Shuffle, as he will at the beginning, you will return to the position you were in at bedtime that night and soothe him. You might want to go by his crib briefly to calm and caress him before you return to that evening position. After we walk through the Shuffle, in my Problems and Solutions section I'll talk about some specific reasons that babies at this age wake up at night and how to address them.

You should follow the Shuffle schedule, moving on to the next position even if your child has had a bad night or two, fussing or waking more frequently. Don't be surprised if there's a little regression or protest the first night of each new chair position. If your child gets sick during the Shuffle, you might want to pause and "freeze" or maintain your position until he's feeling a little better. You might even have to move a little bit closer during an illness to offer more comfort. But then resume your sleep shaping when he recovers.

NIGHTS 1–3. Once bath, stories, bottle/nursing, and songs are over, sit in a chair right next to your baby's crib. If he cries or fusses, you can stroke or pat him intermittently but don't do it constantly or you'll just create a new negative association. (You can do more touching on night one, then taper off.) It's also important that the parent control the touch. Instead of having him hold your hand or finger, you should pat his. Make sure that you do not caress the child too steadily; do it on and off. You don't want to swap one negative association, like rocking, for another, like your constant touch or the sound of your voice. Don't depend too much on touch because on day four, you will be farther away and won't be touching as much. (The no-snuggles or no-picking-up-the-baby edict does not apply to a child who is sick, frightened, or startled by a loud noise, but make sure you don't do so much snuggling that he will expect it even when he is feeling better.)

Try not to pick him up—but if he's extremely upset go ahead and pick him up, over the crib if possible. Hold him until he's calm but keep it brief. Put him down again while he's still awake. You can sing during the get-ready-for-bed stage, but once it's time for sleep, you are better off making lulling "sh-sh" or other soothing sounds. You might want to try closing your eyes. That makes it easier not to talk to him too much and it also conveys a sleepy-time message. Don't stimulate him—bore him. Stay there until he falls asleep.

NIGHTS 4–6. Move the chair about halfway to the door. (If the room is small or the crib is close to the door, then move all the way to the doorway as in night seven.) Continue the soothing sounds, but stay in the chair as much as you can. Get up to pat or stroke him a little if necessary, or make the same soothing sounds as you have used the past three nights. Again, try not to pick him up unless he's hysterical, and if you do pick him up, follow the technique I described for the first three nights. Stay in the chair until he falls asleep.

NIGHTS 7–9. Move the chair to the doorway or the doorjamb. You should be dimly lit but still in his view. Continue the same soothing techniques from your chair, remembering to intervene as little as possible. Don't worry if he cries a little bit; keep quietly reassuring him. He'll know that you are there, and he will fall asleep.

NIGHTS 10–12. Move farther from the doorway, into the hall, but make sure he can still see you. You can keep making those "sh-sh" sounds, not constantly but enough to let him know that Mom or Dad is close by and responsive. Stay until he falls asleep.

A few things to remember. Children get ritualized easily. Make the changes every three days—or less. Dragging it out makes it harder, not easier, for your baby. Give it more than three days and he'll expect you to stay exactly where you are—and get mad or upset when you try to double that distance.

NIGHTS 13 AND ON. A significant number of babies start falling asleep and staying asleep by now. But most parents have one more step to take: giving him the opportunity to fall asleep without you being present. Leaving him to fall asleep without a parent in his room may seem like a huge leap for you, but it's not so big for him. All that chair moving has given him nearly two weeks of preparation. He has given up some negative associations and he has learned that you are near.

Most parents stay in the hallway or in a very nearby room, where the child cannot see them but can hear them. You can make some reassuring "sh-sh" sounds, not constantly but enough to let him know that Mom or Dad is close by and responsive. If he cries, try checking on him from his bedroom door—without going all the way into the room. Be calm and reassuring. Make some comforting sounds, conveying that you are not far away and that you know he can put himself to sleep. I find that this final step is often harder for the parents than for the child. Try not to convey anxiety about possible tears to your baby. Give him credit for what the Shuffle has helped him achieve. Your baby really can soothe himself to sleep—if you give him the opportunity. Occasionally a baby will cry a little for a few nights, but don't rush in and rescue him prematurely. Let him calm down and nod off. If you check on him from the doorway, try to be fairly unobtrusive about it and don't check too frequently. You want to calm him, not stimulate him into getting more awake each time you approach. It should get easier on you quickly.

PROBLEMS AND SOLUTIONS

Many babies have *negative associations,* or *sleep crutches,* which they need to get themselves to sleep or back to sleep. They may want to be fed, held, rocked, and so forth. Work on eliminating these associations at bedtime and when your baby wakes up during the Shuffle. These directions emphasize the first three nights, when you will sit right beside your child and comfort him. From night four on, if your child has not yet discarded the crutch, go to his crib side and comfort him very briefly, and then return to your bedtime Shuffle position for that night. If your child wakes up once in a while after the Shuffle, I usually recommend that you make a quick, reassuring visit to his crib side, make sure he's okay, and then return to the hallway or your bedroom, whichever makes you feel more comfortable. Don't forget to use the lovey.

If despite following the advice in this section your child is still waking up at night, take another look at his routine. Are you putting him to bed a little too drowsy? If so, he may have learned to put himself to sleep at bedtime when you've done much of the sleep preparation work for him, but he can't get himself back to sleep at night without your assistance. Try putting him down at bedtime when he's a tad less drowsy, and a bit more awake so he can perfect those self-soothing skills. You might also try moving bedtime earlier by 15 minutes or a half an hour, and maybe create a little more separation between that last nursing or bottle feeding and bed. Try leaving a soft light on while you nurse, it will help him break that suckle-sleep association.

Eliminating Nighttime Feeding

One of my hardest tasks is convincing mothers that most healthy six- to eight-month-old babies on a normal growth curve don't need to eat at night. Even a smart, thoughtful mother who knows this in her head may still have a fear in her gut of letting her child go hungry. "My baby was in the ninety-eighth percentile for weight and I still worried about starving her," one mom I worked with told me. Check with your pediatrician, but the overwhelming odds are that the main reason your baby still gets up in search of breast or bottle is that you allow it! Don't be hard on yourself if your baby developed this habit. You have loads of company. It is a time-tested way of getting you and your baby back to sleep quickly, but now you can try some alternatives.

Families I've worked with have tried several techniques for eliminating nighttime feedings and you are welcome to try the most gradual to the most abrupt; however, I'll warn you that very gradual techniques don't work for everybody. Choose what feels right for you. Even if you start with the gentler steps, please read this entire section because you'll find some tips on soothing your baby or adjusting mealtimes that may be helpful. Also, please check with your pediatrician and make sure that your child does not have a medical or growth issue that does require more frequent feedings. Some babies who haven't yet outgrown their reflux, for instance, might still need more frequent, small meals, but even with these babies, try to do as much of the feeding as possible during the day or else you'll be living with the sleep-disrupting side effects of reflux long after her tummy problems are over.

Whatever approach you take, it will be easier if you try to reset her hunger clock so that she takes in more calories by day and is not looking around for more at night. I know some babies, even this young, who do a remarkable job of resisting food all day so they can feast all night. Review your daytime feeding schedule, and keep a written log of her diet. Talk to your doctor about whether she's getting the right mix of milk and solids. Try to nurse or bottle feed her in a quiet, dim place without television, phone calls, or other distractions. That may help her feel more like it's a night feeding. This advice holds true during growth spurts too. She may need an occasional night feeding midspurt but by concentrating on enhancing daytime feeding, you'll minimize the nighttime ones.

Overnight, try cutting down on nursing time. If she usually feeds for twenty minutes, give her fifteen. Keep cutting back every few days until she's ready to give it up. Make sure you are unlatching her when she finishes eating heartily; don't let her just gently suckle and doze. Get her back to bed while she's drowsy but awake. Same with a bottle. Let her eat, but don't let her play with it. With a nighttime bottle, you can also try to switch to a smaller bottle, put less formula in the bottle, or gradually dilute the formula so that when it gets very watery she might decide it's not worth getting up for. But when you cut the nursing time all the way back to five minutes, or the bottle to just three ounces, it's time to stop. Anything smaller is just a tease.

If you, or your pediatrician, think your baby still needs to eat at night, or if you want to cut back nighttime feedings but aren't ready to eliminate them altogether, restrict it to once a night. Feed her quickly, and avoid other interaction that will encourage her to stay up and play or cling to you. You can try what we call a *dream feed*, which means you wake her for a final feeding before your own bedtime, probably around 11:00 p.m. Or you can wait until she wakes up, as long as it's at least eight hours after her last feeding, which usually means around 3:00 or 4:00 a.m. *But be consistent.* Choose one approach and stick to it. And only feed her once at night, and not again until at least 6:00 a.m. If you cave in, you are just giving her intermittent reinforcement and mixed messages and making it harder for her in the long run. If she wakes wanting food at a time you don't plan on feeding her, find other ways of soothing her. Go briefly to her crib, then return to your Shuffle position and comfort her. Keep reminding yourself that she is a healthy, well-fed baby, not a starving waif.

Some parents find that when they get on more consistent schedules, the babies just start skipping this final feeding on their own. Other parents use this one feeding as a temporary solution, a bridge for a few nights between multiple feedings and eliminating the night feedings.

When you are ready to eliminate the nighttime feedings, go in and comfort your baby when she gets up but don't nurse her. Try not to pick her up unless she's hysterical, and then only pick her up briefly. Some babies adjust in three or four days. Some take a little longer, but if you are consistent, the tears will ebb quickly and she'll wake less frequently. Having the father, who can't nurse, comfort the baby at night often makes this adjustment go more quickly.

> *At seven months, Anita was still getting up to eat several times a night, migrating among her crib, car seat, and parents' bed. She had never slept through a single night of her life. Penny and Jim tried limiting the feedings to once a night, at 4:00 a.m., but it didn't help. Anita didn't understand why they would not feed her when she woke and cried in the dark at midnight or 2:00 a.m. but would feed her at 4:00 a.m. "Looking back, I realized it was confusing her," Penny said. It was classic intermittent reinforcement—rewarding Anita with food just often enough to motivate her to keep waking in search of it.*
>
> *With my help and her pediatrician's support, Penny overcame her lingering doubts about whether Anita still needed to eat at night and became confident that she could wean Anita at night without having to stop nursing altogether. Penny still nursed at bedtime, but she nursed at*

the beginning of the bedtime routine, not the end, to weaken the nursing-sleep association in Anita's mind. When Anita woke up at night, Penny or Jim—they decided that they would not leave it all to Jim—would soothe her but would not feed her. I gave them the choice of staying in her room until she fell asleep again or going in and touching base and then leaving. Penny chose the second approach, but only up to her comfort point. "I was able to go in, spend a few moments with her and then leave. If she was crying a lot, and it was becoming more intense, I could go back in and soothe her again. If she was crying a little but it seemed like she was about to fall asleep quickly on her own, I didn't go back. It wasn't based on strict time limits and rules; it was based on how I felt and how I thought Anita felt." On those nights when Penny did return to Anita's room, she was careful not to pick Anita up. That could have just teased Anita into thinking she was going to be nursed, creating more frustration when those hopes were thwarted. It could also have led to a new negative association, with Anita waking up at night and expecting to be picked up and rocked and snuggled back to sleep.

Even at seven months, Anita quickly decided that if she wasn't going to get fed, she wasn't going to bother waking up. By the fourth night, Penny had to go in for only one brief check. By the fifth night, Penny heard Anita get up briefly and stir, and then drop right back to sleep on her own. From then on Anita slept all night and was happier, and more well rested during the day. She even began eating better during the day, further reducing the incentive to get up at night. "I was amazed," said Penny. "That's all it took!"

Phasing Out Walking and Rocking to Sleep

Many of us walk or rock our newborns to sleep—or start this habit when we find that nursing doesn't get them to sleep anymore. But if your child is six months or older it may be time to phase it out. You'll know it's a problem if your child needs to be walked for more than a few minutes at bedtime, if she wakes up again as soon as you stop walking, or if she needs to be walked each time she wakes up at night. The same goes for rocking.

Start by focusing on bedtime, when you are most awake and better equipped to follow through consistently. Begin by doing all the walking or rocking in her bedroom, not all over the house. This helps create a positive association between the bedroom and sleep. Scale back the amount of time you walk—even if she isn't entirely asleep when you stop. In other words, if you usually walk thirty minutes, try walking twenty minutes for two or three days, then scale back to fifteen minutes for two or three days, then ten. Put her down when she's drowsy but awake—think about that seven or eight on the drowsiness scale. This is the point when parents usually look at me with alarm and say, "But if I put her down, she'll cry." Yes, she might. Stand or sit by her crib and soothe her. Don't engage too much, just whisper some gentle reassurances and stroke her a bit now and then. If you do pick her up, do so very briefly to calm her and then put her back down. Continue your reassurances, and maybe try rocking her body a little bit with your hand while she's lying down. Some babies this age still find comfort in being swaddled with their arms free when you put them back down, or in having the top of their head rest against the crib bumper. It makes them feel like you are still holding them.

> Erin, whom you met earlier, needed to be walked—and walked and walked—at bedtime and for her nap. At first her mom, Corinna, didn't mind all that much—newborns are so snuggly and all the pacing was good post-pregnancy exercise. But Erin got heavier and heavier, and walking got harder and harder. Jeremy devoted a special pair of deck shoes to baby walking. Corinna developed pain in her arms. "I lost all my baby weight fast but my arm was about to break!" Corinna said. They didn't follow the phase-it-out approach. They just stopped the walking. But to prepare her, they first made some schedule adjustments. Her bedtime had been around 9:00 or 9:30. When they moved it up to 7:00 or 7:30, she wasn't so overtired and therefore didn't need her sleep crutch so much. They also got her up at a more consistent hour in the morning, moved her nursing and solids closer together, and rescheduled her naps so she wasn't going as many hours without some rest. When they were ready to make the change, instead of making a long march around the house, they just included a brief and calming stroll around her room as part of her bedtime routine. They put her down awake, sat next to the crib, and soothed her as they did the Sleep Lady Shuffle. There were some tears, but not nearly as many as they had feared.
>
> "I thought it was going to take two hours that first night. I made Jeremy come home from work early and we were going to order a pizza," Corinna said. "But it took a half hour, and it got easier each night after that."

Erin was a little unusual in that she didn't demand to be walked if she woke up at night—and she didn't wake up every night. Often babies who want to be walked to sleep at bedtime will insist on the same nocturnal promenade in the middle of the night. If your baby gets up crying, go to her immediately and reassure her. Stroke her a bit and whisper "sh-sh" or "night, night" or a similar soothing sound. But avoid lifting her out of her crib, and definitely don't cave in and start walking. If, despite your reassuring presence, she gets really hysterical—if she reaches the point where she is crying so fervently that she can't remember what she is crying about—go ahead and pick her up. Help her calm down—but keep her in her room. Build pleasant associations between her room and sleep. Don't pace the halls, don't hand her any new crutches to replace the walking. Hold her gently for a little while until she is calm. Put her down calm and drowsy but awake. Let her do that final piece of falling asleep on her own. You can sit beside her as she does.

> Donna rocked her eight-month-old daughter, Elsa, to sleep in her arms. Elsa then woke up to nurse three times a night, and still got up between nursings wanting to be rocked back to sleep. She was also a poor napper and needed a pacifier at bedtime. Donna began by focusing on putting Elsa to bed while she was drowsy but still awake, and soothing her while she fell asleep without her pacifier. She initially scaled back nursing to every five hours, and around the fourth or fifth night she stopped nursing at night. The pediatrician said this was fine, Elsa was very petite but healthy. Donna still nursed Elsa at bedtime but instead of rocking her after she ate, she would burp her, kiss her, and put her into the crib, sitting next to her and soothing her. By the end of the first week, Elsa was waking up only once at night instead of four, five, or six times, and she went back to sleep easily without nursing, rocking, or using her pacifier.

Pacifier Withdrawal

Pacifiers are great for the first month or so of life, when newborns really need all that extra sucking. After that, I think pacifiers still have their place—but their place is not in the crib overnight, unless your baby is one of the rare ones who uses one to go to sleep at bedtime but doesn't seek or demand it when he gets up in the middle of the night. At six to eight months, it's fine if your baby is using a pacifier to calm himself, but not as a sleep crutch. If he spits it out, leave it out. Don't assume he wants it back. He'll let you know if he does. Make sure that you are not blocking his blossoming efforts to communicate with you by plugging it in all the time, especially during the day. And try to make sure that the pacifier isn't becoming a security object.

Encourage attachment to a lovey instead. But if your child is sending you scurrying after his pacifier all night long, I generally recommend that you take it away. Pick a night when you are ready to cope with a little unpleasantness and put him to bed without his binkie. Make sure you have an especially nice and calming bedtime routine, and try to get him to bed drowsy but awake. Stroke or soothe him instead of giving him the pacifier, using techniques similar to those I advise for parents who are breaking the nighttime nursing or walking habits. Do the same thing each time he wakes at night. Be consistent. Keep in mind, if you cave in once after he's cried for an hour, you aren't teaching him to sleep without the pacifier. You are teaching him to cry for an hour in order to get a pacifier.

I realize many parents don't feel comfortable taking away the pacifier, particularly if they are making other changes to their baby's sleep behavior and routines. Once he can handle the pacifier himself, at about eight or nine months, an alternative is to leave several pacifiers strewn around the crib. The baby has an easier time finding one without waking up completely or screaming for you to come in and find it for him. If he still isn't able to find it himself, then come in quickly, put the pacifier in his hand, and walk out again without saying a word. Every month or so, try not responding and see if he can do it by himself. By ten months he should be able to. Some families also decide to take away the pacifier at night, but leave it at nap time when it is harder for a baby to settle down.

> I worked with a set of twins who were definitely caught in the pacifier trap. The parents spent so much time traipsing in to replug one pacifier or the other that they finally just took the twins out of their cribs and put them in Pack 'n Plays at each side of the parents' bed. But it wasn't really all that much better—they didn't have to keep running all night into the other room but they were still constantly swinging their arms and replugging "Nuks." We stopped this by adjusting their schedule, moving the babies back to their cribs, and improving the bedtime routine to help them settle down. We used the Sleep Lady Shuffle to improve their ability to sleep without their pacifiers.

Unconventional Beds

Some babies learn to sleep in unconventional places—swings, car seats, and the like. Maybe your baby had reflux, and you placed her upright in her car seat to digest when she was very little, and she got used to dozing off there. Maybe the soothing movement of the swing just helped relax her to sleep. But she can't sleep there forever.

I worked with one little girl, nearly eight months old, who had spent every single night of her life and all her naps in a moving swing. If she woke up at night, her mother nursed her and then put her back in the swing. This child was actually quite advanced developmentally, crawling at five months and standing at six months. But she didn't have a clue as to how to sleep lying down. It took her three weeks to learn.

Her parents did the Sleep Lady Shuffle. They would lay her down in her crib, she would promptly sit up, and fall asleep sitting. Then she'd fall over, which naturally would wake her up—mad. She'd sit up again, fall asleep again, topple over again, and wake up. One of her parents sat nearby, soothing her, but avoided picking her up unless she was really frustrated. They would go through this ritual several times at bedtime, and several times when she woke up in the middle of the night. Eventually she would get so tired that she would lie down and go to sleep, although she wasn't particularly happy about it. But within a few days, she was waking up less frequently, and less furiously. It was only taking her parents five to ten minutes to get her back to sleep.

Initially, her mom kept the swing for naps, although she turned the swing off when the baby fell asleep, phasing out that feeling of being rocked. By the end of the first week, she had made enough progress that her mom put her in the crib for naps as well. It took another two weeks for all the problems to resolve but her parents noticed that when she began napping in the crib, instead of the moving swing, she seemed to be much better rested. The motion of the swing, like the motion of a moving car, interferes with deep sleep, so she had not been getting the full benefit of her naps. (I also talk a lot about swings, car seats, etc. in my chapters on newborns; some of those ideas may help at this age too.)

Early Birds

Early risings sometimes have a very simple solution. If too much light is coming into the baby's room, buy room-darkening blinds (also good for napping). If an external noise—garbage trucks, songbirds, or a dad with a long commute who has turned on the shower—is waking him, you might want to try a white noise machine or a fan. Unfortunately, it's not always so simple.

If your child is awake at 6:00 or 6:30 a.m., cheerful, refreshed, and ready to start his day—even if you aren't—you'll probably have to live with it. That's a common and biologically appropriate wake-up time for a baby or small child. Remember to adapt the meal and nap schedule to suit his early hours. The first nap should be one and a half to two hours after he wakes up. You might also try making his bedtime later, shifting it in fifteen-minute intervals to see if that will coax him into sleeping later, but be careful. He may still wake up at 6:00, but be more tired and cranky because he's no longer getting enough sleep at the front end. Pay attention to his sleep window, his sleepy signals and behavior. Don't force him to stay up when he really needs to go to sleep or he won't be able to fall asleep when you want him to. If you do make a trial run on the later bedtime, try letting that third little afternoon nap run a little later so he isn't too overtired when you put him down. You may also use the techniques I outline below for problematic early risers, but they may or may not work for a child whose early wake-up time is appropriate for his own internal clock.

Babies who wake up before 6:00 a.m., or who wake up cheerful at 6:00 or 6:30 but are a total grump by 7:00, are a different story. You need to intervene and coach him to sleep later. The longer you endure early risings, the harder it is to change the pattern, so I strongly suggest you address it now, even if it takes a few weeks to see results. Once they're older, it can take months. Make sure your early riser is getting enough daytime sleep because nap deprivation can cause poor night sleep and early awakenings. You can try adjusting an early bird's morning nap, moving it later in half-hour increments. This might help shift his whole body clock and coax him into sleeping later. But be careful. Watch his sleep windows and use your intuition, because you don't want to postpone his nap so long that he is too wired to fall asleep. If you think he is waking up very early because he is hungry, try waking him for a final feeding about 11:00 p.m. as an interim step, and also work on making sure he takes more food during the day. (See Eliminating Nighttime Feeding on page 91 for more help on improving daytime feeding.)

When you hear your early bird stir, go to him very quickly. Try to soothe him, and offer him a lovey. Try to get him and his lovey back to sleep without taking him out of his crib. Even if he doesn't doze off again, do not turn on the lights or let him out of his crib until 6:00 a.m—even if he wails with impatience. When I say 6:00, I mean 6:00. I don't mean 5:45 or 5:50. Or even 5:59. Letting him get up earlier, while it is still dark, sends a confusing message, and is another example of intermittent reinforcement. He cannot understand why he can get up in the dark at 5:45 a.m. but not at 2:15 a.m. Also, many parents I've worked with have learned the hard way that if they let him get up at 5:45 a.m., he'll gradually wake up earlier and earlier.

At this age, I usually recommend that the parent stay in the room while the child gets back to sleep in the early morning. But keep your interaction minimal. Try sitting in a chair with your eyes closed. Say that Mommy (or Daddy) is still sleeping and act like baby should be sleeping as well. When the clock finally strikes 6:00—and it can seem like it takes forever—leave the room for a minute or two. He may cry but it's only one minute. You'll be right back.

Whether you've been out for a minute or much of the last hour, when you reenter the room, do a *dramatic wake-up.* Open the blinds, turn on the lights, sing a cheery morning song—a reverse lullaby. Think of it as a morning routine, just like you have an evening one. The idea is to help the baby distinguish between day and night, to know when it is really time to get up and start his day. Your message must be clear: "I'm getting you out of the crib because it's morning time—not because you were crying."

(If you feel your presence is encouraging him to stay awake, as often happens with older children, you can try leaving his room and see if he falls asleep again on his own. Stay out until 6:00, or check on him periodically until 6:00. At 6:00, reenter and follow the dramatic wake-up advice above.)

Napping

Napping is hard for babies. Nap training is almost as hard for parents. Nighttime problems are usually solved reasonably quickly. Most families begin to see progress in just a few nights and they see considerable improvement or total resolution of their problems in two to three weeks. Fixing day sleep requires more patience and more perseverance.

Like adults, many babies simply have trouble sleeping when it is not dark. Our brains are programmed to be awake during daylight, and asleep at night. In addition, babies aren't yet very good at helping themselves switch gears from active to restful. And even at this young age, they can resist sleep. They fight it off because they would much rather stay up to play, explore, and be with you. That doesn't mean they are having separation anxiety problems, it just means they are forming nice healthy attachments.

Nap training is hard on parents because it is time consuming and usually involves tears. I'm going to give you some techniques for improving your baby's daytime sleep. I'm also going to give you some shorter-term fixes to help you and the baby get through the day if full-fledged nap training is just too much for you right now.

NAP READINESS · Remember that babies from six to eight months need two naps a day, about one and a half to two hours apiece. The short third nap in late afternoon is optional as long as they are getting two decent naps earlier in the day. If not, you'll need the third nap until daytime sleep improves. Start by reviewing your child's schedule, paying attention to the correct timing of naps and her daytime sleep windows. Create a good nap environment, both in terms of stimulation levels and physical surroundings. Don't go directly from a stimulating activity, like dancing her around to your favorite radio station, straight into the crib. Give her some wind-down time, maybe an abbreviated version of her bedtime routine. Read a book, listen to some quiet music. Nursing or bottle feeding sometimes helps to create this transition time, but try not to let her fall asleep while eating. Remember to put her down drowsy but awake—although she can be a little bit drowsier than at nighttime.

Napping success often depends on a dark, quiet room. Experiment with turning off the night-light or leaving only a very dim light on. Some babies need near total darkness to nap, even if they want a little more light at night. If you live in an especially noisy home you might want to try a fan or place a white noise machine on low volume across the room from the crib. If you are concerned that she will get so dependent on the machine that she won't be able to sleep without it, use it only for naps and slowly reduce the volume as her sleep improves.

Follow the same basic rules as bedtime to avoid early attempts at power struggle and delay. If she stands up in the crib, put her down once; if she stands up again, ignore it. Don't feel obligated to feed her before every nap, particularly if you are working on breaking a food-sleep association. If you've been rocking or swinging her to bed, concentrate on phasing it out at nap time. Cut the rocking or swinging time in half at the beginning, and work on getting her down drowsy but awake.

THE LONGEST HOUR · Even if you do everything right to set the stage for nap time, brace yourself. You may have to devote the next full hour (twice a day if you are training for morning and afternoon naps) to getting her to sleep. Use the Sleep Lady Shuffle, and if she cries—and she probably will—sit by her, soothe her, "sh-sh" her, pat her, reassure her as you did at bedtime. Don't overengage; don't keep picking her up. If you do have to pick her up, keep it brief and put her down again as soon as she is calm. Do what you must to console her—and yourself. However, if your presence is making her stay awake instead of falling asleep, if she's either trying persistently to engage you or she's getting madder and madder that you are there but won't do what she wants, then you should try leaving the room. Come back to check on her frequently, every five to fifteen minutes, whatever feels right to you. That's what worked for Corinna and Erin.

> *Corinna stopped walking Erin to sleep at nap time and just put her down in her crib. Corinna sat right outside the room with a magazine and said, "It's okay, Mommy's right here." She entered the room briefly about every fifteen minutes for some additional reassurance. Then it got to the point where she could put Erin down, then move away from the hallway and do some things around the house. She would still check on her every fifteen minutes. It never took a whole hour for Erin to fall asleep, and over a period of a few weeks, she fell asleep faster and faster.*

If you have an older child to take care of, you may have to leave the baby's room and make frequent checks. I had to do this when my second child was an infant and my first was three and at home in the afternoon needing Mommy. For me it was quite difficult because I felt pulled between my two children, and the younger one, Gretchen, was crying more than I really wanted. Marianne, who'd had three kids in three years, was convinced that each baby was a more capable napper than the one before simply because she didn't have as much time to rock, sing, and soothe the youngest at nap time. She had to leave the littlest one, Ally, in her crib at nap time and go to deal with whatever toddler antics needed her attention.

> *Donna couldn't sit next to Elsa's crib for an hour twice a day for the Shuffle because she had four-year-old Kit to attend to—and some of Elsa's natural nap windows coincided with the time she had to take Kit to preschool. Donna did the best she could, which meant working around the preschool schedule and leaving Elsa in her room when Kit was home. She checked on Elsa frequently (more like the Ferber method). It wasn't easy on any of them, and it took forty-five minutes of coaxing to produce forty-five minutes of napping. But forty-five minutes of sleep was still better than Elsa's earlier little dozing sessions, and gradually the naps lengthened as Donna stayed as consistent as she could be under the circumstances. With two parents around to share child-care responsibilities, Elsa napped better on weekends, and those longer and easier weekend naps probably helped her overall progress.*

If after a full hour, your baby still hasn't fallen asleep, leave the room for at least one complete minute—that's sixty seconds, not ten seconds—even if she complains. No matter how little tolerance you have for tears, you can manage sixty seconds. Come back in and, with a little drama and flourish, take her out of her crib and act like nap time is over, much like you do at morning wake time. You want to convey the idea that when she gets up it's because you've decided it's time, not because she has been crying. Even if she doesn't sleep, move your Shuffle position every three days, just as you do at bedtime. (It's okay if you start nap training days, weeks, or even months after the bedtime Shuffle. You don't have to be in the same position at naps as you are for bedtime and night wakenings.) If she doesn't sleep a wink during the morning hour, try to get her down for her afternoon nap earlier than usual because she's going to be overtired. Watch her sleepy clues, and catch her when she's ripe for a nap, maybe in as little as forty-five minutes.

CATNAPS · Ideally, your baby will sleep for an hour and a half or more, but often they sleep less than forty-five minutes. I call these *disaster naps*, because they are less than a full sleep cycle. All those little naps do is give her just enough oomph to resist sleep, but she'll be cranky and tired again in no time.

You have a few options to try to prolong those naps. Remember that if she's getting up after thirty or forty-five minutes, she might not really be fully awake; she may be experiencing a partial awakening. Instead of taking her out of her crib as though her nap was over, go to her quickly and try to soothe her back to sleep for another half hour or an hour ideally. If this works, gradually give her more opportunities to resettle herself without so much assistance from you. As she develops this skill, you won't have to jump in so quickly when you hear her stir. A little "sh-sh" from the hallway might do the trick. Gradually, with your help and consistency, she will start sleeping for longer periods of time on her own.

If you can't get her back to sleep and she has only slept twenty or thirty minutes, you should modify her schedule for a while until napping improves. If she takes a brief morning nap, make her afternoon nap earlier. She's not going to manage to stay awake for three hours until the second nap if she's running on vapors, not without driving both you and herself crazy. Use both the clock and your child's cues to make adjustments before she falls apart. She may need her "afternoon" nap at 11:30 or noon, and then need a brief third nap later in the afternoon. Don't let her take the third nap too late, or else it will throw dinnertime and her evening routine so far off that you'll be back to where you started. Be flexible at this stage. If you try and fail to get her to nap at 9:00 or 9:30 a.m. but at 10:00 or 10:30 she seems sleepy, try again.

But if your child skipped a nap, or only dozed briefly either in the morning or afternoon, you need to implement an emergency backup plan to make sure she sleeps one way or another for a decent interval in the afternoon. You don't want a baby so completely miserable and sleep deprived that you undo all the progress you've made at bedtime—even if it means temporarily ignoring all my rules about no motion sleeping. Put her in a car, or the stroller or her swing, whatever works to get her a nap. You can try nursing her, and if she falls asleep, put her back in her crib, tiptoe out, and thank your lucky stars. But be careful what backup technique you choose. Don't backslide into one of the habits you have just broken. For instance, if you have been working on ending co-sleeping at night, don't put her in your bed for this nap emergency. Try a car ride instead. If you have been phasing out rocking and walking at night, don't walk or rock at nap time. Find another nap tool, and rely on it for the short term. If motion sleep is part of the short-term fix, try to minimize it. If you use a swing to get her to sleep, turn off the motor once she's out and let her nap with it off. Ditto for the car. Drive around to lull her into sleep if you must, but then pull over or come back home so she can sleep without the car's motion. Transfer her to a crib if it won't wake her, or sit out there with her, in the car or right nearby if the weather permits, and let her sleep. Read a book, or snooze yourself—tend your garden if the weather's nice. I'm not too comfortable with letting a baby sleep in a car unattended, even in "safe" neighborhoods.

Unfortunately, after everything you went through to get her to nap, you can't let her nap too late or your evening will be even rougher than your day. Wake her by 4:30, 5:00 at the absolute latest, and keep bedtime at its normal hour.

PARENTAL STRAINS · Just about every parent I've worked with has found nap training tedious, but emotional reactions vary. Some parents tolerate daytime tears, finding it easier emotionally to have a child cry when it's not dark.

> *Penny found Anita's crying easier to take at nap time than at night. "I wasn't so exhausted; I wasn't trying to sleep myself," she said. "And I knew Anita was exhausted; I knew she really needed this nap. That allowed me to put up with some crying. She cried for forty-five minutes once, but that was the worst. Usually it was twenty to thirty minutes, and even that stopped in a week and a half." Anita began sleeping for a solid hour, and then gradually extended her nap to an hour and a half.*

Other moms report exactly the opposite reaction, that they can't take being alone in a house with a screaming child when the other parent is off at work and unable to provide on-site support and encouragement. Caretakers at home, whether a nanny or a grandma, often find it hard to deal with the nap routine or the tears. My advice then is don't push it. If it's too hard on you, if it's too hard on your caretaker, if it's creating more tension instead of less, then don't worry about it right now—as long as your child's nighttime sleep is improving. Use backup measures, temporary fixes, or improvised solutions to get your child some daytime sleep for the short term. Nurse her, pat her, swing her, do what you have to do. But don't give up on naps completely or convince yourself that she doesn't need them. She absolutely does need them and she will need them for another three to four years. But don't feel guilty if you can't follow all my advice right now. Give yourself (or your babysitter) permission to let the training slide for now and just do what you have to do to get your child some daytime sleep, preferably at predictable times. As nighttime sleep improves, the daytime sleep might fall into place on its own. If not, take a deep breath and try the training again in another month or two. Keep reminding yourself that good daytime sleep promotes better nighttime sleep; it helps you get through it.

You may go through a stage when some of your nap tricks no longer work. Don't panic. It just means that changes in her bedtime and overnight sleep are helping her discard her sleep crutches. It may mean she's on the brink of learning to nap better, with a little more coaching from you.

Co-sleeping

If you started out co-sleeping but have found that it is not right for you, or if you start the night with the baby in her crib but end up bringing her into your bed after she wakes up once or twice even if it's not what you intended, please turn to Chapter 10, Co-sleeping and the Family Bed, for help in making changes. I'll also give you advice in that chapter for how to improve sleep if you want to continue sharing the family bed but are finding that no one is sleeping very well in it.

Many of the families I work with do see extremely swift results, particularly with babies this age. They detect some improvements in just a few days, and they experience very significant changes in as little as a week or two. Some of you will have to be more patient, and bear in mind that the first few days of my program can be quite tiring. I think it helps to consider Adam's story.

Adam's Story

Adam had a host of developmental, health, and sleep problems in the first months of life. His parents were overwhelmed. Robert and Margaret consulted quite a few doctors and experts before they came to me. They'd even had a sleep study done, electrodes and all, at a major teaching hospital. Some of Adam's problems were treated. Others he grew out of. But he still wasn't sleeping. Looking at how Adam's parents coped, how they adapted my system to fit their own rather extreme needs, how they found their own new comfort zone for tears may be helpful as you craft your own sleep solutions. Robert's very structured approach to how and when to stroke, pat, and comfort Adam also wonderfully illustrates my advice about touching or patting your child on and off so he doesn't develop new negative associations.

From early infancy, Adam needed to be walked, rocked, bounced, held, and nursed—and even that wasn't enough. A full-term, seemingly healthy baby, Adam in fact had a number of developmental delays and digestive difficulties that were not immediately apparent or swiftly diagnosed. Neither his hearing nor his vision developed properly at first, so for the first few months he heard and saw less than other babies. He also had a severe, but somewhat atypical, form of reflux that was hard to diagnose. Instead of spitting up, he would pant and gasp as acid reflux hit a spot in the back of his throat, closing his trachea. Sleep was almost impossible.

"I knew from the time he was five days old something was wrong," Margaret remembered. "By the time he was ten days old I was keeping a log. I had to hold him constantly, eighteen to twenty hours a day. He never slept more than twenty minutes at a time."

By the time six months had passed, Adam's reflux was under control and his hearing and eyesight had caught up. But the early difficulties had created poor sleeping habits, depriving him of the chance to learn to self-soothe. Margaret and Robert went through one or two hours of bedtime contortions every night, finally getting him down at 8:30 or 9:00. He would sleep reasonably well for three hours or so and then wake up repeatedly for the rest of the night. He spent lots of time in their bed, nursing and dozing, but seldom getting much deep sleep. Daytime wasn't much better. Naps seldom lasted more than twenty minutes. An overnight sleep study in a clinic shed some light on his idiosyncratic sleep patterns. Even when he seemed to be awake and thrashing he was in fact neurologically asleep. From that, his parents learned that sometimes they were actually stimulating him into being more awake when they thought they were lulling him to sleep. But even armed with more knowledge about Adam, nights didn't get any easier.

The family sought me out when Adam was seven and a half months old. Within three weeks, we had him going to sleep in his crib in a matter of minutes with minimal tears. It wasn't perfect. He still woke up once or twice many nights, but now the awakenings were brief and far less upsetting and disruptive. Everyone was getting more rest and feeling much happier.

Robert took the lead in the Sleep Lady Shuffle, with a few minor adjustments to suit Adam's needs. We developed an extremely detailed and structured nighttime routine. We wanted Robert to give Adam enough of the physical contact he craved so he could feel secure, but not so much that it prevented him from changing sleep patterns. From a chair near the bed, Robert patted Adam's back intermittently for thirty seconds, with his hand through the crib slats. He said, "Sh-sh. Go to sleep," the same sounds he would make consistently each night. Then Robert paused, and patted Adam again for another thirty seconds. When Adam tried to stand up, Robert removed his hand and did not interfere with Adam's movements. He said, "Sh-sh. Go to sleep" again, followed by another thirty seconds of patting. The first two nights, he did this for an hour and a half before Adam fell asleep. When he woke up during the night, Robert did exactly the same thing, making sure that Adam got an utterly consistent message.

By the third night, Robert followed the same routine, but it only took forty-five minutes. On the fourth night, Robert patted Adam for ten-second intervals, and made sure he paused for at least twenty seconds in between. He did this pat-stop, pat-stop routine for a total of only five minutes. After that, he continued to make his reassuring "sh-sh" sounds, but he had moved farther away from Adam now, and did no more patting. Adam fell asleep in half an hour (as did Robert in his chair!). The fifth night, Robert did one sequence of "sh-sh" and ten seconds of patting when he initially went in. Then he waited a full minute. Then he did another ten-second sequence, and waited a full minute. He followed this cycle five times, and then sat quietly in the chair in Adam's room, occasionally still murmuring a reassuring "sh-sh." Adam fell asleep in thirty minutes.

On nights six and seven, Robert and Margaret could see the difference. Robert put Adam down and said, "Sh-sh. Go to bed," once. Then he just sat in the room, a few feet from the crib. Adam cried but fell asleep within an hour on night six—and in twenty minutes on night seven. On the next two nights, Robert was able to move the chair farther from the crib, reaching the door on the ninth night. He stayed there, at the door, for another four or five days (a little longer than I usually recommend), and finally was able to leave the room. Adam cried, but his mother described it as a normal wind-down crying: quiet whimpering with a few bursts of harder tears, but decreasing in intensity. None of that ear-piercing shrieking they had earlier endured. And it was only for a few minutes, not the hours they had experienced in the past.

Encouraged, Margaret and Robert decided that they were ready to stop going in to him when he woke in the middle of the night, to see if he could get himself back to sleep on his own. This was a change for a couple who had earlier rushed to respond to his every tear. They braced themselves—but he only cried softly for five or six minutes and then drifted back to sleep. They decided it was less disruptive for his sleep and theirs if, instead of getting out of bed and interacting with him and risking waking everybody up even more, they just let him cry those few minutes and put himself back to sleep. He still woke up but his whimpers never lasted very long. They followed this practice into toddlerhood. Adam never became a perfect sleeper, and he still has some hypersensitivity issues they may want to explore before he starts school. But the best measure of how much their life improved was their decision to have a second child. They had a little girl—and she is a much better sleeper!

NINE TO TWELVE MONTHS

Please take a few minutes to read the first three chapters of my book, which give an overview of my system and include some helpful hints that apply to all age groups. It won't take long and you'll have much better results.

○ ○ ○

BABIES AT THIS AGE ON AVERAGE need eleven hours of sleep at night and three during the day. At nine months, babies should nap for about an hour and a half in the morning and about one and a half to two hours in the afternoon. Most have given up that brief, third late-afternoon nap. By twelve months, the morning nap is about an hour and the afternoon nap is about an hour and a half.

Many of the problems and solutions encountered in babies from nine to twelve months old are quite similar to those found in babies from six through eight months old, but there are a few sleep-related developmental differences. These babies are more mobile, crawling and pulling themselves up in their cribs, and can pop up each time you put them down at bedtime. Some walk by their first birthday, a major developmental milestone that can temporarily disrupt sleep. Increased activity can tire them out, so you have to pay very close attention to their sleep window, when they are most ready and able to fall asleep. Some can fight sleep, and conceal that window. If you wean during this period, that can also alter the rhythms of bedtime.

The families you will meet in this chapter had experiences that are quite typical for this age. Though not a first-time mother, Greta had trouble letting Frederick cry, and she nursed him constantly, day and night. Christina had difficulty with that final phase of nighttime weaning, and even after she did wean, Sally kept waking up all night wanting Mom. Brad refused to nap more than twenty minutes at a time. Bruce's parents held him virtually every waking minute (and believe me, there weren't too many minutes that weren't waking) for four entire months. They let him stay up until 10:00 every night visiting with his grandmother, and then they put him to sleep in a bouncy chair—which they then placed in their bed. Amy was actually a good little sleeper from about five months until about ten months when first she got sick, then a tidal wave of separation anxiety overwhelmed her. Linda, an X-ray technician who had to be cheery and comforting to orthopedic patients bright and early in the morning, and Miguel, a state trooper whose shifts were always changing, were so exhausted that they used to take turns trying to get at least a little sleep with Amy on a basement couch while the other parent got some desperately needed shut-eye upstairs. Jason's mom, Tess, whom you met in the Introduction, had to confront her own demons before she could withstand teaching her child to sleep.

Many of these families expected their babies to resist sleep changes far more fiercely than they did, and they anticipated having a lot more difficulty in coping with tears. All of them found the baby responded better than they expected. The parents found that the tears were not as intense as they had feared, and they didn't feel so bad about letting him shed them as long as they were by his side.

> *"The key to success with sleep training was realizing that crying wasn't abandonment, it wasn't torture," Megan said. "We learned that sleep was so important to his growth and development that not teaching him to sleep was hurting him. We thought we would be bad parents if we let him cry. But we learned that ten minutes of crying didn't hurt him. We realized he was okay and that made us feel so much better. You've got to just tell yourself over and over again, what you are doing is right."*

 DEVELOPMENTAL CHANGES

Separation Anxiety

Babies have peaks of separation anxiety at about nine months, when they are crawling and sitting, and at twelve months, when they are standing, walking, and climbing. Those physical leaps often make them wake up more at night, at least temporarily, and the accompanying cognitive leaps make them more aware of strangers, places, and change. Right around the first birthday, babies experiencing these anxiety peaks often start to test their parents to see what the response will be. One common test is to start bawling when the parent, particularly the mom, leaves the room at night. They are saying, "What are you going to do if I cry? Can I make you come back and stay with me?" This can make bedtime a more wrenching time for both the child and the parent, even with babies who had been going to bed easily at a slightly younger age.

Amy had slept quite well from around five months until around ten months. Then a bad stomach virus and a wave of separation anxiety combined to wreak havoc with her shut-eye. "Whatever it was, it came with a vengeance," her mother, Linda, remembered with a grimace. Amy started waking up at night, once, then twice. Then she started fighting going to bed at all—she wanted Mom and Dad. "We tried walking, talking, rocking. Eventually the screaming would get so bad that one of us would take her down to the basement and lie on the couch with her, and the other would stay upstairs and try to get some sleep." Their home and work life got more and more stressful. They followed my program, which made Amy feel more secure and sleep better at night.

Loveys

If your child has not already grown attached to a lovey, encourage one now. The lovey makes the baby feel safe and secure, particularly at bedtime or when he wakes up at night. Put a few stuffed animals or blankets in his crib, and see if one has special appeal. Or try to choose one matched to his own habits and preferences.

One mom noticed that her son kneaded her fingers as she nursed him to sleep. She got him a little stuffed cow, and with a little steering from her, he gradually shifted his kneading habit from her finger to the cow's horns. After that, he was able to use his little cow to soothe himself at night.

To encourage the bond with the lovey, hold it between you and the baby when you are nursing or bottle feeding him, and include the lovey in bedtime games like peek-a-boo. You may want to wear it inside your own shirt for a few hours to impart that *eau de Mom*. If he doesn't bond despite your efforts, try a lovey again in a month or two—or maybe he'll choose one from among the presents he is sure to collect on his first birthday.

New Mobility

Most babies can now pull themselves up and stand—which creates some new twists at bedtime or nap time when you put them down in the crib and they can pop back up again. I usually tell parents not to intervene, or to put the baby down once, but only once. Babies do tend to learn how to get up before they can get back down, so let them practice during the day. Let her stand up and try to get down holding on to a coffee table—after you babyproof the corners and put some pillows or soft landing pads around if needed. Games like ring-around-the-rosy are also good for developing up and down motions. But do the practicing games out of the crib, during awake time, not at naps or bedtime.

Eating and Sleeping

Introduce a cup before the first birthday, even if you are still nursing, and even if you plan on nursing for some time to come. As babies get older, they can get emotionally attached to the bottle or breast. It basically becomes a lovey and that can contribute to an ingrained habit of waking up at night in search of it. Nurse or bottle feed at set times, and use the cup at set times, giving him water, milk, soy milk, formula, diluted juice, whatever your doctor recommends. Most moms find that they and the baby both like nursing in the morning and evening, and using the cup during the day, especially with solids at mealtimes. Don't let him fall asleep on the breast or with the bottle, don't let him be dependent on nursing to fall asleep or stay asleep or you'll be up nursing him back to sleep all night for months to come. To facilitate the switch from bottle to cup, make sure you keep encouraging the attachment to a lovey.

Some mothers wean their babies in the nine-to-twelve-month range, and some babies basically wean themselves no matter what their mothers intended. If your baby is looking around a lot while nursing (or taking a bottle), mouthing the nipple without sucking, trying to slide off your lap before you finish feeding him, or impatiently looking like he's got better things to do, that's the signal. Whether you do it now or in a few more months, weaning should be a natural, easy transition. But nothing is easy and natural when you are dealing with a sleep-deprived, overtired baby, particularly one who hasn't learned how to fall asleep without a breast or bottle in his mouth.

CREATING A SCHEDULE
Sample schedule:

7:00–7:30 a.m. Wake up. Nurse/bottle/cup and breakfast.

9:00–9:30 a.m. Start the morning nap. If your child is sleeping 11–12 hours uninterrupted at night he might be able to stay awake until 10:00 a.m. (or 3 hours after waking up). Some children need a small morning snack after the nap.

12:00–12:30 p.m. Lunch with nurse/bottle or cup.

1:00–2:00 p.m. Start the afternoon nap. Snack upon awakening.

5:00–6:00 p.m. Dinner with nurse/bottle or cup.

7:00–7:30 p.m. Bedtime with nurse/bottle.

Although I don't believe in completely rigid schedules, young children do need consistency and predictability. During the first weeks of sleep scheduling, you are better erring on the side of too much rigidity than too little. This section gives you detailed advice on how to set up a schedule for this age group. (If you want to read even more about the art of scheduling, and about the relationship between food and sleep, review the scheduling section in the previous chapter.) Schedules obviously vary somewhat from one child to the next. A baby who wakes up at 6:30 a.m. will have a slightly different timetable than one who gets up at 7:30. But this is a good model, so try not to deviate too much. Especially don't let the baby stay up too late at night, no matter how much fun he seems to be having. Remember Dr. Weissbluth's mantra—sleep begets sleep. A well-rested child sleeps better than an overtired one. Babies who don't get enough sleep during their naps, or who don't go to bed on time in the evening, tend to wake up more frequently in the middle of the night, and to wake up earlier in the morning.

"One of the first things Kim did was talk to us about schedules, map out the interval, when Amy should be awake, when she should be napping. That was news to us! She had always been a catnapper. Talking about an actual schedule was a big thing," said her mother, Linda.

The big scheduling differences between younger and older infants center on eating. Check with your pediatrician, but healthy children from nine to twelve months on a normal growth curve can almost always go eleven to twelve hours at night without a feeding. If your child is still waking to eat frequently, you probably have to either adjust his body clock or change his habits.

Separating food time from sleep time, and creating recognizable meal and snack times instead of nonstop nibbling, helps create a sleep-friendly structure. Your pediatrician has probably recommended a variety of solids by now. Feed her at recognizable mealtimes: breakfast, lunch, and dinner. Many babies also have morning and afternoon snacks, but you want to get away from the idea of constant feeding and grazing all day (and all night). If your baby goes to bed or takes a nap right after a meal, make sure there is some time between nursing or bottle feeding and going into the crib. You want to break that suckle-snooze association, and teach her that milk is part of mealtime, not part of sleep time.

WAKE-UP · A good time to wake up is 7:00 to 7:30 a.m., although some children do get up earlier for the first few years. Even if your child tends to sleep later, it's generally a good idea to start waking him by 7:30 to regulate his sleep rhythms and avoid pushing naps and bedtimes too late. (If he sleeps later but takes good naps and sleeps well at night, don't worry about it, just give him plenty of time to adjust when he gets older and has to wake up for preschool.) Just like you have bedtime rituals, create morning ones. Throw open the blinds and greet the new day with special games or songs. Sleep experts call this a *dramatic wake-up* and it helps him better define in his own mind the difference between waking time and sleeping time. This can be a good opportunity for some of those active, stimulating games, like flying baby, that dads like to play but that aren't a great idea in the last five minutes before bed. It's also nice for parents who get home from work late to start their day having fun with the baby.

MORNING NAP · Give him some wind-down time to prepare for his nap. It doesn't need to be as long as the bedtime ritual but he does need time to transition from all that revved-up morning activity to morning sleep. Try to get him down by 9:00 or 9:30—a little earlier if he's an earlier riser, a little later if he sleeps an uninterrupted eleven or twelve hours at night. But don't let him stay up for more than a three-hour stretch. Watch for his sleep windows.

Many babies yawn, suck their thumb, or rub their eyes. Others have more idiosyncratic signals like twirling their hair or just getting a zonked-out glassy-eyed look.

> *"Amy rubs her eyes, that's a sleep clue. But she's a sleep fighter; she is good at masking her cues. We had to learn to pay very careful attention to her cues because she would push and push and fight as hard as she could, so we thought that she wasn't tired, that she just didn't need a lot of sleep. In fact, she needed two or three hours more than we had been giving her. She was sleep deprived," Linda said.*

The morning nap should be about one and a half hours for a nine-month-old and an hour for a twelve-month-old. If your child sleeps longer, but still naps well in the afternoon and makes it to bedtime, don't worry about it. If, however, he takes a long morning nap, then has trouble sleeping in the afternoon and is a wreck before bedtime, knock off fifteen to thirty minutes from the morning nap. The afternoon nap is generally a longer and more important one, and it's the one he's going to keep after he gives up the morning nap a few months from now.

The interval between the morning nap and lunch is often a good one to go run some errands or get outside and play. He has just slept and is less likely to doze off in the car or stroller and throw off his afternoon nap schedule. Some kids need a small snack right after the morning nap, others wait until lunchtime.

LUNCH · Lunch is around noon or 12:30. At this age it's usually solids, with nursing or a bottle or, even better, a cup. Try to have some playtime after lunch, or a walk. Don't have lunch so late that you go directly to the afternoon nap; you are trying to weaken associations between food, particularly the bottle, and sleep.

AFTERNOON NAP · The afternoon nap usually starts between 1:00 and 2:00—or around three hours after the morning nap ends. This nap should last one and a half to two hours for a nine-month-old, and one and a half hours for a twelve-month-old. He'll probably want a snack when he gets up. Remember to keep an eye out for that sleep window, and give him some wind-down time to transition to sleep after a period of active play and exploration.

DINNER · Keep dinnertime early, between 5:00 and 6:00, even if both parents aren't home or aren't ready for dinner yet. Your life will be saner and his sleep will be much better if you keep him on an early schedule. I find that babies have an eating "window" (much like a sleep window), and if you miss it, they eat poorly. Either they wake up hungry in the middle of the night—or we wake up worried that they didn't eat enough.

BEDTIME · Bedtime should be at 7:00 or 7:30 and by bedtime, I mean in the crib, not in the bathtub or on your lap reading stories. Babies this age can fight sleep much more vehemently than younger infants. I worked with one who would shake his head vigorously to stay awake at the tender age of nine months. Make sure you leave plenty of time for him to unwind, and develop ways of cueing his brain that it's time to sleep. You should start brushing his teeth at this age, even if there aren't many teeth. Some parents like to get the toothbrushing out of the way before they begin the rest of the bath and bedtime routine. If the baby hates having his teeth brushed, you don't want to get him all cuddly, cozy, and ready to sleep only to have him kick up a great big stimulating fuss over his dental hygiene. After his bath, make sure the bedtime routine is in the bedroom, not wandering all over the house, and keep the games and stories pretty much the same every night. Some babies, especially when they get a little older, will insist on exactly the same routine every night, down to the last detail, and heaven forbid that you try to vary the story. Allow about fifteen to twenty minutes. Babies are getting a little more interested in picture books and simple rhymes and songs now, and they like peek-a-boo and other simple games. Remember to include the lovey in the games.

> *Christina and Andy had a pretty good bedtime routine for Sally even before I met them. We tweaked it a little, mostly eliminating a feeding too close to her bedtime. She would have dinner, a bath, then a story and to bed. That was at nine or ten months and it worked so well for her that at nineteen months, her routine had hardly changed—a little extra playtime with Dad, and two stories instead of one. "Andy has tried to put her down without those stories but she won't go," Christina said, laughing. "Rituals! I swear by them."*

Keep any bedtime music soft and quiet. Use music to set the mood and cue the brain for sleep, but turn it off before she gets into her crib, or soon after. You don't want her so accustomed to lullabies that she can't sleep without them. If you've been playing music until after she falls asleep, slowly ease it out. Lower the volume and try to turn it off before she's fully asleep. If the tape runs out, don't restart it. Similarly phase out bedtime use of toys with noise and lights.

If you walk or rock your baby, keep it brief and stay in her room. Put her down drowsy but still awake so she can learn to do that final part of falling asleep on her own. The goal of getting her down drowsy but awake is crucial. If your baby has trouble with it, focus your energy first on getting it right at bedtime. It's not less important at 2:00 a.m. but it's a lot easier for parents to follow through when we are not half asleep ourselves. Once you get it right at bedtime, it will be easier for you to carry this out consistently at other times.

BEDTIME FEEDING · It's okay to nurse or give your baby a bottle right before bed as long as she doesn't rely on it to nurse herself to sleep and you aren't nursing her back to sleep when she wakes up at night. If she does depend on nursing, and many babies do, try to put the final nursing earlier in the bedtime routine, say, before a song or story. (More on nighttime nursers in a minute.) Try not to let her fall asleep at the breast. Remember, drowsy but awake! Some moms find it easier to create that separation by no longer nursing in the baby's room. See if it's a good tool for you. If you want to remain in her room, try keeping the light on while you nurse and turning it off when you want to signal her it's crib time.

Megan and John had no schedule whatsoever for Bruce—unless you call haphazard twenty-minute naps and a 10:00 p.m. bedtime a schedule. You'll hear more about Bruce in this chapter, because he had quite a number of sleep issues, and schedule adjustments alone would not have fixed them. But Megan and John wouldn't have solved the other problems without fixing the schedule. Bruce had had severe colic for his first four months, and an extremely kind grandmother used to come over and help every day, comforting the baby and giving Megan and John a bit of a break. Once he was over the colic and feeling better, she'd still come over to play with him almost every night. What baby will willingly crawl off to bed when his grandma is around to cater to his every whim? He used to rub his eyes and yawn a bit around eight o'clock, but nobody paid much attention, even though his sleep window was gaping wide open. After all, he was wide awake and having so much fun. "He was enjoying himself so much, acting like a crazy man the entire evening," Megan said. Later they realized that Bruce was clearly telling them he needed to go to bed at 8:00 but when nobody responded, he got a rush of cortisol, a second wind, to stay up until 10:00. No wonder it was so hard to get him to sleep when Grandma finally went home. Along with sleep coaching, they put him on a more consistent nap schedule and told Grandma that although they and Bruce loved her dearly, she had be out the door at 7:00 p.m. when he was in his bath—or stay all night and deal with the consequences.

THE SLEEP LADY SHUFFLE

Many families I work with, including those in this chapter, use the Sleep Lady Shuffle to help the baby shed these negative associations. I introduced the concept in Chapter 1, but we'll review it here, paying particular attention to the needs of this age group. When your child wakes up at night during the Shuffle, go to his crib to comfort him briefly and then resume the position you had been in at bedtime that evening. We want to respond consistently to all wakenings. Use the tips I offer in the Problems and Solutions section to address your child's sleep crutches or habits that make it hard for him to fall to sleep again on his own during the night.

You should follow the Shuffle schedule, moving on to the next position even if your child has had a bad night or two, fussing or waking more frequently. Don't be surprised if there's a little regression or protest the first night of each new chair position. If your child gets sick during the Shuffle, you might want to pause and "freeze" or maintain your position until she's feeling a little better. You might even have to move a little bit closer during an illness to offer more comfort. But then resume your sleep shaping when she recovers.

NIGHTS 1–3. Once bath, stories, and songs are over, sit in a chair next to your baby's crib. If she cries or fusses, you can stroke or pat her intermittently (especially the first night), but don't do it constantly or you'll just create a new negative association. You can sing during the get-ready-for-bed stage, but once it's time for her to sleep, stick to calming "sh-sh" or other soothing sounds. You might want to try closing your eyes. That makes it easier not to talk to her too much and it also conveys a sleepy-time message. Remember, if she stands up in the crib, put her down only once or pat the crib to see if she gets the message.

It's also important that the parent control the touch. Instead of having her hold your hand or finger, you should pat hers. Make sure that you do not caress the child too steadily; do it on and off. You don't want to swap one negative association, like rocking, for another, like your constant touch or the sound of your voice.

Don't be too quick to pick her up during any stage of the Shuffle—but if she's really upset and you do need to pick her up, go ahead and do so, over the crib if possible. Hold her until she's calm, but keep it brief. Put her down again while she's still awake. Tell her that it's okay, and stay in the chair until she falls asleep.

NIGHTS 4–6. Move the chair about halfway to the door. (If the room is very small, or the crib is close to the door, then move all the way to the doorway as in night seven.) Continue the soothing sounds, but stay in the chair as much as you can. Get up to pat or stroke her a little if necessary, or make some of the same soothing sounds as you have used the past three nights.

NIGHTS 7–9. Move the chair to the doorway or the doorjamb. You should be dimly lit but still in her view. Continue the same soothing techniques, remembering to intervene as little as possible. Don't worry if she cries a little bit; keep quietly reassuring her. She'll know that you are there, and she will fall asleep.

NIGHTS 10–12. Move farther away, usually to the hallway or by the entrance of another room, but still within her direct line of vision. Make your "sh-sh" sounds, not constantly but enough to remind her that Mom or Dad is close by and responsive. Stay there until she falls asleep.

A few things to remember. Children get ritualized easily. Make the changes every three days—or less. *Dragging it out makes it harder, not easier, for your baby.* Give it more than three days and she'll expect you to stay exactly where you are, and get mad or upset when you double that distance.

NIGHTS 13 AND ON. It's time to leave your baby to fall asleep on her own—if she's not sleeping already. Don't panic, it's probably harder for you than for her. She's had two weeks to prepare for this. She has surrendered some of her sleep crutches and is more secure in her sleep skills. She recognizes your support and responsiveness.

You now need to move away from your baby's room. How far away you go is up to you. You should be out of her sight, but it's fine if you want to stay within earshot, down the hall or in a nearby room. If she's whimpering or crying a bit, try calming her from the bedroom doorway. See if you can soothe her with your voice from the doorway. But if you find you must go to her crib, do so briefly. Then return to the hallway out of view, but close enough that she can hear your soft soothing sounds. Listen to your intuition and check on her again from the doorway in a few minutes if you think she truly needs you. But try not to intervene too much or backtrack on all the great work you—and your baby—have done.

Very rarely do babies cry for more than a few minutes after experiencing the Shuffle. Keep in mind, she has gained confidence that you are nearby and responsive. She's ready to master this skill.

> *Remember Amy, the baby with all those nighttime separation problems? Her parents put her on a more regular nap schedule, lengthened what was basically a good bedtime preparation routine, and began the Shuffle. She cried at first, and she cried a lot the night they moved the chair to the doorway. But Linda and Miguel had been dealing with hysterical crying for the past two months and at least now they could see that she was adjusting to the bedtime arrangements. Within about ten days, they were out of her bedroom and able to give her verbal encouragement and instructions from their own room across the hall. "We'd say, 'Lie down, lie down,' and she would lie down and go to sleep," Linda said. Through the measured paces of the Sleep Lady Shuffle, Amy had regained trust that her parents were nearby, that they would check on her and be there if she needed them. But she also figured out that they weren't going to take her out of the crib, even if she screamed, and that she had to go to sleep. When Amy got a little older, fifteen months or so, she would sometimes take charge of her own bedtime when she got tired early. "She'd pull herself out of my lap and point to her crib!" On the other hand, if Miguel's or Linda's parental antennae picked up a little anxiety one night, they could bend the rules a bit. They didn't pick her up, they didn't return to the earlier chaos and the basement couch. But one parent would occasionally sit on the floor in her doorway at bedtime and give her the little extra reassurance she needed. This let them keep those normal peaks of separation anxiety in check, without disrupting her whole sleep routine. It's a good example of how parents can be flexible and respond to their child's needs, once their baby has mastered the fundamentals of independent sleep.*

PROBLEMS AND SOLUTIONS

Babies who have trouble getting to sleep and staying asleep often have *negative associations,* or sleep crutches. These aren't actually bad behaviors per se; they only become negative when they block sleep independence. For instance, children should be hugged and snuggled. But if they are hugged and snuggled until they fall asleep, and each time they wake up at night, they will never learn how to fall asleep on their own or get themselves back to sleep at night. Similar negative associations involve a pacifier that has to be replaced constantly; walking, rocking, serenading, or swinging a baby; or nursing or feeding a baby even when he is seeking food purely for comfort, not out of hunger. Our job as parents is to help the baby erase these sleep-harming associations and create positive new ones that will help him get the sleep required by his growing body and that miraculously expanding mind.

If despite following the advice in this section your child is still waking up at night, take another look at his routine. Are you putting him to bed a little too drowsy? If so, he may have learned to put himself to sleep at bedtime when you've done much of the sleep preparation work for him, but he can't get himself back to sleep at night without your assistance. Try putting him down at bedtime when he's a tad less drowsy, and a bit more awake so he can refine those self-soothing skills. You might also try moving bedtime earlier by 15 minutes or a half an hour, and maybe create a little more separation between that last nursing or bottle feeding and bed. Try leaving a soft light on while you nurse, it will help him break that suckle-sleep association.

Eliminating Nighttime Feeding

Many parents who are still feeding nine- to twelve-month-old babies all night look at me with a great deal of skepticism when I tell them this, but healthy babies this age who are on a good growth curve don't have to eat at night. Not even once. Not even a little bit. They can go eleven to twelve hours or so without a feeding. Check with your pediatrician, but if your baby is still waking up to eat at night, you're dealing with a habit, not a nutritional need. Either your child's hunger clock needs a little readjusting, so he eats more during the day and doesn't have a growling tummy at night, or he is using nighttime nursing or bottle feeding as a sleep crutch. It's a good idea at this age to shorten the nursing sessions, and make sure your child is nursing, not just dozing with the nipple in his mouth. If it's hard for you to see whether he's actively nursing or just suckling, watch the clock instead. Remember, babies are more efficient eaters now than when they were newborns, and twenty minutes or less is usually plenty of time. At this age, I usually recommend that you simply stop the night feedings. Instead, comfort the child, sitting by his bed and patting him intermittently, murmuring "sh-sh" or making other reassuring sounds. If that's too abrupt for you, do a *dream feed* for two or three nights. Wake him at about 10:00 or 11:00, about three hours after he goes to bed but also before you turn in for the night, for one last feeding. Don't feed him again until morning. He will wake up very hungry and eat better during the day, which in turn will help him eat less at night. I know a lot of us have anxiety about not feeding our children at night; we are afraid that we are hurting them, that we are leaving them with severe pangs of hunger that they can't articulate. We aren't. They will be fine. If you are consistent—meaning you don't cave in and feed him some of the time at night—he'll probably give up those nighttime feedings in just three to four days. If you are inconsistent, it's just going to be more difficult, more pro-longed, and more confusing for him. If your baby takes more than three to four days, don't worry, there is nothing wrong with him; just stay calm and consis-tent and he'll adjust and be fine. (If this is a particularly anxiety-provoking topic for you, go back and review the Eliminating Nighttime Feeding section [page 91] where I go into more detail, particularly about how to increase food intake during the day.)

> Greta and Matt used the Ferber technique successfully with Jordan, their first son, but with Frederick, their second, it was a disaster. "He cried for forty-five minutes, and I couldn't stand it. Plus the crying seemed to stimulate him, to keep him up more," Greta said. But at eleven months, Frederick was "nursing a hundred times a night," or at least once an hour. He would end up in his parents' bed, often dozing on top of his mom, who did not find this a restful arrangement. Greta and Matt combined the Sleep Lady Shuffle with a complete halt to overnight nursing. Greta continued to breastfeed the rest of the day, but not so frequently. Less nursing meant that he ate more solids, which in turn meant he wanted to nurse less. Giving up the constant nursing, Greta could concentrate on developing alternative soothing skills and give Frederick more of a chance to develop his own self-soothing skills. At bedtime, Greta also had to train herself to make sure he didn't fall asleep on the breast, so she could put him down drowsy but awake.
>
> Greta and Matt moved through the Shuffle fairly quickly, sometimes moving every two days instead of three, because Frederick was so easily ritualized. In other words, after two nights, he expected his mother or father to be sitting in a specific place and got upset when they changed the chair's position. If we had let it go to a third night, it would have been even harder for him to adjust to the changed chair position. They also recognized immediately that they should keep the touching and patting to a minimum, because it seemed to make him more alert, not more sleepy. "It didn't help to have my hand on him. It worked better if I stood nearby and occasionally said something or touched him," Greta said. Bedtimes improved really quickly but night wakenings took a little longer. When

Frederick woke up, Matt went very quickly into his room to soothe him. After eleven days, he began sleeping through the night, although it did take a good deal longer to get him to sleep later in the morning.

◌   ◌   ◌

Daytime weaning came easily for Christina and Sally, but at ten months Christina was still having trouble cutting out her daughter's two last breast feedings. At bedtime, Christina nursed Sally to sleep in a rocking chair, staying there until she was sleeping soundly enough to be gently transferred into the crib. At 4:00 a.m., Sally woke up and Christina and Andy took her into their bed to be nursed again. Contemplating doing anything that would upset Sally was very difficult for Christina, who had about zero tolerance for tears and who interpreted every cry as a sign of hunger. "She was my little baby and I couldn't let her cry," Christina recollected. "I nursed her too much; every little cry, I thought she was hungry. I never let the poor child cry. I didn't realize that crying was part of her way of communicating."

Christina was apprehensive about the Sleep Lady Shuffle and the prospect of tears but had become convinced that she owed it to herself and to Sally to help her daughter learn to sleep. She and Andy considered which one of them should be the one sitting in the chair, and Christina decided that as hard as it would be for her to listen to Sally's tears up close, it would be absolutely unbearable for her to listen to them from farther away. "I knew if I was watching her, I would know she was okay."

Sally was a classic example of an easily ritualized baby who just swapped one sleep crutch for another. She gave up her nighttime nursing— but within two nights was demanding bedtime patting instead. It was very hard for Christina to keep the touching intermittent, to let Sally go to sleep without Mom's hand resting on her through the crib. Christina also had to resist—and she didn't at first—putting Sally down over and over again when she stood up. Sally would keep doing it, because she knew Mom would rub and pat her as she got her to lie back down, and Mom would keep doing it because Sally would cry if Mom stopped. Sally cried a fair amount the first three nights, even with her mom being much too involved. The first night was a tough forty-five minutes, the second was thirty, the third twenty. (This is why it helps to keep a log, because twenty minutes seems really rotten until you look at your log and see that night three was less than half the tears of night one.) On the fourth night, it was time for Christina to move the chair to the door—and things began to fall into place. It took the rest of the week, but the wakenings grew shorter and less frequent. Within a week, she was sleeping through the night. Her mom said, "She became an awesome nighttime sleeper."

Phasing Out Walking and Rocking to Sleep

When nursing no longer does the trick, or when we cut out nighttime nursing because we know it interferes with sleep, some of us end up walking or rocking our babies to sleep instead. A few minutes of walking or rocking at bedtime is fine, but if he demands prolonged rocking or a five-mile hike, or if he needs to be walked and rocked repeatedly during the night, it's time to stop.

As with so many sleep problems, the easiest time for you to institute changes is at bedtime, when you are more awake and more likely to be consistent. Begin by doing all the walking or rocking in the bedroom, not all over the house, to create a positive association between the room and sleep. Scale back the amount of time you walk or rock, for instance by slicing off ten minutes or so every few days. Stop walking when he's reached a seven or eight on the ten-point drowsy scale, and put him down in his crib. We want him to be aware that he is going into the crib. We don't want to somehow secretly slide him in or trick him, because when he has a partial awakening he'll get mad if he thinks he went to bed in your arms but now he finds himself stuck in the crib. Sit by the crib and soothe him. If he gets really hysterical, pick him up briefly and put him down as soon as he's calm. If he calms down in two seconds once you've picked him up, you know you've been had! He didn't need to be picked up as badly as you thought he did. Offer swift comfort when he wakes up, but don't start the walking and the rocking again. Resume your Shuffle position and be consistent.

I worked with one little girl who slept poorly during the day and more poorly at night. Her mom nursed her much too often but by this age, nursing no longer guaranteed that she would fall asleep. Instead her parents spent an unbelievable amount of time bouncing her to sleep in their arms. They bounced at bedtime, they bounced at nap time, and they bounced each time she woke up at night. An extremely alert baby who hated missing out on any of the action, she even learned to jerk herself awake when she started falling asleep midbounce. We addressed it by cutting bouncing time in half for two days, and then cutting it back drastically. They would bounce and give her kisses as they turned off her bedroom light, and then they would bounce her over to and into the crib.

That was it. She wasn't too happy at first but her parents were comforting yet consistent. Luckily, she was a resourceful little thing and soon learned to hum herself to sleep!

Pacifier Withdrawal

Pacifiers are great for the first month or so of life, when newborns really need all that extra sucking. After that, pacifiers have their place, but their place is not in the crib, unless your baby is one of the rare ones who uses it to go to sleep at bedtime but doesn't seek or demand it when she gets up in the middle of the night.

If you are "re-binking" all night, as one mom put it, you can either wean your child off the pacifier or, if that seems too harsh or difficult to you, you can let her keep it but help her learn to put it back in her mouth by herself. You've probably noticed that she can put Cheerios, banana pieces, and teethers in her mouth; there's no reason she can't handle the pacifier. To make it easier, leave several in her crib so one is always within easy each. If your child has not yet learned how to "re-bink" herself, when you retrieve the pacifier, put it in her hand, not her mouth. For a few nights, you might have to guide her hand to her mouth, but at this age they learn pretty quickly if they don't know already. Some children this age want one in each hand. If you do let her keep the pacifier, she may well attach to it as she would to a lovey, and you may eventually have to confront pacifier withdrawal more directly. But some parents prefer to wait until their children are a little older to cross that hurdle. I would encourage you at this point to limit the pacifier to crib and car so that your child will experiment with other forms of self-soothing. Some parents take the pacifier away at night, but leave it at nap time when it is harder for babies to settle themselves.

If you decide to go without the pacifier, or if you try to let her take care of her own pacifier but she resists and still wakes up in search of it repeatedly, pick a night when you are ready to cope with a little unpleasantness. Make sure you have an especially nice and calming bedtime routine, and try to get her to bed drowsy but awake. Don't give her the pacifier. Stroke or soothe her, just as you would a child you were weaning. Instead of giving her the pacifier, use techniques similar to those I advise for parents breaking nighttime nursing or walking habits. Do this each time she wakes up at night. Consistency counts. Keep in mind, if you cave in after she's cried for an hour, you aren't teaching her to sleep without the pacifier. You are teaching her to cry for an hour in order to get a pacifier.

Unconventional Beds

In the early months, many babies sleep anywhere except their crib—car seats, bouncy chairs, cradles, bassinets, and wicker baskets that have been passed down for generations. But they can't fit in a basket or bouncy seat forever, and by the time your baby is nearing the end of the first year, he really should be in his crib (unless you are committed to long-term co-sleeping). If your child is still spending his nights in a less conventional setting, change it now. Use my Sleep Lady Shuffle to get him into a crib, and keep him in the crib, consistently, when he wakes up at night. Use that lovey to ease the transition.

Bruce, the baby who had those evening playdates with Grandma, was walked, rocked, held, and put to bed in an unusual manner. His parents had held him almost 24/7 in the first four months—partly because he was colicky, partly because they thought it would make him grow up to be an affectionate person, and partly because they just couldn't resist holding their beautiful first child in their arms. "We were so amazed by him, we just held him and stared at him," Megan recalled. Eventually she and John decided they needed to put Bruce down—but by then he had his own thoughts on the matter. Sure, he was fine in his crib—playing with an excessively interactive mobile that did a better job of waking him up than calming him down. But sleep in the crib? Forget it. Bruce slept in a bouncy chair—and they placed the bouncy chair in their bed. Even so, he was up several times every single night, and they would either bounce him back to sleep in his chair or take him out and walk him and then try to "secretly sneak him back into the bouncy chair before he knew it." As his first birthday approached, they decided something had to give. They did the Sleep Lady Shuffle, and although it wasn't an overnight fix, the worst they ever faced was a half hour of crying. Within two weeks, it was bye-bye bouncy chair; he was cheerfully going to sleep in his crib and staying there all night long.

Early Birds

If your child is awake and raring to go at 6:00 or 6:30, you'll probably have to accept that, even if your own preference is to sleep another hour or so. Many babies do wake up early, and feel fine that way. Remember to adapt the meal and nap schedule to suit his early hours. The first nap should be one and a half to two hours after wake-up. (For a baby who sleeps eleven hours uninterrupted at night, the nap can be three hours after wake-up if he doesn't seem too tired or cranky before he hits the three-hour mark.) You might also try shifting bedtime later in fifteen-minute intervals to see if that will coax him into sleeping later, but be careful. He may still wake up at 6:00, but be more tired because he's no longer getting enough sleep at the front end. Pay attention to his sleep window, and his behavior. Don't force him to stay up when he really needs to go to sleep or he won't be able to fall asleep when you want him to. Room-darkening blinds may help, and white noise machines can be useful if there's a lot of noise—birds singing, garbage cans crashing—early in the morning around your home. You may also try the techniques I outline below for problematic early risers, but they may or may not work for a child whose biological clock is set just fine for him, but not for you.

That laissez-faire approach doesn't hold for a baby who wakes up *before* 6:00 a.m., or who wakes up cheerful at 6:00 or 6:30 but is falling apart by 7:00. You need to step in and teach him to sleep later. As Greta and Matt can attest, the longer you endure early risings, the harder it is to change the pattern. Address it now, even if it takes several weeks to see results. If you wait until he's a toddler or preschooler, it can take even longer. Make sure your early riser is getting enough daytime sleep, because nap deprivation can cause poor night sleep and early awakenings. You may have to change his nap schedule too, to make his morning nap a little later. Try moving it back a half hour or so, but don't let him get so overtired that he is too wired to nap.

When your early bird stirs, go to his room immediately. You want to try to get him back to sleep ASAP, not let him scream himself awake. Give him his lovey and try to soothe him back to sleep without picking him up. Even if he doesn't doze off again—and not all babies will at first—do not turn on the lights or get him out of his crib until 6:00 a.m. no matter how much he protests. Getting him up earlier, while it is still dark, sends a confusing message and is another example of intermittent reinforcement. He can't understand why he can get up in the dark at 5:45 a.m. but not at 2:15 a.m. Also, many parents I've worked with have learned the hard way that if they let him get up at 5:45 a.m., the next thing they know it's 5:30, 5:15, etc.

At this age, I usually recommend that the parent stay in the room for this early-morning routine. If, however, you feel your presence is encouraging him to be more awake, as often occurs with older children, you can try leaving his room after a bit of reassurance and see if he falls asleep again on his own. Check on him every ten to fifteen minutes. If you stay in the room, keep the interaction minimal. Try sitting in a chair with your eyes closed. When the clock finally strikes 6:00 and he's not falling asleep—and it can seem like it takes a very long time to reach 6:00—leave the room for a minute or two. He may cry, but try not to let it bother you, you will be right back in a minute.

When you come back in, make a big deal out of "good morning" time. Do your dramatic wake-up. The morning routine is the flip side of the bedtime-routine coin. Your goal is to help him distinguish between day and night, to know when it really is time to get up. Your message must be clear: "I'm getting you out of the crib because it's morning time—not because you were crying."

> *While Frederick's nights were increasingly easy, early morning was not fun. He woke up at 5:00 a.m with a high-pitched scream. "It was the toughest time to deal with, because you knew you were less likely to go back to sleep," said Greta, voicing a sentiment I hear often from parents. Either Greta or Matt would go to him and tell him to lie back down. Sometimes he would fall asleep right away. Sometimes he'd cry the whole hour. "It was very unpredictable." But they didn't pick him up. Then at 6:00 a.m., they'd leave the room for two minutes. When they came back, they would say, "Good morning!" and act like the previous hour of protest had never occurred. It took longer to change this early-waking pattern than it had to get rid of that constant nighttime nursing, but eventually Frederick began sleeping until 6:00. His parents would love to have him sleep another hour, but they keep reminding themselves that he's getting eleven hours of solid sleep—and they relish that extra fifteen or thirty minutes he occasionally grants them.*

Napping

Parents often wonder why overtired children don't nap easily. The answer is that they are too tired! Their high cortisol levels make them feel alert, even wired, no matter how sleep deprived they actually are. This applies to babies who go to bed too late at night, babies who wake up too early in the morning, babies who nap in moving cars and strollers, babies who skip naps, and babies who take short catnaps instead of longer, restorative naps. You need to review your child's schedule and get him on a nap schedule consistent with his natural sleep windows. I confess, nap training is my least favorite part of sleep training but it's an absolutely essential one.

Children this age still need two naps—one in the morning, and a longer one in the afternoon. The transition to one nap usually doesn't come until around fifteen to eighteen months—don't attempt it too early. Don't let your baby sleep too long in the morning or else he'll have trouble sleeping in the afternoon, and there is no way a nine- to twelve-month-old can make it all the way from morning nap to evening bedtime without making everyone in the family pay the price. Limit the morning nap to one and a half hours for the nine-month-old, one hour for the twelve-month-old. Get that afternoon nap started about three hours after the morning one ends. An occasional exception is okay. If he's been sick, or slept poorly one night, or had an unusually active morning exercising brand-new crawling or walking skills, he might need a longer nap once in a while, but don't make it a habit. By nine months, most babies give up that third late-afternoon mini-nap. If he's still taking that third nap but it doesn't interfere with bedtime, don't worry about it; he'll give it up soon. Similarly, if he's not napping particularly well earlier in the day, let him keep the mini-nap while you work on lengthening and improving his two main naps. However, if he is taking the mini-nap and then having trouble getting to sleep at a reasonable bedtime, you are going to have to force the issue and not let him take that late-afternoon snooze.

Nap training isn't fun, and it often involves tears. Some of us as parents can cope with a crying baby in daylight more easily than we can at night. We are more rested and we just don't feel as bad leaving them alone when it's not dark. But some of us have a terrible time doing nap training ourselves at home when our spouse or partner isn't there for moral support. I always tell families to try the nap training—and try it for more than a day or two. But if a little voice inside your head is saying that you really can't do this, listen to it. Give yourself permission to stop the training. That doesn't mean you should abandon your efforts to get your child to nap, or that you should convince yourself that your child doesn't need to nap. He does need to nap, even if he is trying his level nine-month-old best to convince you otherwise. For instance Ilan, my co-author's son, stopped napping at ten months. He wouldn't nap for her, he wouldn't nap for his father, he wouldn't nap for his loving babysitter who had gotten dozens of babies to nap in her long child-care career. He'd occasionally doze off in the car, picking his big brother, Zach, up from school, or even slump over in his high chair late in the day. His parents finally concluded he was one of those rare babies who just didn't need to nap. They were wrong. I didn't work with Ilan's family until he was almost two but then we did get him to resume napping for two, two and a half, or sometimes three hours on weekdays. (Weekends, when he was excited that Zach was home, remained a problem.) The moral of the story is that if you can't stomach the tears, you don't have to. But you can't give up on napping altogether. Put your energy into improving his nighttime sleep, and use whatever tricks you have up your sleeve to get him to sleep during the day, even if that means bending my rules and relying in part on some motion sleep. You may find that when nighttime sleep improves, daytime sleep will follow. Or you may find that you have to return to nap training again a few weeks or months from now. But once you see that these techniques really do improve nighttime sleep and make your child happier, it may be easier for you to stick to nap training the second time around.

Here's nap training in a nutshell (read the Napping section in Chapter 5, Six to Eight Months, if you want more information, including how to adapt the Shuffle for daytime). Put your child in a crib drowsy but awake and give him an entire hour to fall asleep at the morning and afternoon naps. If you want to stay with him and do the Shuffle, even if it takes the whole hour, that's fine. If you want to leave the room but go back and comfort him every fifteen minutes or so, that's fine too. If you want to sit right outside his doorway, where he knows you are nearby, and use the hour to read, knit, stretch, do leg lifts, or balance your checkbook, that's fine too. Don't stay in the room, though, if you sense that your presence keeps him awake. Not all babies will take that full hour, or they may only take the full hour for the first few days. Have a backup plan for the afternoon. Give him that hour to fall asleep but when the hour is up and he's still awake, do a dramatic wake-up. Then do whatever it takes to get him to sleep, including a car ride if necessary, because letting him get even more overtired will just add to your vicious no-sleep cycle. If he falls asleep but only catnaps, waking up after twenty or thirty minutes, resettle him and start your sixty-minute count again.

A common error is to offer the child a brief "comfort nursing" right before nap time. What often happens is that the baby dozes off after about fifteen minutes while nursing—sort of a little "power nap" on the breast. It gives him just enough sleep to fight off a genuine nap. Moms should either eliminate pre-nap nursing, or schedule it earlier in the day.

Irene got Brad off the nighttime bottle and out of her bed extremely quickly but nap training took two stressful months. "The nanny was reluctant to do it, so I did it when I was home but I wasn't home every day, so it took a long time and was very difficult," she said. Still, her perseverance paid off and Brad finally abandoned those unhelpful twenty-minute catnaps and started taking two solid naps every day. When he got older, his transition to one nap went quite smoothly, and at eighteen months he was napping—for Irene or the nanny—two to three hours every afternoon.

◌ ◌ ◌

While Bruce's nighttime sleep improved quickly, naps were tough. Some days, Megan bundled him into the car and drove until he fell asleep, which usually didn't take long. She didn't want to risk waking him up by trying to carry him back into the house through the cold winter air, but didn't want to keep driving either, knowing that he would not sleep as deeply in motion. So she'd take along a bunch of blankets . . . and her laptop. When he fell asleep, she'd drive home, park in her driveway, drape herself in blankets, and get some work done for a job at a local magazine.

Co-sleeping

Co-sleeping is a sensitive topic and I discuss it in great detail in Chapter 10. In it, I try to help those of you who wish to continue co-sleeping improve the quality of your family's sleep. If you have been co-sleeping but want to stop, I give you suggestions on how to follow through. If stopping is on your agenda, age nine to twelve months is a really good time to do it, before the heightened separation anxiety that occurs around the first birthday.

Jason's Story

You met Tess briefly in the opening chapter, where she was struggling with her mother's chemotherapy and her son's sleeplessness. Jason was ten months old at the time, and usually slept with Tess, while her husband, Ron, unable to sleep with a baby in the bed, exiled himself to the guest room for eight months. Jason nursed and nuzzled all night long. "It was an all-you-can-eat buffet, all night long," she said, laughing. "And I was his walking, talking comfort item."

Tess knew she was going to have to make some changes, but she wanted them to be ever so gentle, and I didn't want to push Tess beyond her emotional limits. So we tried just getting rid of the 2:30 a.m. feeding, we tried having her place a pillow between her and the baby and turning him away from her, we tried having her wear extra layers of clothing at night. "I'd be up from two a.m. to five to skip that two-thirty feeding, rocking him, blind with exhaustion. I knew deep down that it wasn't going to work, but Kim let me go through all of that because I needed to. It was about exorcising my demons. Then, with my mother sick, I was on the verge of collapse."

Tess had her own emotional baggage. As a child, she had experienced sleep terrors and sleepwalking, and slept with her parents until she was eight. *"I have my own memories of being in my room and going into my parents' room. I think I would have dropped dead if they had said, 'No, you can't come in.' I was the third child by fifteen years so I got away with a lot."* She had also endured two devastating miscarriages before Jason, so all the normal anxieties of motherhood were magnified in her mind. And of course she was dealing with a seriously ill mother she was very close to. On the other hand, she knew her tear aversion was a little over the top.

"I'm a lawyer. I'm a prosecutor. I can be cold-hearted. But I can't stand to let my baby cry. I was insane!"

Finally ready for more direct action, she got Jason a lovey, a "taggy" blanket. She kept one at her home and one at her mother's New York home. *"He loves tags; every toy we got him, he just went for the tag."* They co-slept on the floor in his room for nearly two weeks, more than the two or three days I usually recommend, but there was so much situational stress here, we needed extra emotional padding.

When the time came to put Jason into his crib, she handed him to his father and checked into a hotel, where she spent the night explaining to a friend on the telephone that she was afraid letting her baby cry might make him feel abandoned and turn him into a serial killer someday. Meanwhile Ron, not exactly a tear warrior himself, invited one of his friends over to the house for moral support. The baby cried for an hour, and Ron stayed in the room but did not pick him up. Yet despite that difficult bedtime, Jason woke up only once overnight when he cried for twenty minutes. The next night was easier—twenty minutes of crying at bedtime, and he needed only brief checks and reassurances from his dad. The third night, Tess checked out of her hotel and took her turn. Jason cried less than night one, but more than night two, and although Tess still found tears distressing, she had seen the evidence with her own lawyerly eyes that he was not hurt, that he was "his usual happy self" and that he was already sleeping better. She sat near him, saying "sh-sh" and murmuring soothing things to him, but kept her distress in check and let him cry.

Over the next week or so, it kept getting easier. Jason would go to bed without much fuss, and wake up only once or twice, crying but not needing to nurse, falling asleep again within twenty minutes. The first few nights

Tess sat by his bed, but then discovered he fell asleep more easily if she just went in to make sure he had his pacifier and blanket, and left again. Usually he'd fall asleep right away. On the rare nights when the tears ramped up, those moments when he cried to the point where he probably forgot what he was crying about, one of his parents would soothe him and he'd go back to sleep.

"It was only ten days of trauma—although it felt like a year. And then it was such an amazing turnaround. In three days he went from nursing all the time to not nursing the entire night, from sleeping with me to sleeping in his crib. It took ten days to consolidate, but the change in the first three days was amazing," Tess said.

"I let the sleep issues get completely out of control because I was so unwilling to let him cry, I waited much too long to deal with what was a real problem. Now I look back and don't know what I was thinking."

7
THIRTEEN TO EIGHTEEN MONTHS

Please take a few minutes to read the first three chapters of my book, which give an overview of my system and include some helpful hints that apply to all age groups. It won't take long and you'll have much better results.

૦ ૦ ૦

*A*T THIS AGE TODDLERS NEED *an average of eleven and a quarter hours of uninterrupted sleep at night and two and a quarter to two and a half hours during the day. Children at the younger end of this age bracket take two naps, in the morning and afternoon, but by eighteen months they consolidate to one midday or afternoon nap.*

Early toddlers are prone to have behavioral sleep problems. Their increased mobility (including walking), a peak in separation anxiety around the first birthday, and emotional attachment to such objects as bottles and pacifiers can all complicate bedtime and contribute to nighttime awakenings. At around fifteen to eighteen months, toddlers transition from two naps to one. That's a tricky stage because there is usually a point when one nap is not enough and two naps are too many. The result is an overtired child who doesn't sleep well at night. This chapter will give you techniques to help speed up and smooth out that transition, but you will probably still face a bit of crankiness for about three weeks as her body adapts.

As if that wasn't enough, temper tantrums often emerge at this age, and toddlers start testing their parents. Bedtime is a common battleground for toddler titans flexing those emerging willpower muscles. A soothing bedtime routine is extremely important for children this age, and adhering consistently to routines and setting clear rules is essential—because the next stage is only tougher. We'll cover all this ground as it pertains to this age group, and I'll walk you through a toddler's typical day.

In this chapter, you will meet James, who was adopted from Korea at six months and who remained a shy and somewhat fearful child who woke up repeatedly every night. With my help and his parents' perseverance, he became what his mom called an "Olympic sleeper," and loved his bed so much that he would indicate to his mother when to put him into it. It took Chloe's mom a long time to wean her at night—but Chloe still kept waking up over and over again demanding a bottle after she gave up the breast. Alex, who had been sleeping with his parents, had a tough time learning to nap on his own, and his task was made even harder because his body was getting ready to drop one of the naps he was learning to take. You met Teddy when he was about seven or eight months old, and he's still sleeping well at this age; his mom had some wisdom to share about toddler naps. Joshua never, ever, ever slept through the night, and his mom, Carol, rocked, nursed, and held him for hours at a time—anything to avoid having him shed a tear. "I thought that if you ever let your baby cry, you were a terrible mother. But then neither of us ever developed a repertoire of soothing skills," she said. When she finally backed off a bit, he not only became a better sleeper, he became a happier, more energetic, and much less clingy child.

 DEVELOPMENTAL CHANGES

Separation Anxiety

Separation anxiety hits a peak right around the first birthday. Saying "night-night" to parents can be tough. That nice long transition to bedtime, good focused time with one or both parents, helps ease the fears. Although one-year-olds can't say much, they understand an awful lot, so give plenty of verbal assurances about how Mommy and Daddy are nearby. Some parents like to stay in the room as the baby falls asleep to help with the separation. That's okay as long as she doesn't wake up at night needing you to go and sit there again and again. If you don't stay in the room, it may help if you reassure the toddler that you'll be nearby—and then keep your word. Instead of going downstairs to clear the kitchen, which can seem awfully far away to a baby alone in her crib, stay in a nearby room on the same floor so she feels your closeness as she nods off.

Loveys

Loveys, usually a special stuffed animal or security blanket, are very useful at this age as children cope with separation anxiety. Many families have told me their babies resisted all attempts to have them bond with a special toy the first year, but quickly attached to an object around age one. They may choose one of their own at this age, maybe from among that batch of first birthday presents. They may also abandon the lovey they favored in infancy and choose a new one.

"Alex had a whole cribful of animals and we had been trying to get him to attach to one since he was six months old. He ignored them, wouldn't even touch them. But when he got older, he got interested. While we were concentrating on his sleep, we chose one, a Good Night Moon *bunny, and tried to use it consistently. When he got a little older, he started asking for a different animal each night," his mother, Adele, said. It wasn't a typical pattern but it was a successful one. He was able to happily snuggle up with whichever one he selected as his evening's companion.*

ᴑ ᴑ ᴑ

Teddy had been sleeping pretty well since you met him as an infant, but he just didn't take to a lovey. At thirteen months, he suddenly got attached to two plastic teethers. He wasn't teething, he just wanted to grip one in each hand when he went to sleep. The problem was they were so small that they'd fall through the crib slats, and he'd wake up and scream if he couldn't find them. "It wasn't easy to keep crawling under the crib to get them," Lisa recalled. She began a concerted effort to transfer his affections from the teethers to a Barney. It took a while, but Barney eventually trumped the plastic rings and was much less likely to end up on the floor.

To encourage the bond, incorporate the lovey in bedtime and nap-time rituals. For instance, if you play peek-a-boo before bed, the lovey should play peek-a-boo too. If you stroll around the room saying good night to favorite objects, the lovey should say good night too. Tuck the lovey in with her in the crib at bed and nap time. At some point, your baby might mimic bedtime activities for the lovey, giving her lamb or teddy bear a good-night kiss and tucking it in. Even if the lovey bond hasn't stuck before, I strongly recommend making another effort now. Toddlers often get emotionally attached to the breast, their bottle, sippy cup, or pacifier, and they may wake up often at night wanting a bottle or cup, not because they are really hungry or thirsty but because it helps them feel secure. Easing the attachment to the breast, bottle, etc. goes hand in hand with strengthening the attachment to the lovey—you'll have trouble fostering the lovey bond if you don't reduce the previous attachment simultaneously. Snuggly toys help toddlers get themselves back to sleep independently at night. In contrast, attachment to a breast, bottle, cup, or pacifier often makes kids wake up and call for you to nurse them, give them a bottle, refill their cup, or find their pacifier. An additional plus for loveys is that they don't lead to very wet diapers in the middle of the night! Dr. T. Berry Brazelton, in his 1992 book, *Touchpoints,* suggests tying the bottle or pacifier to a doll or a lovey to help the transition from one security object to another.

Some parents worry if a toddler starts lugging the lovey around with him all the time. That may be a minor inconvenience, because you have to remember to take the lovey with you, but I don't regard it as a problem. Pacifiers are a little different, and I don't recommend having toddlers walk around with them all day. It may interfere with communication and speech development. Consider getting rid of the pacifier, or restricting it to bedtime and naps.

Eating and Sleeping

As parents, we have to adjust to the idea that milk isn't the heart of our children's diet anymore. By the first birthday, they get most of their nutrition and their calories from table foods or solids. Pediatricians usually recommend they take two to three glasses of milk (18–24 ounces)—the advice varies a bit so consult your doctor about what's right for your child. Remember, she's not an infant anymore, so feeding her lots of milk right before bedtime will not prolong her sleep. To the contrary, it might just fuel her habit of associating milk with sleep, and wanting to drink all night. It may also invite her to wake up and let you know loudly that she has a soaking wet diaper. Introduce a cup now if you haven't already, regardless of whether you plan to continue nursing. Offer the sippy cup—of water, milk, formula, diluted juice, whatever your doctor recommends—at each meal.

If you wean, and many mothers do around the first birthday, I recommend going from breast feeding to a cup, not to a bottle. Weaning should be an easy, natural transition. It seldom disrupts sleep, but sleep that is already disrupted can make weaning harder for an overtired, unhappy baby. Weaning is more difficult if she has not learned how to fall asleep without a breast or bottle in her mouth. There's no "right" way to wean, but the most common advice is to drop one daytime feeding one week, drop a second one the second week, and so on. Many mothers continue nursing the first thing in the morning and once at bedtime well beyond the first birthday. That's only a problem when the baby can't go to sleep, or back to sleep, without being breastfed. (The same applies to bedtime bottle feeding.) In that case, you are facing a sleep issue, not a weaning issue, and I'll talk more about how to change those patterns later.

If your child is using a bottle rather than a sippy cup, I'd strongly consider making the switch now, particularly if the bottle is a sleep crutch. Check with your pediatrician; if there are any growth concerns and the doctor recommends sticking to the bottle for a while, you can still address the sleep associations. Give the bottle when your child is awake, after a nap for instance, instead of right before nap or bedtime.

The transition from bottle to cup can be gentle and gradual. Start with the first morning bottle. Fill it with only three or four ounces, and then move quickly to breakfast. After a few days, offer a sippy cup of milk. Then start reducing the amount of milk in the bottles that you offer before (or after) lunch and dinner. Give him a cup with his meal instead. You may find that if you give him the bottle after his meal, he won't really want it much anymore, he won't be hungry.

If your child becomes fussy during the day and asks for a bottle, look at the clock and your sleep log. Is he really hungry or does he want the bottle for comfort or out of habit? And can you comfort or distract him some other way? Maybe he's overstimulated and needs a few quiet hugs from you, or a few minutes on your lap with a book. Maybe he's tired and it's time for his nap. Perhaps he is signaling that he needs to go to bed a little earlier than usual. Don't assume that the bottle is the only thing that will make him feel calm and happy.

When you are ready to wean him from the bedtime bottle, follow a similar strategy. Reduce the amount every two or three days, from eight ounces, down to six ounces, to four, to two. Then offer him a sippy cup of water instead. Sometimes a baby protests when he hits that four ounce mark because it is no longer enough fluid for him to suck himself to sleep. Find other ways of comforting him, and stick to your plan.

Some families deal with the bottle-cup issue before they start sleep shaping, but it's often best to do them simultaneously. You can modify the Sleep Lady Shuffle slightly. For instance, you might want to add one night at the cribside (so you would be right next to the crib for four days, not the three I usually recommend). Night one you might cut the bottle to six ounces, night two to four ounces, night three to two ounces, and on the fourth night, take the bottle away but stay by the crib to give him a little extra help adjusting. The next night, proceed with the next phase of the Shuffle, moving away from the crib. There are other ways to modify this, and you may want to tweak the system a bit to fit your family, but keep in mind that if the bottle is the child's sleep crutch, you will have to help him give it up so he can learn how to soothe himself to sleep.

CREATING A SCHEDULE
Sample schedule:

(Shift earlier if your child wakes between 6:00 and 7:00 a.m.)

7:00–7:30 a.m. Wake-up and breakfast.

9:00–9:30 a.m. Start of one-hour morning nap if she's still taking one. She'll probably want a snack right before or after the nap.

11:30 a.m.–12:30 p.m. Lunch (depending on morning-nap timing).

12:30–1:30 p.m. Start of afternoon nap. About 1.5 hours if it's a second nap, about 2 to 2.5 hours if it's the only nap of the day. Snack after nap.

5:00–5:30 p.m. Dinner.

6:00–6:30 p.m. Start bath/bedtime routine.

7:00–8:00 p.m. Asleep.

As you know if you've read my earlier chapters, I do believe that children need regular nap times, regular bedtimes, and three recognizable mealtimes. Their bodies need the routine to regulate day and night hormone cycles, and to keep them in sync with their internal clock. Their little hearts and minds need certainty and predictability to feel secure. But I also believe in some flexibility. The sample schedule is a good starting point, but you can adjust it. For instance, if your child is an early riser, move the morning nap earlier. You may also have to play with the schedule a bit to accommodate the needs of your other children. Sleep times are averages. Some kids sleep more, some sleep less, but the variations are a lot less than many parents think. If your child is napping and sleeping poorly, chances are you are underestimating how much sleep she needs. Even when you do achieve a nice workable schedule, natural variations inevitably occur. Some days she will eat or sleep a little more and some days she will eat or sleep a little less. Growth spurts, runny noses, new teeth, or just a bad mood—toddlers have their off days just like we do—can all create minor variations in his daily routine. But don't let the schedule get totally out of whack. As you learn to read her sleep cues and she becomes better rested, you will be able to tinker with the schedule more easily. Watch her daytime behavior. If she's easy and content, she's probably on a pretty good schedule. If she's fussy and demanding, she may need longer naps, an earlier bedtime, a later wake-up time—or all of the above.

If you have to skip a nap because of a doctor's appointment or some other essential interruption, most toddlers fare better missing the morning nap than the afternoon one. You can move the afternoon nap up a bit to compensate for a missed morning one.

Barring unusual dietary or health concerns, thirteen- to eighteen-month-olds should have three recognizable mealtimes a day. Most snack twice a day, either before or after the morning nap (usually before, but it depends on your child's precise schedule) and upon awakening from the afternoon one. Check with your pediatrician, but healthy children in this age group on a normal growth curve can almost always go eleven to twelve hours at night without food. If your child is still waking to eat frequently, you have to adjust her body clock, change her sleep habits, or both. I'll give you some tips on how to do that later in this chapter. Don't give a bottle at bedtime in the hope that it will make her sleep longer—those days are long over.

WAKE-UP · A good wake-up time is anywhere from 6:00 to 7:30. Remember that one of the basic rules of sleep hygiene is to wake up and go to bed at about the same time every day. If your baby wakes up before 6:00, the Early Birds section (page 148) will help you teach him to sleep later.

Some toddlers sleep past 7:30. If it works for you and your family—and by works, I mean that she is getting good naps and at least eleven to eleven and a half hours of uninterrupted sleep at night—that's fine, leave it alone. When she gets closer to starting preschool make sure you leave plenty of time for her to gradually adjust to an earlier wake-up. But an 8:30 or 9:00 a.m. wake-up throws off many toddlers. They nap too late or inconsistently, and they go to bed too late and don't sleep well at night. You can either just start waking her at 7:30—gently at first—or you can adjust more gradually. Get her up about ten minutes earlier than usual, hold it there for two or three days, then another ten minutes earlier, and so on.

Morning rituals, the counterpoints of your evening ones, are still a good idea to reinforce her understanding of wake-up time versus sleep time. Throw open the blinds, switch on the lights, sing some cheery good-morning songs, and start your day. It's your choice whether you feed her immediately or have some playtime. Parents who come home late from work (usually, but not always, fathers) often make mornings their special game time.

MORNING NAP · While she's still on a two-nap-a-day schedule, morning nap should begin around 9:00 or 9:30. If she's sleeping well at night, the morning nap should be two to three hours after she woke up. Watch the sleep windows to determine exactly what time is right for her. Remember to provide that wind-down time to get ready for sleep, maybe a book or two or an abbreviated version of her bedtime routine. She will probably sleep about an hour, maybe an hour and a half. I discourage longer morning naps because the afternoon nap is usually the more important one, the one that she will hold on to for another two or three years. If she sleeps two or three hours in the morning, consider waking her after ninety minutes or else she is going to have a tough time going down for her afternoon nap. After the morning nap is a nice time to visit the playground, go for a walk, or do some shopping. She will be refreshed and less likely to doze off in the car or stroller and throw off her afternoon nap schedule.

LUNCH/AFTERNOON NAP · Lots of parents don't realize that toddlers get hungry more quickly than we do. Lunch is often at 11:30, almost always by noon or 12:30. You've usually got some playtime after lunch and before the afternoon nap. Usually you will aim for two to three hours between the end of the morning nap and the start of the afternoon one. Again, watch her sleep signals to get her down at the right time. The afternoon nap usually lasts about one and a half hours. Once she consolidates to one nap, aim to get her down sometime between 12:30 and 1:30, and she'll probably sleep two to two and a half hours. A pretty typical afternoon nap runs from about 1:00 to 3:30, but it can vary thirty minutes in either direction. When she gets up, it's time for another snack and some playtime before dinner.

DINNER · An early dinnertime, 5:00 or 5:30, is usually wise, even if that means she doesn't eat with her parents. She can always have fruit or dessert with you while you eat dinner. The early schedule helps both her food and her sleep. I find that children have eating windows too, and if you feed them too late, they don't eat very well. The last thing you want is a poor dinner eater who then wakes up demanding a midnight snack. (You'll get enough of that in adolescence!)

BEDTIME · Aim to have her asleep—asleep, not getting ready for bed— between 7:00 and 8:00. Watch her cues and trust your own intuition. You might move bedtime a little later, 8:00 or 8:30, after she has begun sleeping consistently through the night and at nap time, and has caught up on all her missing sleep. Remember, she still needs, on average, eleven hours and fifteen minutes of sleep at night.

Toddlers need a lot of transition time to prepare for sleep, both in terms of brain hormones and emotional readiness to separate from their parents until morning. Bedtime routines must be structured and predictable, and they absolutely cannot be rushed. Leave enough time—maybe it will be half an hour for your child, maybe it will be an hour (including bath time)—and make it a fun and loving time, a time she eagerly anticipates. Keep the bed-time routine in her bedroom, not all over the house, so she incorporates the message that it is time to slow down and get ready to sleep. It's okay to start downstairs with some pre-bedtime evening rituals, but as soon as the bath is done, stay in the bedroom. Get any unpleasant aspect of bedtime over at the beginning, so you can spend the rest of it calming down in enjoyable ways.

As I mentioned, she won't need a feeding prior to bedtime, but some tod-dlers still like to nurse briefly or have a cup of water before bed. If she's taking a bottle at bedtime, switch to a cup and think about water instead of milk. You can do this gradually if you like, moving from an eight-ounce bottle to a four-ounce bottle and then to a cup. Some people use milk or formula and dilute it for a few nights before switching to water. If you walk or rock your baby before sleep, keep it brief and keep it in her bedroom. If she still listens to music at bedtime, start phasing it out before she actually gets into her crib. Put her down drowsy but still awake. I'll give you more tips on how to achieve this later in this chapter.

Relatively minor changes in bedtime routine can sometimes make a big difference for a toddler. Adele and Geoff used to read Alex a book in their bed, but they moved his story time to his own room, which helped him transition to his crib. They also got much more attuned to his sleep windows. "I got more hyper about paying attention. He pulls at his eyelids—which I hate. And he pulls his hair. Sometimes he just gets really

*wound up or can just be staring and walking around and out of it. I began
to recognize that any of those signs meant he needed to go to sleep," his
mom said.*

Now that your baby is standing and probably walking, be prepared for
some crib gymnastics. Many babies stand in their crib; you put them down,
and they bounce right back up. For a one-year-old, this is literally stand-up
comedy. But no matter how hilarious she thinks it is, try not to join in
the merriment or she'll play jack-in-the box all night. Pat the mattress, lie
her down once, and then pat the baby. If she gets up again, keep patting the
mattress as a signal to her, but don't keep lying her down. She'll get down
when she's ready, and she'll be ready faster if you don't help her turn it into a
game.

*Ellen and George adopted James from Korea when he was six months
old. He bonded quickly with his new parents but remained shy, somewhat
fearful, and apprehensive about change. He was also a terrible sleeper,
waking frequently and needing lots of help to get back to sleep. Severe
chronic ear infections made the whole situation worse, because he woke up
often, in pain and in need of comfort. At eighteen months, Ellen and
George worked with me to change his schedule. They shifted the 9:30
bedtime to 7:30, but made only very minor changes to what was already a
specific and stable bedtime routine. "We bathed him every night, instead of
every other night, and then we put on his pajamas, gave him a cup of
water, and read three books—the same three books every night in the same
sequence. We put on the music box for two minutes; we hugged him and
put him in the crib," Ellen recalled. Before working with me, they had
rocked, walked, or patted him until he fell asleep, and then tried to gingerly
slip him into the crib without waking him. I think that usually
backfires—if a toddler goes to sleep in one place, he's going to open one eye
at some point and then bolt wide awake when he finds he ended up
somewhere else. In addition, James had co-slept with his foster parents in
Korea. When he got to the United States, Ellen and George didn't take him
into their bed, but they didn't teach him to fall asleep on his own either. At
bedtime and when he woke up at night, they had to walk, pat, or rock him,
over and over again. "He was totally reliant on me to get him to sleep," his
mother recalled.*

THE SLEEP LADY SHUFFLE

Many families I work with use my Sleep Lady Shuffle to change sleep habits, to gently and gradually have the parent fade away from the bedside. Let's see how it applies to a child at this age. Night wakenings usually taper off during the Shuffle, but when she does wake up, pat or comfort her briefly by her crib then resume the position you were in at bedtime that evening (we want a consistent response to all wakenings).

You should follow the Shuffle schedule, moving on to the next position even if your child has had a bad night or two, fussing or waking more frequently. Don't be surprised if there's a little regression or protest the first night of each new chair position. If your child gets sick during the Shuffle, you might want to pause and "freeze" or maintain your position until she's feeling a little better. You might even have to move a little bit closer during an illness to offer more comfort. But then resume your sleep shaping when she recovers.

NIGHTS 1–3. Once bath, stories, and songs are over, sit in a chair next to your baby's crib. If she cries or fusses, you can stroke or pat her intermittently, but don't do it constantly or you'll just create a new negative association. You can touch more on the first night. You can sing during the get-ready-for-bed stage, but once it's time for her to sleep, stick to calming "sh-sh" or "night-night" sounds. You might want to try closing your eyes. That makes it easier not to talk to her too much and it also conveys a sleepy-time message. Stay there until she falls asleep. If she gets up, remember not to keep putting her back down.

Make sure that you, the parent, control the touch. Instead of having her hold your hand or finger, you should pat her. Make sure that you do not caress her too steadily; do it on and off. Count to yourself if it helps—count to ten touching, then count to sixty not touching, then touch for another ten counts. You don't want to swap one negative association, like rocking, for another, like your constant touch or the sound of your voice.

Try not to pick her up—but if she's really, really upset, go ahead and pick her up, over the crib if possible. Keep it brief and put her down as soon as she seems calmer. Don't let her fall asleep in your arms. Tell her that it's okay, and stay in the chair until she falls asleep. Do this for each wakening.

NIGHTS 4–6. Move the chair about halfway to the door. (If it's a very small room, you may move all the way to the door.) Continue the soothing sounds, but stay in the chair as much as you can. Get up to pat or stroke her a little if necessary, or make some of the same soothing sounds as you have used the past three nights.

NIGHTS 7–9. Move the chair to the doorway or the doorjamb, where you are dimly lit but still in her view. Continue the same soothing techniques, remembering to intervene as little as possible. Don't worry if she cries a little bit; keep quietly reassuring her. She'll know you are there and she will fall asleep. It's okay to go briefly to the crib to touch when she initially wakes during the night, but then return to your chair.

NIGHTS 10–12. You want to be a little farther away, in the hallway or maybe the entrance to a nearby room, but still where she can see you. Keep making those "sh-sh" sounds. Stay until she falls asleep.

NIGHTS 13 AND ON. Many toddlers have started falling asleep and staying asleep by now, but most parents have to take one more step and leave the toddler alone for five-minute intervals. This may seem like a huge leap for you—but she's ready. All that chair-moving has given her nearly two weeks of preparation. She has given up some sleep crutches and has learned "Mommy is there for me even though I can't see her" and "Daddy is nearby and loves me."

You have a little flexibility in how to handle this stage, but don't go too far away the next few nights. Most families stay on the same floor, down the hall or in a nearby room. She may be able to hear you a bit but she shouldn't be able to see you. Other parents move farther away, doing what I call a "job check," telling the child where they will be, what they will be doing, and promising to be back very soon: "Mommy is going to get her pajamas, I'll be back in five minutes" or "Daddy is going to brush his teeth, then I'm going to come back and blow you another kiss." These checks work best with older toddlers who have more developed language skills. Whether you are sitting nearby or doing a "job check," make sure you do go back every five minutes to the bedroom door. Try not to go into the room; do your "sh-sh" calming sounds from the doorway. The toddler may cry for a few minutes, but you'll be back to reassure her— but keep the reassurances brief, too, don't get drawn in. You don't have to leave her more than five minutes and, unlike the traditional cry-it-out approaches, don't keep extending the intervals. In fact, keep a close eye on the clock so you don't exceed five minutes and upset her more. She may complain the first few nights you leave her but it's quite unusual for a child to cry for more than a few minutes after experiencing the Shuffle. For the last two weeks, you have been teaching her that you are nearby and responsive and she's got the confidence to learn this new sleep skill.

Some families stay in this position for a while; the toddler still needs those ten or fifteen minutes of reassurance. Others get to the point where they can put the child to bed, say good night, and leave. Sometimes they need to come back for one last "curtain call" before she goes to sleep, but the goal is to reduce the number of checks. Use your instincts about what will work best for your child. You might have to let her regress a little once in a while. For instance, if you are leaving her to fall asleep on her own, and she does it successfully, she may still have a spell now and then when she needs a little more reassurance and you have to stick closer by her for a few nights. I don't mean going back to the start of the Shuffle but you might have to hang out in the hallway one or two nights, or revert to making checks briefly before you can leave her on her own again.

A few points to stress: Children get ritualized easily, so make your changes every three days, not every four, six, or eight days. *Dragging it out makes it harder, not easier, for your baby.* She'll get accustomed to you sitting in a certain place, and get mad or scared when you try to double the distance.

Diane and Peter had a rough first night with Chloe, then thirteen months, doing the Sleep Lady Shuffle, but then so many of their nights were rough nights with their first-born child. Chloe would fall asleep drinking a bottle in her mom's lap, and often woke up unhappy when Diane tried to place her in the crib. Chloe had been weaned but she had an attachment to her bottle, and woke up several times a night demanding it. Like many babies I work with, Chloe had had severe reflux, and she threw up a lot. There was no way her parents were going to do a cry-it-out program, knowing that if she cried hysterically, she'd start vomiting again. Diane said that people sometimes told her not to worry if the baby threw up one more time at bedtime, to just let her cry. But they didn't understand that if your baby is already throwing up a zillion times a day "you can't stand having her throw up one more time." Plus, neither parent nor child gets to sleep any faster when a baby throws up in her crib. Projectile vomiting is not exactly a spa-like experience. Sheets and pajamas have to be changed and the baby needs to be washed or bathed again.

Chloe did cry a lot the night she began the Shuffle, but with a parent seated by her crib, she stayed just this side of hysterical and didn't throw up. (I had recommended that Diane do the last nighttime feeding a little earlier, before bedtime, which I think reduces the chance of tears leading to vomiting at bedtime.) She stood in her crib sobbing with her arms outstretched, then she'd get tired and "flop down." Then she got up and sobbed some more. The second night was much, much easier. Chloe cried for fifteen minutes, less intensely, although she was up a few times during the night. By the fourth night, she was standing in the crib, pacing and talking, but the hysterics were over. By night six, she went to bed with far fewer complaints and she slept right through until morning. Nap training took longer, partly because she decided to break with the usual pattern and tried to give up her afternoon nap, not her morning one. That doesn't work too well because a thirteen-month-old just can't go that long between nap time and bedtime.

◌ ◌ ◌

The Sleep Lady Shuffle also helped James. Ellen and George took it slowly, knowing that he did have a lot of separation issues and that his adoption a year earlier had already turned his whole world upside down. By the second week they were leaving his room after twenty minutes, and making frequent checks on him. Ellen found that he sometimes did better when they left the room because he became irate when they were present but not picking him up. And when they were in the room, he didn't always want to be touched; he just wanted a parent's silent presence. "He needed to know I was around, but it was insulting to him if I touched him but wouldn't take him out of the crib," she said. That's not at all uncommon; some babies don't like physical contact while they are trying to fall asleep. James's problems didn't go away overnight, but Ellen and George did begin to detect an improvement after only four nights, not enough to make it easy on them—Ellen sometimes bawled harder than James—but enough for them to know they had embarked on the right path. Starting on night sixteen, he slept through for five nights in a row. At about day twenty or twenty-one, he was ready to let his parents leave the room and fall asleep on his own. That's when she dubbed him the "Olympic sleeper," and once his problems were solved, they stayed solved. Not even the birth of a little sister threw him off. Two years later, he had a brief period during which he needed a little extra reassurance at bedtime, when he went through one of those normal periods when preschoolers get the "scaries." But he got over it quickly and returned to his well-established sleep champ patterns.

You might remember Ellen from the first chapter in this book. She was the mom who wrote out the cue cards to use in the middle of the night. Sleep training was really hard on her. It's hard on lots of parents—and think of the extra anxiety an adoptive parent feels. The cue cards reminded her not just of what she had to do—but why she had to do it. "It was my first really tough parenting task but I saw it was bigger than sleeping. It felt like a life lesson," she said. "It was about teaching him to self-soothe; it was the first baby steps of understanding limit-setting. I could see all the parenting issues coming down the road. This is where my husband and I had to step up to the plate and take hold of this problem for him." I admired their perseverance as they tackled bedtime, nap time, and those three or four middle-of-the-night awakenings simultaneously and with impressive consistency.

PROBLEMS AND SOLUTIONS

Babies who have trouble getting to sleep and staying asleep have what sleep experts call *negative associations*, or *sleep crutches*. These behaviors aren't bad in and of themselves, they only become bad when they interfere with sleep—yours or your baby's. For instance, children should be hugged and snuggled, but if they are hugged and snuggled until they fall asleep and each and every time they wake up at night, they will never learn how to fall asleep without being hugged and snuggled. And no matter how much we love hugging and snuggling our children, 3:00 a.m. is not necessarily the preferred time. Pacifiers, swings, walking, rocking, or midnight nursing can also become sleep crutches. Our task is to help our children free themselves from these crutches.

Night wakenings usually taper off during the Sleep Lady Shuffle, but they don't always stop immediately. I've stressed the first three nights, when you will be tackling these problems initially, and you will return to sit by your child's crib side to comfort him. Starting on night four, just quickly go to his crib for reassurance, and then resume whatever position you were in that evening for the bedtime Shuffle. We want to give a consistent message for all awakenings. If your child still wakes up sometimes after the Shuffle is completed, it's generally best to comfort him from the doorway, or give him a quick reassuring pat in his crib and then comfort him from the doorway.

If these techniques don't eliminate those final night awakenings, you might be putting your child to bed when he's too drowsy. Remember, you want a 7 or 8 on that drowsy-but-awake scale. Maybe you are at a 9. It's easier for a toddler to put himself to sleep at bedtime than in the middle of the night—particularly if he was 90 percent asleep before his head hit the pillow. Try putting him down when he's a bit more alert, even if it means backing up and doing a few more days of the Shuffle. You may find that an earlier bedtime also helps him conquer the night awakenings. Try moving bedtime a half hour earlier. If you are still nursing at bedtime, try doing that feeding a little earlier in the evening to further weaken the link between suckling and sleeping. Sometimes it helps to keep a low light on while you nurse to help her break that suckle-sleep association.

Eliminating Nighttime Feeding

As you know, healthy toddlers should be able to go from dinner until breakfast without a feeding, eleven or twelve hours. Check with your pediatrician, but if your baby is still waking up to eat at night, you are probably dealing with a habit, not a nutritional need. Either you need to adjust her hunger clock so she eats more during the day—or she is using the bottle or breast as a sleep crutch. Or maybe both. If she's still nursing, shorten feeding sessions so that she is actively nursing, not just sucking or dozing with the nipple in her mouth. Adjust your nursing schedule so she's not falling asleep on the breast. If she is using a bottle, consider switching to a cup.

With infants, I often recommend a gradual elimination of nighttime feedings but after the first birthday, it's usually best to just stop it cold. When she wakes up wanting to nurse or take a bottle, sit by her side and find other ways to calm and comfort her. Pat her or her mattress a bit, whisper "sh-sh," tell her it's night-night time. Don't cave in and feed her or the inconsistency, the intermittent reinforcement, is going to make the change more prolonged and difficult for her. If you can't bear stopping cold, try a *dream feed* for a few days, no more than a week. That's when you wake her, or half wake her, sometime between 10:00 and 11:00 p.m., for one last feeding to help tide her over. It usually doesn't take more than a few days at this age to wean a child overnight, from either the breast or bottle. If you don't feed her at night, she'll wake up hungrier in the morning. If she's hungry in the morning, she'll eat more during the day. If she eats more during the day, she won't wake up as hungry in the night. It's the opposite of a vicious circle.

Phasing Out Walking and Rocking to Sleep

If you are still walking or rocking your child to sleep, and having to walk or rock him back to sleep over and over again all night long—stop it. There are easier ways to get weight-bearing exercise that don't involve serious sleep disruption! A few minutes of walking or rocking before bedtime is fine if you can then put him down without him squawking and if he doesn't wake up at night demanding another stroll. But if walking and rocking have become a sleep crutch, just get rid of it. It's time. Make sure you have a nice long and comforting bedtime routine. You can incorporate a wee bit of walking or rocking in it, just don't let it be the sleep crutch. A few minutes in the rocking chair while you read a book, or a brief stroll around the room saying good night to favorite toys is fine. Then put him down, drowsy but awake. If he wakes up, go to him quickly but don't walk or rock him. Sit by his bed and pat him, stroke him, whisper soothing words, but leave him in his crib. Whichever parent is least likely to cave in and rock him should be the one to do the crib-side duty the first few nights.

At fourteen months, Joshua was still getting up many times a night, and Carol was having a lot of internal conflict about the attachment-parenting model she had chosen for herself. Each time Joshua woke, it would take an hour or an hour and a half to get him back to sleep. She and her husband, Daniel, tried everything—nursing, rocking, holding him. Nothing worked consistently. Making changes was difficult for Carol because she felt she had to hold and nurse Joshua all the time. She was at a total loss when it came to setting any boundaries or limits, and she felt very guilty if he cried. "I was always putting that boob in his mouth. It soothed him, but it wasn't what he needed," she said. "I was a major rescuer."

Carol knew she would have to make some difficult emotional adjustments if she was going to follow my advice, but she knew the time had come. She and Daniel were a wreck, and Joshua himself was a clingy, cranky, lethargic baby who got sick a lot. "I just knew that wasn't his real personality," Carol said. "We wanted to get some sleep ourselves and we wanted to get him functioning."

Bedtime wasn't Joshua's biggest problem, middle-of-the-night awakenings were. When Joshua woke up, Daniel would go into Joshua's bedroom and sit next to him, pat the crib, and say over and over again in a calm, soothing voice, "Night-night, time to go to sleep." He stayed as long as it took for Joshua to get back to sleep. Joshua didn't improve the first few nights, but then his parents began noticing changes. He was still waking up but the crying was tapering off, and he was going back to sleep faster. Within a few weeks, he was usually sleeping through the night.

Pacifier Withdrawal

Most pediatricians recommend weaning your child off the pacifier by eighteen months to two years, but if your child is waking up a lot at night seeking his paci, you might want to choose to tackle it now. Be prepared for a few nights of unpleasantness. Comfort her, and encourage the bond to a lovey or other alternative. As you take the pacifier away, say something like "It's not paci time but Teddy Bear is here and wants to hug you." That distracts her from the pacifier, and provides a security substitute.

If you don't want to take away the pacifier yet, you should still be able to train your child to find it herself so you don't have to keep chasing it for her all night long. Leave a few pacifiers scattered around the crib so she can find at least one of them in the middle of the night while she's still half asleep. I do encourage restricting pacifier use to sleeping, though, because research suggests 24/7 use can interfere with other aspects of development, including speech. Some families get rid of the pacifier at night, but use it for naps.

At this age, however, lots of babies go through the pacifier-as-missile stage. They love to hurl it out of their crib and make you go after it. Ignore it. She may get very enraged if you don't go fetch, but if you pick it up, she'll just throw it again. (If you don't believe me, try it!) Wait until her complaints reach their crescendo and when she seems like she's ready to lie down, tell her that if she lies down you will get her the paci. You'll have to experiment a little to get the right rhythm for this little dance; the key is to discourage the throwing and to reward the calming down. Even low-tear-tolerance moms can often cope with this crying because they are tears of temper, not fear or despair. Even the calmest and happiest babies have occasional tantrums. Our task is to learn to distract and calm them instead of fueling their fires.

Early Birds

If your toddler is up at 6:00 a.m., cheerful and happy, it may be a strain on you but it's not a crisis for her; 6:00 is a common wake-up time for young children. If she's up at 6:00 but cranky by 6:30, or if she wakes up consistently before 6:00, it may be a symptom of sleep deprivation. I know that sounds odd, but young children who go to bed too late wake up too early. Try getting her to sleep between 7:00 and 8:00 p.m., and ensure that she is getting enough nap time. You might move her morning nap later (in thirty-minute increments). This might help shift her whole body clock and help you conquer the early awakenings. Be careful and use your intuition. This is a dance between pushing her nap later but not postponing it so long that she is too wired to sleep.

But if she is waking up before 6:00 a.m., you are going to have to teach her to sleep later. After the first birthday, if early rising is an established habit that has gone on for a few months, it will probably take at least three to four weeks of parental consistency to change it. In some cases, it takes longer and it can be draining for you.

When she gets up, respond immediately. Your goal is to get her back to sleep quickly, not to let her scream herself into total awakeness. Give her the lovey and try to soothe her back to sleep without picking her up. No matter how much she protests, and she may protest a great deal, don't turn on the lights or let her out of the crib until 6:00 a.m. Letting her get up earlier, especially if it's still dark, sends a confusing message and is a clear-cut instance of intermittent reinforcement. How can a one-year-old understand why she can get up in the dark at 5:45 a.m. but not at 2:15 a.m.? Be firm about 6:00 a.m., too, or you'll find that if you get her up at 5:55 a.m., next it will be 5:45, then 5:30, and you'll be back to your undesirable starting point.

Sleep training at 5:00 a.m., when we are being pulled out of a dream sleep ourselves, is really hard. It's up to you whether you stay in the room or leave, and you may have to experiment to see what works best for you and your child. Some parents find that their presence stimulates the child into being more awake. In that case, soothe her a bit and then leave and see if she dozes off again on her own. You can come back in and make some checks if you want.

If you decide to stay in the room, keep the interaction minimal. Try sitting in a chair with your eyes closed or return to your Shuffle position. That helps you keep from engaging with her, and it conveys a message that it's still night-night time. Some parents who stay in the baby's room may even lie down on the floor or on a guest bed mattress and be able to at least doze for a few minutes.

> "The early rising is the area that took the longest to train, and it still fluctuates; he regresses," Joshua's mom, Carol, said. "If he woke up before six, we would go in and say, 'It's still night-night time.' Eventually we got to the point where we wouldn't go in, and he would go back to sleep or play quietly."

If she's still awake when the clock finally strikes 6:00—and it can seem like it takes forever—leave the room for a minute or two. She may cry, but try not to let it bother you; you will be right back in a minute. If you're already out of the room, now's your cue to come back. Put on a good-morning show when you reenter. Open the blinds, turn on the lights, sing a cheery morning song. You want to send a very clear message: "I'm getting you out of the crib because it's wake-up time—not because you were carrying on."

As I said, if it took your child months to get into this early-rising pattern, expect it to take at least a few weeks to get her out of it. You aren't going to feel very good at 5:00 a.m., dealing with a crying baby, so prepare yourself. Use cue cards, give yourself a pep talk, whatever works. Having two parents take turns, so one isn't always exhausted and resentful, is also a good idea.

Napping

I'm going to talk about two aspects of napping. First I'll try to help the toddlers who don't nap well or who don't nap at all. Then I'll tackle the whole problem of nap consolidation—how to know when the time is right, and how to make the transition less difficult for all concerned. The two problems do overlap—nap training is hard and it may be harder if her body is getting ready for a nap transition. If you need a reminder of how hard nap training can be and everything it entails, read the Napping section of Chapter 5, Six to Eight Months, on page 100 (including daytime Shuffle instructions) but I'll stress the important elements for this age group here.

This advice applies whether your child is on a two-nap or one-nap schedule. Remember, when she's taking two naps, the morning one should be about an hour, and the afternoon one about an hour and a half. A little variation is okay, but don't let her sleep so long in the morning that she can't go down in the afternoon. When she consolidates, the afternoon nap (which may be at midday for a while during the transition) is about two and a half hours up through eighteen months. Nap needs will slowly shrink to about ninety minutes by age three.

Keep in mind how hard it is for children to switch gears and get to sleep in daylight, particularly toddlers who are perpetual motion machines. Set the stage for her in a quiet, dim room. Listen to some quiet music, read a book or two, or play some gentle games before putting her in the crib. Put her down drowsy, even a little drowsier than she is at night, but awake. You can wait until her eyes start to roll back, but not until they close.

It's up to you whether you stay in the room doing the Sleep Lady Shuffle and soothe her, or leave. If your presence calms her, stay. If your presence stimulates her, leave but don't go too far away and check on her every 10–15 minutes. Either way, don't converse, just say things like "sh-sh, nap time." Resist picking her up unless she is about to reach that "point of no return" hysteria, and then pick her up briefly and put her down as soon as she is calm. Give her an entire hour to fall asleep. She might cry an entire hour, and you'll hate it, but try to make yourself get through it. If she doesn't sleep in an hour (or even less if she's crying nonstop and you can't take a full hour of it; remember, you don't have to push yourself beyond your limits), leave the room and come back in and do your dramatic wake-up, whether or not she's slept. Throw open the blinds and make a big deal about wake-up time. However, if she did not sleep during the morning nap, try to get her down for her next nap earlier than usual, because she's going to be overtired. Look for sleepy cues to know when to try again, maybe in about forty-five minutes. Try the same approach for the next nap. If the afternoon nap doesn't go well either, trigger your emergency backup plan. Even though I usually advise against motion sleep, this is a time to make an exception to the rule because you have to get her to sleep. Take her for a car ride, put her in the stroller, do whatever it takes but avoid returning to your original sleep crutch. Otherwise she will be too overtired to go to bed at night and you'll be back to that downward spiral of sleep deprivation generating more sleep deprivation. Go back to the nap training again the next day; eventually she'll get the message that when you put her in the crib, it's time to sleep.

If she's a catnapper, sleeping less than forty-five minutes, attempt to prolong the naps. Also try to lengthen naps beyond forty-five minutes if she wakes up tired and cranky. If you hear her stir after twenty or thirty or forty minutes, she may be having a partial awakening, not a full awakening. You need to gently resettle her, and help her go back to sleep, which can be quite difficult for her. You want to respond quickly enough that she doesn't have time to awaken fully, but gently enough that you don't stimulate her into thinking nap time is over. It's a bit of a balancing act, but you'll get attuned to her cries and her rhythms. When you respond, you can be in your Shuffle position in her room, or you can stay in the doorway. Try to give her a full hour to fall asleep again, if you can. Keep doing this every day, for both morning and afternoon naps if you have to. If she doesn't get more than a catnap, use your backup plan to make sure she gets at least one decent nap in the afternoon.

Adele had a good schedule for Alex, but it was a tough task getting him to follow it. It would take her at least thirty minutes to get him to sleep, and he had to fall asleep on her. Then she had to ease him into his crib so he wouldn't wake up. Nap training was really hard for her, "grueling," as she put it, but she knew that she couldn't put it off any longer. "He'd cry for an hour in the morning, cry for an hour in the afternoon; we'd get in the car and drive him around." Adele chose not to stay in his room while he cried; he would try too hard to engage her in conversation or activity. She checked on him every fifteen minutes or so. Some moms find tears easier to deal with during daylight hours, but for Adele it was agonizing to be home alone with a crying child while her husband was at work. It took a month for Alex's naps to improve—but then they improved a lot, although they still ran on the short side. In retrospect, we learned that Alex was on the brink of consolidating his naps, and that probably made it even harder for him since Adele was trying to train him right as he entered that betwixt-and-between stage. Luckily the transition itself went pretty smoothly.

Moving to One Nap a Day

Consolidating from two naps to one is a definite physical and psychological transition, and almost all children undergo the "one nap is two little, two naps are too many" phase. Lots of parents get very nervous about this, and even in the best case scenario you will probably have a little bit of crankiness and disruption for one, two, or maybe even three weeks. *The trick is to know when your child is ready to make the transition to a single afternoon nap and to make sure that she doesn't get so overtired during the transition that she crosses the line between mildly cranky and totally sleep-deprived.* As you know, sleep deprivation means she won't nap well, she'll have more difficulty at bedtime, and she might start waking up again during the night or very early in the morning. Try to get your child to bed earlier than usual for two weeks or so during the transition—maybe 7:00 or 7:30 p.m.—to cushion her from being overtired.

An extremely common error is for parents to try to consolidate naps prematurely—and sometimes they try to scrap the afternoon one, not the morning one. For instance, many parents will let a twelve-month-old take a two- or three-hour nap in the morning. The child will then refuse to sleep in the afternoon, but there's no way she will make it from the end of that morning nap all the way until bedtime without melting down. At this point, she still needs two naps. In order to preserve that afternoon nap, you'll have to shorten the morning one. Experiment a bit to find the right amount of time for your child, but generally it's roughly one hour in the morning and ninety minutes in the afternoon.

Toddlers usually get ready to drop the morning nap somewhere around fifteen to eighteen months. A little earlier or a little later is normal, but remember to watch your child, not the calendar. Especially watch for changes in her morning nap patterns. It may take her longer to fall asleep or she may wake up earlier from the nap. She may also sleep so long in the morning that she won't sleep in the afternoon, meaning you'll have a very overtired toddler by bedtime. Don't mistake one or two abbreviated morning naps for the sign that she's ready for the change; that might happen now and then as she gets older. But when this pattern becomes pretty consistent, when many or most of the morning naps are truncated, the time is probably right to help her start the consolidation.

Your goal is to have one nap starting around 12:30 or 1:00 p.m. It should last two and a quarter to two and a half hours (although it will grow shorter during the next two or three years). But you need to get her there gradually over a period of about seven to ten days; just skipping the morning nap and trying to keep her up until 1:00 p.m. is not going to make anybody happy. Start by pushing her morning nap a bit later. Delay it until around 11:00 a.m. for two or three days, then 11:30 for a few days, then noon, and so on. Don't let it get stuck in late morning. You want her on that early afternoon schedule within seven to ten days, although it may take another week or so for her body's wake and sleep rhythms to fully adjust. If your child is in day care or preschool part of the time, try to synchronize the afternoon nap at home with the timetable at school (assuming she sleeps at school at a reasonable time).

If she sleeps for only one hour and wakes up tired, which often happens, then try to soothe and resettle her back to sleep. (See the tips on nap training in the earlier age chapters). If all else fails, use one of your emergency backup nap techniques, like putting her in the car or stroller, to get her some more sleep. Remember not to let her sleep past 4:00 or 4:30 p.m. Even if she naps later than usual, don't delay her bedtime; keep it on the early side. If you've been working on this consolidation for a few days and you see that she is a bit "off," that she is too tired, feel free to let her take a "two nap" day to catch up. I know I keep telling you to be consistent, but in this particular situation, your priority is to see that she's rested, to keep her from crossing into that exhausted but wired state. After the "two nap" day, get back on the one nap consolidation path.

One last suggestion—if your child is not yet sleeping through the night, work on that before you tackle nap consolidation. When she's slept through the night consistently for a few weeks, then you can begin altering the nap schedule if you see that she is ready.

> *Despite Carol's valiant attempts to improve Joshua's napping at around fourteen to fifteen months, he remained a spotty daytime sleeper, particularly in the morning. She was relieved when the time came to drop that nap, at about sixteen months. "We started skipping his nine a.m. nap, which wasn't a good one anyway; it was so depressing. One nap worked so much better. We moved the one p.m. nap earlier (while he adjusted to one nap) and then pushed it back again," she said. "We try to keep one p.m. consistent but you need to catch him at the moment he's tired, and if you miss it, it's gone. Sometimes he'll get tired at ten-thirty and sometimes not until two. I got better at picking up the signals—I can see it in his eyes. He blinks a lot; he just looks tired and lethargic."*

Co-sleeping

Co-sleeping is such a complex topic that I've devoted a whole chapter to it (see Chapter 10). I try to help families who remain committed to co-sleeping improve the quality of their family's sleep. And if you have been co-sleeping but want to stop, I give you suggestions on how to follow through.

Matthew's Story

When Lizette and Carl watched newborn Matthew sleep peacefully in his crib, they didn't understand all the talk about sleep deprivation. Matthew slept through the night pretty often at three months, and just about every night by four months. But at five months, after a severe ten-day virus, his sleep deteriorated. "During his illness, I got so used to running in there where I hadn't before; that was the beginning of the end," Lizette said. "Every time he made a peep, I'd run in."

By nine months, they too were experts on parental sleep deprivation. They tried to Ferberize Matthew. But the baby just planted his sturdy little feet in his crib, pulled himself up, and gripped the top bar. He screamed bloody murder for ninety minutes the first night, even longer the next two nights. Lizette and Carl gave up. "It tore my heart out and I swore I would never do it again," she said. Instead, they were in his room on and off all night, rocking him, giving him bottles, and replugging his pacifier. If he woke up three or four times before 11:00 p.m., they would bring him into their bed, where he would twist and thrash and keep them awake, until they tried to put him back into the crib, only to have him wake up and demand rocking, bottles, and a pacifier all over again. "You name it, we did it," his mother said. Lizette and Carl convinced themselves that this was normal and adopted an "if it ain't broke, don't fix it" attitude.

After the September 11 attacks, Carl was summoned to homeland security duty in New York City with the Coast Guard Reserve. He only made it home once or twice a week. Matthew, then thirteen months and going through the normal separation anxiety for that age, felt his father's absence acutely. Lizette could no longer cope. "Carl's down in New York Harbor in some boat, patrolling, and I'm on the phone in tears. It got so bad." She knew it was time to fix what was broken.

She consulted me and, after a few minor adjustments to Matthew's bedtime routine, she began the Sleep Lady Shuffle. Carl helped on the nights he was home, and over time he took on many of the bedtime responsibilities. Matthew responded much more positively than Lizette had expected. The first two nights he fussed but did not cry as he had earlier when they left him alone. "He kind of whimpered and wanted to know why I wasn't picking him up," she recalled. "He was complaining but he never wailed; it wasn't like when we tried Ferber. I put my hands on the mattress and whispered, 'Lie down, lie down.'" Finally he did.

Matthew rebelled on night three. Kids often do that, once they figure out, "This is for real!" "He sort of said, 'I'm not really digging this,'" his mom said, laughing. He threw everything out of his crib—the pillow, the five pacifiers Lizette was now putting in his crib, everything. Lizette put the essentials back in the crib, very discreetly because she didn't want him to think it was a game and do it all over again. He finally slept. The next three nights, as she moved the big rocking chair to the middle of the room, then toward the door, he protested, but it got milder each night. By night twelve, she was sitting on the floor out in the hallway. "I sat outside and verbally assured him. I said, 'Sh-sh, night-night, Mommy loves you.' Sometimes I would sing so he knew I was there. Having me there was the key."

He continued to wake up at night, though less frequently, and she would return to her bedtime Shuffle position for that evening. He still needed his parents to touch base, but he no longer demanded that they come into his room or pick him up or rock him. As long as he heard one of them in the hallway, he was fine. Soon, he started sleeping all night, and even began looking forward to bedtime. "He'd have both arms out, diving into his crib, wanting it, loving it, excited to go to sleep. I never thought that would happen."

Simultaneously, Lizette worked on decreasing Matthew's use of the pacifier, and switched him from a bottle to a cup. She started with a cup of water before naps, as she rocked him briefly. Then she switched to the cup for the rest of the day, and kept only one four-ounce diluted bottle at bedtime, which he drank as they read books, before lights out.

Unfortunately, as nights improved, early mornings deteriorated, and Lizette found the process excruciatingly difficult. "That was the hardest, having to get up and sit in the hallway at five a.m., but we had to do that," she recalled. But that too improved over time.

Nap training was the low point of Lizette's day. "I would get so exasperated; naps would take everything out of me." Mornings weren't so bad; he took that nap pretty well. But afternoons were a misery. Lizette later realized that she had been reading Matthew's sleep windows wrong. "He would go down in the morning fairly well. He'd wake up at six-thirty and nap at nine or nine-thirty, but afternoon was a whole different story. I thought rubbing his eyes meant he was ready to go to sleep, when in fact *rubbing his eyes meant it was too late! I had to look more at the clock and know that he needed to be asleep within three hours of waking up. I was underestimating how frequent and how early the naps had to be."*

Some days she couldn't get him to nap. He'd flail and resist and even strike her. Other days, he would sleep for just forty minutes, wake up, not know how to put himself back to sleep, and scream. Sometimes if she couldn't settle him back down she'd take him for a car ride, not a good long-term solution but an acceptable stopgap. The rides helped his body get into the rhythm of sleeping twice a day. Soon the afternoon nap became a habit, not a struggle.

No sooner did she get napping solved than she struck the dreaded "one nap is too little, two naps are too many" phase. "He was giving me a hassle about going down in the morning. He loved his morning nap. He was like Rip van Winkle, sleeping two hours in the morning, two hours in the afternoon, and going to bed at seven. Then all of a sudden, he didn't want to go to sleep in the morning. He'd play in his crib until nine-thirty or ten, and not go to sleep until ten-thirty. That was late, so then he wouldn't go down for his afternoon nap." Lizette recognized that this was his signal; he was ready to give up that morning nap. She began keeping him up in the morning, and putting him down at midday. Gradually he made the adjustment.

Every once in a while, there is naturally still a bad nap or nighttime sleep, and some tears. But Lizette learned that it really helps to keep an eye on her watch. "It may feel like he's crying a long time, but when I look at my watch, I realize it's only thirty seconds!"

ONE AND A HALF TO
TWO AND A HALF YEARS OLD

Please take a few minutes to read the first three chapters of my book, which give an overview of my system and include some helpful hints that apply to all age groups. It won't take long and you'll have much better results.

✿ ✿ ✿

AN EIGHTEEN-MONTH-OLD ON AVERAGE *sleeps eleven and a quarter hours at night and two and a quarter hours during one midday or afternoon nap. At age two, sleep requirements drop to eleven hours at night and two during the day. Over the next year that will drop to ten and a half hours at night and one and a half during the day. Remember these are averages but variations should not be huge. Watch your child's daytime behavior for clues to whether he or she needs more sleep.*

Toddlers and early preschoolers are lots of fun but bedtime can be a challenge. They are learning to follow simple directions, yet they also test our rules and their limits. Curious about their world, they are extremely eager to explore, leading to more limit testing and boundary breaking. They climb, crawl, crash, and clamber, standing on furniture, knocking down gates, trying to scramble out of the crib. Yet as they push their limits, they rely on their parents to keep setting boundaries, seeking safety, reassurance, and security. Their language skills are blossoming, but they understand more than they can say, leading to frustration and tantrums. Their favorite words seem to be *no, I do,* and *mine,* and they are particularly possessive about their toys and their parents. As their language skills improve, they just love to stall, bargain, and negotiate, particularly around bedtime. They may go through periods when they have the "scaries" of the dark, thunder, monsters, and the like. Nightmares and night terrors may start, and be a recurring problem for the next several years. Potty training can also complicate bedtime behavior, if you let it become a battle of wills rather than a cooperative venture. To prevent bedtime from becoming a war zone, make sure that you have a very, very consistent, predictable, and soothing routine. Clear rules and parental consistency are essential, along with plenty of love, cuddles, and kisses.

All too often, parents rush to get their child out of a crib or into a bed, as though it were a sign of achievement, maturity, or their guaranteed success as adults. One woman I worked with even reported an unspoken competition in her playgroup to see which baby could move first to a bed. Children who switch too young to a bed may experience sleep disruptions, and difficult bedtimes with tears and tantrums. Safety is also a factor. I worry a lot about a twenty-month-old roaming around in his room at night, pulling out drawers, unplugging lamps, exercising all that wonderful but potentially hazardous curiosity. Even if the child is trying to climb out of the crib, I almost always advise parents to keep him in as long as possible, definitely until two and a half, and preferably until three. By then, a child has the verbal skills to understand the "big bed" rules and to communicate when he has gotten out of bed for the twentieth time that night. This chapter is written with crib-sleepers in mind, but I do recognize that a few children do successfully transition to a bed at a young age, and some of you may have already made the switch before learning that it may not be ideal. So if your child is in a bed, you may want to review some of my suggestions in the next chapter on older children and see if you can adapt them for your child.

One of the hardest aspects of sleep shaping for one-and-a-half- to two-and-a-half-year-olds is that parents are a little skeptical that they can change deeply ingrained habits, and they are often so exhausted after two years of sleep deprivation that the required nighttime consistency is taxing. I've met parents who have literally fallen asleep on the floor in the middle of the night as they've tried to carry out these changes. But as you will see, children can and do learn to discard their sleep crutches; they give up their bottles, their midnight nursing, their need to be rocked, walked, or snuggled to sleep. They can become excellent sleepers, or at least reasonably good ones.

Joel, who had frequent ear infections and who still needed a bottle to fall asleep, stayed up until 10:00 p.m. and woke up repeatedly every night. His parents had been very firm about not letting him into their bed when he was an infant but were now so drained by the sleep battles that their eighteen-month-old ended up with them at some point in the night. Barry, who slept with his mom while his dad ended up in the guest room, could only fall asleep if he had a bottle and twirled, twirled, and twirled his mother's long hair. Madison was another hair twirler and milk guzzler, plus she demanded to be rocked, walked, or bounced for at least forty-five minutes before bed and again when she awoke during the night. At twenty-eight months, Suzanna went to bed easily and independently, but nevertheless woke up over and over again all night. Approaching his second birthday, Ilan was a sunny, smiling, easy baby—except at 10:00 p.m., midnight, 2:00, 4:00, and 6:00 a.m. (sometimes he awoke on the odd-numbered hours too), when he screamed, squirmed, squiggled, burrowed, bellowed, and occasionally bonked his parents on the head if they dared hand him a sippy cup of water when he was still demanding the milk that he had long ceased to need at night.

 DEVELOPMENTAL CHANGES

Separation Anxiety

Separation anxiety may have peaked at the first birthday, but prepare for another big wave at about eighteen months, and then spells of it throughout early childhood. A nice, long, gentle, predictable transition to bedtime, quality time with one or both parents who are really focused on bedtime rituals, and not on the telephone, washing dishes, or paying bills, helps soothe those worries. At some point, your child may begin to articulate that he wants you to stay with him at bedtime. It can be heartbreaking to hear him plead "Mommy, sit," or "Mommy, stay." Be gentle but firm when the time does come to say good night. If your child isn't talking yet, she can probably still understand your verbal reassurances about how Mommy and Daddy love her and will be nearby. Many children find it easier to fall asleep if you stay in a nearby room, not on another floor of the house. They can't see you but they know you are there.

Young enough to still experience some separation anxiety at night, and old enough to suspect they may be missing excitement if they are asleep, children this age excel in stalling and delaying tactics at bedtime. I've heard some sleep doctors call these "curtain calls" because they aim to get the parent to come back over and over and over again to the bedside. When a child repeatedly seeks to be tucked in, kissed, given a blankie, etc. after normal, reasonable limits have been reached, the parent should respond once. Define what you consider reasonable limits for your child, balancing his separation fears with his gift for manipulation! Maybe you want to say good night once and that's it; maybe you don't mind going in three or four times. But once you set those limits, make them clear to your child and remind him "This is the last time." The next time, if there is a next time, your response should be neutral but firm. Say "Now it is time to go to sleep" or "I love you, sweetheart, but you know it's time to go to sleep now." A parent who says "last time" better mean it's the last time, because children absolutely pounce on adult inconsistency.

Loveys

Loveys, usually a special stuffed animal or blanket, are very important for those children who are gaining independence but still need that extra helping of security. Loveys help with separation, with fighting the scaries, and with breaking lingering emotional attachments to bottles, cups, or pacifiers. Even children who have spurned loveys in the past may embrace one now. They may want a lovey, like Clifford or Elmo or Blue, from a favorite book or video. With their blossoming imaginations, they also like including loveys in games, including bedtime and nap-time rituals. For instance, if you look out the window and say good night to doggies or cars, have the lovey say good night to doggies and cars too. Tuck the lovey in with her for bedtime and naps, and when she wakes up at night remind her that she has her lovey to snuggle.

However, if your child's lovey is a pacifier, a bottle, a cup, or your breast, she may not accept a new lovey as easily. As you wean her from the bottle, or start to weaken the association between nursing and sleep, she will be more receptive to a new security object, but it takes time. Parents may worry if their child wants to carry the lovey everywhere. If the lovey is a pacifier, restrict it first to the house, then to nap and sleep time. But if it's a toy or blanket, I don't regard carrying it as a problem before age two. Then you might want to restrict it to the house and car, or maybe a special occasion such as going to the doctor or an anxiety-provoking unfamiliar place or situation.

Loveys can also help you address other bedtime quirks. Barry at two and a half could not get to sleep or back to sleep without his bottle or twirling his mother's hair, a fixation he had formed when he was only six months old. Helene took Barry to one of those workshops where you can make your own teddy bear; they have them at malls and crafts shops. Helene made Barry a "fireman bear" to match his fireman bed theme, while Barry made a pink "wishes" bear for his mom. His excitement made it easy to weave the fireman bear into the bedtime routine, and ease out of the bottle drinking and hair twirling. "Making it himself really got him

*invested in it," Helene said. Later Barry adopted a long-eared bunny as a
lovey, and yes, he twirled its ears to his heart's content. Barry, whose own
hair was too short to twirl, still wanted Mom's hair when he was sick
or particularly tired, even after she got a short tousled cut. "I don't know
why he likes it so much; he is always telling me, 'I love your hair.'" But
while it still may be a habit, it is no longer a constant need that disrupts
his sleep.*

New Mobility: The Change from Crib to Bed

I like keeping toddlers in a crib as long as I can but they sometimes have
their own agenda. If your child starts climbing out, dissuade him by making
the climb harder by lowering the mattress. Put pillows on the ground for
safety in case he attempts Olympic-style hurdling. Remove large toys or
stuffed animals from the crib that might serve as a launch pad. If he does get
out, put him right back in the crib with minimal interaction—except to say,
"No climbing." Be firm, but don't yell at him. Try stationing yourself outside
the bedroom door, out of his line of vision if possible, and peek in. When he
starts to raise his leg again say, "No climbing." Sound like you mean it, and
keep putting him back in the crib if you have to. You may also try to put him
in a long T-shirt or nightshirt, which makes it harder for him to climb. If your
child still seems determined to get out, particularly if he's under age two, try a
crib tent, a zipped mesh cover that lets him see out but not get out. That may
buy you a few months before you switch to the bed, although if your child
hates the tent, and some do, don't push it.

> *Madison's parents noticed that she moved around a lot in her crib,
> and thought it might be too small for such an active sleeper, that she
> might sleep better if she had more space. They took her out of her crib at
> the unusually early age of fifteen months, and gave her a mattress on the
> floor. That gave her more room but it didn't solve any of their problems,
> and it created a lot of new ones. She still tossed herself around, slept
> perpendicularly, and woke up a lot, but now she wanted her mom in
> her bed with her.*

Children who move from the crib too early don't necessarily have the verbal skills to understand bedtime rules. Then they keep getting out of bed over
and over again, and you may end up having to gate the doorway or even shut
the door, which sometimes provokes the tears and tantrums that you were try-

ing to avoid. They may also miss that feeling of cozy containment in their crib. I know some families who regretted moving the child to the bed and managed to get him back to a crib, particularly if he was talking about his crib or trying to climb into a younger sibling's crib. That's not regression. It is listening to your child.

Some kids do hate cribs and start talking about "big boy" or "big girl" beds. If they can articulate it, that's a reasonably good sign that they have the verbal ability to understand big-bed rules. To make the transition easier, read the "New Mobility: Switching to the Big Bed" section of the next chapter (page 201). Use a bed rail if he might fall out. Remind him that with the privilege comes rules—like staying in bed all night. Sticker charts are wonderful behavior incentives for older children, and sometimes children this age respond as well. Children who don't yet understand a chart may like wearing a sticker in the morning.

Even as an infant, Ilan had never seemed to like his crib, perhaps because Zach, the much older brother he idolized, did not sleep in one. The summer before he turned two, and a few weeks before my first meeting with his parents, the family spent a week at the beach and instead of struggling with a portable crib that they knew he would never stay in, they threw a single mattress down on the floor. Elated, he slept better than he did at home—in other words, he slept poorly but not disastrously. He never tried to come into Joanne and Ken's bed at the beach, which is where he often ended up at home, although he did sometimes want Joanne to come into his bed. The first few nights back home in a crib were miserable; he let them know loud and clear that he hated being back behind bars. That's when I met them. We talked about the pros and cons of cribs and beds but their instinct was to try a mattress on the floor like at the beach. He was only twenty-two months old, but had excellent verbal (and comedic) skills, as you'll see in a moment. A few days earlier they had been in New York, where Ilan had been entranced by a huge line of fire trucks shrieking down Park Avenue, so when Joanne saw sheets decorated with bright, bright, bright red fire trucks, she knew Ilan would be thrilled. They moved him out of the crib the same night they started sleep shaping with me. The timing was perfect. He embraced the bed as well as the new sleep rules, figuring it was a package deal. Although it took a very, very long time to get Ilan sleeping consistently through the night, we solved several of his sleep problems in a matter of days, and he stayed in his new "big boy" fire truck bed all night long right from the start.

Eating and Sleeping

When our babies are little, we strive to get them to bed on a full tummy, hoping it will help them learn to sleep longer at night. That's no longer necessary. Those youngsters who are still breast feeding may want to nurse briefly before sleep. That's fine, unless she must nurse in order to get herself to sleep at bedtime, nap time, or when she wakes up at night. (I'll talk more about how to gently modify night feeding when we address specific sleep solutions.) In general, children this age should be able to go twelve, even fourteen hours from dinner until breakfast, without a bedtime snack except perhaps a glass of water. Most pediatricians recommend limiting milk to eighteen to twenty-four ounces a day maximum (three or four six-ounce cups). Kids who drink milk (or juice) all day tend not to be hungry at mealtimes and don't get enough solid foods, or enough of a variety of solid foods, to meet their expanded nutritional needs. Barring any unusual dietary or health concerns, children eighteen to thirty months should have three recognizable mealtimes, breakfast, lunch, and dinner, plus snacks in the midmorning and following the afternoon nap. Some will want a third nibble but keep it very healthy if it's close to a meal. Remember that healthy childhood eating patterns help shape healthy eating patterns later in life. Toddlers and preschoolers begin to recognize and ask for sweets and junk food but you should keep them as a special treat, not a staple.

If you haven't already introduced a cup, do so now even if you are still nursing. Offer the sippy cup, of water, milk, toddler formula, diluted juice, whatever your doctor recommends, at each meal. If he takes a bottle at night, switch to a cup, and if he takes milk at bedtime, switch to water. You don't want the milk bottle to become a sleep crutch, something he needs every time he tries to fall asleep.

Joel, whom you'll hear about more at the end of this chapter, was very small for his age and a poor eater. Dorothy worried about him a lot, and kept giving him bottles of milk when he got up at night long after she stopped nursing at nine months. "My doctor said not to feed him all night but I didn't believe him. I was just so happy to see Joel have the calories." Dorothy also acknowledged to herself that as a working mother carrying more than her share of guilty feelings, she wasn't quite ready to give up that cuddly warmth of bottle feeding her baby, even though she knew he was perfectly content to drink from a cup at day care. Once I persuaded Dorothy that the bottle had to go as part of an overhaul of Joel's whole eating and sleeping routines, she found that he gave it up much more easily than she expected. The one odd side effect—and I've run into this with a few other children— was that he would no longer drink milk from a cup at home! He'd drink a cup of milk in school, he'd take it in his cereal, he just would not drink it from a cup offered by Mom, not even with chocolate! Thankfully, Dorothy took a very pragmatic approach to this and instead of turning it into an issue, she made sure he got enough calcium from other foods.

The Scaries

Children at this age may get the *scaries*, conjuring up all sorts of gremlins and monsters at bedtime. Remember that the fear is real, even if the monsters aren't. Do what you need to console him, to convince him that there are no monsters. But don't let the monster business get so drawn out that it pushes bedtime back too long. There are no hard and fast rules; trust your instincts and see what works. Try shining a flashlight into the closet, or under the bed. Enlist that lovey to help you look. "See, your snuggly bear says there are no monsters under your bed and now snuggly bear will get in bed with you and you'll both be safe and sound." One of my clients found a "boo-buster" anti-ghost spray bottle on the Internet, and you could probably make your own with some pleasantly scented water. Maybe your child can help you decorate the spray bottle, making him feel a little more powerful against whatever is frightening him.

> *When Barry occasionally got scared and came looking for parental reassurance, Helene walked him back to bed and simply said, "I'm right across the hall if you need me."*

> ☼ ☼ ☼

> *Teddy, whom you met as a seven-month-old, slept well for many months but began experiencing some bedtime fears just shy of his second birthday. Although Teddy used to like to sleep in total darkness, Lisa now found that a small night-light helped. "He'll ask me, 'Mom, are monsters real?,' and I'll say, 'Are there monsters? No, they are only in your imagination.' We have to go through this every single night."* He also clung to the book It's OK! Tom's Afraid of the Dark! *and she read it to him every night for many months.*

Potty Training

I don't see any problem doing sleep training and daytime potty training simultaneously, as long as the child is ready, able, and reasonably enthusiastic.

Indeed, children often have a "window" between eighteen and thirty months (later is not abnormal, don't worry) when they are quite interested in at least starting toileting and you should seize that moment or you might have to wait months for another chance. I'm not going to get into all the different theories and techniques of potty training, except to recommend that you start with day training. At nap time give him a diaper or pull-up until he stays dry for several naps in a row. Leave nighttime for last. In fact, as far as I'm concerned, you can leave a diaper or pull-up on at night all the way up to age four or five. (I address bedwetting for older children in Chapter 13, Medical Problems.) Children often learn to stay dry at night on their own in time, and it makes no sense to expend all this energy teaching a child to sleep all night and then confuse him by waking him up to go to the bathroom! I do know one mom who put the little potty chair in the bedroom at night, so her son would have it nearby when he wanted it.

Ask your child to sit on the potty before naps and before bed (but don't insist). If your child starts using "I need to go potty" as a stalling tactic at bedtime, bring him to the bathroom once, and only once. But keep it boring. No talking, no games, no show-and-tell. Then put him in a diaper or pull-up, reassure him it's fine to use the diaper at night, and get him to bed. If he gets in the habit of having a dirty diaper at about 5:00 a.m, change him (change him in the crib if you are agile enough) but leave the lights as dim as possible and make it clear to him that it's not yet morning, that he gets up when it's morning time, not because he had a dirty diaper. Help him get back to sleep. (My section on Early Birds at the end of this chapter will help you with that.)

Potty training is a major developmental milestone, so expect temporary social, emotional, feeding, and sleep disturbances. You may occasionally hear about a child who trained in just a few days, but don't worry if your child takes months, that's perfectly normal. Be patient and celebrate achievements!

CREATING A SCHEDULE
Sample schedule:

(Shift earlier if your child wakes between six and seven.)

7:00–7:30 a.m. Wake-up and breakfast.

12:00–12:30 p.m. Lunch.

12:30 or 1:00 p.m. Start afternoon nap. Snack upon waking.

5:00–5:30 p.m. Dinner.

6:00–6:30 p.m. Start bath/bedtime routine.

7:00–8:00 p.m. (Sometimes 8:30, depending on age and nap schedule.) Bedtime.

Children need regular nap times, regular bedtimes, and reasonably regular mealtimes. Their bodies need the routine to regulate day and night hormone cycles, their little hearts and minds need the certainty and predictability to feel secure. But I also believe in some flexibility. Sleep times are averages but the variations are a lot less than many parents think, and your child may well need a lot more sleep than he's getting. Even when you do develop a nice workable schedule, you will experience some natural variations. Some days she will nap, or snack, a little more and some days she will nap, or snack, a little less. As you learn to read her sleep cues and recognize her sleep windows, you'll be able to adjust the schedule more easily. Watch her daytime behavior. If she's easy and content, she's probably on a pretty good schedule. If she's fussy and demanding, she may need longer naps, an earlier bedtime, a later wake-up time, or all of the above.

As toddlers turn into preschoolers, they may be able to skip an occasional nap without falling apart. Don't be fooled into thinking that she's outgrown naps completely. Most kids need about an hour or an hour and a half until age four.

WAKE-UP · Give her a *dramatic wake-up*. Throw open the blinds, switch on the lights, sing cheery good-morning songs, and start the day. Create morning rituals, just like you have evening ones, to reinforce her understanding of wake-up time versus sleep time. Any time between 6:00 and 7:30 is normal for this age group. (I'll talk later about children who wake up too early.) If she sleeps much later than 7:30, start waking her up earlier to get her on a more age-appropriate schedule. Usually sleeping later just pushes the rest of her schedule out of whack, particularly if she attends preschool. With younger children I change wake-up time in ten-minute intervals over several days. At this age, do it faster because they adapt well. Either just wake her up at 7:30 and put up with a little crankiness for a day or two, or make the adjustment by about half an hour a day. If your child is sleeping late because she is up several times a night and then has to fill up her sleep tank, shift her wake-up time earlier and follow my program for eliminating night wakenings. On the other hand, if your child goes to bed a little late, sleeps a little late, but still naps regularly and sleeps well at night, go ahead and leave it alone if it's working for your child, your family, and your preschool or child care.

MORNING NAP · By eighteen months, most children have consolidated to one nap, usually afternoon or midday. If yours hasn't yet done so, don't worry, it's uncommon but not abnormal. Read the "Moving to One Nap a Day" section in Chapter 7, Thirteen to Eighteen Months (page 155), to make that rough spot a little less bumpy.

LUNCH/AFTERNOON NAP · Lunch is usually around noon, give or take a half hour. Afternoon naps for this age group usually start around 12:30 or 1:00, maybe 1:30. They'll cut back from two and a quarter hours at eighteen months, to two hours at age two, to about one and a half by age three. A little variation is normal. Don't worry as long as the rest of his schedule is fine; tweak the napping schedule a bit if it's causing other sleep problems. For instance, if your eighteen-month-old naps for three hours but is cheerful and sleeping well, leave it alone. But if she's taking those long naps and then doesn't want to go to bed on time, gradually shorten the nap or move it a little earlier in the day. Aim for about a four-hour gap between the end of the nap and bedtime for an eighteen-month-old; it will get closer to five hours as you near age three.

> *Barry, the hair twirler, took very long late naps, and then stayed awake until 10:00 p.m. After a lot of trial and error, Helene settled on a schedule that is later than most kids' but works for Barry's family, particularly since Larry gets home from his restaurant management job late. Barry goes down for a nap at about 2:30 p.m., and Helene wakes him up at around 5:00. Otherwise he'd sleep another hour or so. Bedtime is 9:00 p.m., and he sleeps until 7:00 a.m.*

DINNER · Fight the temptation to keep young children up late so the whole family can dine together. Feed them around 5:00 or 6:00, even if that means eating without the rest of the family. The early schedule better matches their natural rhythm for eating and sleeping. If an early dinner means less family time, find other ways to compensate, such as building in a little more parental playtime in the morning. There's no reason you can't read good-morning books, as well as good-night books. And those stimulating daddy games, like space rocket baby, are better suited for dawn than dusk anyway.

BEDTIME · A soothing bedtime routine is a must, so give yourself plenty of time to prepare her for bed, physically and emotionally. By that I mean leave time not just for bathing, toothbrushing, and pj's but also for calming down and getting ready to separate from you for the night. First let's talk a bit about bedtime mechanics, the whens and wheres, including a few minor differences between being in a crib and a bed. Then we'll see how to create that calm, soothing transition to dreamland.

Bedtime, meaning asleep in bed, not thinking about going upstairs, should be between 7:00 and 8:00. Figuring out the exact time for your individual child is one part watching sleep cues and one part backward math. Start with her average wake-up time, and count back the hours she needs. For instance, if your eighteen-month-old wakes up at 7:00 a.m. and needs eleven and a quarter hours of sleep, she should be asleep by 7:45 p.m. Start putting her down at around 7:00 or 7:15, depending on how long her bath and routine take. If your two-and-a-half-year-old wakes up at 7:00 a.m. and needs a tad less than eleven hours sleep, get her to sleep around 8:00 p.m., maybe a few minutes later, meaning you should probably be heading upstairs around 7:15 or 7:30. These are averages—your child may need a half hour more or a half hour less. Watch her for signs that she is getting tired, and make sure she's in bed before she's overtired.

The bedtime routine should be in the bedroom, not all over the house, so she knows it's time to slow down and prepare for sleep. You still need to get her down drowsy but awake. As I mentioned, she no longer needs a feeding prior to bedtime but some toddlers still like to nurse briefly or have a glass of water before bed. Just don't nurse her all the way to sleep or let her use her sippy cup as a sleep crutch. If you walk or rock your baby, keep it brief and keep it in her room. Keep any bedtime music very soft. Use it to cue her that it's time to sleep but turn it off or let it run out before she gets into bed, or soon after. You don't want the lullaby to be a sleep crutch, so that she can't get to sleep or back to sleep without it. Ditto for toys with music and lights; phase them out before she falls asleep. At this age, they often like a moment or two of deep-pressure hugging before you put them into bed.

Either parent should be able to put the child to bed, and it's okay if Mom and Dad have slightly different styles. Both parents, however, should put the child to bed at the same time, and should display a consistent response to such bedtime behavior as crying, throwing toys, etc. The united front sends a clearer, less confusing message that discourages such antics and lays the groundwork for all the co-parenting to come.

The routine should be literally a routine. Young children are very ritual-oriented. In fact, your child may well demand that you keep to the exact same routine each and every night. This may include singing the same song, playing the same game, or reading the same book over and over again. They get to the point where they notice if you try to skip a page or truncate a sentence!

Each of my kids had her own rituals at this age. Carleigh liked to kiss a flying cow she had hanging in her room. Later we made up a "two things" game, where we talked about two things about her day. She liked to hear stories about my childhood, or about when she was a baby. Gretchen and I had our own silly little game. She liked me to kiss my pinkie and make it "buzz" like a baby bee. The bee would then kiss her nose. I always told both girls that I would check on them again before I went to bed—a promise I still make and carry out every night even though they are both now in school.

Telling children what to expect, particularly as they get older and more verbal, helps fills their craving for predictability while underscoring the rules. "Now I am going to tuck you in and give you a big hug and then you are going to go to sleep and have wonderful dreams." If they start stalling and negotiating, you might want to "blame the clock" instead of getting into a power struggle. For instance, if they want to read three more books, point to the clock and say, "It's ten minutes before eight, when we have to turn out the light. Let's see how many books we can read in ten minutes." You may also try to make her feel invested in her bedtime, which becomes even more important in the next two or three years. For instance, Barry and his long-eared bunny like to watch the fish tank in his room and Helene permitted Barry to decide whether the fish should have their little light on or not. Joanne always gave Ilan a two- or three-minute reminder before story time was over, and then she let him put out the bedside lamp by himself (at least, he thought his little hand was flicking that switch all by itself).

Talking about fun things that happened during the day, or about pleasant things to anticipate the next day allays bedtime anxieties. You can even make a list of sweet things to dream about. Starting at about age two, tell her how sweet and cozy she looks when she sleeps. Children love to hear that; it also reassures them that you are watching out for them while they sleep.

Joanne made up two bedtime songs for Ilan. One, based on "Skip to My Lou," stayed the same every night, and included the names of his parents, brother, aunts, uncles, cousins, and grandparents. The other she adapted from a thank-you song he knew from a tot religious service. She kept some verses the same every night, for consistency and reassurance, but the rest she improvised to suit his mood, the day's events, even whether he needed to eat more yummy vegetables. If he was rubbing his eyes, she kept the song brief; if he was still pretty wide awake she could throw in more verses and allow him more time to unwind. They did their snuggling at story time, but once the light was out, she gradually moved a little farther from him as they sang their special songs together. That quiet time in the dark helped calm him down and get used to the darkened room while he still had his mother's company. When Joanne had to work late, Ken would sing the same songs and he would usually stay in a rocking chair in the room until Ilan fell asleep because the little boy got a little anxious when Mom wasn't home for bedtime. Ken could stay there because Ilan did not associate him as strongly with going to sleep or getting back to sleep in the middle of the night; his father was less of a sleep crutch.

Even if you do everything right at bedtime, your child may well go through phases where you put her down and she gets right back up again. If a toddler in a crib stands, put her down once. If she bounds up again like a jack-in-the-box, ignore it. She thinks it's hilarious and if you keep responding, she'll keep doing it. By eighteen months, most babies know how to get themselves back down from a standing position. If she doesn't, she will figure it out soon enough, even if her technique isn't particularly graceful. If she tries to climb out of the crib, lower the mattress and review page 164 for advice on keeping her in the crib.

If she's in a bed and gets out looking for you after good night, walk her back in a no-nonsense way. You don't need to scold, but don't play or interact or talk a lot either. Tuck her in and do what you need to do to make her feel safe and comfortable but do it quickly; don't linger. If she gets up repeatedly, put a gate on her door, or at least threaten to put up a gate if the threat alone suffices.

Ilan at twenty-two months had adapted beautifully to his new big-boy bed and to an earlier and more structured bedtime routine. But soon after completing the Sleep Lady Shuffle, he went through a phase where he always had one pressing errand every night. Those same verbal skills that enabled him to stay in bed now became his vehicle for getting out of bed! He was always very matter-of-fact about his mission, and his parents and big brother, Zach, had a tough time reserving their laughter until Ilan was asleep.

"I go to McDonald's," he said nonchalantly as he strolled to the bedroom door one night. This came as a particular surprise as Joanne had never taken him to McDonald's. She put him back in bed and made a mental note to talk to Ilan's otherwise absolutely perfect babysitter about the fat content of French fries.

"I go to Max's," he announced the second night, naming a kid-friendly restaurant he liked. Joanne briefly explained that you don't go to Max's in pajamas and put him back in bed.

The third night, he abandoned that restaurant strategy and for the next few nights he tested a series of sporting events. "I go play hockey" and "I go fly kite, Mom" were particularly ingenious.

When the athletics didn't work, he got even more creative. He announced that he was doing whatever he thought his mom did in the evening, figuring that if it was a good enough reason for a grown-up goose to be up and around, it should be an equally valid excuse for a toddler gander. "I go check my email, Mom" was one memorable example. "I go spill water, make mess." Next he aimed for tasks the family does in the morning, which must have made a lot of sense to him, because these were things you do when you get out of bed. "I go get newspaper, Mom." "I go make coffee." When the coffee ploy failed, he knew he was defeated and from then on he stayed in bed. Joanne put a gate up protectively, in case he had another spurt of imagination. He didn't mind the gate at that age, although at around age three, when Joanne only used it when he needed some reminders of "big boy" stay-in-bed rules, the gate became an irritant. He would climb over it or body slam it out of the doorway until he finally learned to simply unlock it.

By the way, one other little stalling trick you see at this age: strip teases. If she pulls her diaper off, duct tape it! Or try a pull-up if it's harder for her to remove. I know some parents who have even taped zippers closed on pajamas, or put the pj's on backward to thwart attempts to take them off.

THE SLEEP LADY SHUFFLE

Many families use my Sleep Lady Shuffle, a gentle and gradual way of teaching children to fall asleep on their own. I explain my Sleep Lady Shuffle here for toddlers who are still in cribs, but it's quite similar to the Shuffle for those in beds, and I outline the modifications on page 174. As always, we try to minimize tears but I can't promise to eliminate them completely. Don't rush to pick up a whimpering child during the Shuffle, but go ahead and pick him up briefly if he's really upset, especially the first night. Night wakenings taper off during the Shuffle but they don't always disappear immediately, so when your child calls for you in the middle of the night, resume the position you were in at bedtime that night as you calm him back to sleep. It's okay if you briefly soothe him or pat him in his crib before you return to your bedtime position. We want a consistent response to all awakenings.

You should follow the Shuffle schedule, moving on to the next position even if your child has had a bad night or two, fussing or waking more frequently. Don't be surprised if there's a little regression or protest the first night of each new chair position. If your child gets sick during the Shuffle, you might want to pause and maintain your position until he feels a little better. You might even have to move a little closer during an illness to offer more comfort. But then resume the Shuffle when he recovers.

NIGHTS 1–3. Once bath, stories, and songs are over, sit in a chair next to your child's crib. Stroke or pat him intermittently if he fusses or cries but don't do it constantly or he will form a new sleep crutch or negative association and will need you to pat him constantly for him to sleep. (I'm a little more liberal about how much touching you do the first night, but by the second night make sure it's more sporadic.) Closing your own eyes conveys a sleepy-time message and makes it harder for him to talk to you or try to engage you, particularly at this age when he is probably going to try very hard to get you to interact. Stay there until he falls asleep. If he stands up, pat the mattress and tell him to lie down. Once he does get down, stroke or pat him if he finds it comforting.

Some children in this age group resist. That usually doesn't happen during the first few nights; it's more likely to occur a little way down the road when they realize this isn't a passing whim of yours, that it's their new reality. He might start throwing his toys out onto the floor. Then he'll want you to pick them all up and put them back for him. Then he'll throw them out again. It's both a way of expressing frustration at you for making new sleep demands—and a way of engaging you. Don't fall for it. Let everything stay on the floor. If he throws out his lovey or pacifier and then gets upset about it, tell him you will give them back as soon as he lies down.

> *Be careful that you don't create new sleep crutches. One mother, using the Shuffle to teach her son to sleep without being rocked on and off all night, introduced a new song about the night sky, which immediately assumed the same psychological importance for him as the rocking had! Within a few nights, she found herself singing it three times, then four times and then five, because the instant she stopped, he roused himself from semi-slumber and demanded, "Sky! Sky! Sky!" He also demanded the song each time he woke up at night.*

NIGHTS 4–6. Explain, particularly to an older child who can understand better, that he has done such a wonderful job of learning to go to sleep that you are now going to move your chair farther away but that you will still stay with him until he falls asleep. Move the chair about halfway to the door. (If the room is very small, or the crib happens to be very close to the door, you should instead move to the center of the room or sit in the doorway.) Continue the soothing sounds, but stay in the chair as much as you can. Get up to pat or stroke him a little as needed, or make some of those same soothing sounds that you've been using. Try not to pick him up—but if he's really upset and you do need to pick him up, go ahead and do so, over the crib if possible. Hold him until he's calm but keep it brief and don't let him fall asleep in your arms or on your lap. Sometimes a minute of deep-pressure holding really helps them calm down. Stay in the chair until he falls asleep.

NIGHTS 7–9. Again, explain he is doing a great job and tell him that you are going to move the chair again. Sit close to him and hug him for a minute before you make that move, but don't get so entwined that you have to struggle to get loose. Then move to the doorway, or the entrance to the hall, so that you are in his view, although dimly lit. Continue the same soothing techniques, intervening as little as possible. He may cry a little bit but gently reassure him and he will fall asleep.

NIGHTS 10–12. You are now going to move out into the hallway, but where he can still see you. Explain this move carefully before you make it, and praise him again for what a good sleep boy he is becoming. You can keep making those "sh-sh" sounds from the hallway—not constantly but enough to let him know that Mom or Dad is close by and responsive.

NIGHT 13. A fair number of children start falling asleep and staying asleep by night seven or ten—occasionally even sooner. But most parents have to take one more step and leave the child alone for five-minute intervals. Tell him that you will keep checking on him until he is asleep. Leaving the child may seem like a radical change for you but think about it. All that chair shuffling has given him nearly two weeks of preparation. He has given up some sleep crutches and he has learned "Mommy is right down the hall even though I can't see her." Or "Daddy is sitting on the floor right near my room and he loves me." Describe exactly where you will be sitting and explain that you will be close by even though he won't see you. Don't go too far away. Stay on the same floor, maybe in a nearby room, maybe just read a magazine or a book for the first few nights. He may cry for a few minutes, but keep going back every five minutes to reassure him. You don't have to leave him more than five minutes and, unlike the cry-it-out approaches, you don't keep making the intervals longer. In fact, I strongly encourage you to keep a close eye on the clock so you don't exceed five minutes and upset him more. They don't really understand what five minutes is, so for the older toddlers you can explain in terms of what I call "job checks." "Mommy is going to change her clothes and then I will be right back to check on you." Or "Daddy is going to brush his teeth but I'll be right back." (If your child gets stimulated and more awake each time you come to check, you may want to consider longer intervals, or you may want to start with five minutes and slowly lengthen it.) He may cry a bit the first few nights but very rarely do children cry for more than a few minutes after going through the chair routine. If he does cry, check on him from the doorway. Be reassuring but calm. Keep in mind, he has gained confidence that you are nearby and responsive. He's ready to learn this skill.

A few things to remember. Children get ritualized easily. Make the changes every three days—or less. *Dragging it out makes it harder, not easier, for him.* Give it more than three days and he'll expect you to stay exactly where you are—and get mad or upset when you try to double that distance.

Some parents decide this is as far as they want to go for now, and they stay in the hallway a few feet away from the child's room. That's fine—as long as it's not taking an hour and the child doesn't need you in the doorway on and off all night long. Other parents gradually move away and phase out the checks. If you are using checks or job checks, always return as promised. Eventually most families get to the point where they can say good night and the child won't call for them; they can dispense with those five-minute checks.

> *You might have to experiment a little until you find a "job" that he doesn't find threatening. Ilan did fine when Joanne reached the hallway in the Shuffle but resisted and cried when she tried to go to clear the*

kitchen or work at her computer. He would plead, "No go computer, stay with Ilan." One night she had a brainstorm. She said she had to go help Zach, Ilan's beloved big brother, with his homework. At twenty-three months, Ilan did not know what homework was but figured that if Zach did it, it had to be cool. He let her go without any tears or argument. That worked for about three months until he had a brainstorm of his own. "No, Mommy stay with Ilan," he said sweetly. "Daddy go help Zachy homework."

The Sleep Lady Shuffle for Children Sleeping in a Bed

The basic Shuffle is the same, so read through the directions for a crib-sleeper. Sit by the child's bed, and keep moving the chair away every three days. If you've put his mattress on the floor, or if he's in a low toddler bed, sit nearby on the floor, not on a chair. Explain that you are going to move—that's even more important with toddlers in bed than in the crib, because they usually have better verbal skills and you want them to understand that they must stay in the bed.

When the child gets upset, try to stay in your chair. Instead of reaching to touch him, try using soothing words and sounds. "Night, night. Sh-sh. Mommy loves you." Don't talk too much; he'll suck you into a sleep-postponing conversation. Close your eyes if it helps. But if he gets really upset, get up and give him an occasional brief pat. If you absolutely have to pick him up, do it briefly, and do it close to the bed. When he calms down, put him back down and return to your chair. Don't let him fall asleep in your arms, and don't lie down in his bed, not even for a minute.

Like the crib-sleeper, he may well throw toys and blankets at you. Ignore him; only return the lovey if he promises to stop. However, he may also get out of bed and come to you, or try to crawl into your lap.

Give him a big hug and return him to bed. If he does it again, take him back to the bed. Don't talk, don't reason, don't explain, don't get exasperated. Just put him back, as many times as it takes. If he keeps climbing into your lap, you may have to move a little more quickly through the Shuffle, for instance three days by the bed, three days by the door and then the hallway.

When you get to the point where you are sitting in the hallway, where he can hear you but not see you, you might have to deviate from the basic plan a bit. Some kids will be fine with your position, but others will keep trying to come out and join you; they'll get really frustrated that you are close by but not with them. Try putting up a gate and staying in the hall. If he sits or stands by the gate and cries, you may have to skip the step where you stay in the hallway and move to the next phase where you leave and do checks every five minutes. You have to find your own comfort level. If you don't want to skip ahead to the checks, explain that if he gets back into bed, you will tuck him in. Climb over the gate, give him a quick tuck-in, and then go back to the hallway. If he keeps demanding more tuck-ins until you reach the exasperation point, just stay in the hallway without any more tucking in. Stay there until he falls asleep, which may well be on the floor near the gate. You can move him to his bed once he is sleeping soundly; children usually give this up reasonably quickly. Use your intuition and your knowledge of your child's temperament to figure out which works best.

Sometimes even children who have successfully gone through the Shuffle and learned bedtime independence regress a little. Maybe their routine was thrown off, or they have been sick, or they experienced one of those normal little spikes of fear or insecurity. Don't go back to square one and return to whatever prolonged and convoluted bedtime techniques you had used before the Shuffle. Instead, return to the sitting-in-the-doorway or hall stage, where your child can see you. That allows you to be present and comforting, without abandoning all your progress. Stay there for two or three nights, then move on and complete the final steps of the Shuffle. It should go pretty smoothly. See Chapter 14, Routine Busters, for more advice.

With the lovey and an earlier bedtime, Helene and Larry did a great job of laying the groundwork for Barry's Shuffle, but they had to do some improvising. They carefully explained to Barry that they had met the "Sleep Lady" and she had helped them make new sleep rules. They made a sleep manners chart and told him they were going to do a better job now of helping him sleep. He was very forgiving. "I am not mad at you for not teaching me how to put myself to sleep," he said sympathetically.

Larry took on most of the sleep coaching because Barry associated his hair twirling and co-sleeping with Helene. (If Helene tried to do the Shuffle, Barry would just get out of bed and giggle.) But Barry didn't like the Shuffle. If his dad wasn't going to engage him in his room, he didn't want him there. "Go away," he demanded, and he meant it. This is a great example of how a couple blended my framework with their instincts about their child. They skipped to the second part of the Shuffle, Larry sitting by the doorway in Barry's view for a few days, then out of sight in the hall, then "job checks." It went pretty well. Sometimes he would regress and get out of bed looking for one of them or asking for his bottle. But most of the time he fell asleep and stayed asleep.

◊ ◊ ◊

Before working with me, it would take an hour and a half or two hours of all sorts of acrobatics to get Ilan to sleep, and then he would wake up repeatedly at night, often every hour or two. Through the Sleep Lady Shuffle and improvements to the household evening routine (difficult when both parents work irregular hours and there's a much older sibling who needs help with math homework while his baby brother needs a bath), Ilan's bedtime improved extremely quickly, and the night wakenings diminished. He also started napping great for his babysitter, and okay for his mom, despite having given up all but an occasional catnap when he was only ten months old. But it took a very long time to get his night wakenings to go away completely. Joanne, who was always quite tears-averse in the middle of the night, partly because sustained crying just made it harder for both Ilan and her to get back to sleep, kept trying to shrink nighttime intervention. She cut back and cut back until she was just sitting in the hallway and saying "sh-sh." Although Ilan was an extremely cheerful child without any unusual separation angst, it was very hard for him to give up that one middle-of-the-night Mom sighting. She just continued telling him he had to stay asleep in his own fire truck bed, and devising new incentives as he got older and understood more. She would finally get him sleeping all night, sometimes for several blissful weeks, but then each time he ran a fever, got an ear infection, or the family traveled for even a weekend, he'd get thrown off again. This continued to be a very stubborn pattern with Ilan. Sometimes retraining him would take just a day or two but sometimes it took a few weeks. Interestingly, when his much-loved babysitter moved on and he started preschool—child care at two years and ten months, his sleep improved dramatically. Lots of kids regress when they start school or have a change in care. Ilan, in contrast, equated preschool with a new independence that carried into his sleep. This worked for two solid months—until the next break in his routine.

PROBLEMS AND SOLUTIONS

Many experts who subscribe to the crying-it-out approach to sleep training contend that once children learn how to fall asleep by themselves at bedtime, they somehow magically start sleeping all night. I think we have to help them make that magic by addressing their night wakenings, giving them a consistent message as we go through the Sleep Lady Shuffle. In this section I give you specific techniques for helping toddlers let go of their sleep crutches. If we address bedtime and night wakenings consistently, most children do start sleeping through the night by the time they finish the Shuffle, although it sometimes takes a little longer if patterns have been ingrained since birth. Occasionally I find toddlers and preschoolers like Ilan who easily acquire new bedtime sleep skills but nevertheless have a harder time applying them in the middle of the night. Keep watching for negative associations—the bottle, the pacifier, a music tape you had running at 7:00 p.m. but don't have on at 4:00 a.m. Rule out any medical factors (see Chapter 13) and make sure she is going to bed early enough, sleeping late enough, and napping enough during the day. Overtired children wake up more at night.

Think about whether you are putting her to bed when she is a little too drowsy. She may not be getting enough opportunity to learn how to put herself back to sleep at night. Put her to bed when she is a tad more alert (See Drowsy but Awake, on pages 20–21) so she can become more adept at falling asleep on her own at bedtime or in the middle of the night.

When a child does wake up and cry at night, either because you haven't totally eliminated all night wakenings through the Shuffle or because your child is backsliding a bit, I believe parents should respond quickly. That helps reassure her, and makes her feel safe, secure, and listened to. It lets you serve as her "secure base," to use the vocabulary of the attachment theorists. It's also much easier on you, the parent. By going to her, you can reassure yourself that she hasn't gotten sick, her foot isn't stuck in a crib slat, the blanket isn't around her neck, the diaper isn't soaked, her socks haven't "whoopsed," as Ilan used to say when his slipped off. You can make sure her lovey is in reach. If she absolutely positively needs to be picked up, or hugged, then pick her up or hug her but keep it brief and put her back down as soon as she is calm. The goal is to get her back to sleep—not to have her scream herself wide awake. Hysterics make everyone feel bad, and it's harder for both the child and the parent to get back to sleep. But you have a few choices as to exactly how you respond, striking a balance between what feels right to you as a parent and what helps your child learn to sleep. You can:

- Sit by her side or in a chair in her room and comfort her. Don't lie down with her. Try to soothe her with loving sounds and phrases more than with patting and touching. However, if you sense that she is continuing to wake up one or more times every night in order to get you there, if just seeing you has become her sleep crutch, which is often the case, you'll have to back off a bit. Maybe sit in the hallway instead.

· Go to her room quickly to calm and reassure her, then sit in the doorway or hallway until she falls asleep again or gets drowsy enough for you to leave without setting off more tears.

· Go to quickly reassure her but then return to your own room.

· Let her cry if you think she'll get herself back to sleep quickly and you are comfortable with this approach. I've found that families usually know instinctively if and when they've reached that point where the child does a better job of getting herself back to sleep after a spurt of tears than they do when they rush in to rescue her. But in most cases, if the child could get herself back to sleep you would know it by now!

Whichever method you choose, remember to interact as little as possible, and keep it soft and gentle. Don't scold. If your child is getting out of bed, walk her back to bed, tuck her in, and then choose one of the above strategies.

> Sheila and Randy's daughter, Suzanna, was two years and four months old when they consulted me. She had been going to bed quite easily and independently since early infancy—but she was still waking up three times most nights. "She just wanted to say 'Hi, Mom,'" Sheila said. Usually all Sheila had to do was go in and sit there for a moment or two and give her a pat, but it still disrupted everyone's sleep. Ignoring her to see if she could fall asleep again on her own made matters worse. "She'd cry more and more. She was still in her crib then, and she'd be standing and would not sit down. Once it escalated, it would take much more time to get her back to sleep. She'd want to get out of her crib, we'd have to rock her, and then we'd put her down but she'd wake up again."
>
> Working with me, Sheila learned that Suzanna was too tired to sleep! We worked on her naps and her early-morning wakenings, using methods I will share with you later in this chapter. Sheila also realized it was time to get her daughter off a nighttime milk bottle, and when she got a little older and moved to a bed, they made sure she knew how to reach the water cup, tissues, pacifier, and teddy bear, right by her bed. Suzanna was old enough to understand the new sleep rules that Randy and Sheila repeated to her over and over again, day and night, and she loved her sticker chart.

When Suzanna woke up at night, one parent would go to her bedroom door and just say, "You need to lie down." They would reward her with a sticker in the morning when she put herself back to sleep. As she made up for her lost sleep, she became less dependent on seeing Mom at night. Her awakenings became less frequent, and then stopped. (See more about the sticker chart in Chapter 9, Two and a Half to Five Years Old.)

Eliminating Nighttime Feeding

A bedtime snack or milk will not prolong or improve children's sleep at this age. To the contrary, it may actually disrupt sleep by making them seek a cup, breast, or bottle every time they stir all night. That said, many kids do still have the nighttime milk habit, possibly because we as parents were so concerned about getting that last meal in them as infants that we haven't let go of it now that they are toddlers. In those cases, feeding and sleeping patterns may still be closely entwined. Let's talk first about the nursers and then we'll address those who take their nightcap in a cup or bottle.

There's a subtle but important difference between nursing at bedtime and nursing to sleep. Some moms breastfeed until age two or older, and bedtime may be the nursing time they hold on to the longest. Avoid letting your child fall asleep at the breast. Either nurse until he's drowsy but still awake and then put him down or, better yet at this age, nurse him as part of the bedtime ritual but not as the last activity. In other words nurse, and then brush teeth, play a quiet game, read a book, or sing a song. Do something to create a little space between nursing and sleep. Try keeping a light on while you nurse, so he is less likely to link breast-feeding with conking out.

With cups and bottles, you want to move from a bottle to a cup, from milk to water, from in bed to shortly before bed. How fast you make those changes depends on your temperament and your child's, but your end point is a cup of water before lights out. (Or no drink at all, eventually, but you don't have to push that.) Some kids switch in a day if you explain it to them, no problem. Others take it slower and may resist a little, but even a gradual transition should not take more than a week to ten days. The more they resist, the more emotionally attached they were to the cup or bottle.

If he now takes a bottle of milk at bedtime, switch to a cup, and when he adjusts to the cup, switch the milk to water. Alternatively, cut the amount of milk in the bottle in half before you switch to a cup, and then make the switch from milk to water. Give the cup at story time, not after lights are out. Don't give him any milk during the night, neither in a cup nor a bottle. You can give

him a cup of water if he's really fussy. Once you weaken the food-sleep association at bedtime, night wakenings often—not always but often—stop by
themselves. Once some toddlers realize they aren't going to get milk anymore,
they don't bother waking up at night for water. However, if your child keeps
waking up despite these bedtime beverage shifts, help him adjust his internal
hunger clock. Encourage him to eat more at regular daytime meals. But you'll
probably also have to tackle the nighttime awakenings more directly.

At this age, the best tactic is usually to stop the night feedings. Comfort
the child when he wakes up wanting the breast, cup, or bottle. Explain at
bedtime, or even during the day for a few days before you make the change,
that he is a big boy now and no longer needs his milk at night. (Children at
this age generally need two or three servings of milk or dairy products a day.
Check with your pediatrician.) Tell him he is going to sleep better and feel
better if he doesn't wake up for milk anymore and that Mommy and Daddy
are going to be very proud of him. When he does wake up wanting that
dairy fix, go to his room. "Sh-sh" him, stroke him a bit, even pick him up for
a moment for a big, deep, comforting hug. Keep encouraging that bond with
the lovey, to replace the bottle. Then put him back down and stay quietly
in his room until he falls asleep again. If you want to try more gradual
approaches, check out the techniques I recommend for younger babies, age
six to eight months, in Chapter 5. They sometimes work at this age but you
may find that you'll need a more direct approach. But you'll be surprised at
how fast they adapt. (If you need help moving from a bottle to a cup, see
page 112.)

*Ilan had reflux as an infant and stayed on a newborn-style feeding
schedule for months, since he could only hold down small amounts of food
at a time and therefore continued to eat small, frequent meals pretty much
around the clock. Even after the reflux diminished—his was pretty severe
until ten months and some problems lingered until he was almost three—
milk at night had become a deeply-ingrained pattern. His parents
switched him to water, but it didn't stop his night wakenings. And his
bedtime water cups, much more than his stuffed bear, were his nighttime
security objects. A stickler for symmetry, he clutched one cup in each fist to
go to bed, and called them his "one-two cups." He needed water each time
he woke up at night, often four or five times a night even as he approached
age two. Joanne tried every gradual technique she and I could think of.
Finally she realized she had to just take away the water, not at bedtime,
but in the middle of the night. He cried and protested and got mad at her*

but she sat with him and cuddled and soothed him, maybe a little more than she should. He gave up the night water in three nights.

Every few months, he would wake up demanding his water again. With a two-year-old it was hard to tell whether he was regressing and wanting the one-two-cup security again, or whether he was genuinely thirsty after a little too much soy sauce in his broccoli that night. He also asked for water when he was sick. If he was quite insistent, and Joanne couldn't be 100 percent sure if she was dealing with a dry throat or a security pang, she'd usually give him the water. The next night, if he slept through, she knew she'd made the right call, that he really had been thirsty. But if he started the whole cycle all over again, getting up seeking his one-two cups, she knew she'd been outsmarted and she'd have to tackle it again. Sometimes a little gentle coaxing would suffice or she could distract him with the lovey. But sometimes she would have to force the issue again. Each time she dreaded it but it was always easier than she had anticipated, and it got easier each time they had to go through this drill. He would wake up and cry or yell at her once or twice, but that was it: no more plaintive cries at 3:00 a.m. for "More water, Mommy." While she addressed the middle-of-the-night drinking, she never tried to flat-out break the bedtime water habit, because it never caused significant problems. At three, he learned to leave an ounce or two in his cup and entrust one of his stuffed animals to "hold" it in case he wanted it later.

Phasing Out Walking and Rocking to Sleep

Many of us walk and rock our newborns to sleep, but after eighteen or twenty-four or thirty months, it gets a little old—and they get very heavy. I often use the Sleep Lady Shuffle to break this association at bedtime. If they get rocked in the middle of the night, but not at bedtime, explain to your child that you will sit in his room and help him get himself back to sleep but you won't rock him anymore. Then gradually phase yourself out of the room as in the Shuffle. We aren't eliminating cuddles, we are just eliminating cuddles as a sleep crutch. You can have your child nestle into your lap while you read stories or sing songs with the lights on. But don't let him fall asleep in your arms or your lap, he must fall asleep in his own bed.

At twenty-one months, Madison, as her mother, Beth, put it, "had every bad sleep habit in the book." They had a nice sensible 7:30 p.m. bedtime, but then it all fell apart. Beth and Vince would have to rock, walk, or "bounce around" with her for about forty-five minutes every night to get her to sleep. She also demanded milk in bed, and insisted that her mom stay with her to get her to sleep. Like Barry, she had a thing about twirling her mom's hair, but rejected all the substitutes her mom offered, including Groovy Girl dolls with yarn hair, and blankets with fringe. She would wake up after three hours, and her parents would have to rock her for another forty-five minutes. Three hours later, when she woke up again, they were usually too tired to deal with another rocking marathon so Beth usually ended up sleeping with Madison. But Beth did not get much sleep with a child who wriggled and moved all the time, and she missed sleeping with her husband. A professional counselor who worked with teens, Beth knew a lot about what was wrong but didn't know how to make it right. She had tried Ferber when Madison was eight months old, with fairly good results. But when Madison got thrown off after being sick for a few days some months later, they were never able to get her back on track. A second attempt at Ferber failed dismally. Madison screamed for hours and instead of crying herself to sleep, she would throw up.

Before we started the Shuffle, Beth switched Madison from milk to water at bedtime and stopped lying down with her to get her to sleep. She also made sure to keep her head out of hair-twirling reach. On the nights Vince put Madison to bed, long hair wasn't an issue.

They moved through the Shuffle quickly, changing every two days instead of three because Madison was easily ritualized. "She's one of those kids that if she sits in a certain chair when she watches a certain TV show, she has to sit in that same chair every time she watches that show," her mom explained. They didn't want her to get used to having a parent seated in a specific position and then get upset at the change on the fourth night. At first she still woke up once or twice at night, but all she needed now was for Vince to sit in her room for a few minutes. She didn't scream, she didn't request milk, and she didn't demand her rocking and snuggling. Her night awakenings did not go away 100 percent, but they became briefer and much less frequent.

Pacifier Withdrawal

If your child's pacifier habit interferes with his sleep, particularly if he wakes up calling you to fetch it, the time may well have come to break the habit. Many pediatricians agree this is a good age to deal with it. Unfortunately I haven't found any sweet and gentle ways to do this (although I do have a backup plan for the squeamish). Tell him it's time to give up the binkie, paci, or Nuk, whatever he knows it as. Give him a little while to get used to the idea, and then pick a day to act. When he fusses or cries, calm him, soothe him, pat him, stroke him. Expect a few rough nights and naps. Make sure you work on strengthening his bond with his lovey. "It's not paci time but Teddy Bear is here and wants to hug you." That both distracts him from the pacifier and provides a security substitute. Better yet, try getting him a brand-new lovey as you take away the pacifer; the newness might further distract him. You could even try taking him shopping and letting him choose his own new bedtime pal. If he's old enough, read some books about children who get rid of pacifiers, such as *The Story of Binkyland* (at www.binkyland.com) or *The Last Noo-Noo*. Some pediatricians have advised parents to keep cutting the tip of the pacifier more and more until it's so mutilated the child no longer wants it. And I know one mom who had her son put it inside a Build-A-Bear and he slept with the bear! Whatever you do, once you send it away or give it away or throw it away, don't go out and buy another one after an hour of whining.

> *Sheila tried to get Suzanna to bond to a security blanket and encouraged the little girl to put all her pacifiers in a nice bright-colored envelope to send to a family friend's new baby. It worked brilliantly—for one whole day. Then Suzanna wanted her pacifiers back, and in an uncharacteristic moment of intermittent reinforcement, Sheila gave in and decided not to press the pacifier issue at this time. Suzanna never did bond to that blanket, and Sheila may have made it harder to get rid of the pacifier the next time she tries.*

Lots and lots of parents do not feel comfortable taking away the pacifier, preferring to wait and see if he gives it up on his own. There's a good chance you will have to take it away eventually but if you aren't ready now, I would restrict the pacifier to bedtime and nap time. Don't let him keep carrying it around all day. He's old enough to find it by himself by now if you put several pacifiers in his crib or bed with him, or in a little basket within reach. He should be able to grab one, and get back to sleep without calling for you. The first few nights, you might have to remind him from the doorway to reach for it himself. Don't get it for him—or if you do get it for him a few times, put it in his hand, and let him then put it in his mouth. Don't keep doing this; remind him at bedtime that he has to find it himself and if necessary show him again where it will be. You should still encourage the lovey; it is really more useful for him to hold on to at night than the pacifier and will eventually help him give up the pacifier.

Early Birds

Early rising, at 5:00 or 5:30 a.m., remains very common at this age, and children who get up very early are often exhausted and fussy by midmorning. It may sound counterintuitive, but early rising is often caused by a late bedtime. Rather than being up bright and early because they are so ready to start their day, they are actually sleep deprived! The first thing you should do is get him to bed earlier. Shift bedtime a few minutes earlier each day, so that the child is going to bed between 7:00 and 8:00 p.m., which for most children remains a good target bedtime up until around age five. Make sure he is napping enough. If early awakenings have been going on for months or even years, as is sometimes the case with children this age, it may take three to four weeks to change it. Some families—not many, but some—have found that it has taken a few months until the child sleeps in consistently. Parental consistency is hugely important. *Consistency,* in this context, means utter consistency and a little more rigidity than other aspects of my program. Intermittent reinforcement at 5:00 a.m. is just not a good idea. Some parents give up trying to teach the child to sleep later, and instead are satisfied if they get him to stay in his room and play quietly until 6:00. That might work in some cases, but usually children do better and get less tired during the day if you can get them to sleep that extra half hour or hour.

Respond quickly when he wakes and calls for you. Letting him stew or scream will only make him more awake, while your goal is to teach him how to stay asleep. Go to him, saying "It is not time to wake up" or "Mommy and Daddy are sleeping." Don't turn on the light or raise the blinds. Give him his lovey and reassure him, including a hug if that's needed, but don't pick him up. With younger babies, I give the parents the option of staying in the room. At this age, it's usually better if you leave because your presence will probably stimulate him into trying to stay awake. Check on him every fifteen or twenty minutes, until he falls asleep again. If he comes out of the room looking for you, take him back to his bed. Promise you will check on him soon. If he gets out again and again, consider putting a gate on the door. You might want to sit or lie just on the other side of the gate, a compromise between leaving him alone and staying in the room. Children will sometimes end up falling asleep on the floor near the gate. Don't worry about it; he'll be fine there. You are working on changing his internal wake-up clock, and when that occurs he'll naturally prefer his comfy bed to the hard floor.

If you really feel you need to stay in the room, go ahead and try it. But your child may get more riled up if you do stay but refuse to get him out of bed or ignore what is certain to be his very determined attempts to engage you in conversation or activity. If he's still in his crib, you might need to stroke or soothe him. But just like bedtime, do it sporadically, every few minutes, so he doesn't get dependent on it. If he's out of the crib, he may try to come over to you and clamber onto your lap. Try a deep-pressure hug for a moment or two, then put him back in bed and return to your chair. He may need a little stroking or soothing, but once again, do it sporadically. Don't lie down with him or touch, sing, or pat him completely to sleep. You may have to experiment for a few days to see which approach works best for your family, but do consider leaving the room.

Ideally, he will fall asleep again, and if you are lucky you can get some more sleep too. But often he will stay awake—and probably complain about it loudly. Keep him in bed, or at least in a dark room, until 6:00 a.m. When I say 6:00, I mean 6:00. I don't mean 5:50 or 5:40, or else you'll find that the wake-up time keeps getting earlier and earlier and you aren't making any progress. At 6:00 a.m., if you are in his room, go out for a minute or two and then come back. If you are already out of the room, then 6:00 is the time to return. (If he's asleep, don't wake him, and if he's awake but quietly content you can wait until a little later than 6:00.) Go in and have a *dramatic wake-up* to start the day. Make a big deal about turning on the light and opening the shades. Or let your child turn on the lights with you. Sing a cheerful good-morning song. Basically, you want to have a good-morning ritual, just like you have a bedtime ritual, although the morning one is more stimulating, of course. You want to convey the message that it's time for him to wake up because it's morning, not because he was crying or whining for you.

At some point in this age range, usually as they approach two and a half, try using the clock in one of several ways. Instead of having your child mad at you, blame the clock! "The clock says it's not time to wake up yet, sweetie, you need to stay in bed until the clock says get up." You might be able to teach him to recognize 6:00 on a digital clock, and not get out of bed or call for you until he sees that number. A variant is to set a musical alarm for 6:00, and tell the child that if he wakes up before the music starts, he has to stay in bed. These clock-related approaches are all a little hit or miss at this age; some kids get it and others don't until they are three or four. Once you get him sleeping until 6:00, you can try to push it back to 6:15 or 6:30 using the same techniques, but it may or may not work—6:00 is a natural and common wake-up time for young children. Many early risers will begin to sleep later on their own in another year or two but there's no guarantee. Some tend to wake on the early side throughout childhood but will develop the ability to sleep in a little on occasions when they've gotten to bed late.

> *Suzanna woke up much too early, sometimes at 4:30 a.m. Sheila and Randy tried several strategies and finally settled on the clock radio. When she awoke early, they gave her a very precise and consistent message. "We'd go in briefly and say we aren't coming to get you until the music is on your radio. It's still dark out and Mommy and Daddy are sleeping." Over the next few months, as she became a better nighttime sleeper and napper, her mornings steadily improved. She stayed in bed until she heard her music, and later did not need the radio, sleeping until about 7:00 a.m. on her own. When she gets a little off track, for instance after an illness or the time changes in Spring and Fall, her parents return to the clock radio for a few days. As she slept later in the morning, she awoke less frequently at night.*

In many families, the toddler wakes up at 6:00 a.m. cheerful and happy—but the parent accustomed to sleeping until 7:00 or 8:00 is grumpy and not so happy. You can try training him to sleep later if you want, using the techniques I outline above for children who wake up too early. But you might have to accept it for a year or two more, and try to get to bed earlier yourself. You can also try to teach him to stay in his room and play quietly or look at a book until you come to get him. Reward him if he does, but don't be mad or punitive if he doesn't. It's a hard skill to learn at this age. He wants to see Mom and Dad after being away from you all night, and he may also be hungry, wet, or in need of a little help reaching that bathroom light.

If he wakes up at 6:00 but is cranky and irritable by 6:30 or 7:00, then he is getting up too early. Consider it a sign of sleep deprivation, and use the advice above for early risers to train him to sleep for another half hour or hour. Make sure he gets to sleep between 7:00 and 8:00 at night, and that he naps enough during the day.

> *Sometimes, your child is not an early riser until you embark on a sleep-coaching program. Before Joanne and Ken started working with me, Ilan woke up consistently between 5:00 and 5:30 a.m. demanding a bottle of milk or later a cup of water. Usually Ken, who had an easier time*

getting back to sleep at that hour than Joanne, would fetch him, Joanne would give him his cup, and they would all go back to sleep in the family bed. Ilan would then sleep until 7:00 or 7:30, sometimes later. When we started sleep shaping, his bedtime got much easier, his napping improved and his night sleep got significantly better, but the early risings got worse. That was very hard on Joanne. He would get up at 5:00, and she would sit in his bedroom instead of letting him come into her bed. She stayed in the room—he would work himself up into incredibly intense crying if she left—and sometimes she could get him back to sleep and sometimes she couldn't. Joanne's own body clock never adjusted to a 5:00 a.m. wakening. She was one of those people who could function if she woke up at 6:00 but was a complete wreck if she was up at 5:00. Yet she had trouble getting back to sleep herself if she was up and around at 5:00; some switch in her brain was activated and wouldn't turn itself off. Sometimes Ilan fell asleep again; often he didn't, and he could make it a pretty unpleasant hour, demanding to get up and she trying to just gently get him back to sleep without responding to his determined provocation. After three months, she tried letting him sleep with her after 5:00 in a guest bed in his room. That worked for both of them for a few days. Then he started waking up three, four, or five times a night again, demanding that they both get in the "big bed, a guest bed nearby." This is very common—and precisely why I warn you not to lie down with your child in the morning. Joanne gave up the morning snuggle, and went back to sitting in the room and trying to calm him. Finally he reset his body clock and began sleeping until 6:00 or 6:30 most of the time. And on those days he still woke at 5:00, he found it easier to get back to sleep.

About six months later, he began waking up at 5:00 again after the family's schedule had been disrupted by both travel and illness. She tried sitting in his room with him but was so exhausted that she just fell asleep in the "big bed" and he climbed in with her. He was older now, though, about two years and eight months. She very painstakingly explained that this was a special almost-morning big-bed snuggle but that the rest of the time Ilan had to stay in his fire truck bed. He had the language skills and the cognitive ability to get this abstract idea. Once or twice when he woke up in the middle of the night and said, "Big-bed snuggle," she said, "No, Ilan, go back to your fire truck bed, it's not time for our special almost-morning big-bed snuggle yet." It worked. He didn't wake up at night demanding her (at least not until the next time he got sick) and when he did wake up at 5:00 or 5:30, he'd call for her, they'd both stumble into the big bed and get back to sleep quickly. This helped get him an extra hour or two of sleep a day, shielding him from that spiral of overtiredness that causes more early rising. He began sleeping until 6:15 or 6:30 most of the time. On those days he still woke up earlier, they could both get back to sleep quickly. All of a sudden, in late summer, he began sleeping until 7:00 or even 7:30 and once even until 8:15. Naturally that was exactly one week before big brother Zach started middle school, meaning the whole family had to be up at 6:00 or 6:30 and now had to tiptoe around and sacrifice using the coffee grinder to avoid waking up Ilan!

Napping

Most children this age have consolidated to one nap a day, or will do so shortly. Usually, they nap from roughly one to three in the afternoon. As you no doubt know, napping can be difficult for children, just as it is difficult for many adults to sleep during daylight. They need plenty of time to change gears, to get ready for rest. You should have a whole routine, shorter in duration but similar to the bedtime routine. Quiet stories or songs in his room are good pre-nap activities.

Children this age still need naps, even if they think they don't. You may have to train them—which as I've said before is my least favorite aspect of sleep shaping. (See Chapter 5, Six to Eight Months, for details of nap-training techniques.) Get the child ready for his nap, and then put him in his room and have him stay there for an hour, whether he falls asleep or not. Stay with him, sit right outside his door, or check on him every ten or fifteen minutes or so, whichever feels right to you as the parent. But don't engage or converse, try not to pick him up, and do make him try to stay in bed or at least in his room, for the full hour. (If he's already switched from crib to bed, you might have to gate the door. One mom who hated gates would read a book in the room across the hall from her son's room. If he came out, she'd meet him in the hallway and immediately walk him back to bed.) If your child still hasn't fallen asleep after an hour, do a dramatic wake-up and get him out. But then use an emergency backup system, such as a drive in the car, to get him to sleep. Motion sleep is not the most restful sleep, but it's better than no sleep while you are nap training. Try again to get him to nap the next day. Use nap stickers, logic, bribes, whatever it takes, but keep him in that room and coax him to sleep. Sometimes the child will learn to sleep for a parent but not a babysitter who may not be willing to do her share of the training. Sometimes the reverse is true, and the child naps angelically for the sitter, saving the napping power struggles for Mom.

Getting him to sleep may only be half the battle. Some kids won't stay asleep. Catnapping, though more common with younger babies, can still occur at this age. That's when a child takes several naps, each less than forty-five minutes. That's not a complete sleep cycle and it's not refreshing. You want him to sleep about two hours (a little less by age two and a half). If he wakes up after thirty or forty-five minutes, go to his crib or bed and reassure him but don't let him get up. Tell him it's still nap time and he has to stay in his bed. Stroke him a little if that helps him get back to sleep. Don't get him out of his crib or room for at least an hour, whether he falls asleep again or not.

If he sleeps longer than a thirty-minute catnap, but his naps are still on the skimpy side, use these techniques to try to get him back to sleep. You want to stretch those naps out to ninety minutes or more, particularly if he still seems tired. On days when your child does not nap enough, try the backup nap plan and if he falls asleep late in the day, wake him after forty-five minutes or by 4:00 p.m. Get him to bed early, around 7:00.

Nap training is often very hard on the parent, usually the mom, who is home without the assistance or moral support of her husband at that time of day. And even for those parents who cope with tears in daylight better than they do at night, nap training can seem incredibly time consuming, and you'll have to stick around the house at nap time. If nap training is absolutely too much for you—or a child care provider—then give yourself permission to give up for now. Keep using your backup temporary solutions so you don't have such an overtired child that bedtime falls apart again. Try nap training again in a few months.

Helene began a more disciplined approach to napping, including paying more attention to Barry's sleep window, catching him when he was tired but not too tired. Before, she had spent a good chunk of her day lying down with Barry, trying to get him to sleep. Sometimes she would put him in the car. Now, she would not lie down with him and she made him stay in his room for an hour. Sometimes she would then have to take him for a drive, but he didn't wake up when she moved him into his bed. Gradually he adjusted to a better daytime sleep routine except when Larry, whose job running a restaurant meant erratic hours, was home. Barry would resist napping if it meant missing a minute of Daddy time. On those days, Helene and Larry tried to get him down but resorted to taking him for a drive if they saw he was determined to stay up. Getting him to sleep was more important than being a purist about how he slept. "If he misses naps for two or three days he gets sick, and even he has begun to understand that," Helene said.

○ ○ ○

Madison was another recalcitrant napper. She hated it if her mother left the room before she fell asleep, and would cry hard enough to keep herself awake. So Beth stayed with her, and if Madison started to get out of bed, Beth would tell her to lie down again or else Mommy would leave. That usually worked and she would fall asleep. Some disruptions in her schedule—a cross-country move, a stay at her grandmother's house during renovations on her new home—disrupted naps. Later her preschool schedule also posed an obstacle. If she missed her 1:00 p.m. get-ready-for-nap window, she often failed to sleep. But on the days she attended preschool, she didn't get home until after 1:00. By the time she had a snack and settled down, it was 2:30. Either she couldn't fall asleep by then, or if she napped it was so late that it threw off the rest of her schedule and she was even worse the next day. On those afternoons, Beth did enforce quiet rest time, which wasn't as good as a nap at that age but it did help her keep it together. "If she doesn't nap, she gets cranky at about five, but it's a fifteen-minute meltdown and then she's okay until bedtime," her mother said. Beth was also diligent about getting Madison to bed early on no-nap days.

○ ○ ○

Suzanna's nap was a challenge for Sheila too, and it got even worse when she switched to a bed before turning three. This little girl had no intention of napping, and even less intention of staying in bed for a nap she wasn't going to take. Sheila tried gating the room but said, "It made her more upset than it was worth." Instead Sheila allowed Suzanna to play in her room, while Sheila shut the door and read a magazine in the hallway. If Suzanna came out in pursuit, Sheila would calmly tell her to go back into her room or else Mommy wouldn't sit so close anymore.

"I couldn't force her to nap, so I let her play in her room. Sometimes she would just conk out on the floor," her mom said. As Suzanna got accustomed to napping, maybe even understanding on some level that her body needed it, she gave up on the floor and went to bed. Again, the better rested she was by day, the better she slept by night.

Co-sleeping

Lots of families who co-sleep decide that they've had enough at this age, and the Shuffle can help end the practice. Similarly, some families who never planned on co-sleeping find their toddler in their bed now that he's old enough to wander in on his own. Co-sleeping is so complex that I've devoted a separate chapter to it (Chapter 10, Co-sleeping and the Family Bed). Please refer to that if you've been co-sleeping since birth and want to stop, or if you've been taking your child into bed for all or part of the night because you think it's the only way you can get him to sleep. For those of you who choose to continue co-sleeping, that chapter gives you some tips on how to improve the quality and quantity of sleep in a shared bed.

Joel's Story

Remember Joel, the boy who wouldn't drink milk in a cup from Mom? I met Dorothy and Jack when Joel was nineteen months old. He was their first child, although he had a much older half-sister from Jack's first marriage who lived with them part-time. Joel had never been a great sleeper, partly because he had frequent ear infections as an infant and Dorothy rocked and held him to sleep when he was sick. They had tried to let him cry it out, but he'd throw up if he cried too much, which was not exactly a soothing and sleep-promoting experience. Dorothy and Jack had agreed early not to co-sleep but at about sixteen months, an exhausted Dorothy, who was also dealing with guilt about being a working mom with a long commute to her engineering job, started bringing Joel into the family bed some of the time. Musical beds didn't solve the sleep problems and it created marital friction. A move to a new house, job changes, and business travel for Jack added to the stress.

"We started a bad pattern. I felt guilty being back at work and I compensated a lot. I'd come home, and I was tired and Jack was away, and Joel would get sick and I'd just take him into bed. I thought it would be just for a few days, but I couldn't reverse it; if I put him in his crib, he'd just cry and cry. And I tried letting him cry but he'd throw up. And if he did fall asleep, he'd be up again in an hour and a half. Plus he needed a bottle all the time," said Dorothy, who as you recall, was also very worried about his small size and nutrition.

Dorothy also disliked schedules. "I'd come home late, I was tired, I wanted some wind-down time, I wanted to be with my baby. I didn't want to walk in and have it be bedtime." She didn't like watching the clock or worrying about when to go upstairs. She often made an attempt to get him to sleep early with a bottle but if that didn't work, she carried him around with her until trying another bottle around 10:00 p.m.

I helped Dorothy understand a little bit about sleep cycles and hormones, which made it easier for her to start keeping a closer eye on the clock and on Joel's sleep signs. She also realized it was finally time to give up the bottle, which was far easier than she imagined; Joel didn't need it as much as she thought he did, or maybe as much as she needed to give it to him. We began the Sleep Lady Shuffle, concentrating those first few nights on putting him into his crib while he was drowsy but still slightly awake.

The first two nights were difficult and I'm not sure Dorothy would have stuck it out if she wasn't so afraid of admitting failure to Jack. Joel cried for more than an hour. But he didn't throw up; he never reached that point of complete hysteria. "He was crying but he wasn't completely inconsolable. It was different having me in there with him," Dorothy said. "He finally did fall asleep—people say babies can't fall asleep standing up but he did." Dorothy caressed him a little but was very mindful of my advice not to create any new sleep associations. "He would reach out to me—he still does. That was hard. He was reaching out and I wanted to hold and cuddle him, but I tried to comfort him with words." She also kept some calm music running in the background, but that wasn't a problem because music is a mood setter, not a sleep crutch, for Joel. It helps him prepare for sleep but he doesn't need it to stay asleep or get back to sleep at night.

The third night was much different, a good thing because the first two had been very hard on Dorothy. Joel cried briefly, but then fell asleep right away, this time lying down. I think part of the change was that Dorothy was getting much better at her new nighttime routine, at reading Joel's signals and getting him into the crib when he was "really, really drowsy but still awake." When she moved the chair farther away, he fussed a bit but not too much. He still woke up in the middle of the night, but as they went through the Shuffle they went in to quickly comfort him and then they could leave. "It wasn't an ordeal; he went back to sleep in his crib and we were able to go right back to sleep." Gradually, he woke up less frequently. He still wakes up now and then, but not most of the time.

Even when Joel's schedule was disrupted—when Dorothy regressed (sleeping with him for a few days when he had a high fever), when a job crisis meant an eighty-hour workweek, when Jack was on the road again and a frightening kook in the neighborhood was going around banging on everybody's doors at midnight—Dorothy managed to get Joel back into a good sound sleep routine in less than two weeks.

"I learned that if I wanted to cuddle with him, I could still do that, but while we read books, not while I was getting him to sleep. I learned the difference between a tired child and an overtired child," she said. "I learned that even if I hate routine and consistency, even if I find them difficult, Joel needs them."

TWO AND A HALF TO FIVE YEARS OLD

Please take a few minutes to read the first three chapters of my book, which give an overview of my system and include some helpful hints that apply to all age groups. It won't take long and you'll have much better results.

♻ ♻ ♻

BETWEEN AGES TWO AND THREE, *average sleep needs drop to about ten and a half hours a night, plus an hour-and-a-half afternoon nap. Four-year-olds need eleven and a half hours at night, and most no longer nap daily although they do need about forty-five minutes of quiet time each afternoon and possibly an occasional nap. Five-year-olds sleep about eleven hours a night and afternoon quiet time is still beneficial.*

Preschoolers still need a lot of sleep, but they are immensely clever at devising reasons not to get it. They stall and evade with amazing ingenuity, which for parents can be frustrating, or comical, or both. They engage in philosophical discussions worthy of a junior Socrates, and they voice enough curiosity to rival a little Einstein. "Why do bats fly at night?" "Was the sky always blue?" "What does God eat for breakfast?" Of course, none of these thoughts and questions hold any interest for them at 4:00 or 5:00 in the afternoon when they are busy playing, but become an all-consuming need to know as soon as they hear the word *pajamas*. I worked with one couple that dubbed their oldest daughter "Captain Loophole" for her brilliance in delaying bedtime.

Sleep shaping for this age group requires a mix of the techniques you are already familiar with from earlier chapters and new ones designed for older and more verbal children. As parents, we need to inject some discipline into bedtime but still keep it warm and cozy. We need to help them with those bouts of the scaries that can make bedtime difficult even when they aren't turning stalling into a competitive sport. As they begin to cut back and eventually outgrow their naps, we have to keep tinkering with their sleep and wake schedules and introduce afternoon quiet time unless we enjoy meltdowns before dinner. Solutions to ingrained problems that date back to infancy can take some time. You aren't going to undo four years of night wakening or pacifier dependency in three days, so keep in mind my advice about patience and consistency. If some new problems emerge at this age, like a demand that you lie down with her at bedtime, address it quickly, before it becomes a long-term ingrained behavior. Luckily, from about age three on, sometimes even a few months earlier, children understand on some level that they need sleep, that sleeping poorly is a problem, that you are upset about it. They can then become an ally in your attempt to change things and begin to "own" the solutions.

Among the children you will meet in this chapter are Cliff, whose sleep wasn't all that bad until he endured all sorts of changes and disruptions shortly before his third birthday; Ariella, who just didn't seem to get the idea that she wasn't supposed to wander all around the house in the middle of the night; Isabel, whose parents literally went through a song and dance to get her to sleep; and Sam, whose determination to get out of bed every night prompted his parents to put not one but two gates on his door—until he wore them out.

 DEVELOPMENTAL CHANGES

Separation Anxiety

Children this age often still experience lingering separation anxiety at bedtime, which is why so many of them demand that you lie down with them at bedtime or they'll wander out of bed looking for you. If they have basically sound sleep habits they can learn to settle down more easily with a lovey, a dim (four-watt) night-light, and some reassurance. A good, comforting bedtime routine is essential. Don't rush through it, but don't let him keep stalling, negotiating, and bending the rules. A promise to check on him again before you go to bed is very reassuring. And if you say you are going to check on him, make sure you really do. Children love it if you tell them how snuggly and cozy and peaceful and beautiful they look when they sleep. I think they take it as a confirmation that you really are checking on them and watching over them while they are asleep, that you aren't that far away, that they are as safe and sound as you promised.

Loveys

Preschoolers and kindergarteners shouldn't need to schlep around a security blanket, stuffed animal, or favorite toy wherever they go, barring perhaps exceptionally stressful or unfamiliar situations. But they are definitely not too old for a lovey at bedtime. To the contrary, I encourage it strongly. My own daughters both still have them. The lovey helps them cope with separation and nighttime fears. Some children are and always will be indifferent to loveys, but lots of kids will get attached now, even if they spurned one toy after another when they were younger. Include the lovey in your nighttime games, stories, and rituals. Be creative, and give your child a role in choosing her lovey. Go shopping together, or make a lovey together on your own or at a workshop at a local craft store. Some children switch alliances, first bonding to this bedtime toy, then latching on to that one. That's fine; it's their way of satisfying their own evolving tastes and needs. One little boy outgrew his baby lovey and started lining up all his macho action-hero toys around his bed to keep him safe at night. No monster would dare cross Spider-Man, Superman, and a big green Hulk!

If your child sleeps with the same lovey every night, make sure you tuck it in with her and say good night to them both. If she likes different loveys, let her make that night's selection pretty early in the routine or else it becomes another excuse for stalling at lights-out.

> *Each night Ariella would choose one of her baby dolls to sleep with. In a brilliant flash of intuition, Marcy used the doll to persuade Ariella to stay in bed. "I would remind her to stay in bed, and tell her that baby doll Rachel needs her. 'If you get up, baby Rachel won't have anyone to be with her.' That made Ariella feel good and strong."*

Many kids this age have some kind of self-soothing ritual that involves the parent. They may want to twirl Mom's hair (surprisingly common!). They might do something a little more eccentric, like poking fingers in Dad's belly button. Try to transfer this habit to a lovey. One mother of a hair twirler went to a fabric store and made a lovey out of satin with a tassel. Others have found stuffed animals, blankets, and dolls with fringes or other twirlable features. She may not accept the substitute immediately, but ease her into it. Let her do her little ritual, like the hair twirling, for a few minutes while you are reading good-night stories but then slowly start to move away, letting her gradually hold the lovey instead.

New Mobility: Switching to the Big Bed

Most children move out of the crib by age three, although I don't personally think there's anything wrong with keeping a child in a crib until age four. If you'd like to try to keep him in a crib a little longer, particularly if he does not yet have the verbal skills to understand big-bed rules, review my tips on prolonging crib sleeping on page 164 in the previous chapter. You might try a mesh cover called a *crib tent*. Some kids hate them, but others stay in the crib a few extra months with the tent. But if your child is climbing out of his crib frequently and is also talking about wanting a "big boy" or "big girl" bed, make the switch. If you want to do it in several steps, start by leaving the crib railing down, with a stool at the side so he can get out by himself. You might want some extra pillows around on the floor for safety. You can either put a bed in his room with the crib or remove the crib and put the bed where the crib stood. You might want to put the bed in the corner of the room, so the child still has that sense of being safely contained. It's often a good idea to put up a bed rail so he doesn't fall out, and you might want to put some pillows or extra blankets on the floor to shield him if he does fall. Putting a gate on the bedroom door, at least at the beginning, is usually a good idea both as a training device and a safety measure. The gate delineates boundaries, helping a child understand that he has to stay in his bed. It also prevents him from wandering around and possibly getting hurt in a dark house in the middle of the night.

Let your child make a big deal about the transition to the big bed. Let him pick out some cool sheets. (No matter what design scheme you have in mind, there seems to be an inordinately high chance your little girl will want pink and purple and your little boy will want fire trucks. Just go with it.) Explain the privileges but also review the rules. Let him understand that you will still put him to bed, but then he's expected to stay there. Be consistent from day one. If he gets out of bed, take him right back without any fuss. Reward him for staying in bed. Give him lots of stickers and let him call his grandparents or aunts or cousins to brag about the new bed.

You met Suzanna, Sheila and Randy's daughter, in the previous chapter when she was a little past two, and still in her crib. Her sleep improved after I worked with them, but the little acrobat got very adept at scrambling out of her crib no matter what her parents tried. "Every morning we'd wake up and she'd be standing at the edge of our bed. It was farcical," her mom recalled. A few months before Suzanna turned three, she started showing lots of interest in "big girl" beds. She was sleeping well now, and had good language skills, so her parents decided she was ready for the switch.

"She knew a lot of her friends were in 'big girl' beds. When we went somewhere to play, she'd go to the 'big girl' bed to play, so I told her, 'You are getting your "big girl" bed.' We put pillows next to the bed in case she fell out, and I got sheets with purple butterflies and flowers. She was very excited to have her 'big girl' bed," said Sheila. Sheila explained the "big bed" rules very clearly and rewarded Suzanna with stickers for staying in her bed and not wandering out to look for her parents. The transition went very smoothly.

If you are about to embark on my Sleep Lady Shuffle or other major nighttime changes, like taking away a bottle or pacifier, consider whether it would be easier if you kept him in the crib a little longer. It keeps him in a safe and familiar environment while you are changing other aspects of his sleep, and it may be simpler if you don't have to worry about him getting up and out of bed while you are trying to teach him how to sleep in it. But I have also found that many of these older children do better if you change everything all at once. You give him the privilege of the new "big boy" bed, and incorporate the changed sleep expectations into the "big bed" rules. There's no right or wrong decision here, just trust your instincts about which approach is a better match for your child's temperament.

If your child, even up to age four, still likes the crib even with the railing down, leave it alone. You can bring up the topic occasionally. You can look at beds and sheets, but there's no rush unless, of course, your child's weight exceeds the crib's limit. He'll move when he's ready, and he'll be ready soon enough. Some families use toddler beds as an interim step but I don't see a need for it. If he really wants one, fine, but it's certainly not an essential investment. The one advantage is that they are usually too small for you to fit into alongside him, which children often demand when they move into a bed of their own.

Some preschoolers go through a phase when they don't want to sleep in their bed; they want to sleep or nap on a little couch, or a pad on the floor, or a beanbag chair, whatever. It may happen right after the transition from the crib, it may happen later. You can use some kind of system of rewards and incentives to lure him into the bed, such as reading his favorite story together in the bed, or giving him an extra backrub in bed, or something like that. Probe whether something in the bed is frightening him. Maybe he's afraid of falling off, in which case you can put extra pillows on the floor or get bed rails for the side. But I would ask myself if it's worth fussing over. If he's sleeping reasonably well in his room, I wouldn't worry about it and he'll probably move into the bed himself pretty quickly.

"I spent three hundred dollars on custom-installed, room-darkening shades to get my son to nap," one mother lamented. "He did begin napping again—but only on the living room couch in the brightest room in the house!"

Eating and Sleeping

Children this age should have a regular meal routine: three meals a day plus healthy snacks in the midmorning and midafternoon—after nap if they still take one. They just do not need a bottle anymore. Sucking on one at night is not good for their sleep, their teeth, or their overall nutrition. If you need help getting rid of it, review the nighttime feeding section later in this chapter. At bedtime, she can have a cup of water, but no milk or juice in bed. I'd prefer you give her the water during story and song time, not after lights out. If she makes you fill the water cup a zillion times at bedtime, set clear limits, explain them, and stick to them. You can leave a cup of water by her bedside overnight (I'd recommend a sippy cup or a sports bottle, not a baby bottle or an open cup, until she gets used to groping for it in the dark). But again, explain at bedtime that this has to last her all night; you aren't going to keep coming back to give her more. Remember how Joanne convinced her little boy to leave a few ounces in his nighttime water cup. Ilan gave it to a stuffed animal, his "backup lovey" who slept near his bed but not in it, to hold for him in case he needed it.

Stalling and Curtain Calls

That father who called his eldest daughter "Captain Loophole" pretty much summed it up. Children this age are brilliant procrastinators, and any separation anxiety or nighttime fears only hone their skills. The best defense is a sensible bedtime, a good routine, and the ability to gently disengage when they start to pepper you with all sorts of questions and requests. If your child wants you to tuck him in three hundred times, try to do it just once or twice. Tell him what you expect, when "last time" will be. Then stick to it. You can come back to his doorway in a few minutes to quickly praise him for understanding and following the bedtime directions. Once you've given him that dollop of praise and reassurance, leave before he starts trying to engage you all over again. Skip this step if it makes matters worse. Use your judgment. Put up a gate if he insists on coming out of bed a zillion times; he'll get the message. You can even tell him that if he stays in bed you'll be back in a few minutes to take down the gate.

Sometimes children know exactly which maternal anxiety button to push. I know one little boy who got out of bed and told his mother his tummy hurt. She was naturally solicitous and fussed over him a bit as she got him back to bed. A half hour later he wandered out again, this time declaring that his hair hurt!

> *"She stalls, stalls, stalls," Marcy said of Ariella. "She's so smart; she says she needs certain things and she chooses things that push my buttons. It all seems so rational to me, she asks for such normal things. I'll ask her if she really needs a glass of water, and she'll tell me she didn't get that toothpaste taste out of her mouth. She'll tell me she needs a new diaper, she has pee-pee and can't sleep, so I go back in and change her. She'll say she needs that fuzzy blanket, it's a lot warmer. I try to plan ahead, I try to think of what she'll need at bedtime and set her up for total success. But she always manages to think of one last thing."*

If a child says he is hungry, it's very hard for a parent to say no and then guiltily wonder if he was truly hungry. If he's a picky eater, or seems to have added epicurean demands to his stalling repertoire at bedtime, just firmly say, "No, you had dinner. We'll have breakfast when you wake up tomorrow." If it's a real aberration and you think he might genuinely be hungry, give him a quick, healthy snack but explain very carefully that you are doing this tonight but won't be doing it every night. The next night, consider a preemptive strike. Ask him if he needs a snack right before you start his bath and bedtime routine, and tell him he can have the snack now but not after bath and toothbrushing. Encourage enough eating during the day and have a sensible meal schedule.

The Scaries

Almost all children at some point in this age bracket experience vague fears in the evening: monsters, ghosts, shadows, or just things they can't quite put a name on. You need to acknowledge those fears, without allowing your child to turn them into an excuse to prolong bedtime, or to get out of bed repeatedly during the night. Try not to ridicule the fears. They aren't ridiculous to the child. Tell her that there are no monsters, and then show her there are no monsters. Spend a minute looking under the bed or in the closet, if that's what she needs you to do. You might hold hands and check together, unless that seems to intensify her fear. Make the lovey a part of the search team. The lovey can help you check the room and then snuggle into the child's arms and say, "See, everything is safe and sound. There are no monsters, bears, ghosts," whatever she fears.

> *"Wes has never mentioned being scared of monsters or ghosts but he's afraid of the dark. We use night-lights in his room, the hallway, adjacent bedroom, and bathroom. He also takes a lovey and Blackie the bear to bed always as security, which helps," Amanda said.*

> *At three and a half, Sam began saying he was afraid of voices outside. Nora thought he might be using it as a ploy to delay bedtime, but she gave him the benefit of the doubt. "We reassure him that we've locked and double checked all the doors, and that we are downstairs to keep anyone out. And when we're at my parents' house, we do the same thing and also tell him that their dogs won't let anyone in."*

Giving the child a physical prop to reassure himself can also help. Not a weapon, of course, but something he can see or hold or touch to know he will not be left at the mercy of the scaries. James, for instance, was a great sleeper but he started experiencing bedtime anxieties when he was three and a half. He was a small child with a very soft voice, so Ellen gave him a bedside bell. He could ring it, knowing that Mom or Dad would hear it right away. They even rehearsed during the day so he could see how quickly Mom and Dad would respond. Other moms have found Boo Buster or Monster Go Away! sprays on the Internet, or you can make one out of a water spray bottle and some light, safe scent. Let your child help you decorate the bottle in a way that she feels confident will scare off those scaries. Spray the room together at bedtime and then leave the spray by her bed in case she needs it at night. You might also want to leave a flashlight in reach, unless you think she will stay up all night playing with it. Look through my list of recommended bedtime books to find stories that may help shake off her fears.

I gave my second daughter, Gretchen, a prop she could wear. She had used a blanket as her lovey since she was a baby, and even when she was very little she used to wrap it around her head. Naturally, this worried me and I would unravel her when I went in to check on her every night. Lots of children like some kind of pressure on them, it is comforting, and when she got old enough to talk she would ask me to put the blanket on her head to make her feel protected and snuggled. One December, when she was about three and a half, she saw a picture of a man with a sleeping cap in The Night Before Christmas. *We decided I would design a cap for her, one that would give her that snuggly feeling but finally relieve Bill and me from all those suffocation nightmares. I'm not a great seamstress but I took a rectangular piece of polar fleece, folded down the two top corners, and sewed it into an envelope shape. I put it down on her pillow, she sticks her head in the "flap," snuggles with her blanket and stuffed animal, and tells me it keeps away monsters.*

Obviously, if your child is truly terrified, give her the extra comfort she needs. It's usually better to sit by her and stroke her and hug her rather than lie down and go to sleep with her. If she really needs lots of physical reassurance, hold her in your lap for a moment or two and then put her back down and continue patting her. (If your child is one of those rare ones who can have you lie down with her once in a while without demanding that you do it all the time, go ahead and bend this rule but be careful; try to get out of her bed before she's fully asleep because you are on a slippery sleep slope.) You can also do lots of snuggling and cuddling with the lights on, before the final stage of bedtime. You may have to spend a few nights sitting in the doorway while she falls asleep, rather than leaving her completely alone.

If your child has a nightmare, return her to bed and offer extra reassurance. Help her turn her thoughts away from the nightmare and to more pleasant images—"rainbows and flowers," as my older daughter used to say. Rita used to circle Isabel's bedroom saying, "Bad dreams go away!" Occasional nightmares are normal; just about all kids have them. Read Chapter 12 on nightmares and night terrors for more tips on coping.

Sometimes a child who is not normally afraid will have a few days of palpable anxiety. Depending on her verbal skills, you may be able to tease out what's bothering her—a schedule change, a classmate being mean at preschool, an upcoming event that is worrying her. She may have transferred that anxiety onto imaginary ghosts or monsters.

Children's anxieties begin to expand as they become more aware of the larger world around them, especially in the early school years. They may begin to worry about personal harm, being hurt, or robbed. They worry about one of their parents or grandparents getting sick. They start to worry about school, or their friends, or their pets. They can absorb far more than you may realize from even a brief glimpse of television news or a snippet of a radio report, and be quite worried about wars, earthquakes, hurricanes, and the like, however distant. In our post-9/11 world, particularly if you live in a place like New York or Washington, or near an airport flight path, many youngsters will also have explicit fears or perhaps a more vague unease about terrorism. Assuaging anxieties can sometimes be as simple as talking to your child and getting the fears out in the open where they don't seem so terrifying. But the depth of childhood anxiety is often underestimated. Don't overreact—a little bit of fear and anxiety is normal at this age, and being afraid of a monster doesn't mean your child is going to grow up to be her generation's Woody Allen. But if your child seems excessively fearful, or phobic, talk to your pediatrician and her preschool or school teachers and consider if you need professional intervention.

Potty Training

I don't think there's any problem with working on changing sleep patterns at the same time you are potty training, as long as you don't turn potty training into a tug-of-war. Focus on daytime training, and leave a diaper or pull-up on at nap time until he stays dry for several days in a row. At night, I think it's fine to keep a diaper or pull-up on until age four or five; they can do a lot of that overnight training on their own if you give them time. I just don't see any point in confusing your child—if you are trying to teach him to stay in bed, don't then tell him he's got to get up and out of bed in the middle of the night to pee! For more information on potty training, see Chapter 8, One and a Half to Two and a Half Years Old; and for bedwetting in older children, see Chapter 13, Medical Problems.

With a newly trained child, however, the potty itself can become yet another stalling tactic. When a child says he has to "go potty," you are of course going to let him get out of bed and go potty. But don't let him do this more than once, and do your best to make the trip to the potty brief and efficient. If he says he has to go potty again five minutes later, tell him that he's out of luck, it's too soon to go again, he can wait until morning. Remember to have him go potty before getting into bed in the first place, and make sure he knows there's nothing wrong with using a diaper or pull-up overnight.

PARTNERING WITH YOUR CHILD

Parents have an array of techniques available to them to help shape their toddler's sleep habits and routines. At this age, children can get vested in improving their own sleep and can feel pride and self-worth when they achieve it. Positive reinforcement goes a long way for this age group. In fact, I may be a therapist but I know when a little bribery is in order. Wait until you hear about how I got my oldest daughter to stop sucking her thumb to get to sleep. (Hint: it involved the kindergarten class hamster.)

The Family Meeting

Start with a family meeting where both parents sit down with the child and talk about sleep in an age-appropriate manner. Choose a time when your child is happy and receptive. Sunday morning after pancakes is a lot better than 5:00 p.m. on a weekday when she skipped her nap and is starving for dinner. Tell her that you consulted (or read a book by) the Sleep Lady and learned about how children can sleep better. That way you can blame me for any changes or rules she doesn't like. For instance, if your child begs you to lie down with her you can say the Sleep Lady said we can't do that but we can stay with you in your room. Some children get furious with me. "The Sleep Lady can't come over to play with me!" "I don't like the Sleep Lady." They may pick up this book and throw it! But when they succeed, when they start feeling good about their new sleep skills, they often want to call me on the phone and tell me how proud they are of themselves! They can even send me an email at proudkids@sleeplady.com and I'll tell them how proud I am!

Keep the discussion upbeat and positive. You don't want your child to feel she has a problem, or that she's doing something wrong. To the contrary, you should portray it as your problem, your responsibility. "Mommy and Daddy should have helped you learn to put yourself to sleep earlier, and we are sorry we didn't. But the Sleep Lady helped us understand that and now we are going to help you learn." Explain that children who go to bed without fussing and who sleep all night feel better in the morning and have more fun during the day. Encourage her to brainstorm about how she can participate, maybe by deciding what she can take into her bed to touch, hug, or twirl, or what extra game she will get to play in the morning if she uses her good sleep manners at night. You want her to have a stake in success. You may be surprised at how sensitive children already are to sleep issues, and how quickly they pick up the lingo. Many children are relieved when parents bring this up.

They know that something is wrong, that Mom and Dad are frustrated and want them to sleep differently. They are happy to know you are going to help them fix it.

If you think it will help, you can give your child examples, preferably of an older friend or cousin she looks up to. Say something like "We are going to teach you how to put yourself to sleep and sleep all night long in your own bed, just like Cousin Johnny and Cousin Jenny and Gramma and Aunt Rachel." Be careful; you want to frame this in a positive way, not to make your child feel ashamed.

> At four, Isabel had trouble falling asleep, and seldom slept through the night. She usually ended up in a sleeping bag on the floor next to her parents. Her little sister Deirdre, in contrast, didn't mind just hanging out in her crib for a half hour or so until she fell asleep. Rita and Elliott put up with Isabel's problems until their third child, Rebecca, was born, and then it just got too hard to deal with three young children, two of whom were up half the time. Rita and Elliott convened a family meeting and learned that Isabel was already well aware of the problem.
> "I told her that Daddy and I found out we were supposed to have taught her how to fall asleep by herself, like Deirdre. We said we talked to a lady who is an expert and she gave us some ideas. Isabel said she wanted to go to sleep like Deirdre. She was totally intrigued," Rita remembered.

Explain clearly what changes your family will make so the child knows what to expect. Warn her about an earlier or more structured bedtime, or a new routine. "Daddy is not going to lie down with you anymore, but Daddy will stay with you until you fall asleep." Or "If you come to our bed at night, we are going to tell you we love you and give you a big hug and take you back into your bed where you can snuggle with your teddy bear." Adapt the script to the appropriate sleep challenge, but you don't have to give a lot more detail. You can introduce the idea of a sticker chart as a reward.

> Marcy said of her three-year-old daughter: "Ariella is a real creature of habit, so I always prep her about change. If I do something one night, she'll expect it the next night. She'll say, 'Why don't you have your hand on my leg, you had it there yesterday.' I prep her all day long, letting her know about change in advance. I'll say, 'Tonight we're going to do this but tomorrow it's going to be that.' If I don't tell her, she starts asking about tomorrow."

Sticker Charts

Kids love stickers, stamps, and stars, and they work great for this age. As an extra incentive, you can let them choose their own stickers. Children can have toothbrushing sticker charts, potty sticker charts, eating-vegetables sticker charts, putting-away-toys sticker charts, not-screaming-for-a-cookie-during-communion sticker charts. And of course they have sleep sticker charts. But start with the sleep sticker chart. Later on you can introduce charts for other behaviors (or combine them—you can include tooth-brushing as an item on the sleep sticker chart if you want). I don't want them to get a sticker for something relatively simple, or at least simple for adults to enforce, and then lack the motivation to earn another sticker by doing something much harder, like modifying years of sleep behavior. Nor do I want sleep modification to get tangled up with other power struggles, over cleanup for example.

I like to call it a *sleep manners* chart, instead of *sleep rules*. Rules imply judgment, or even potential punishment. *Manners* connotes being nice, earning praise. Also, it's a reminder that we want to incorporate manners in our life all the time, not just when we are getting stickers.

How elaborate your sticker scheme is depends on your child's age and temperament. Some kids, particularly younger ones, are perfectly happy to just get a star or a sticker stuck on a piece of paper or on their shirt so they can wear it and show it off all day. (Remember to remove them before you do the laundry!) Later you can create a more complex chart and your child can decorate it. If you want, you can do a one-page chart for each week so he can see his track record and maybe get a little extra bonus at the end of each week. Ariella, for instance, got an assortment of stickers but the special sparkly gold one was her reward at the end of a good week. To make a weekly chart, turn the paper horizontally, put the days of the week along the top, and the manners across the left, or short, side. You can even leave a little space to jot down a simple log: what time he went to bed, how long he slept, etc.

Choose three to four manners that best apply to your child. You can change them over time if you need to, but not so often that you confuse your child about his goals. Phrase the manners in positive terms—"do's," not "don'ts." In other words, say "Lie quietly in bed," instead of "Don't make noise in bed." Here are a few examples:

- "Lie quietly in bed." (This means no shouting or yelling; talking or humming quietly to themselves or their stuffed animal is okay.)

- "Put yourself to sleep."

- "Stay in your own bed all night long."

- "Sleep until 6:00 a.m." (or whatever realistic time you choose). Or "Sleep until the music starts on the radio."

- "Go back to sleep without calling for Mommy or Daddy in the middle of the night."

- "Take a nap or quiet time."

In the beginning, include one relatively easy bedtime rule so they can always get some positive feedback. For instance, one category can be "putting on your pajamas without making Mommy have to chase you around the room!" This is a competence builder. It helps her feel she can live up to the new sleep expectations, that it's not too hard for her. However, if your child is satisfied with that easy one, raise the bar. Tell her she is so very, very good at getting that sticker that she will now have to focus on a new manner. Get her invested in the new chart—give her a bunch of stickers as a "graduation" present for that item, if it helps, or let her go to the store with you and select the stickers she will earn for the next task. (There are some good online sites and catalogues where you can buy cheap stickers in bulk, or try your local dollar store.)

> Hillary positively beamed with pride when she got her stickers, but after a good start in modifying her poor sleep habits, her progress stalled; she even regressed a bit. Her mom, Hope, changed the chart. She took off that easy "Brush your teeth and put on your pajamas," and replaced it with "No yelling out for Mommy and cooperate more with Daddy at bedtime." Hillary was not pleased. She called out fifty-five times for Mom (Hope counted) that night. She finally asked for a book instead of Mom, and Hope gave it to her. She then fell asleep.

Give the chart some good focused attention every night at bedtime, even if she appears to be ignoring you. You can talk about it during the day too, emphasizing her successes, gently reminding her of expectations but not dwelling on failures. But the nighttime review is essential. In the morning, give out the rewards promptly, not just the stickers themselves but praise and hugs, which mean even more to her than those cherished stickers. Try not to make her feel that she is bad if she failed, just tell her that she can try again that night and that you know she can do it. Remind her of some other achievement that she is proud of, sleep related or not. If she's done a really good sleep job, you can give her an extra sticker for her jacket or her hand so she can show it to her grandmother, babysitter, preschool teacher, or the bank teller.

Rewards

Some parents promise a reward, a gift or trip, if the child earns a certain number of stickers. This isn't always necessary—the stickers, the praise, the hugs, the sense of accomplishment can be adequate rewards themselves. If you do want to give an extra reward, or if you've been using the sticker chart for some time and need a little extra pizzazz, go ahead and add a carrot, but start small and be realistic. If you promise a trip to Disney World, what are you going to do for a follow-up? With a small reward, you can withhold it if he regresses, but are you really going to cancel a trip to Disney World if he wakes up a few nights and climbs into your bed? You are probably better off just promising him a pizza!

Occasionally children, particularly when they are a little older, need sticks in addition to carrots—although I'm not big on punishment, so maybe we should talk about "twigs" instead of sticks. They may also need some privileges taken away to get them to change sleep behavior. It can be a little thing, like not letting them turn the kitchen light on in the morning if they woke you up before 6:00, or not so little, like taking away a favorite video, computer time, or morning TV if she still gets up in the middle of the night. I use this as a last resort, usually with older children, and I don't use it very often. And I never use the twig without the carrot. When I take away a privilege I continue to offer lots of praise and positive reinforcement for what the child is doing right.

Laurel ended co-sleeping and improved Kerry's sleep when he was about two and a half, but a few months later he began getting out of bed repeatedly. She tried all sorts of solutions, but she wasn't a very good limit setter and he knew it. We worked on giving Kerry lots of choices about things during the day—but making him understand that he didn't get to make the rules at bedtime or nap time. Laurel eventually began taking a toy away from him when he wasn't cooperating. I suggested that instead of a toy, she take away an activity or privilege, like the computer. I also urged her to talk to Kerry about the consequences of breaking the rules shortly before lights-out—but not get into threats, recriminations, or even any discussion while he was misbehaving and getting out of bed.

I'd like to encourage you to think about family outings and activities as rewards, instead of toys and games. Tell your child that if he earns his sleep chart, he can decide whether you are going out for pancakes Sunday morning or for pizza Saturday night. Treats can be free. Tell him Daddy will take him for an extra trip to the playground, or they can go sledding twice in one day. (Don't promise sledding in July; you want the reinforcement of a reward to come quickly after the behavior.) You can say Mommy will read three extra stories one afternoon or watch a special video with him twice. You have enough plastic junk in the house already, and time with you is more valuable to your child than anything you can get at the store.

CREATING A SCHEDULE

Scheduling isn't as elaborate or as difficult for these children as it is for younger ones, and the schedule may well be shaped largely by his preschool hours. Generally, you want your child to wake up between 6:00 and 7:30 a.m. Six is quite common and, unless they are tired by 7:00, that's perfectly acceptable. I'll address later how to help a child who persistently wakes up before 6:00.

Usually preschoolers need a midmorning snack, and then have lunch around noon or 12:30. If they are still napping, a common time is about 1:00 to 3:00 in the afternoon. When they stop napping, usually at around age four, they should still have some quiet time in the late afternoon.

As napping decreases, bedtime becomes earlier. If your three-year-old has been going to bed at 8:30, when she eases out of the afternoon nap she'll probably need to go to bed at around 7:30. By age five, you probably want her to sleep from about 8:00 p.m. to 7:00 a.m. Adjust it, of course, depending on your family schedule and her school start time, but aim for at least eleven hours of unfragmented overnight sleep. When you see her sleep window open, get her to bed. Common sleep cues at this age include yawning, rubbing their eyes, sucking a thumb or pacifier, or just general fussiness. If she falls asleep on the floor, you probably missed the cue! Take note, however, that preschoolers are adept at hiding their sleep cues so you must also pay attention to the clock. If you miss the window and she gets that cortisol-fueled second wind, you should probably get her to bed a half hour or so earlier the next night. Avoid that vicious cycle where the less they sleep the less they sleep. Similarly, if she dozes during her bedtime routine or falls asleep the very second you turn out the lights after story time, you are probably putting her to bed too late. Move bedtime earlier by fifteen to thirty minutes.

Kids themselves at this age learn to pick up on the sleep-window concept. Occasionally, they'll just say, "Mommy, I'm ready for bed," or "Nye-nye," or just crawl into bed by themselves. But that's not too common, even with much older children. Perceptive children might pick up on the sleep-window concept and try to outsmart you. One night when he was about three, Ilan went to bed with unusual ease, and Joanne went to spend what she thought might be a few rare quiet moments with her husband before getting their older son, Zach, to bed. No sooner had she settled herself on the living room couch than a very small blond guy in blue baseball pajamas zoomed through the living room at about a hundred miles an hour shouting, "I missed my sleep window, Mom!"

Bedtime Routine

For this age group, the bedtime routine is typically the most challenging part of the day. Now that your child is older, you may want to modify her routine a little but make sure it remains soothing and predictable. Bedtime preparations should be in her room (or perhaps the early stage can be in a younger sibling's room), not all over the house. Include stories, songs, or games that soothe, not stimulate. Make sure the rules for how many stories, or how long you will read, are completely clear and nonnegotiable. Avoid wild, fast-moving games, and scary stories. Leave plenty of time, at least a half hour, for her to unwind, and to get the attention from you she needs. If you rush it, she'll be more likely to run out of bed or stall or manipulate you into staying longer. If she starts bargaining for an even longer time with you, more stories or more songs, blame the clock. Tell her the clock says you have to stop reading at 8:00, and it's ten minutes to. If two parents take turns at bedtime, you don't have to follow an identical script but you should have a similar routine, style, and response to bedtime power plays, fears, or manipulation.

"We used to have to go in his room for a half hour to play before we did our routine, but that's not necessary anymore," said Amanda, who was able to reshape her son Wes's troublesome sleep after his apnea was corrected with adenoid surgery when he turned four, an experience you can hear

more about in Chapter 13, Medical Problems. "He goes into his room to play by himself and then we go in for ten or fifteen minutes. We read books, say a prayer, and have a quiet talk about our day. That's all he needs."

○ ○ ○

Ariella is a champion negotiator who always tries to con Marcy into just one more story. It's a quandary for Marcy and Doyle because they know they need to be consistent, but sometimes if they don't succumb Ariella gets so worked up and hysterical that it becomes that much harder to get her to sleep. "It jacks her up; she gets more awake." Recently Marcy has been using my advice to blame the clock. "I started showing Ariella the time, and at first I thought it would be more stress and pressure, but I was wrong. It was a great idea. I can show her the time and tell her, 'You have to hurry or else you'll lose your book time.' " While most of Ariella's sleep issues are resolved and she generally sleeps through the night now, the stalling hasn't gone away completely, although it's not totally out of control either. The clock promises to be another useful tool in containing it.

It's often a good idea to warn your children a minute or two before lights-out. "We have a few more pages in this book, then Mommy is going to turn out the light." Sometimes they like to turn out the light themselves. It's another way they can "own" bedtime. You might want to blame bedtime on the clock. "Oh look! The clock says eight-thirty. Lights-out time. We can't read any more books tonight. We'll have to get upstairs earlier tomorrow night so that we can read more books." If your child doesn't respond to the sight of numbers, you might try a clock radio or a timer. "Oh, the music went on" or "Oh, the bell rang, it's time for bed." If the clock ploy doesn't work, feel free to blame me! "It's eight-thirty. The Sleep Lady says we have to turn out the lights now."

Some children will say, "I can't do it; I can't put myself to sleep." Explain that everyone has trouble going to sleep sometimes, even Mommy and Daddy, and then teach them some simple relaxation techniques and creative visualization. (See the Resource Directory for some suggestions on age-appropriate guided visualizations and relaxation exercises.) Children have such wonderfully active imaginations, they are actually better at visualization than we are. They may not understand the word *visualization* but they certainly get *pretend* and *imagine*. They can learn how to think relaxing thoughts at bedtime, how to close their eyes and imagine playing at the beach, building a snowman, taking a summer walk with their cousins in Vermont.

Try to build on the images in their favorite illustrated book and have them imagine entering the book to play with the characters (as long as there are no scary themes). My own girls loved playing "in" *Angelina Ballerina*. The mouse house illustrations were so inviting and warm. Your children will come up with their own suggestions and will pleasantly surprise you with their creativity. I had one client tell her daughter about my own girls' Angelina Ballerina game. They tried it, and then the little girl chose books of her own to "go into." She even had her mother call me on the phone so she could recommend it to my family. You might also want to teach your child deep-relaxation techniques, the kind you do at the end of a good exercise class or before going into labor! Have her relax her toes, her feet, her ankles, shins, knees, etc., all the way up her body. If you don't want to do this yourself, you can play a relaxation CD (see my list of suggestions at the back of the book).

Children also like applying their imaginations to a dream agenda. "Tonight I'll dream about playing basketball." Or "Tonight I will dream about building a sand castle." Or "Tonight I will dream about being a beautiful ballerina." It helps them feel more in control of what happens to them after they fall asleep, particularly if they are worried about having nightmares.

THE SLEEP LADY SHUFFLE

My Sleep Lady Shuffle is still a useful tool for this age group. But I'll warn you that it isn't as easy doing the Shuffle with a three- or four-year-old in a bed as with a six-month-old in a crib. The Shuffle is gentle and gradual but older children still get upset and fight the change. Don't get angry, but don't give up either. Keep reminding him that he can learn to put himself to sleep in his wonderful "big boy" bed without Mommy lying down with him.

Throughout the Shuffle we try to minimize tears but I can't promise to eliminate them completely. Luckily, by the time our children are three or four most of us aren't as worried about tears damaging our children. We've inevitably had to listen to our share of tears by now and we find it easier to cope with crying now that our children can also use words to communicate their wants and worries. To keep the tears in check, give lots of reassurance, lots of love, lots of praise. In addition to reviewing rules and expectations every night at bedtime, you should also pay your child some sleep compliments during the day. Don't dwell on his sleep failures, but keep praising his sleep achievements.

(The directions here are for children in beds. If your child is still in a crib, follow the version of the Shuffle in the previous chapter but do a little more explaining about each step, which helps an older child with better verbal skills buy into the Shuffle. If he climbs out of the crib, put him back just like you would a child in a bed.) If your child wakes up in the middle of the night, and he probably will at first, pat or soothe him briefly in bed and then return to where you were sitting at bedtime that night until he falls asleep again. We want to give a consistent response to every wakening. I give tips later in this chapter on ways of dealing with specific bedtime and middle-of-the-night sleep crutches.

Keep moving every three days, even if he had a bad night, woke up frequently, or protested a lot. Expect some regression or resistance each time you move a little further from his bed. But stick to it, particularly with this age group, it's essential not to backtrack or give mixed signals. If he gets sick during the Shuffle, give him lots of extra hugs and kisses and then maintain or "freeze" your Shuffle position or sit closer if needed. When he starts to feel better, continue with the Shuffle. Try not to drag it out too long.

NIGHTS 1–3. Once bath, stories, and songs are over, sit in a chair or on the floor next to your child's bed. Stroke or pat him intermittently if he fusses or cries but don't do it constantly or he will form a new negative association and will need you to pat him constantly in order to fall asleep. You can be a little more generous with touch the first night, when the whole system is new to him, but be careful about creating difficult new patterns, starting on the second night. Children this age will almost certainly try to engage you. Try closing your eyes, which not only conveys an unambiguously sleepy message but also makes it easier for you to resist getting drawn into a conversation or philosophical seminar about the nature of the universe. Stay there until he falls asleep.

Some children get quite upset even on this first night if you won't lie down with them. In desperation some parents have put their head down on the pillow next to their child. Try not to do it, and if you do, please restrict it to the first night or you aren't going to make much progress. You will not be changing your child's ritual, or teaching him to learn new skills if you are sharing a pillow! Be careful to stroke, pat, sing, or hand-hold intermittently, not constantly, at least after the first night. You will just be replacing one crutch with another. You should be in charge of the touching, not the child. For instance, if he grabs your hand, gently remove it but then touch his hand sporadically. Close your eyes and "sh-sh" him. Remember, in three more nights you won't be sitting next to him and won't be able to touch him constantly. You want to be able to fade out of his sleep picture, not add to his fury each time you make a change.

NIGHTS 4–6. Children this age do better when they know what to expect, and they also respond to positive reinforcement. Tell him what a good job of sleep learning he has been doing, what a good night-night boy he has been. Tell him you are going to move farther away but that you will still stay with him until he falls asleep and that you will continue to check on him. Move the chair about halfway to the door. (If the room is very small or the bed is right by the door, your next step would be to sit at the door, where he can see you.)

Continue the soothing sounds, but stay seated as much as you can. Get up to pat or stroke him a little as needed. Try not to pick him up but if he gets really overwrought, pick him up briefly, as close to the bed as possible. Give him some deep-pressure hugs, and remind him that you aren't going to leave him, that you'll stay until he falls asleep. Put him back down. Don't let him fall asleep in your arms or lap, and don't lie down with him in his bed. Keep telling him what a good job he's doing, how proud you are, that he's going to earn lots of fun stickers.

Some children try to fight the Shuffle by getting out of bed and coming to you, trying to crawl into your lap. Give him a big hug and return him to bed. If he does it again, take him back to the bed. Don't talk, don't reason, don't explain, don't get exasperated. Just put him back, as many times as it takes.

Usually they get tired and stay in bed, particularly if they become more confident that you are going to stay there until they fall asleep. But if he doesn't stop getting out of his bed, explain very clearly that if he keeps it up, you will have to leave. You can say something like, "If you don't follow your sleep manners and lie quietly in your bed, then I am going to have to leave your room and go read in my room." You can substitute the phrasing, and say you are going to go downstairs or to the kitchen or whatever will strike the right note with him. Remind him that if he does stay in bed and follows his sleep manners, you will stay there as long as he needs you to fall asleep. Most children then agree to stay in bed. If yours absolutely doesn't, you'll have to leave and put a gate on the door so he doesn't follow. You can stay near the door if you want, and tell him that if he gets back into bed and stays there you will come back into the room. If even that tactic fails, skip to the last two stages of the Shuffle, involving sitting in the hall until he goes to sleep. Again, tell him you'll come in and tuck him in if he gets in bed and stays there. If he falls asleep on the floor near the gate, move him later when he's in a sound sleep. If gates stop working, some parents close the door or threaten to close the door. Parents don't like this and children don't like it, and I would never insist that you do it. But some parents who reluctantly have taken this step found that it works in about thirty seconds. The child jumps right into bed and you can then keep the door partly open and sit nearby until he's calm.

NIGHTS 7–9. Again, explain that he is doing a great job and tell him that you are going to move the chair again. Sit close to him and hug him for a minute before you make that move, but don't get so entwined that you have to struggle to get loose. Then move to the doorway, so that you are in his view, although dimly lit. Continue the same soothing techniques, intervening as little as possible. He may cry a little bit, but gently reassure him and he will fall asleep. (If he keeps getting out of bed, follow the advice for nights four to six.)

NIGHTS 10–12. Move a few feet farther down the hallway, but still in his sight. Keep praising him again on what a good sleep boy he is becoming. You can even give him an anticipatory sticker if you think that will help. "I'm giving you this sticker because I know you are going to be such a good boy now while I sit outside." You can keep making those "sh-sh" sounds from the hallway, not constantly, but with enough frequency to remind him you care. Some kids have trouble with this, and keep coming out to find you. Just keep taking him back to bed, unless it gets excessive, in which case you might want to put up a gate.

If this step upsets him, having you so near and yet so far, you might want to skip it and proceed directly to the next phase of the Shuffle. Trust your instincts to figure out what's best for your child.

NIGHT 13. A fair number of children start falling asleep and staying asleep by night seven or ten—occasionally even sooner. But most parents have to take one more step and leave the child alone for five-minute intervals. Tell him that you will keep checking on him until he is asleep. Don't go all the way into the room, stay at the doorway when you check on him.

Since children don't really understand what "five minutes" means, and it may seem like a very long time to them lying in bed, explain exactly where you will be, and describe what you will be doing. Some parents sit down the hall out of sight for a few nights. Others do what I call *job checks*. Tell him that you will check on him in a few minutes after you've brushed your teeth, or changed your clothes, or some other brief but comprehensible task that helps him understand that you will be back quite soon. They sometimes like it if your "jobs" have to do with getting yourself ready for bed too. Always return as promised.

Leaving the child may seem like a radical change for you but please remember that he's had nearly two weeks of preparation. He has given up some of his negative associations and gained quite a bit of sleep independence. He is old enough to understand that you are close by even if you are out of sight. Don't go too far away—stay on the same floor, in a nearby room and just read a magazine or a book for the first few nights. Gradually you can move a little farther away. If he cries, you'll be back every five minutes to reassure him. Try not to go in more than that; he'll just get more stimulated and more upset if he has to say good-bye to you every two minutes.

Unlike the crying-it-out approaches, you don't keep stretching out the intervals for longer than five minutes. The only exception is if you sense that five minutes is too brief for your individual child, that having to see you but separate again every five minutes is making him more agitated. Then experiment and see if he finds it less disturbing if you check on him every ten or fifteen minutes. Parents often resist this idea; they are so worried about harming their children by being away from them, they have trouble adjusting to the idea that some children actually need a little more distance to calm themselves down and fall asleep.

He may well cry a bit the first few nights—he may even cry a fair amount for one or two nights. But very rarely do children cry persistently after two weeks of the chair routine. If he does cry, check on him from the doorway. Remind him to hug his lovey. Be reassuring but calm. Keep in mind, he has gained confidence that you are nearby and responsive. He's ready to learn this skill.

Cliff slept reasonably well until he was about two, when a series of changes, including a new baby sister and the start of day care, threw him off. Dislocation because of home remodeling was the last straw. The family stayed at Cliff's grandmother's house, with mom, Hailey, sleeping upstairs with the baby, Janice, while Cliff and his dad, Harry, camped out in the living room, one on a cot, one on the couch. When they went back to their own home, Cliff was much clingier. He also experienced night terrors sometimes. His parents let him stay up until 9:30, by which time he was overtired but wired. It took forever to get him to sleep, and Harry often fell asleep in Cliff's bed before Cliff did. "Hailey would come in at eleven-thirty or midnight and tap me on the shoulder and say come to bed, he's asleep now!" Harry recalled.

About two months before his third birthday, Hailey and Harry told Cliff that the "Sleep Lady" had given them new bedtime rules. "I don't like the Sleep Lady," he declared. They began taking him upstairs between 7:30 and 8:00 p.m., for a shorter and more structured bedtime routine. They still snuggled but now they snuggled during the lights-on stage of the bedtime routine. When they started the Shuffle, Cliff, whom Harry described as a "very spirited child," was not at all pleased. Cliff did okay the first few nights, when Harry was beside his bed. He tried to coax his dad into his bed, but he acquiesced when Harry declined. But the farther Harry moved away, the unhappier Cliff got. "When I moved the chair, he *would plead; he would look sad and cry quietly. That was worse for me than having him screaming mad at me."* But because they had shifted his bedtime and improved their routine, Cliff still fell asleep an hour earlier than usual. When Harry neared the end of the Shuffle, standing by the door and then leaving to make checks, Cliff screamed and ran out of the room. Harry said it felt like he ran out a million times, but in fact it was only about three. Then he'd go to bed. Within a few weeks, he stopped protesting at bedtime. His father made checks every five minutes for a while, and after about two weeks, noticing that the checks sometimes caused Cliff to stir when he was almost asleep, Harry switched to one check after five minutes, which Cliff liked, and then he wouldn't come back for another twenty minutes, by which time Cliff was almost always asleep.

Cliff's night wakenings also decreased during the Shuffle. When he did wake, Harry checked on him quickly to make sure he was okay, and then reminded him to snuggle with his special blanket and stuffed animals. He'd tell him, "The Sleep Lady says you have to sleep all night." It didn't make Cliff a fan of mine but he listened! Soon, all that Cliff would need when he woke up was a quick reassuring look at his father, then he'd roll over and go back to sleep. The first week of the Shuffle, Cliff woke up two or three times each night. The second week, he woke up only two times during the whole week. The third week saw a little regression; he slept through three nights and woke up once or twice the other nights. That was it; he began sleeping through pretty consistently, except of course if he was sick. Some mornings he did talk about having been up briefly but was very proud that he could get himself back to sleep. He'd say, *"I didn't cry out for you, Daddy,"* so Harry knew that Cliff had woken up, taken his blanket, and gone back to sleep. *"I gave him lots of praise for that,"* his father said.

A few things to remember. Children get ritualized easily. Make the changes every three days—or less. *Dragging it out makes it harder, not easier, for him.* Give it more than three days and he'll expect you to stay exactly where you are and get even more frustrated and angry when you try to double that distance.

Some parents decide to stop the Shuffle at the point when they are sitting in the hallway a few feet from the child's room. If that feels right to you, go ahead and try it, as long as it's not taking an hour and the child doesn't need you to come back to the doorway on and off all night long. Other families continue to make the five-minute checks for weeks or months, if that's what makes everyone comfortable. That's okay as long as he's sleeping through the night and falling asleep reasonably quickly, that he's not using those checks as an excuse to keep himself awake so he can keep seeing you. But most families do get to the point where they can do their bedtime routine, say good night, and leave.

> *"Even now I can't go downstairs until Wes falls asleep," Amanda said, months after Wes sailed through the Shuffle and began sleeping beautifully. "I can be somewhere else on the same floor but I can't go down and do the dishes. Luckily there's always enough for me to do upstairs, believe me. But he likes me to go in and check on him from the doorway, it's very reassuring to him."*

Sometimes even children who have "graduated" from the Shuffle and sleep well regress a little. Routines get disrupted, illnesses occur, they experience normal waves of fear or insecurity. Don't return to whatever prolonged and convoluted bedtime techniques you used before the Shuffle. Be particularly wary of relapsing into co-sleeping. Instead, sit quietly in the doorway for two or three nights, where he can see you. That allows you to be present and comforting, without abandoning all your progress. Then move on to the final steps of the Shuffle. It should go pretty smoothly.

PROBLEMS AND SOLUTIONS

Many sleep experts maintain that once children learn to fall asleep by themselves, they will sleep all night. In my experience, that is often but by no means always the case. I have found that night awakenings become much briefer and less frequent in one to three weeks after starting the Shuffle, and that the children go back to sleep much more quickly with less help from us. But the awakenings don't necessarily totally evaporate, particularly with older children whose sleep problems may date back a few years. In this section, I will help you address specific middle-of-the-night sleep crutches that may linger after bedtime problems dissipate (or that you may want to understand better as you go through the Shuffle). Your child may still want you to lie down with her at 3:00 a.m., even if she no longer needs that at 8:00 p.m. She may want to be snuggled or given yet another cup or bottle when she wakes up at night. She may still be sending you scurrying to find that pacifier under the bed. Dealing with the normal nighttime fears and worries of the preschool years, a child may just wake up to say, "Hi, Mom, just testing! Just checking to make sure you're where you're supposed to be!"

I believe in responding when our children need us. Leaving them to scream in the dark does not promote good sleep for them or for us. Checking on them makes them feel better, and it makes us feel better. (You do need to make sure she's truly awake before you rush in to "rescue" her. If she's whimpering or crying out briefly during a partial awakening, don't charge in with parental sirens blaring when she's about to drift back into a deeper sleep on her own.) But we don't want to overdo it. We want to give our children enough comfort so that they feel safe and can go back to sleep, but not so much reinforcement that they have no incentive to give up these awakenings. Make sure she's going to bed early enough, and getting the naps she needs at her age. Overtired children are more likely to wake up at night.

When your child wakes up at night during the Shuffle, give her a brief reassuring pat and return to the position you were in that night at bedtime. If you are dealing with awakenings after the Shuffle, quietly return her to her bed, and sit in a chair or stand in the doorway. You might want to start in the chair, and then after a night or two move to the door, similar to what you did during the Shuffle to fade yourself out of her middle-of-the-night picture. Remember—do not engage her, bore her. Do not take her into your bed. Do not get into her bed. Do not pick her up and walk around the house. Do not criticize or scold or talk about consequences or punishments or disappointments at this particular time. In fact, do not talk at all except for a few soft phrases like "Night-night" or "I love you, go to sleep." Hand her the lovey and give her a quick hug and a kiss but don't do too much hugging, patting, and cuddling or she'll keep waking up every night wanting her fix of snuggles. Leave as soon as you can without engendering hysterics.

The exception to the rule: some children do better if we don't respond, if we do let them cry—not for hours but for a few minutes. These are kids who get more awake, more stimulated when you come in at night. Occasionally I've come across couples so utterly convinced that their child can't get back to sleep without them that they have trouble recognizing when the opposite is true, when the child actually goes to sleep better without them in the room. But most parents know instinctively when they should leave their child alone and when they do belong at her side, or at least in her doorway.

Bells and Whistles

Occasionally, children sneak into your bed during the night but you don't even notice until much later. Hang a plastic kitchen utensil or a bell from your bedroom door and close the door enough so the child has to push it to enter.

The bell or spoon will probably make enough noise to wake you up. Warn her that you are going to do this, and let her hear what it sounds like, so it doesn't terrify her in the middle of the night.

> One mom said it didn't really bother her if her two-and-a-half-year-old snuck into her bed, she didn't even notice, and everybody slept. She had second thoughts after the night her daughter crawled into bed with some unsuspecting houseguests.

Gates and Doors

Some parents use gates on the bedroom door, either to keep children from popping out of bed repeatedly at bedtime or as a safety measure to prevent nocturnal wandering. Some kids respect the gate as a boundary; they like the visible limit. Others climb over it, knock it down, or figure out how to unlock it. A few families I've worked with have even put up two gates, if they are dealing with particularly agile climbers or future safecrackers. Some kids detest the gate so much that their parents don't even have to use it; they just say, "If you get out of bed again I'll put up the gate," and that does the trick. Or instead of threatening, they entice. They put up the gate but say, "As soon as you lie down quietly in your bed and stay there, I'll take down the gate." Parents may choose to sit or lie down on the other side of the gate as a transitional step once they have reached the hallway stage of the Shuffle. That enables you to reassure your child that Mom or Dad is there, while reinforcing the message that she has to stay in her room after lights-out.

> Sam had been a pretty good sleeper for more than two years. His mom, Nora, a labor and delivery nurse, found Dr. Marc Weissbluth's explanations of infant sleep cycles helpful and she successfully followed his crying-it-out technique with Sam at four months. But in his second year, Sam had all sorts of changes: lots of travel, some separation from his father due to a job change, then a move from Washington to California, and yet more travel. His mom also discovered she was pregnant during all this transition, so Sam had both a new home, a new routine, and a little sister on the way. His sleep deteriorated and even though Nora knew a whole lot about newborns, Sam's nighttime problems stumped her and she didn't think leaving him alone to scream was going to help.
> He was just about three when we did the Shuffle. It was successful up to the point where they left him alone in his room. Two seconds later, he

would appear. They tried to reason with him but, guess what, reason didn't get them very far. So they made up the "two-strikes" method. The first time Sam came out of the room, they told him, "Strike one," and returned him to his room. When he marched out the second time, they'd say, "Strike two," and put up two gates, one on top of the other because he was an incredible climber. He got the hang of this pretty quickly and would march out of his room shouting, "No gates!" But he wasn't able to get around the double barrier. "He could climb over one but he was a little gun-shy about climbing over two," Nora said. He sometimes would fall asleep on the floor with his pillow by the door and they would put him in bed later.

His sleep improved but another round of holiday travel to relatives and the birth of his sister threw him off. By now, he literally had worn out the gates. Nora shut the door. "I held it shut and he wigged out. My husband was freaked out that my son was freaked out. I held it for about thirty seconds and you could tell I made my point." All she had to do after that was threaten to shut the door and he'd hop back into bed.

But in the next few weeks after Lizzie's birth, Nora's instincts told her to compromise—but to have a definite plan for ending the compromise. Lizzie is co-sleeping with her parents, so Sam gets to come into Mom and Dad's room too. He isn't allowed in their bed; he has a special little sleeping place on the floor, and he brings his special fleece, his stuffed pig, and his water bottle. As soon as Lizzie gets to the point where she's only nursing once a night, she'll be out of their bed, and Nora will put both kids in Sam's room. She knows that Sam might then require a little refresher course in sleeping, but thinks this arrangement is best for him right now, and doesn't anticipate that retraining him will be all that hard, especially with his little sister in his room. "I'm letting him sleep near us because it's finite. Then there will be no kids in our bedroom until morning. That's easier than having different rules for different kids," Nora said, adding, "I think he'll like being in the room with her. He loves her, loves her, loves her; once she's in there, things might take care of themselves."

Eliminating Nighttime Feeding

If your child still takes a bottle, it's definitely time to get rid of it. Explain that she is a big girl now and doesn't need a bottle. She may well realize this herself by now. Offer her a cup of water during story time and if she cries for her bottle, soothe, comfort, and distract her but don't give her the bottle. In fact, you should get the bottles out of the house or at least out of sight. Focus on strengthening her attachment to a lovey as you remove the bottle, or let her choose a new lovey as a reward or incentive. Alternatively, you could try the bottle-to-cup advice I give for younger babies in Chapter 7: Thirteen to Eighteen Months (pages 137–139). If you plan to continue nursing, try to separate it from sleep. Nurse with a light on to weaken that sleep association.

If she is emotionally attached to the water cup and it has become a sleep crutch, help her learn to go back to sleep without it. Go to her when she calls for it in the middle of the night, but either just quietly point to the cup you left by her bed and encourage her to take a sip or two and go back to sleep, or just try to soothe her into going back to sleep without it. Don't refill the cup. It will probably take a few nights, and you'll probably have some tears but you can sit with her, stroke her intermittently, "sh-sh" her, and comfort her like you would a younger child. If all else fails, offer her an extra sticker instead of her cup!

Phasing Out Walking and Rocking to Sleep

By this age, children aren't usually rocked like they were as infants, but some still like to be lulled to sleep on their parents' laps during or after story time. Use the Shuffle to try to break that habit, just as you would for a child who wants you to lie down with him. Rock or hold him during the bedtime routine, while you read books and sing your songs, but don't rock him to sleep after lights out. If he tries to climb out of bed and get in your lap, just put him back to bed and soothe him. If he wakes up at night wanting to be rocked or held, return to your Shuffle position. I have very rarely encountered a child who still wanted the rocking in the middle of the night after learning to do without it at bedtime. If yours still wakes up, soothe him but don't let him get onto your lap again. (And try not to fall asleep in his bed either at story time, or he'll expect you to be there all night.)

Pacifier Withdrawal

If you still aren't ready to get rid of the pacifier, at this age definitely restrict it to sleep. Hide it or at least keep it by the bed but out of reach during the day, except at nap time and bedtime. If she wakes up one or more times during the night summoning you to help her find her pacifier, put several in and around her bed, or leave a spare in a little basket or bowl where she can find it herself. If she demands that you get it for her, go to her and gently remind her where they are and reward her for learning to do it by herself. If she absolutely cannot find it herself, then as an interim step you should retrieve it but hand it to her and make her put it into her mouth by herself. Try again to teach her to retrieve it herself when she's a few months older. Most kids over age three can manage this.

Now that your child has pretty good verbal skills, consider eliminating the pacifier completely. Talk to her about the decision; she's old enough to be part of it. Choose a time when she's relatively rested and relaxed—not right after she's been sick, when you've been traveling, or she's in her first week at preschool. Work on transferring some of her attachment to a lovey, and expand the lovey's role in bedtime rituals.

If you haven't already restricted the pacifier to bedtime and naps, do that first before you get rid of it completely. You'll get a little resistance, but distract her and praise her for not using it. When she adapts to not having it during the day, take it away at bedtime, but let her keep it for a while longer at naps. Pick a "big day" when she will no longer have the pacifier. Give her a few days to get used to the idea. She may agree to it—but then get very upset when the big day arrives. Get the pacifiers out of the house; she can't demand them quite as much and you can't give in if they just aren't there anymore. If you yield when she cries, she will learn that you don't really mean it and the next time you try to wean her from the pacifier she will cry and fuss even more.

I've heard lots of creative ways to get the child to invest in getting rid of the pacifier, like mailing it to a new baby, or leaving it by the chimney so Santa can take it for the reindeer. Some kids wrap it up in a box and save it for their own children, although that can be a little abstract for most preschoolers. I even heard of one child who gave hers to the goat at a petting zoo, although I'm sure that could not have made the zookeeper very happy.

Once you have disposed of the pacifier, brace yourself for a few rough naps and bedtimes. She will probably cry. Give her that lovey and offer extra reassurance. Cuddle a little longer before lights go out, or sit by her bed until she falls asleep. Don't do this for more than a week or you will be stuck by her bedside indefinitely. If you've been sitting by her bed for several days, you might want to do a truncated version of the Sleep Lady Shuffle again to get out of her room. If it's the second (or third!) time you've done it, move through it quickly: just one or two nights in each position or go straight from her bed to the doorway. Use your instincts and your judgment, but try to do it on the speedy side. Offer lots of praise and keep encouraging attachment to a lovey.

I worked with Charlotte's twins, Ethan and Nathaniel, when they were just a few months old, and you can read about their experiences in Chapter 11, Twins and Siblings. But Charlotte and Ed decided at the time that they didn't want to get rid of the pacifiers—a decision that they later regretted! After spending three years chasing two sets of pacifiers, Charlotte finally got rid of them around the boys' third birthday. "They didn't have pillows yet, but they saw a friend who had a toy under his pillow and they wanted one. I said sure, you can have a pillow and put a toy under it, but you have to get rid of the pacifiers first. They were fine with that—for about ten minutes and then they wanted the pacifiers back. I said, 'I'm sorry, it's too late.' That was it. They weren't pleased. There were rough nights, and rough naps, but I stuck with it. One of them screamed really hysterically for two weeks straight and then he sort of said, 'Okay, never mind, I'm going to sleep.' The other was really sad and hung on and almost stopped napping but eventually he got used to it."

Thumbsucking

If your child is still sucking his thumb, I don't think he'll outgrow the habit on his own. I've even met a few middle schoolers and teenagers who still suck their thumbs, braces and all. Age four or five is a good time to address it because your child now has the language skills to communicate with you about what can be a several-month process. He also may be getting a little self-conscious about his habit.

My daughter Carleigh was a determined thumb sucker and Bill and I decided to address the habit when she was five, already in kindergarten. She had started sleeping through the night when she was only eight weeks old but she had sucked her thumb since then too, and had the callous to prove it! She had a lovey, a small pillow she'd used since she was a baby, but instead of being a substitute for the thumb, it was a companion. When she snuggled against that pillow, the thumb went right into the mouth. I enlisted her dentist's support in encouraging her to stop sucking her thumb because she was going to get "big girl" teeth soon and we wanted them to grow in straight and strong and beautiful. Use whatever words and images will reach your child and get her invested. Her father and I empathized a lot and told her we knew it was very hard and were very proud that she was going to try. We also enlisted other people, including her grandmother, to share their memories of how they stopped sucking their thumbs as children, and how proud they felt.

Praise and encouragement will, however, only get you so far. Bribery will get you the rest of the way. We asked Carleigh what she wanted as a prize or reward. Her first choice was pierced ears, but I managed to dodge that bullet for a few more years. But I let her talk me into her second choice: adopting the class hamster at the end of kindergarten. I wasn't thrilled, but at least it wasn't a class snake. We found a picture of a hamster that we pinned on her bulletin board so she could see it from her bed. I also talked to her about the hamster a lot, and of course she had the hamster in class as an additional reminder all day. We found an unexpectedly large selection of hamster books at our local library, and I think we read them all.

We started by giving up daytime thumbsucking. Children are often not even aware that they are sucking, so she agreed to let me point it out to her by gently removing her hand. I noticed patterns: Carleigh was much more likely to rely on her thumb when she was frustrated, upset, overstimulated, or over-tired. Once we had cut down on daytime sucking, we got rid of the thumb-sucking at nap time—she still needed an occasional nap at five and a half. (I usually recommend getting rid of thumbsucking at bedtime before napping but I reversed that with Carleigh because at that age her naps were sporadic, while bedtime was daily.) When she napped, and later when she slept, we put bandage tape not just on her thumb but on all of her fingertips. Carleigh, a partner in this process, suggested that herself because she thought she would suck other fingers if we taped just the thumb.

As I expected, the first night in the thumb-free zone was the hardest. Carleigh was generally an excellent sleeper, but I recognized that falling asleep without the familiar association of thumb and lovey-pillow was a struggle that night. She snuggled with her special pillow, looked at books, and talked to me about what she wanted to dream about. I told her I would check on her a lot that night, which I did. I reassured her that she could do this, that she would love having a hamster. It was hard for me as her mother to watch her that night, but she eventually did fall asleep. We kept the tape for several weeks and slowly reduced the number of fingers. Carleigh told me which fingers she would be most likely to suck at night. We then went tapeless but still didn't bring the ham-ster home until she was no longer sucking any fingers when we checked on her at night. Her callous disappeared, the nail changed shape, and she even said her thumb no longer tasted as good! (Someone once told me a sucked thumb does taste different than an unsucked thumb; it has something to do with the oils in the skin. But I confess I don't recall seeing any scientific confirmation of this phe-nomenon!) We finally celebrated Carleigh's accomplishments and brought home the hamster. (That hamster, alas, died, as did two of his successors.)

Although this plan worked for Carleigh, it took several months. We might have been able to do it faster but I think it would have meant more tears, more trauma, and probably a higher risk of failure. Be patient and be creative. Involve your child, and respect her insights; she may know well what will help. I can't imagine doing this with a younger child, or one who lacks good language skills.

Early Birds

Early rising is a little more complicated once they switch from crib to bed because children can get up and try to begin their day whether you like it or not. It is a hard pattern to change, and it usually takes three or four weeks of very consistent coaching, longer if she's had early wake-ups for more than six months. Children sometimes wake up too early because they are actually over-tired. Remember that sleep-begets-sleep idea we talked about in Chapter 2? She may find it easier to sleep later if you make bedtime earlier by a half hour or so. (Very rarely, if a child wakes up early but acts fine all day and doesn't doze off in late afternoon or in the car, she may need less sleep than average. Slowly move bedtime later and see if she sleeps later in the morning. But as I said, this is rare so don't rush to try it unless you are quite certain that your child has below-average sleep needs.)

Remind her at bedtime every night that she has to sleep until at least 6:00 a.m. You may be able to teach her to recognize "6:00" on a digital clock, or you may train her to stay in bed until her radio starts to play music. You can blame the wake-up rules on the clock, or blame them on me: "The clock says it's still night-night time." Or, "The Sleep Lady says you will feel better if you sleep until six." Sticker charts help a lot with early awakenings. Keep reminding her that she can't get up because Mommy and Daddy (and brothers and sisters) are still sleeping. She'll feel better if she knows she isn't missing a party!

If she gets up at, say, 5:00 or 5:15 and comes looking for you or calling you, get her back to bed with minimal conversation. Remind her that it isn't morning time yet. Decide whether you will stay in her room until 6:00, or whether you will leave and check on her every ten or fifteen minutes. Base your decision partly on which approach is more likely to get her back to sleep—or even get her to stay in her bed. You don't want her chasing you every thirty seconds if you leave, and you may need to gate her door. Nor do you want her to keep talking and chatting and trying to engage you if you stay in her room. You can try both approaches for a day or two to get an idea of which will work, but don't keep switching back and forth. Choose a system and stick to it for a while. You may find a two-stage approach works best. Stay in her room in the morning for a while, maybe a week or so to communicate that she has to stay in bed. Then leave the room to give her more space to fall asleep again on her own.

Ideally, she should get back to sleep until 6:00 or later and you can snooze in a chair, lie on her floor, or get back to your own bed. If she does sleep, let her wake up on her own (as long as it's after 6:00) and then start the day with your dramatic wake-up. If she doesn't get back to sleep, wait until 6:00. Then come back into her room (if you are already in the room, leave for a minute or two but explain you'll be right back) with your dramatic wake-up and morning routine. Convey the message that she is starting her day because it's 6:00 a.m.—not because she cried, fussed, and screamed.

For children who wake up at 6:00 and are perfectly content, you'll probably have to live with it. It's a common and appropriate wake-up time for young children, even if you'd rather have her sleep until 7:00. You can try to teach her to stay in her room and maybe put out some special toys that she only gets to play with in the morning if she stays in her room and is quiet. However, if she wakes up at 6:00 but is cranky and miserable by 7:00, then she needs to sleep later. Try putting her to bed earlier in the evening and/or use the early-bird techniques described above to teach her to sleep later.

Some children naturally start sleeping later as they get a little older and outgrow napping. If that happens, it will happen on its own; you can't force it. You should not take away or shorten naps in the hopes of persuading her to sleep later (unless her naps are much longer than typical for her age). That usually backfires and you just end up with an even more overtired child, who will still wake up early and be even grouchier.

Napping and Quiet Time

Sleep needs shift year to year for this age group. As their naps shrink and disappear, they need to sleep a little longer at night. You'll have to adjust bedtime, unless they naturally begin to sleep in a little later in the morning. Even when they stop napping, quiet time in the late afternoon or before dinner is a must for four-year-olds, and a wise idea for five-year-olds, unless you actually like watching your child melt down.

With the two-and-a-half- or three-year-old, you still need to be vigilant about daily naps. He can skip an occasional one, but put him to bed earlier that night. Naps also remain essential for older children who aren't sleeping through the night or who are obviously tired during the day. You may have to nap coach. You can do a Shuffle for naps in this age group, or you can just put him in his room and check on him every ten to fifteen minutes. Every day, promise that you will come get him as soon as his nap is over. Make him stay in his room for an hour, every day. He may protest, and you may have to put a gate on his door. Some parents sit outside the gate at nap time with a book; it helps the child stay calm and get to sleep. Don't let him nap too late. Leave at least four hours between the end of the nap and bedtime or he'll have trouble falling asleep. (Nap training is hard. If you need more encouragement and advice about backup plans, read about napping for younger age groups.)

You may find that your child no longer needs a daily nap but still needs a "nap day" every three or four days. Carleigh napped daily until age five, and slept every other day after school for the first few months of kindergarten. That's longer than most children, but I could tell by her behavior that she still needed that extra sleep in the afternoon. Gretchen, in what was probably a more typical pattern, stopped napping at home when she was about three and a half, but still napped at preschool. The simplest way to tell whether a preschooler or kinder-gartener needs a nap is to watch him. If he gets a lot of nighttime sleep and is cheerful and easygoing during the day, he probably doesn't need to nap. If he is cranky or teary or frequently melting down, he probably needs at least a few naps a week. Car behavior is also a good clue. If he conks out every time you start your engine, he probably still needs that afternoon snooze.

> After they moved, napping was a struggle for Sam, and Nora never found a wholly satisfactory solution. His bedroom overlooked a high school with indecently loud and frequent bells, so she let him nap in her room, which she knew was not ideal. "Once I got him to sleep, he'd often sleep for three hours," she said, which is really too much for a three-year-old. But she had a hard time getting him to sleep. "It was a fight at nap time. He'd tantrum and wear himself out. Even when I gave him time, he still needed some tantruming to get out that last bit of energy and fall asleep."

If your child is getting about eleven hours of unfragmented sleep at night and seems well rested during the day, it may be time to go from naps to quiet time. You might want to cut out naps every other day, rather than eliminate them completely, or you may find that he naps great on the days he's with his sitter or at preschool but won't nap on days he's with you (or vice versa). Children who were good nappers but who now take a very long time to fall asleep in the afternoon may also be ready to phase out the nap and start quiet time.

> *When Kerry was two years and nine months, Laurel abandoned her struggle to make him nap on the days he was home with her, but he still napped beautifully on the days he had a sitter. A few months later, Laurel noticed that he was much more difficult at bedtime on nap days. "I'd put him to bed and he'd be up and out of bed six times. It more than made up for the nap," she said. "Everybody would be angry—I felt so bad for him." Although I usually urge families to continue the nap until around three and a half or four, in this case Mom's instincts were right. When they cut out the nap, bedtime became simple and pleasant. "We can shut the light and say good night and he goes to sleep," Laurel said.*

Quiet time is exactly what it sounds like, about forty-five minutes of structured, solitary play, preferably at about the same time every afternoon. It's a time for children to rest their bodies and, to a lesser extent, their minds. It helps pave the way for a peaceful dinner hour and easy bedtime. Good activities include looking at books, watching an age-appropriate, calm children's video (leave fast-paced, action-packed cartoons for another time), coloring, or playing in their room with dolls, trains, trucks, or the like. The activity should not need a lot of adult interaction or supervision, so make sure the child is in a safe place.

Co-sleeping

Some of the families you met in this chapter co-slept with their children for at least part of the night, and as you've seen the Shuffle can help end that practice. But co-sleeping is a complicated subject so I've devoted a separate chapter to it. Please refer to Chapter 10, Co-sleeping and the Family Bed, if you've been co-sleeping since birth and want to stop, or if you've been taking your child into bed for all or part of the night because you think it's the only way you can get him to sleep. For those of you who choose to continue co-sleeping, I'll also give you some advice on how to improve the quality and quantity of sleep in a shared family bed.

Isabel's Story

> *When Rita and Elliott had that family meeting with Isabel, they faced a daunting agenda. Isabel was four and had been a poor sleeper since*

birth, waking up every night and resisting napping anywhere but in a stroller. For the past year, her parents had had to sing and dance her to sleep, making up all sorts of silly Isabel songs and doing their own customized adaptation of "Kumbaya." Even with all that, she still ended up sleeping on the floor of their bedroom or sometimes crawling into bed with them.

Rita had tolerated this until her third daughter, Rebecca, was born. "We had learned to live with it; if she wants to live in a sleeping bag on the floor, fine. But now with one child on the floor and a newborn screaming in our bedroom, it was too much."

They held their meeting, made their chart, decorated it with little illustrations of her goals, and began the Shuffle.

"Instead of singing I told her I'd keep her company until she was having a good dream. We talked about things that were nice to dream about," Rita said. Isabel resisted the Shuffle only two or three nights. Mostly she was "really excited and pleased in the morning" when she put her stickers on her chart.

At first she still woke up some nights and came to them. "We'd walk her back to bed. We'd sit there if she needed us to. She was just so tired, all she would do was crawl back to bed and fall asleep. If she was really awake and distraught about something, I would end up staying with her." But within a few weeks, she stopped waking up.

Juggling three little girls in four years, Rita is ecstatic to have a "blessedly simple and short" bedtime. She gives Isabel and Deirdre their dinner and bath, then reads them books, with baby Rebecca on her arm. She puts Deirdre, the easier sleeper, in her crib first and says good night. Then they go to Isabel's room and she gets to pick out a few books of her own for Mom to read. "She gets into bed, gets a big hug and kiss and I say good night. She likes me to leave the door open, but she doesn't need me in the room anymore." No more singing and dancing.

Mary Catherine's Story

Mary Catherine did the Shuffle in stereo—two daughters at once. Ashley, like her much older brother, had been "Ferberized" as a baby, and slept reasonably well until she moved into a bed too early and her sleep fell apart. Then her baby sister Mimi was born. Mary Catherine had not co-slept with her first two children, but her whole life was different now; she was a stay-at-home mom and wanted to have her kids around her all the time. She co-slept and nursed the baby, but Ashley figured out that little sister was upstairs in bed with Mom and Dad, while she was stuck by herself downstairs. Eventually she joined the gang in the family bed. They all went to bed at around 9:00 p.m., Mom in the middle, one girl on each side, both girls twirling Mom's hair. Dad usually ended up in the guest room. Mimi also had a pacifier. A poor sleeper who seldom napped after the first year, Mimi was often overtired.

After about a year, Mary Catherine realized this was not a truly restful experience. "The girls were getting bigger and kicking and thrashing around. They were both very light sleepers. When I would get up to go to the bathroom, they would follow. If the TV was on, they were watching. If I was reading in bed, they were awake. I was suffocating and getting very frustrated."

Their pediatrician recommended that she separate the girls, "put locks on the doors on the outside and let them cry." That was way too much for Mary Catherine and Keith, so they tried all sorts of bribes—even a brand-new bunkbed for the girls. When Mary Catherine found Keith in the bottom bunk and the girls still in her bed, she knew they had hit rock bottom. She called me and took charge.

They had a family meeting with the girls, now three and five, and explained the new sleep scenarios. Mary Catherine introduced the new tassled satin pillows she had made for them to use as loveys they could twirl instead of her hair and explained that they would have each other for company in their shared room. She also bought some material like curly sheep fur (her own hair was very curly) as a backup. Brand-new Barbie sheets were an extra incentive, along with sticker charts and a system of rewards. Ashley understood the sticker chart; Mimi didn't quite get it, at least not enough to make it work for her at first.

Mary Catherine began the Shuffle sitting between the girls, first comforting one child, then the other. She also rolled up some blankets and put them on the sides of the bed to make the girls feel more snuggly and nestlike as they got used to sleeping without two or three other bodies in bed. The first five nights were hard, particularly on Mimi, and Mary Catherine felt sad about her daughters' obvious distress. In a stroke of unfortunate timing, Ashley had just started asthma medication that made her heart race and inhibited sleep. But Mary Catherine stuck it out, knowing that she needed to make this change, and knowing that the girls were getting a lot of comfort from each other. "Ashley became a little mom and would reassure Mimi," she said.

The Shuffle went reasonably well although she had some problems when she reached the hallway. One or both girls would want to come out after her, and Ashley fell asleep in the hallway a few times. If they got out of bed later or tried to make their way into their parents' bed, Mary Catherine would silently return them to their room. On a few very rough nights Mary Catherine threatened to close the door, and that definitely motivated them to stay in their room. It took three weeks before both girls slept through the night—Ashley, who started to twirl her own hair, would have done it earlier, but Mimi would wake her up, sometimes crawling into her big sister's bed. It's now been three years, and the girls sleep well, but Mary Catherine is still careful to enforce clear rules, including no sweets after 6:00 p.m. "Bedtime routine is not as strict as it was when we were laying down the law, but we're still consistent."

Part Three

CO-SLEEPING AND THE FAMILY BED

W
HEN I WORK WITH PEOPLE who are expecting a child, the subject of co-sleeping, or the family bed, always arises. That's not surpris-
ing. Co-sleeping is one of the most hotly debated child-rearing issues these
days, one that can push some intense emotional buttons. Some people argue
that it's the right and natural way to raise a child, that when parents and children share a bed they will have stronger bonds and a more secure attachment.
Others will tell you just as forcefully that it's risky, ridiculous, or simply not
what they want for their family.

My task is to help you figure out the right and comfortable sleep-
enhancing decision for both the parents and the child. I encourage parents to
make a decision before the baby is born, reserving the option to change their
minds without any guilt if your decision turns out not to be the best one for *you*.

It's important to understand that co-sleeping is not magic. Although
some proponents of the family bed would disagree, I have worked with
numerous couples whose babies did not necessarily sleep deeper or longer
because their parents were close by. In fact some parents found that their child
slept longer and woke less frequently when they stopped co-sleeping and
moved him into his own crib. In this chapter, I will help you take steps to help
your child improve his sleep skills in or out of the family bed, and I will guide
you in moving your child out of your bed and into his or her own crib or bed
if you need help in making that change.

CO-SLEEPING CATEGORIES

I divide co-sleeping into three categories—the committed co-sleepers, the short-term co-sleepers, and the "we didn't plan it this way" co-sleepers.

The committed co-sleepers are couples (also lots of single moms) who choose the family bed as a philosophy and lifestyle. Many are influenced by the child-rearing philosophy known as *attachment parenting* popularized by William and Martha Sears. These parents consciously decide to have the baby (or later, all the children) sleep with them until he expresses a desire for his own bed, even if that takes several years.

The short-term co-sleepers want the baby with them the first few months. They like the bonding and they like the convenience of having the newborn right there when they are nursing frequently. As new parents are often anxious parents, they may also feel less worried if the baby is by their side. (In the interest of full disclosure, Bill and I initially planned on co-sleeping with Carleigh for the first few months but I was so worried about rolling over on top of her that I didn't sleep a wink. She also made a lot of noise, even as a tiny baby. We put her, and later her sister, in her own room early on.) I recommend that if you choose to co-sleep with your newborn, plan to transition to the crib at about three months. During the three months in which you are co-sleeping, you should have the baby nap in his crib or bassinet consistently. Having him sleep on his own at nap time will make the eventual switch to nighttime sleep in the crib much smoother. It also makes it much easier for him (and you) to master the self-soothing skills for newborns I discuss in Chapter 3, The Right Start for Newborns and Infants.

The "we didn't plan it this way" co-sleepers are also called *reactive co-sleepers*. These parents end up with the baby in the bed part or all of the night, not by choice or philosophical commitment but because it's the only way they can get their baby to sleep at bedtime, or back to sleep in the middle of the night. Some started out as short-term co-sleepers but never figured out how to stop it. Others put the baby in the crib at bedtime but take her into their bed when she wakes up at night. And there are those who are ambivalent and either can't decide where they want the baby to sleep or are conflicted, with one parent advocating the family bed and the other wanting to put the baby in the crib. Disagreement on this issue usually results in a mishmash of crib sleeping and co-sleeping, which can make even a very young baby confused about where and how she is supposed to fall asleep. Even the most enthusiastic proponents of the family bed don't promote reactive co-sleeping.

WHAT'S RIGHT FOR YOU

When you are deciding whether long-term co-sleeping is right for you, an array of practical and emotional issues bear consideration. Think about your own childhood, your nighttime fears, your feelings of closeness to or isolation from your parents. Mothers working outside the home need to consider whether they want the extra closeness at night because they feel guilty or are afraid they are hurting the baby by being away from her during the day. I don't mean to imply that all parents who co-sleep do so out of guilt. But understanding your motives can often clarify your decision.

You need to think carefully about how having a child in bed with you all the time will affect your marriage. Think too about how you will deal with a growing family, when two or three children are in bed with you. If you are a single parent, consider the implications of integrating a new partner into your life when your child is sharing your pillow.

Keep in mind that co-sleeping is a long-term commitment, a practice that you will need to continue until the child *chooses* to transition to her own bed. Sometimes that takes a year or two, sometimes seven or eight. Reid and Julia, for instance, co-slept with their first two children and it was easy, pleasant, and emotionally gratifying. Both children quickly transitioned to their own beds. Then along came Todd, their third child, who was a very disruptive co-sleeper and didn't want to move until I helped them ease him into his own room at fourteen months.

Also take more mundane matters into account. How light a sleeper are you? Will a wriggling baby keep you up at night? Will you worry more if he's with you or away from you? Will you miss being able to read in bed with the light on, or watch television late at night? Will a baby in bed disrupt your marriage?

If you change your mind during the first three or four months, the transition isn't much of a problem. After that it gets harder, but not impossible. I've worked with many families who have practiced co-sleeping for two years and then decided that they needed to change their sleeping arrangements. I will give you advice on how to transition a two-year-old into her own bed as smoothly and gently as possible, but I must emphasize that I don't recommend letting a child sleep in your bed for two years and then abruptly sending her down the hall to her "own" bed. After all, she thinks your bed *is* her bed. And I definitely don't encourage abruptly ending co-sleeping with one child to make room for a new baby in your bed. (I'll have some suggestions later in this chapter for coping with that situation.)

SAFETY CONCERNS AND PRECAUTIONS

As you consider the pros and cons of the family bed, you should be aware of some safety issues. Some studies have found a higher risk of sudden infant death syndrome (SIDS) in families that co-sleep. The American Academy of Pediatrics and the U.S. Consumer Product Safety Commission (CPSC) has formally recommended against co-sleeping with a child under age two because of the possible risk of death or injury. The CPSC says that an average of sixty-four babies under age two die each year in adult beds, including waterbeds and daybeds, either because of suffocation or strangulation through entrapment. In a January 2003 bulletin posted on their site, the CPSC cited concerns associated with the co-sleeping of adult and baby that include suffocation of an infant who becomes entrapped or wedged between the mattress and another object, suffocation due to airway obstruction when the baby is facedown on a waterbed mattress, and strangulation in rails or openings on beds that allow a baby's body to pass through while entrapping the head.

If you decide to co-sleep, talk to your doctor about the most recent safety recommendations and do everything you can to reduce the hazards. Some experts recommend placing a firm, smooth mattress on the floor, with well-fitted sheets that can't be easily pulled off. Don't use any pillows or blankets in the early months and make sure the baby can't get stuck in a mattress pad. Don't use waterbeds or any other soft and flexible surfaces. Make sure there are no crevices or soft spots where the baby can get caught or smothered.

If your mattress is not on the floor, use well-designed guardrails that cannot entrap a baby. If your bed is next to the wall or other furniture, make sure there is no place the baby can get stuck or smothered.

Some experts, including Elizabeth Pantley, author of *The No-Cry Sleep Solution*, recommend placing the baby between the mother and the wall or rail, not between the two parents. She believes that fathers, grandparents, and babysitters don't have the same "instinctual awareness of a baby's location" and won't respond as well to the baby's needs and positioning. Pantley also says that mothers who are very deep sleepers, who won't wake up at the baby's subtle cues, might want to refrain from co-sleeping.

Do not sleep with your baby if you are very overweight, or if you have been drinking alcohol or using drugs or medications.

Sharing a Room

If you worry about safety but want your baby near you, consider keeping the bassinet or crib in your room or next to your bed where she will still be within easy reach for nursing, comforting, and those middle-of-the-night checks that all parents of infants go through. Various products to facilitate this approach are now on the market, including a co-sleeper that attaches to the bed like a sidecar.

QUALITY SLEEP IN THE FAMILY BED

If you do choose co-sleeping but want to make sure it's not all "co" and no "sleep," you can take steps to improve the quality of everyone's sleep. You can help your baby develop good sleep patterns and at least a degree of sleep independence.

As I mentioned, I very strongly recommend having the baby nap in his bassinet or crib and restricting the co-sleeping to nighttime. (An occasional exception of a parent-child nap will not create a problem.) Not only does this promote better sleep habits for the child, it gives the parent a lot more freedom. If your child naps on his own, you won't have to lie down with him at every nap time, or go to bed at 7:00 every night. (Napping while your baby naps is a great idea sometimes, particularly during those tiring newborn months, but you won't want to be locked into napping with him all the time for several years. It can also create a big child care napping problem if you go back to work or want to get out of the house now and then. It gets really complicated if you have two children napping at different times, or one who needs you to lie down with her and a slightly older one who isn't napping at all anymore and needs your supervision and attention.) If she's in a crib, you also have a little more freedom to move around your home. You don't have to stay in the room every minute to make sure she doesn't get smothered by your bedclothes or, when she gets a little older, roll out of bed.

Some couples who co-sleep but also want to foster a degree of sleep independence in their baby and a little early-evening freedom for themselves put the baby down in her crib at bedtime. Then they move her into the family bed when they get ready for sleep themselves, or the first time she wakes up at night.

Remember that sleep is a learned skill, regardless of whether your child is in your bed or her crib. Helping her develop the ability to fall asleep without being nursed, held, or rocked each and every time is an important foundation.

Try to put her down drowsy but awake at least once a day, as outlined in Chapter 1, The Sleep Lady System, and Chapter 4, Newborn to Five Months. The morning nap is usually the easiest time. This prevents reactive co-sleeping and reduces a baby's need to be nursed back to sleep at each partial arousal.

Try not to sleep with your baby latched on to your breast all night. Even if you are feeding on demand, realize that your baby might not always be demanding to feed. She might be perfectly content with other ways of being soothed and comforted if you give her a chance. If it's too hard for you to break that pattern, sleep in a T-shirt and/or try letting the dad do more of the snuggling and comforting. Remember that your breast is not the only tool in your soothing repertoire and review the suggestions on soothing in Chapter 3, The Right Start for Newborns and Infants.

If your baby is eating much more at night than during the day, keep track of her nursing patterns and then try to shift them. Consult the appropriate age chapter in this book for techniques on cutting back on nighttime nursing, even if you don't want to eliminate it completely, and adapt those strategies to the family bed. For instance, if your child were not co-sleeping, you would nurse her before putting her to bed and keep some separation between the two activities. If you are nursing in bed, you have to find subtler ways of creating that separation. Feed her, unlatch her while she's still awake, turn her away from you, and pull your shirt down. Then place her facing away from you, and put a lovey in her arms. You might also want to create a little space between you and the baby as she falls asleep after nursing. Comfort her to sleep but don't let her have your breast again until a predetermined interval has passed—two hours perhaps until a very young baby needs to be nursed again, four hours for a slightly older one. If she wakes up wanting the breast again sooner than that, use one of your other comforting techniques to help her get back to sleep. If that proves too hard, the mom might sleep in another room between nursings for a few nights, letting the dad comfort and share the bed with the baby.

Moving Out of the Family Bed

Many of my clients are couples who start out committed to co-sleeping and later find it doesn't quite work out for them. I also encounter lots of "we didn't plan it this way" couples seeking help in finally breaking the pattern. These families end up missing their privacy, or they end up just not getting very much sleep. Babies can be very noisy, squiggly sleepers, thrashing around or burrowing down to the foot of the bed, where you then worry about them being smothered in bedding. Some babies may not learn to sleep very well in bed with their parents, nursing frequently because the opportunity is always present, or because they are too stimulated to sleep much of the night simply by being so close to Mom and Dad. It can be a bit of a jolt for a couple who opted to co-sleep because they believed their baby truly needed their constant presence, only to find that this particular child sleeps better without them.

Although I told you my preference is that you make an informed decision about co-sleeping early on and stick to it, if you find it isn't working, do not hesitate to make a change. Don't feel guilty, and don't let anyone else make you feel guilty—or incompetent. You can and will have a strong and healthy attachment with your child even if you don't co-sleep. I'm going to share several families' stories to demonstrate how some couples have dealt with what can be a difficult transition. The switch goes pretty quickly for babies who are less than three or four months old, and I'll guide you through that. For older children, expect the adjustment to take at least three weeks, and then give it another two or three months until you can be confident the change has really taken root.

The one time I do not recommend ending co-sleeping with your child is with the birth of a new baby. It's not ideal to move one child out of your bed to make room for the next, particularly since fears, rivalries, and feelings of displacement are so common even without making dramatic changes. I know a few kids age three and older who have graciously gotten up and out of Mom and Dad's bed to accommodate the new baby but that is really asking an awful lot of them. Either complete the transition a good three to six months before the new baby comes, or keep the older child in your bed for a few more months. You can put the newborn in a bassinet or co-sleeper sidecar nearby. Then simultaneously transition both children to their own room or rooms. Some couples divvy up the co-sleeping tasks, with the mom in one room with the newborn and the dad in another room with the older child. They usually do that for a few months, until the newborn is sleeping through the night, and then end co-sleeping with both kids.

When you do move a child out of your bed, you must be completely consistent. You mustn't cave in and take her into your bed sometimes, not even when it's almost morning, or you are going to confuse her. This can be emotionally difficult for a parent who still enjoys aspects of sleeping with her child. If you miss that little baby head curled against your neck, find another way to satisfy that yearning with some extra cuddling throughout the day.

After a baby has been in your bed for months or years I suggest making changes in several stages over several weeks (though not every family goes through every step): daytime acclimation to her room; daytime napping; sleeping with the child in her room; the Sleep Lady Shuffle, my multistep program for teaching sleep independence. I'll explain each stage in more detail below.

If your child is old enough, try to prepare her by talking through the imminent change. Even a one-year-old may comprehend more than you realize, and certainly from eighteen months or so they can understand a good deal. Letting them know what is coming—and making it sound enticing and exciting—often helps the transition. For an older child, sticker charts and rewards are great incentives.

Stage One: Daytime and Playtime

Start by getting your baby used to his room awake and in daylight. In fact, he shouldn't just be used to it, he should like it. Play with him there, change him there, hug him and kiss him there. If he needs some incentives to venture into the unfamiliar room, or a room he may associate with isolation or fear, buy him some fun new toys or take some books and tapes out of the library. (You can skip this stage if your child is already playing in his room and/or napping there.)

Stage Two: Napping

If she's not already napping in her bedroom, start now. Spend a week or two getting her accustomed to napping in her own crib or bed during the day, before you make the nighttime transition. Go ahead and nap in her room with her for two or three days if your intuition tells you she needs that extra assistance. Then if she has trouble falling asleep in her room, sit with her for the next few days but try to be a fairly neutral presence. Calm and soothe her a bit but don't let her constantly engage you, or all the interaction will be an excuse for her not to sleep. After a few days, you can try the Sleep Lady Shuffle to help her learn to nap on her own. It is up to you whether you want to address the napping first, or napping and nighttime sleep simultaneously—it doesn't matter if you are sitting in exactly the same position day and night at this point. Instead of the Shuffle, you have the option of trying to settle her in for a nap with her lovey and then leave the room, checking on her every four or five minutes if she's crying. If that feels too abrupt to you remember that either approach is fine, and that you should choose the one that feels best for you and suits your child. Read the chapter for your child's age for details on the Shuffle and nap training.

Stage Three: The Sleep Lady Shuffle

When he's ready for night-training—and it will be clear; we're talking days or weeks, not months—you should start the Sleep Lady Shuffle, my method of gradually teaching the baby or child to put himself to sleep without you.

With most babies, you start the Shuffle by sitting right next to the crib or bed. With co-sleeping, I add one more preliminary phase. You can spend a few nights co-sleeping in his room with him, to create a bridge between the family bed and independent sleep. Throw a mattress on the floor, drag in the guest bed, pile up some sleeping bags, whatever is safe and comfortable for both of you.

On the fourth night, stay in his room in your makeshift bed but put him into his bed or crib. He might fuss or cry and want to join you but this is when consistency is critical. Stroke him intermittently, pat and soothe him, but don't relent and bring him into your bed. (If he's in a bed, not a crib, and he gets out and tries to join you, simply put him back immediately without a word. If he does this repeatedly or if you wake up at night and find he has joined you, skip ahead to the Shuffle step where you sit in a chair.) Stay there for two or three nights. If you let it go on longer, he will become accustomed to having you there and will have a more difficult adjustment when you try to leave.

Now you are ready for the Shuffle. Begin by sitting next to your child's crib or bed for three nights to soothe him. Every three nights move a little farther away so that he can gradually fall asleep a little more independently. Move across the room, then to the doorway, then out the door into the hall, and finally you will be able to leave him alone while still checking on him frequently. The fine points of the system vary a little bit by age, so please review my directions in the relevant age chapter.

Below are stories of several families who began co-sleeping—intentionally or unintentionally—and decided to make a change. Some could tolerate tears, and had tears to tolerate. Others were quite committed to attachment parenting, but found the sleep part of it had ceased working for them. All of them got their babies sleeping in their own beds in far less time than they had imagined.

Cynthia (Four Months)

Jayne and Paul were understandably nervous new parents. Cynthia was six weeks premature and spent some time in the newborn intensive care unit and on a home monitor. She was a colicky, fussy baby, requiring her parents to pace with her for three or four hours every night to calm her down. She fussed when they put her in a bassinet, and she balked when they tried to get her into the crib, so mostly she slept with Jayne—or more accurately, she slept on top of Jayne. "I was a nervous new parent and I couldn't sleep. I had to lie on my back with this baby on top of me," Jayne recalled. "I was exhausted and grumpy. It was taking up half my day to walk her to sleep and hold her when she was napping."

When they consulted me, Cynthia was four months old. Our first task was to get her into the crib. To prepare, Jayne revised what had been a far too late nap schedule. Cynthia had been napping from around 4:00 to 7:00 p.m., meaning she was overstimulated, tired, and fussy earlier in the afternoon when she should have been napping, and then up way too late at night. Jayne started having her nap much earlier in the afternoon. She'd nurse her, and put her in the crib drowsy but awake. To make the crib feel more cozy and less vast to a little baby used to being snugly held, Jayne rolled up two receiving blankets, fastened them with ponytail holders, and placed them at the top and bottom of the crib (after reviewing the exact placement and technique with her pediatrician to ensure there was no suffocation risk). She also used a sleep positioner that Cynthia clearly liked, to keep her in place and make her feel more snug.

As Jayne expected, Cynthia cried at first when her mom put her down for her nap. Earlier Jayne hadn't been able to cope with any tears, but now she was more comfortable with letting her cry a little bit. In fact, once Jayne decided tears weren't lethal, she ended up having a higher tear tolerance than many moms I work with (and you don't have to tolerate as many tears as she did if it's outside your comfort zone). Jayne found that if she stayed in the room with Cynthia but did not pick her up and nurse her, Cynthia threw the newborn equivalent of a hissy fit. She screamed and none of Jayne's assiduous attempts to comfort her did any good. But Jayne found that if she worked on soothing and calming and preparing Cynthia for her nap, and timed the nap right, she could put the baby down in her crib and leave the room. Cynthia would cry for a few minutes and then fall asleep.

Having a schedule was a godsend for Jayne. The structure suited her, and she had intuited early on that it would suit Cynthia's temperament. But until we sat down and talked about feeding and sleeping needs and patterns for newborns, she hadn't really known how to establish a suitable schedule. "Cynthia wasn't a 'go with the flow' kind of baby. She couldn't deal when she was tired; she'd just be fussy. I desperately wanted a schedule. I wanted to know, this is when she's going to nap, this is when she'll eat, this is when I can make plans."

Jayne and Paul also revised the evening routine. They fed her at about 6:00 p.m.—when a few weeks earlier she had still been napping. They'd give her a bath, change her, and read her a little book. (Some newborns like books, some don't.) Then they put her down in her crib, sat by her side, patted and comforted her—and she did cry. "I thought this was horrible, it was going to scar her for life, but my husband reminded me that no, it wouldn't, that she needed to sleep, this is something she needed to learn how to do." They ended up leaving her alone but checking on her about every twenty to thirty minutes. It's not an approach that all families I work with like—it's not all that different from Ferber—but it felt right for them because Cynthia actually did better left on her own than with a parent in the room.

Jayne and Paul's goal at this point wasn't to get Cynthia sleeping through the night. It was just to get her sleeping in the crib. So when she woke at night, Jayne nursed her right back to sleep but then put her in her crib, not in her parents' bed. By the end of the week, she was going into her crib without screaming, and was sleeping up to five hours at a stretch. Jayne was ready for stage two, cutting back on the nighttime nursing and encouraging Cynthia to sleep all night. They went from three to two nighttime feedings, and then at six months, eliminated the feedings completely. "I thought she couldn't go that long without food, but once we took the feedings away, we realized she could," Jayne said. If she woke up early, before 5:00 a.m., they would go in and pat and soothe her but not feed her or take her out of her crib until 6:00. They still go through stages when she wakes up on the early side, but in general she's a "super sleeper," going to bed at 7:00 p.m. and staying asleep for twelve solid hours.

Kevin (Eight Months)

Heidi and Steve were "we didn't plan it this way" co-sleepers. Although Kevin was born a big, hearty nine pounds and certainly didn't need to eat all night long, at eight months he was still getting up almost every hour wanting to nurse. His parents ended up keeping him in their bed because it was so much less disruptive to their sleep than having to go to him and nurse every-hour. Kevin did nap in his crib, which helped the eventual transition. But once Heidi decided to stop nursing him at night and keep him in his crib, it was easier than they expected, using the Shuffle. The first night didn't go too well. Kevin cried and Heidi, sitting by his crib, interacted a lot, which is fine the first night, but you have to be careful about not letting him make a habit of it. She rubbed his back, talked to him, and slipped her arm through the crib bars

Co-sleeping Transition for Babies under Six Months

For babies under six months, you don't need the Shuffle or any preliminaries. You can just move her into her crib and sit by her bedside and soothe her to sleep. Don't pat or stroke her constantly. Give her enough contact to feel loved and secure, but not so much contact that it becomes a sleep crutch—that she needs you to be there stroking her all the time at bedtime and during the night. You can then gradually move farther away, in a modified version of the Shuffle, or you can try just putting her down in her crib, offering some love and assurance, leaving, and coming back to check on her every few minutes.

After she gets accustomed to sleeping in her crib, keep your bed strictly off limits for three months or else you'll start the whole cycle all over again, which is not fair to her. Snuggle—but not in your bed. Find a comfy chair or couch somewhere and don't let her fall asleep in your arms. After three months, it's okay to let her snuggle in your bed sometimes but don't let her fall asleep there.

If your child has been going to bed in her crib but ending up with you in the middle of the night, you can't ease out of this habit gradually. You have to stop it, and stop it consistently. You can stroke, soothe, whisper, murmur, and pat your baby when she gets up and expects to come to you, but don't give in, not if you really want to end the co-sleeping. That means you have to keep her in her crib every time—at 2:00, 3:00, 4:00, and 5:00 a.m. If you reassure her but make her stay in her crib at 2:00, 3:00, and 4:00, but take her into your bed at 5:00—you have confused her and possibly trained her to cry longer and harder next time. Babies can't tell time. She can't understand why you take her into your bed sometimes and not others. It's a classic example of intermittent reinforcement and it's only going to make life harder for both of you.

so he could fall asleep hugging it. The next night she patted him and whispered more sporadically, and gave him more space to fall asleep on his own. By the fifth night, he went to bed much more easily, with Heidi sitting in a chair halfway to the door. He woke up only once that night. When he did wake up, she would soothe him but make him stay in his crib. She would not nurse him. They let him keep his pacifier, but when he demanded it at night, they would try to remember to put it in his hand without saying a word and leave. Over the next two weeks, the nighttime awakenings steadily tapered off, until they were the exception not the rule. When he did wake up, Heidi or Steve would still go in to comfort him, but as he got older, they found that if they went in, he would only wake up more, interact, and stay up longer. If they let him work it out himself, he would cry for one or two minutes and then go back to sleep. "I can tolerate the tears now—I know it's not going to damage him forever," said Heidi. "It's two minutes—and then he's asleep." If he cries much longer or more sharply than that, which is highly unusual, they assume he needs them and they respond.

Candice (Eleven Months)

At eleven months, Candice had a severe aversion to her room. She had been co-sleeping with her mom, Patty, while her dad, Don, afraid of squishing her, had been sleeping in another room. When Candice was six months old, her parents had made an attempt at reclaiming their bed and tried to "Ferberize" her. It was a disaster. Candice cried and cried and cried, and the more she cried, the more awake she became. The experience traumatized her so badly she would not even go into her room anymore, not even to play, not even accompanied by parents. She went back into their bed—and Don went back into the guest room. Five more months passed, and her parents finally decided something had to give.

The first step was to reacquaint Candice with her room. Patty put lots of enticing new toys there and the two of them played there together each day. This went on for two weeks. We actually altered the usual order. Instead of working on naps, which were difficult for Candice, we addressed bedtime. Patty put Candice in her crib, while she slept on an air mattress on the floor. When Candice protested or awoke in the middle of the night wanting Mom, Patty was near her, but would not pick her up. Patty would reach through the crib slats to pat and reassure her daughter.

Then Patty and Don did the Sleep Lady Shuffle. Patty noticed that Candice was beginning to develop her own techniques for soothing herself to sleep, twirling her hair, playing with her crib, and using her pacifiers not only to suck on but to play with. Finally it was time for the big move—leaving Candice's room so she could fall asleep on her own. When Patty was ready to leave, she told Candice where Mommy would be, and what she would be doing. There were some tears for four or five nights, but she never got so hysterical that she couldn't calm herself down, nor did the tears ever get so intense that Patty and Don couldn't tolerate them. During those nights, they would check on her from the doorway every five minutes, and if they sensed Candice needed a little more reassurance, Patty would give her a quick hug. That was the last hurdle. Then just when Patty and Don thought

252 · GOOD NIGHT, SLEEP TIGHT

they were done, Candice got sick. They handled it well. Instead of taking her back into their bed and ending up at square one, Patty would sit in a chair in Candice's room until the baby was very calm and drowsy, but not completely asleep. When she recovered, they checked on her from the doorway for a few nights. Candice quickly became an excellent sleeper. Soon Patty and Don could even leave her with a sitter and go out for dinner. "It's a totally different world for us," her mother said. "Now she loves to sleep in her crib."

Alex (Fifteen Months)

Adele and Geoff read every book and tried every technique with Alex before they came to me. By then, he was fifteen months and very confused about what he was supposed to do to get to sleep. "Everything worked a little bit but nothing worked completely," Adele said. They had "Ferberized" him earlier and while it helped him fall asleep, it didn't keep him asleep. Eventually they tried letting him cry it out for those middle-of-the-night awakenings too but it was intolerable; he cried and cried and cried, three or four hours at a stretch. "I couldn't take it. It was two a.m., he was in there crying, showing no sign of stopping, and just crying himself more awake. That panicked me. So I went back to nursing him to sleep. That would work; it would only take five minutes. But I'd have to do it three or four times a night." Later she weaned him at night but it was a slow process, taking about six weeks, partly because he got sick several times around then and Adele would nurse him again while he wasn't feeling well. By age one, the nighttime weaning was over but he was still waking up all night and she wasn't about to put up with all those tears anymore. Desperate, she started taking him into her bed. "He'd go back and forth, shuttling between the crib and the bed. It was horrible and I felt like a complete failure because I had been so anti–baby in bed."

Adele and Geoff realized that they couldn't confuse Alex with any more partial solutions. They decided to do the Sleep Lady Shuffle and stick with it. It didn't take long. Before we started, we made sure he got good daytime sleep so he wouldn't be overtired at bedtime. He napped in his room, and we limited the naps to an hour in the morning and ninety minutes in the afternoon. We wanted to time naps to maximize his readiness to sleep at bedtime. We wanted him tired but not overtired, rested but not so rested that he would fight sleep. We also cut the holding and rocking at nap time in half, right from the start, particularly for the morning nap.

To prepare for the Shuffle, Geoff slept on the floor in Alex's room with Alex in the crib. There, he could comfort Alex when he woke up at night, without bringing him into the family bed. Geoff also took bedtime duty the first few nights of the Shuffle because Alex, like many toddlers, tended to cry less at night with his dad than his mom. But after that, because of work and wake schedules, Adele took weeknights and Geoff took weekends.

"We moved every three nights. It was three nights sleeping on the floor, three sitting by the bed, three in a chair near the door, three in the doorway, three just outside the door. By the time we got to just outside the door, he really didn't wake up for very long and he didn't really cry. He'd fuss and I'd go in and say 'night-night,' and he would lie down. His head would pop up like a turtle to see if someone was still there, but it was very sporadic. Some nights I'd hear him fuss briefly but he'd go right back to sleep," his mother remembered.

When he woke up at night, Adele and Geoff didn't take him out of bed, and they were very consistent about not taking him back into their bed. "I would go in and say 'Night-night' or 'Night-night, go to sleep' and pat him on the back. I'd hand him his animal and, during the first week, I'd sit in his room or lie on the floor," his mother said. Although he did cry during the night, it wasn't the three- and four-hour jags they'd experienced earlier. The absolute longest he ever cried was thirty minutes, and he always had a parent in the room with him comforting him. "He's a crier, he's a screamer. But he quickly learned that crying wasn't going to cut it anymore. He wasn't coming into our bed. He had to sleep."

When Alex woke up at night, he'd often do his screaming standing up. Adele would pat the mattress and encourage him to lie down, but she didn't keep intervening and putting him down. "He was standing, then he'd be sitting, and he'd fall asleep sitting up and fall over like a tree." That didn't wake him, and Adele and Geoff quickly learned to leave it alone. At some point in his sleep cycle, he would wiggle himself into a more conventional sleeping position. But if they tried to lay him down and straighten him out, it would backfire. He'd be wide awake again. It's a lesson many families learn the hard way. Children often sleep in positions that look uncomfortable to us— but feel fine to them. Unless there's a hazard, you are better off not trying to resettle them. If they're really uncomfortable, they'll let you know it! (Do run an unconventional sleep position by your doctor, though, just in case it's linked to apnea and he's adopted that posture to keep his airways open. Read Chapter 13, Medical Problems, for more information.)

Todd (Fourteen Months)

Julia and Reid were committed to attachment parenting, and had enjoyed co-sleeping with their first two children, now both in school. In addition to believing in the family bed as part of a child-rearing approach that fosters bonding and security, Julia also felt she slept better just having to stir briefly to nurse without having to get out of bed and go into another room. With their first two children, both girls, they co-slept from birth but as the girls began settling into more regular sleep and feeding patterns—without much of a nudge from their admittedly schedule-averse mother—Julia and Reid began putting them in their own cribs, with age-appropriate bedtime rituals and routines. If they woke up needing a feeding while Julia was still awake, she'd nurse them in a rocking chair and return them to their cribs. But when the girls would wake up at about 2:00 a.m. for a feeding, Reid would quickly fetch them and bring them back to the family bed. Julia could nurse without having to wake up completely, and everybody then slept contentedly together until morning. As that middle-of-the-night feeding time got later and later, the co-sleeping window shrank. Eventually the girls just slept all night in their cribs, by nine months with one daughter, twelve months with the other. The shift was gradual and easy. Then came Todd. He was fourteen months old when his family consulted me. All was not well.

Todd had a number of health problems, including allergies and one prolonged and severe ear infection that led to surgery to insert tubes. Although those conditions aggravated Todd's disjointed sleep, they didn't fully explain it. And once his ears were better and his allergies addressed, he still didn't sleep any longer or better. He nursed much more frequently than his sisters had, slept more poorly, and had a less malleable temperament.

"Todd wasn't an easily detached baby. We even had to leave a co-op preschool because he didn't separate well," his mom said.

Getting so little sleep with him in their bed, they first tried to move him to a crib at eight months. It didn't work. Instead of Todd napping in the crib, Julia ended up taking thirty-minute walks around the house with the stroller. "It gets pretty boring making endless loops on those hardwood floors," Julia said. Bedtime was a struggle. They had to rock and nurse him to sleep, and he didn't stay asleep unless he was in their bed, nursing and snuggling. "We had to add all these layers of shenanigans on top of all the rituals," Reid recalled. At the same time, they were dealing with two other young children with their own bedtime needs and demands. So they put Todd back in their bed and tried to make the best of it.

Julia and Reid knew that Todd was capable of sleeping all night and in a crib if he wanted to. He had proven that when Julia had surgery for kidney stones and pumped so Todd could have breast milk in a bottle. Todd didn't like bottles, so he just slept all night, albeit not very happily. "That worked until those breasts were back in his world, and that's what he wanted," she ruefully recalled.

When I saw them, we talked a lot about their parenting styles, what changes they would be able to make, what changes just weren't realistic given their personalities, values, and lifestyles. "I am not a schedule person—you give me hours to follow and I come unhinged," Julia said. She identified which tasks she could accomplish, and which she had to turn over to Reid. She agreed to work on limiting feedings to six times a day and to try comforting techniques other than nursing, not an easy task with an agile and determined fourteen-month-old who whenever he got distressed would try to climb up his mom, lift up her shirt, and wriggle himself underneath. They also switched the dinner hour from 6:00 to 5:00, so they'd have plenty of time to eat as a family and to start Todd's bedtime routine at 7:00 and have him asleep by eight. Before, he had gone to bed at 9:00 or 9:30, too late for a one-year-old.

At night, as we began the Sleep Lady Shuffle, we wanted to create a distinct separation between nursing and sleep. Julia nursed downstairs in the sunroom at about 6:30. (Most families I work with nurse in the child's bedroom, being careful not to nurse the child into a deep sleep. In Todd's case, we thought additional separation was warranted.) Julia knew that she wouldn't be able to cope with the initial phase of sleep training so Reid took charge. Todd went down more easily than they expected the first night, with his dad sitting by his side. But he woke up at 11:00 p.m. and again at midnight. The second time was the worst. He screamed furiously for an hour and twenty minutes. Reid sat next to him, calm and consistent. "I knew it was okay to touch him but not to hold his hand. I knew to pat him on the back and then stop, or to pat the mattress gently. It was almost more difficult for me than for him, because you want to reach out, you want to take care of your kid. But I knew I couldn't start out holding his hand because I would be moving farther away in a few nights and I wasn't going to be able to hold his hand when I was five feet away," Reid said.

Julia sat outside the bedroom and tried to empathize through the door until she finally realized that she needed to stop listening, ignore the baby monitor, and try to get some sleep for herself.

The second night, Todd got mad. Reid, who is pretty laid back, remembered thinking, "Oh my God, I've got a demon child in the crib!" Todd threw things out of the crib, and tried to crawl out. They put a really big nightshirt on him so he couldn't get a leg hold.

"I just kept repeating the same reassuring words. I just kept repeating them like I was teaching a dog a trick. 'Todd, you can do this, go night-night. You can do this, go night-night.' By three days, I just shortened it to, 'Night-night, night-night,'" Reid remembered.

The third day Reid saw an improvement. It still wasn't easy but looking at his log, Reid could see that Todd had cried for twenty-two minutes. "That felt like a lot—until I looked back and saw he had cried one hour and twenty minutes the first night. It was bumpy and not a lot of fun but it was getting better." Reid and Julia were still having doubts and second-guessing themselves at this point, but decided to stick with it and gave each other moral support.

By the time Reid reached the point where he had to leave the room, he was feeling much more optimistic. "I realized the next step didn't have to be a big step. I was confident he could do it." Reid came back and checked on Todd every five minutes or so. The nights Julia took bedtime duty, she made less frequent checks because Todd would get furious if he saw her but didn't get to nurse himself to sleep. "It was tough for a few nights," she recalled. "But we knew he was pulling it together."

Julia says she still believes in attachment parenting, still turns to Sears and Sears for child-rearing advice. But she is a little more open to modifications and alternatives based on her children's temperaments, less afraid that she will hurt her children or weaken her bond with them, if she doesn't do everything by the attachment theory book. "I was a Sears devotee and I still tend to be," she said. "But what I found is that before we started sleep training, I had a sweet, wonderful tired little boy. When we finished, I had a sweet, wonderful little boy who wasn't tired." He wasn't less secure, less attached, less loving, or less happy. He was only less exhausted.

Partly because they were still a little ambivalent about the co-sleeping and partly because the family experienced lots of changes and adjustments in the next few months—Reid lost his job when the high-tech bubble burst and the family spent several months traveling around trying to decide where to relocate—they were not always completely consistent. Sometimes Todd didn't cry at all at bedtime, sometimes he'd cry for four or five minutes, but never longer than that and never as ferociously as he had those first two nights. Among Todd's first full phrases was, "Mommy, lie down, bed." And sometimes one parent did give in and lie down with him, particularly while they were traveling or going through one transition or another. "We've had some recidivism," said Reid. "And then it takes a few days to get back. The lesson to be learned is the more you get into a routine and stick to a routine, the easier it is for the kids to know what to expect."

Months later, Todd was generally restricting his bedtime screaming to hotel stays with his sisters. And, his father confided, "He only does that because he thinks it's a riot."

Kerry (Two and a Half Years Old)

Laurel and Richard were classic "we didn't plan it this way" co-sleepers. Kerry slept in a crib—except when he didn't. When he fussed and wanted his mom, Laurel slept with him in the family room or guest room. He was quite young when he moved into a toddler bed where she couldn't fit, but when he got out of bed, as toddlers often do, they often ended up asleep together on the floor.

Philosophically, she didn't object to sleeping with him, only neither of them slept very much. "If I had to sleep with him—well, okay. But sleeping with him wasn't even resolving the issue. He was extremely restless. He would be perpendicular in the bed, kicking me in the head, rolling around a lot. I was so worried about him rolling off, he was moving so much, I couldn't sleep," said Laurel, a therapist who knew about behavioral modification with older children but found it was "a lot different when you are dealing with your own emotional stuff and your own child."

Shortly before he turned two and a half, I urged them to dismantle the toddler bed and leave the mattress on the floor because that's where he was accustomed to sleeping. Before starting the Sleep Lady Shuffle, we tweaked his bedtime routine to change, but not shorten, his snuggle time. They did the bath, toothbrushing, etc., and then Laurel and Kerry snuggled up to read books on a little couch in his room. To earn his last story, his special reading of *Toy Story*, he had to get into bed. "That was the incentive; we could entice him into bed," Laurel said. They also used a star chart for good bedtime behavior.

After reading to Kerry, Laurel turned off the light and began the Shuffle, sitting by his side on the floor. The first night, she kept her hand on him because she knew he was going to need that contact. By the second night she was careful to make the hand-touching more sporadic lest it become another sleep crutch. She returned to his side and patted his hand, without lying down with him, each time he woke those first nights.

Since Kerry was on the floor and was used to having Laurel there as well, she never used a chair. She sat on the floor but she moved through the Shuffle, to the end of the bed, the doorway, then out in the hall. But since he was used to having the door closed, she sat in the hall on the far side of a closed door. "He knew I was right on the other side of it. He didn't really care one way or another; he was already drifting off to sleep on his own."

Kerry had progressed nicely, in less than two weeks. But he was still getting up at night to look for Mom. She would take him back to his room silently. Resisting the impulse to lie down and sleep with him—and it can be a strong impulse when you are tired and want to get both you and your baby back to sleep quickly—she would assume whatever position she had been in at bedtime that night and sit there until he drifted back to sleep. The night wakenings tapered off. There were some bumps, because he'd regress each time he got sick or traveled, but the overall progress was good. I stayed in touch with the family for several months, and as he got closer to age three, I suggested that Laurel, who sometimes had trouble setting limits, be a little stricter. I advised her to give him lots of choices during the day but to enforce extremely well-defined limits around bedtime behavior. That meant an occasional bedtime tantrum, but Laurel learned to set rules and age-appropriate consequences without ever slipping back into co-sleeping.

Two Children (Dylan, Five Years; Leila, Fifteen Months)

While earning her masters in education and working with at-risk preschoolers, Shauna had studied cross-cultural child rearing and become convinced that co-sleeping was the right and natural path. When she and Nick had children, they were drawn to Sears and Sears books and other advocates of attachment parenting. Shauna nursed Dylan on demand, breastfeeding until he was almost two and a half. She carried him in a sling and co-slept, including lying down with him at nap time. Although they had been trying to transition him to a bed, it was not very successful and he usually stayed with them. That's where he was at age four, when Shauna went into labor with his little sister, Leila.

Shauna didn't initially bring Leila full-time into an already crowded bed. Instead she placed her in an adjacent co-sleeper for six months, and then brought her into the family bed. In the meantime, they worked on shifting Dylan into his own bed. They managed to get him out of their bed, but one of the parents often ended up sleeping in his bed! Or they'd get him to sleep, and he'd crawl back in their bed, or someone, somewhere would end up sleeping on the floor to be near someone else.

Exhausted by this routine, Shauna set goals. She wanted Dylan sleeping all night in his own bed. She wanted Leila to stop nighttime nursing and be in her crib at fifteen months. With my help, she and Nick tackled both children's sleep issues simultaneously, with Nick concentrating on Dylan and Shauna on Leila, who was still being breastfed at bedtime and during the day.

They called a family meeting for Dylan, who was now five, and explained their expectations. They made him a star sticker chart with five sleep manners. If he earned all five stars for a whole week, he would get a toy. He also had both moral support and a little peer pressure in his preschool where another little girl had worked with me. She became his sleep buddy as they compared their star tallies.

They began the Sleep Lady Shuffle. "He cried at the beginning. He'd say, 'I want Mommy.' Then he would be really proud of himself for quieting down and falling asleep," Shauna said. If he came to them at night, one of them would quietly walk him back to his own room. "We'd sit in a chair outside the door of his room where he could see us, but there was no talking. If he was having a bad dream or he was scared, we would help him think of happy things," she said. After five years of co-sleeping and emotional ambivalence about ending it, they were not always consistent. They knew it was unwise to lie down with Dylan, but they relapsed, sometimes because their hearts tugged their heads toward their little boy's pillow, sometimes because they were just too tired to do anything else. They had become a sort of hybrid of backsliding "committed co-sleepers" and "we didn't plan it this way" co-sleepers. When Nick traveled overseas, Shauna, by then pregnant with a third child, allowed Dylan to have a "sleepover" in Mom's bed. "He was getting up and walking in and I just let him—I couldn't deal with both his and Leila's sleep issues while I was pregnant and Nick was away. It was just too much for me to handle." She knew there would be sleep consequences but decided to face them, believing she would be able to cope better when Nick was back home and she could get more rest. Meanwhile, Leila was making progress, partly because Shauna was determined to improve Leila's sleep before the next baby came. Nighttime weaning took only two nights. Shauna still nursed her before bed but during the night she would offer her a cup of water; Leila wasn't all that interested in it so Shauna stopped. Then she would pat Leila and hold her until she fell asleep without anything in her mouth. At the same time, she introduced a lovey to distract Leila from touching Shauna's hair as she fell asleep.

Leila had sometimes spent at least part of the night in a crib, but it was in her parents' room. Now they moved the crib to her own room. Shauna and Leila slept on the floor together for one night, but Leila kept trying to sleep on top of Shauna's chest. Although Shauna's own style and preference was to be very slow and gradual, something told her not to sleep on the floor too long, that Leila would start expecting to sleep this way. The next night she nursed Leila until she was drowsy but still awake and then put her into her crib and began the Shuffle.

Leila accepted the changes reasonably well during the first few nights when Shauna was sitting by her side, but once Mom moved that chair away, Leila stood up in her crib and let everyone know she was mad. Shauna at first tried to be a calming, soothing presence, but by the end of a week realized that Leila did better if her mom just left the room. She cried for three minutes— tear-sensitive Shauna clocked it—and then put herself to sleep and pretty much stayed asleep. She woke up too early, 5:00 a.m., so for the first few mornings Shauna lay on a mattress on the floor and her presence helped Leila get back to sleep. Later Shauna would go in and pat and reassure Leila if she woke up too early and then leave the room as Leila drifted back to sleep.

Leila's sleep for the next six months or so was good but not perfect, partly because the family went away for a month that summer shortly after the Shuffle. Leila potty trained early, which has its advantages, but she would yell, "Potty, potty, potty," wanting to get out of the crib at night. She slept through the night for a while, but then began waking up again in the early morning, between 4:00 and 6:00. She also tried to climb out of her crib before age two, but Shauna stopped it. "I wasn't ready for her to get *out* of the crib. I had just gotten her in it!" Like many toddlers, she also went through those spells of separation trouble at bedtime, and Shauna experimented with how to ease those fears. She found that at times Leila sought her presence but not her touch. She sat in a chair in Leila's room at night, and knew that soon she would have to start leaving the room, despite Leila's protests, or else face sitting there for the next few years. Pregnant with her third child, that was not in Shauna's game plan.

Shauna and Nick still believed in co-sleeping but decided to limit it even further with their third child. The plan was to co-sleep for four months, and then get the baby into a crib. With each child, they also paid more attention to how often he ate, and whether he was really seeking the breast or expressing some other infant needs and desires. "I still believe in nursing on demand—but I have to be more aware and recognize what he's demanding, whether he's hungry. I have to be aware when I'm nursing him to sleep," Shauna said.

She's also seen her own attitudes evolve, and keep evolving with each child. She attributes much of Dylan's warm and affectionate personality to his attachment parenting infancy and still can't bear to hear him cry. "If he needs us, we go in." With Leila it's different. Shauna can tolerate more tears, and she doesn't feel the need to be as physically close as much of the time. "With each child, I have more knowledge and experience. I'm still Sears and Sears oriented, I like the attachment parenting philosophy but I'm also fascinated by the science of sleep. It's what my heart wants versus what my brain knows I should do about sleep. What feels natural is not the most sleep promoting, what feels natural often gets in the way."

11

TWINS AND SIBLINGS

MY SLEEP LADY GUIDELINES APPLY whether you have one, two, three, or even more babies, but applying the rules is harder when multiples are involved. Parents need to know how to coordinate two babies' schedules and sleeping styles, to know when the babies should share a room and when they should be apart. In this chapter, I'll pay particularly close attention to families with twins, but I'll also show how families with several children deal with conflicting sleep needs, particularly at bedtime. Be sure to also read the chapter corresponding to your children's ages for specifics on their sleep and schedule needs.

 TWINS

Taking care of two newborns is an awesome task and I encourage families with twins to get their babies on a schedule as soon as possible, particularly for feeding. For guidance, read Chapter 3, The Right Start for Newborns and Infants, and Chapter 4, Newborn to Five Months. Begin the gentle first stages of newborn sleep shaping by the time they are six weeks old (if they were premature, use the adjusted age, counting six weeks from due date, not from birth). Start putting them down drowsy but awake at least once a day and watch their sleep windows. Wake them at the same time in the morning, or allow one to wake the other, so you can get them more in sync early on.

Some moms tandem feed the babies, one on each breast. Others nurse whichever baby wakes up first, and then wake and feed the other one. That way they should still be waking up within thirty, maybe forty-five minutes, of each other.

If your babies were premature, it may take them a *little* longer to sleep through the night. But it shouldn't take much longer, not if they are healthy, gaining weight, and growing well. Check with your doctor, but it's reasonable for them to sleep about eight to ten hours at a stretch by around four months, and to sleep all night by about six months, age adjusted. Don't convince yourself that their prematurity is an excuse for you not to deal with their sleep needs.

I urge all parents, *but especially those with twins,* to keep a simple food and sleep log. It's hard to remember everything about one baby's sleep without writing it down; it's impossible with two. The log will also help you see how their sleep windows, sleep cues, and internal clocks differ, and where they overlap.

From Womb to Room

These babies have been sharing a womb, and it's usually a good idea to have them share a room. Some families even put them in the same crib for a few months, until they start rolling over. Yes, they may grunt, whimper, and make all sorts of strange baby noises, but they almost always sleep through each other's sounds and you want to encourage them to do so. Be careful about responding too quickly if one makes a noise. Parents often rush in as soon as they hear a peep, fearing that one will wake up the other one. You may be reinforcing the troubled sleeper while you protect the one who is asleep. You may be teaching her to make noises so you'll come flying to pick her up all the time. The sleeping twin may be oblivious, or she may stir but then get herself right back to sleep, exactly as you want her to do.

Ethan and Nathanial were both poor sleepers at seven months, waking each other up, demanding to be rocked and held. "Someone had to hold them until they were asleep. You'd put them down, and they'd wake up, they'd be very upset, and you'd have to rock them again," Charlotte remembered. It was bad enough at night with two sleepy parents, and it was impossible at nap time when Charlotte was home alone trying to pace and rock two at once. Working with me, Charlotte and Ed began creating more of a bedtime routine, and learned to put the boys down drowsy but

awake. They'd cry, but Charlotte would come in frequently, sitting in the
room and helping them calm down. She never let them cry alone for more
than ten minutes before she returned to their room. For naps, however,
they did separate the boys, and they kept them apart for nap time
throughout their toddler and preschool years.

In those cases where one twin sleeps well and the other one wakes up so
loudly and frequently that he really does disrupt the other's sleep, I do make
exceptions and separate them at night during sleep coaching. Once the poorer
sleeper is sleeping through the night (or waking for a single feeding if that's
age appropriate and you're satisfied) you can return them to their shared room.
It's usually a good idea to leave the poorer sleeper where he is, and move the
sounder sleeper to another room, using a portable crib if necessary. Good
sleepers tend to be more flexible and can more easily adjust to a temporary
new sleep place, particularly if it's a little noisier or brighter than the babies'
bedroom.

Sandy and Jonathan's twins, Marissa and Sasha, had terrible colic
and probably some gas pains as well. The couple had plenty of help. Four
grandparents lived nearby, but sometimes six adults could not keep up
with two colicky infants. When Sandy first called me, I told her to get
through the colic as best she could and we'd start sleep shaping when it
subsided. At four months, it dissipated swiftly, and we got to work.
At the beginning the girls had slept in a shared crib, in their parents'
bed, and finally in a pair of swings. Sandy treated the swing as a
temporary colic survival measure; she used it a lot from about eight to
twelve weeks and then sensibly began dividing the girls' time between the
swings and the cribs. Sandy and Jonathan also began trying to get the girls
to sleep for longer intervals in the swings, with less frequent feedings,
another wise move that laid the foundation for subsequent progress. As
they got a little older, Sandy and Jonathan began putting the babies in the
crib at bedtime, moving them into the swings only if they had a lot of
trouble getting them back to sleep later at night.
When I started working with the family, at about four and a half
months, we wanted to complete the transition from swing to crib, and cut
back even more on the nighttime feedings, crying, pacifier fetching, and
assorted other interruptions. I urged them not to run in so quickly, and not
to pick the babies up so much when they did run in. Sandy and Jonathan
had always had a video monitor on the twins, so they had been rushing to

the cribs even when they knew nothing was really wrong. They learned to watch the monitor with a more critical eye. "Even at four months I could see Marissa crying, glancing at the door, and crying some more," Sandy recalled. She was looking to see if anyone was coming in! At four months! That told me that I was the one being trained, and after that, we really picked up the effort to reverse it, to train her." Nighttime improved, particularly after the parents decided to stop chasing two sets of pacifiers all night long, at about five months. Marissa slept better before Sasha. Sasha used to throw all her loveys and toys into Marissa's crib, and then scream because she didn't have her favorite things anymore, forcing Marissa to rouse herself and hand the blanket back through the crib, so they could both get to sleep. "They have a lot of empathy for each other. It's really neat to watch," Sandy said. Napping was tough at first, because the girls were not on the same schedule, and if one woke the other one up, it would throw the whole day off for both of them and often cascade disastrously into the next day as well. Sandy separated them for about two months during the day, as she worked on lengthening and coordinating their naps.

Napping

Although I normally keep twins together at nighttime, I often recommend separating them for naps, because daytime sleep is so much more of a challenge for most babies. It's only harder if there's a playmate to distract or be distracted by in the next crib. Some parents keep twins apart for naps for days or weeks, others throughout childhood. Do whichever feels best to you and seems to work for your kids. Nap training duets can be difficult. If you are lucky, one will nap well and you will only have to nap train one, either by using my Sleep Lady Shuffle at nap time or by using the other nap techniques I describe in the age chapters. But if they both need nap training, you'll probably have to calm one, leave him, then go to the other twin and calm him, then after ten minutes or so, go back and check on the first one, and in another ten minutes go back to the second, and so forth. (It's not fun.) If one is napping less than the other, you might have to put him down a little earlier at night, or try to squeeze in an extra short late-afternoon nap if he's under nine or ten months of age.

At seven months, Ryan slept well but Amber did not. "Every time Amber got up, the whole house got up," their mother, Melanie, recalled. "Ryan was not happy." Melanie used to rush in as soon as Amber cried, fearing she would wake Ryan. She tried all sorts of things—holding Amber, putting her in her car seat, reluctantly letting her cry once in a while. Some days the only way Melanie could get Amber to sleep was on her back—on Melanie's back, not Amber's. "It was killing me; she was getting bigger and bigger and bigger," her mother said. When Amber began taking medication for reflux, her nighttime sleeping improved considerably but naps were still a disaster. Melanie separated them, and concentrated on Amber's napping using the techniques I suggest for a seven-month-old (page 100). Amber was mad, and didn't even want her mother to stay by her side at nap time. In those first days of nap training, she would cry for the entire hour. But within about ten days, Amber began taking her lovey and falling asleep for a nice solid nap. Melanie kept the children separate for naps as well as bedtime. The only time they share a room is on vacation—when Ryan enjoys the company but pays a price when his sister wakes him up too early in the morning, no matter how hard he tries to ignore her.

For babies six months or older who are having trouble falling asleep and staying asleep, many families use the Sleep Lady Shuffle, my system of having the parent gradually fade out of bedtime as the child gains sleep confidence. Check out the Shuffle instructions for your children's age. It's obviously easier if only one child needs the Shuffle, and you can temporarily separate the twins while you carry it out. If both need the Shuffle, it's usually easiest if one parent sits in between the two cribs, gently moving back and forth to stroke and soothe each child in turn. By the third or fourth night, you will be relying much more on your voice than on your touch to calm and reassure them. For babies under six months of age, follow the sleep shaping suggestions in Chapter 3, The Right Start for Newborns and Infants, and Chapter 4, Newborn to Five Months.

Bedtime

Bedtime can be quite a juggling act—sometimes ridiculously close to a literal juggling act—with young twins. Melanie, for instance, knew her children needed good focused attention, and nice peaceful stories before bed. Easier said than done. "I can get one sitting in my lap, but not two. I get one down and the other one climbs away. Bedtime is supposed to be this relaxing, wonderful bonding time, but for us it was very stressful." I usually tell parents of twins to close the door, get the pajamas on, and just read. If one gets up, keep reading, try to engage her but don't force it. When it's time for lights out, it's into the crib whether they've paid attention to the story or not. Melanie tried all sorts of variants, depending on their moods and their ages. She usually started out reading and they assumed one of three positions—both on the floor on one side of her, both in her lap, or one on either side of her on the sofa. "I can't say that any of my three systems worked with complete accuracy, but by mixing up the positions, they seemed to stay in one place for the longest period of reading time." When they got older, they began to disagree on what books to read, so Melanie would start them off together on a book, but then let Amber pretend to "read" a book to herself if she turned her nose down at Ryan's choice, and vice versa. "One twin can 'read' the more interesting book while I read the less appealing story to the other child," Melanie said.

When work schedules permit, some parents split bedtime responsibilities. For instance, by eighteen months Kayla and Charlie were out of the crib and in separate rooms. Both were waking up at night wanting to drink bottles of milk (when they got older and went through another round of bedtime difficulties, it was juice in a cup) and wanted their parents to lie down with them at night. Each parent led one twin through the Sleep Lady Shuffle, and later the parents divided up bedtime routines. Charles would give Charlie a good-night kiss and then take care of Kayla, while Molly tended to Charlie, who was a little less temperamental at bedtime. After she said good night to Charlie, Molly spent a few minutes with Kayla before she too went to bed. Kayla took longer to fall asleep, and she had more trouble separating, wanting one of her parents, usually Molly, to sit in a chair in the hallway. On nights when Charles had to work late, Molly read to both children in one room, then put the easier-going Charlie to bed, and then Kayla.

○ ○ ○

Dawn and Clark tried to keep bedtime a whole family time. Now two and a half, the children take a bath, select three books, and snuggle and read with both parents on a sofa in the children's room. Then Allison turns the night-light on. Not to be outdone, Scott then turns it off and back on again. Then they get into their cribs. They may happily keep each other company, sparing their parents some of the stalling and curtain calls typical of children this age. But sometimes Allison decides her brother's company isn't quite enough. "Allison calls; you have to go in, fix her blanket, rub her back. We go through it three or four times, then enough is

*enough. She may cry until she figures out she isn't going to get her way,"
Dawn said. "Scott is more placid. He goes down, no problem, 85 percent of
the time; if she's crying, he'll just lie down and watch her. But once in a
while he'll pick up on some of her little traits, and you'll hear him saying, 'I
need my diaper changed too.' He'll see that she can do that and get
attention."*

◌ ◌ ◌

*Now three and a half, Nathaniel and Ethan still share a room. Their
recent move from crib to bed led to some new bedtime procrastination,
asking for a little more of this and a little more of that—in stereo.
Charlotte and Ed responded immediately by enforcing a very consistent
bedtime routine, which either parent can carry out. The boys bathe, brush
their teeth, read one or two books in the living room, make one last visit to
the bathroom, then to the bedroom for a song, a glass of water, and lights-
out. "With two three-year-old boys, you become a limit setter," Charlotte
said, laughing. "There's no ground to give." Nathaniel recently went
through a period when he was waking up very early—and the first thing
he would do was shout, "Ethan, Ethan," until his brother woke up. His
parents made a sticker chart for Nathaniel; he had to let Ethan sleep until
he could see the sun. If he filled up a whole row of stickers, he could get a
toy. (It's always a good idea to get the sibling a treat too—after all, he was
the one so rudely awakened!)*

Naps

Twins can have different sleep needs, but they shouldn't be wildly different, not more than an hour off from average. Some researchers have found
that identical twins are more likely to need the same amount of sleep than fra-
ternal twins. Either way, you may not get them on precisely the same schedule
but you do want them to be similar. One trick is to make sure they are awake
in the morning within about a half hour of each other. Then coordinate morning naps. For instance, if one twin gets up naturally at 7:00 a.m. and the other
gets up at 8:00, wake the sleepyhead at 7:00 too—or maybe let him sleep until
7:30 while you feed the earlier riser. Then they will both be ready to go down
for their nap at around 9:00 or 9:30. Similarly, if one tends to take a longer
morning nap, start waking him up earlier, so they remain in sync for the afternoon nap. And that afternoon nap is his catch-up opportunity—the one who
needs more sleep can take a longer afternoon snooze, and you will still have a
long enough gap between the nap and bedtime that you can put them down

together. You might have to tweak their schedules periodically because at different times, their sleep needs might diverge a bit more, depending on when each child goes through growth spurts or hits developmental milestones.

> *At five months, Allison and Scott were still in bassinets in their parents' room, near Clark's side of the bed. They had wildly different schedules, and no one in the family slept. One baby or the other always seemed to be awake and nursing—or at least demanding that one parent find a pacifier.*
>
> *I thought it was time to get them out of their bassinets and their parents' room, and into cribs in their own shared room. We introduced loveys, a tiger for Scott, a bunny for Allison. Dawn and Clark cut out the pacifiers, cold turkey, and sat nearby to soothe the babies when they sought their pacis. These babies were growing well and doing fine, and no longer needed to be fed all the time. After checking with their pediatrician, we cut back nursing to just once a night. It took several weeks of tinkering and adjusting but we got them on the same schedule, soothing them without excess nursing as they gradually adapted to new routines. "If one was asleep and the other cried, that was just the way it was going to be," Dawn recalled. "We didn't jump up and pick one up if he or she was crying, we let them learn to go back to sleep." Sometimes, even as toddlers, one would wake up too early in the morning and try to entice the other to play, but usually if Clark and Dawn left them alone, both babies would drift back to sleep within five minutes. "They do amuse themselves," Dawn said. "Every once in a while, you'll hear on the monitor Allison saying, 'Scott look at this, Scott try this,' and then you'll hear 'wheeeeeeeeeeee! thump-thump-thump' and you'll know they are having fun at something."*

The biggest scheduling challenge for many families comes at around fifteen or eighteen months, when the twins start moving from two naps to one. That's a strain when you've got one toddler, but it can be really painful when you've got two transitioning at slightly different speeds. (See Chapter 7, Thirteen to Eighteen Months, for more advice on nap consolidation.)

> *"When one was waking up from a morning nap, we'd wake the other one to make his morning nap short, so they'd both go down together at the afternoon nap. It got kind of complicated, but it was only a few weeks," said Charlotte.*

○ ○ ○

Dawn recalled a similar experience. "Allison doesn't like to sleep as much as Scott, she likes to stay up and jibber jabber, and he learned to just ignore his sister. But when one began switching to a single nap, we dragged the other one along. We had to force it, going by the clock. I could see Scott getting tired; Allison is not as easy to read. But when he went upstairs, she went up too."

SIBLINGS

Bedtime

If you have more than one child, the general rule of thumb is to put the youngest one to bed first (if they are close in age, you may want to apply some of the advice I give for twins). Depending on age, personality, and degree of sibling rivalry, the bigger one may or may not want to listen to the baby's stories and songs and be part of the baby's good-night rituals before going on to her own bedtime. If not, make sure the older child keeps busy with a quiet game or activity so she won't keep interrupting the baby's bedtime in a manner that is disruptive or stimulating. You don't want the three-year-old (or the thirteen-year-old for that matter) running in constantly while you are trying to get the younger one to sleep. That's what I did when Gretchen was a baby and needed a nice quiet pre-bed nursing or bottle, and Bill wasn't home to take Carleigh. But by the time Gretchen was about one and Carleigh three, I could read a "young" book to the two of them in Gretchen's room, and then Carleigh would wait for me in her room while I put Gretchen to bed. As soon as Gretchen was down, I'd go to Carleigh and read her an "older" book and give her some mom time.

If two parents are home in the evening, one may deal with the baby (often the mom if she's nursing) and one takes care of the older child or children. But switch off some of the time, so each child knows how to go through her bedtime routine with each parent. Make sure both children get a few special good-night moments with both parents. It helps if everyone makes the kids' bedtime a priority for an hour or so—take care of other household tasks a little later. Dirty dishes don't bawl in the middle of the night if you neglect them for an hour.

"We stagger our children's bedtimes," said Kathleen, whose children, Maude and Sean, are twenty-six months apart. "That's hard as a working parent, because Maude goes down at seven and I only get an hour and a

half with her on the three days that I work. But I know she needs to go to bed then; kids who go to sleep at nine or ten have a lot more temper tantrums."

While Kathleen is busy with Maude, Sean understands that it's his little sister's special time with Mom. He gets a thirty-minute video, a quiet one suitable for evening, and/or special playtime with his dad. Then he gets to choose if Dad puts him to bed, or if he wants some mom time of his own. The other parent comes in for a final message of sweet dreams and a good-night kiss. The family set up this basic system when Maude was an infant and Sean was two, and it was still working with just a few minor tweaks when he was four and a half.

☉ ☉ ☉

Greta and Matt used to have both boys together for story time. Frederick would just stand up in his crib and happily point at trucks while Dad read books to big brother. When that system no longer worked, when they each needed a more age-specific story, the parents split them up for bedtime.

Some children go through a stage when they only want one parent at bedtime—usually Mommy.

"First I get the baby to sleep, but I often hear Ariella clear across the house; she doesn't want her dad, she wants me. And Peg hears it too, so then I have Ariella stalling and Peg crying. We've tried really hard to let Doyle put the girls to bed, but Ariella really wants me right now, and I have to be with Peg because I'm still nursing," said Marcy. She and Doyle have gently but persistently continued to include Doyle in Ariella's bedtime. He now does baths and dinners and some evening play, although Ariella still insists on Mommy for stories and lights-out. Meanwhile, hoping to avoid a repetition of this pattern with the younger daughter, Doyle has been spending more and more time with Peggy at bedtime, and he's the one who goes in to check on her on those nights when she still wakes up.

Sometimes, as is the case with twins, we worry so much about the younger child's cries waking or upsetting the older one that we rush in too quickly. Try not to fall into this trap, because you are only going to perpetuate her night wakenings by reinforcing her sleep crutches. In fact, you might want to go first to the older child who has been woken up, rather than the one who is bawling. For instance, if you are sleep shaping with a six-month-old, and the baby is waking up your two-year-old, go to the two-year-old first and reassure her, tell her that the baby is okay and she should go back to sleep. Then go tend to the six-month-old. If both parents are home, then divide and conquer, one of you with each child.

As you know from the chapters on toddlers and preschoolers (Chapter 8, One and a Half to Two and a Half Years Old, and Chapter 9, Two and a Half to Five Years Old), when I do sleep shaping with children from around age two and a half on, I encourage parents to start with a family meeting, to explain the expectations and find ways of getting the child to invest in her sleep education. The same holds true when you are training a younger sibling. Explain to the older child what's going on and help her feel like she's a part of it. Depending on the age and sleep skills of the older child, you may even help her think of herself as a sleep role model for the baby. Tell her the baby needs to know how to get herself to sleep, just like her big sister does. Explain that when the baby learns, she won't cry as much, but in the meantime you have to be with her, or you have to go check on her. The older child will let you go more easily if you explain and make her an ally. Hopefully she won't barge in as often with demands on you just as you are finally getting the little one to drift off to sleep. Your goal, as always, is to prevent the older one from feeling displaced. Instead, you want to make her feel even more needed, more loved, more important. (See Chapter 14, Routine Busters, for advice on the birth of a sibling.)

Sometimes if your children are very far apart in age, with eight or ten years between the oldest and the youngest, it seems that life should get a little easier because the big one can help with the little brother or sister, or at least take care of herself. That's true up to a point, but it's also true that the children have such different needs—logistically, academically, and emotionally—in the evenings that you may feel like you are straddling two parallel parental universes. It's tough to bathe a three-year-old upstairs while trying to pry a twelve-year-old away from the kitchen telephone, or to get the little one all cozy and drowsy only to have the big one noisily pop into the bedroom every five minutes with questions about Spanish verb conjugation. I know some families who have enlisted the older child to help put the younger one to bed, or even to pretend that he is going to sleep at the same time, although they aren't always willing or able to go along with that gimmick all the time.

Naps

Scheduling conflicts between your children's naps or activities also create sleep barriers. For instance, you may be trying to get your six-month-old to nap on an appropriate schedule, only to discover that her nap sleep window is wide open exactly when you have to pick up your older child from preschool. See if you can work out a carpool to minimize those disruptions; there's often another parent around who would be thrilled to have a half hour less in the car each day. If you do have to drive and the baby falls asleep in the car seat, either move the car seat inside or, better, work on teaching her how to transfer into the crib: if she wakes up while you move her, stroke and soothe her back to sleep. It takes a little while to acquire that skill, but most babies do get it so don't give up, keep working on it.

Parents often ask me for advice on whether children should share rooms, or how old they should be when they are separated, particularly a boy and a girl (assuming the family has enough space in their home for separate bedrooms). I don't think there's a right or wrong answer; do what feels right for you and watch your children for clues to their preferences. They might be old enough to articulate what they want.

However, when you are doing sleep training with one or both children, it's often a good idea to separate them for bedtime or nap time or both, as with twins. Once you've dealt with the sleep problem, go ahead and reunite them if that's what they want or what you want. If you want to separate them, a natural point might be when they are switching from a crib to a bed. But lots of families wait another year or two without any difficulty. I find that some children are less scared of the dark, of separation, or of those vague under-the-bed monsters and ghosts-in-the-closets if they have a brother or sister in the room. A shared room might be an incentive; you can tell a child he can share with his brother or sister once he has good sleep manners. Make sure that the child sees this as a reward, not a punishment, and that he wants to share the room.

Parents often find that no matter how tears-averse they were with their first child, they have little choice once the second one arrives. For instance, if you are nap coaching an eight-month-old, and your three-year-old is downstairs, it's going to be hard to stay with the baby for a solid hour and leave the preschooler on his own, unless you have a babysitter or a relative who can come over and help at nap time. Even if the preschooler doesn't mind being left on his own (and he probably will mind—an hour is a long time), you are going to be upstairs fretting about whether he's quietly assembling that puzzle you left him, or whether he's dismantling the bookshelf, finger-painting the living room couch, or planning an Alpine-like ascent into the cabinet where you hide the cookies. Chances are, at some point, you are going to be downstairs with the three-year-old while you leave the baby to cry. Try to get at least the pre-nap ritual with the baby done, putting her down drowsy but awake. And check on her every ten or fifteen minutes; you don't want her crying forever. But simply out of necessity, you may have a slightly more Ferber-like approach to naps with a second child.

Marianne and Glenn, whom you met in the chapter on newborns, had three children in four years. Holly was a terrible sleeper, Dean was significantly better, and by the time they got to Ally, it was easy.

> "With Ally, I don't know if I got it right, or she got it right," Marianne said. "She had some mild reflux and she was on medication, but we did everything differently with her. We let her cry a little more, we didn't pick her up at every whimper. We couldn't! We had two other young kids to take care of. At nap time she would cry but I wouldn't be able to get up to her room, and I started realizing she was falling right back to sleep. Maybe there were five minutes of tears. When she gets up now, if I know nap time is over, I'll go get her, but if it's not time for it to be over, I'll leave her alone for five more minutes and she'll go back to sleep."

Occasionally, I've run into families who thought sleep training a younger child would be too stressful on the older child. Ellen, for instance, sent James to his grandparents while she trained Vanessa. Luckily, Ellen had a much easier time with Vanessa than with James, and the sleep coaching took just three days. But usually this isn't a problem; just be attuned to how the older sibling feels about the baby's sleep shaping, or have one parent stay with him and keep reassuring him that the baby won't cry forever, that he'll be sleeping soundly and dreaming sweetly in just a little while.

12

NIGHTMARES, SLEEPWALKING, AND NIGHT TERRORS

NIGHTMARES, SLEEPWALKING, AND NIGHT TERRORS ARE distinct phenomena—and none of them are a sign of serious emotional disturbance or disorder. Nightmares are part of normal development, peaking between ages two and three. This is an age when children have wondrously rich imaginations and some difficulty distinguishing reality from fantasy. Nightmares occur during REM sleep, and the child wakes up feeling anxious or afraid but he recognizes his parents and seeks comfort. Night terrors are less common, occurring in about 5 percent of children, more boys than girls, and can last into the school years. They occur in non-REM sleep, when we do not dream, so the child will not remember the terror. (See Chapter 2, Sleep Basics, if you want to review REM and non-REM sleep.) Night terrors can be disturbing for parents to watch but they are not a sign of serious emotional disturbance or disorder. You may not be able to eliminate them completely, but you can take steps to minimize them. Usually children outgrow them, and they seldom last past early adolescence. Like night terrors, sleepwalking is a partial-arousal parasomnia disorder, which the child does not remember the next day. As the child can wander around, open doors, and climb stairs, safety is generally the biggest concern with sleepwalking.

NIGHTMARES

Nightmares occur toward the end of a sleep period. The child can recall the dream, or at least know she had a bad one, and it may take her a while to get scary thoughts out of her head and fall sleep again. Nightmares are, of course, common after difficult events or when children are experiencing change, stress, or reliving a trauma. They can also occur when a child is overtired, either because she still hasn't learned to sleep well enough or she's been thrown off her routine for a few days by illness, travel, or a change in the family's schedule. But sometimes they occur for no particular reason, just like we as adults may have a bad dream when nothing particularly unusual or unpleasant is going on in our lives. You probably can't prevent all nightmares—they are part of childhood, just as they are an occasional part of adulthood. But you can try to minimize them and make them less frequent. Avoid scary videos, books, games, and stories prior to bed. Don't play scary games, not even during the day if your child is fearful, unless you can turn them into empowering games where your child transforms the scary monsters into giggly monsters or something like that. As I noted in the section on anxiety in preschoolers (page 204), children may pick up more than we realize about frightening events, whether it be a distant hurricane, a fire down the block, or the unsettling news of our post-9/11 world. Through snippets of television news or adult conversation, they may get just enough information to be frightened and not enough to truly comprehend how abstract or distant the threat is to them or their loved ones. Keep your antenna up for what they may be hearing or seeing that may cause fear and anxiety. It's often wise to avoid television or radio news when young children are present.

When a child does have a bad dream, respond very quickly and assure her that she is safe. Hug her and hold her if she needs it, even if you are in the middle of a sleep-shaping program, or the Sleep Lady Shuffle, that asks you to minimize your nighttime physical engagement. Stay in her room until she falls asleep again. It's tempting to lie down in her bed with her, but try to avoid it, or to keep it brief particularly if you are trying to break a co-sleeping pattern, or you have been co-sleeping until recently.

The same rich imagination that contributes to the nightmares may also help combat them. For instance, many three- and four-year-olds have imaginary friends, and you can help the child enlist those friends to ward off bad dreams or monsters. Draw on the lovey too; remind her that the lovey is by her side all night and will make her feel safe and sound. You might want to talk about dreams as part of the bedtime routine, thinking of happy things to dream about. Try saying something like "Maybe when you go to sleep tonight you can dream about having fun at the playground." Or "Maybe when you go to sleep tonight you can dream about playing your favorite game with your friends at preschool." Or something else realistic and soothing. By age five, many children understand that the dream images are not real. But in spite of that cognitive leap, they still need the TLC and reassurance, just as we adults want an extra hug from our spouse or partner when we have a bad dream.

Sometimes kids become fearful of their own room because of the nightmares, or just start stalling more at bedtime or running out of bed more at night. Spend more time playing with her in her own room during daylight so that she feels safer and more comfortable there. At night, allow a little extra time for the bedtime rituals and relaxation. Include bedtime stories about children conquering their fears. (I suggest some good bedtime stories, as well as relaxation guides, in the Resources Directory at the back of this book.) Review her sleep chart, if she has one, to remind her of good sleep manners, and then reward her liberally for following them. If she wakes with a nightmare and comes to your room, take her back to her own bed and stay near her until she feels better.

Sometimes parents sleep in a child's bedroom after bad dreams, but be careful about doing this too long or too often or it will become a negative association, or a sleep crutch, and she will need you to be there all the time. (You may decide lying down with her is worth it if you feel you will be able to retrain her out of that habit fairly quickly, when the fear of nightmares subsides.) At bedtime, if she's apprehensive about bad dreams, tell her you will be nearby, and be very specific. "Mommy will be in her room reading," or "Daddy will be right down the hall hanging up his suits." Promise to check on her frequently and then live up to that promise. Not only will those checks make her feel safer, they will also help keep her in her own room instead of scrambling out every five minutes in search of you. Leave the door open a little if that makes her feel better, and keep a night-light on, or even a little more hall light than usual. Discuss bad dreams if your child brings them up but don't "lead the witness." In other words, you shouldn't be the one to remind her about last night's scary dream, and if she runs into your bedroom at night, your first words should not be, "Did you have a nightmare?" Be sympathetic—don't yell at her for getting out of bed when she may be frightened, but don't plant the idea of bad dreams if it isn't already there.

A few other suggestions follow. Not every idea will help with every child, but experiment to see which works for you, or which leads you and your child to your own helpful variants.

1. Allow a pet to sleep in the child's room.

2. Try letting your children share a room with a sibling as long as they both have good sleep manners and won't keep each other up.

3. Use some kind of "monster away spray" or, if it seems too confusing to be chasing away monsters at the same time as you are trying to teach your child that monsters don't exist, use a "bad thought" spray.

4. Let your child create his own bad-dream defenses. One slightly older girl I worked with, about eight, made a shield with pictures and images that she felt protected her, and kept it by her bed. Another one put up a dream catcher. Several kids I know have arranged their stuffed animals or action figures around their bed in a way that makes them feel protected.

5. Include in your bedtime preparations some kind of prayer for safety if that fits your beliefs, or create a more secular anti-nightmare ritual or mantra. Your child might imagine a guardian angel watching over him, or recite a prayer with you that surrounds him with love, light, and protection.

6. Help your child act out throwing away his bad thoughts in a concrete way that can make him feel they are really gone. Throw them out the window (you don't really have to open the window) or dump them in the trash or flush them down the toilet (just make sure he knows that they are flushed far away, so he doesn't get afraid of the toilet in the morning!). One mom I know made a "worry tree" with her kindergartener. She made the trunk and branches out of brown construction paper and formed leaves out of green stick 'em notes. Each night the child plucked a leaf off the tree, and ripped it up, eliminating a worry.

7. If your child has good enough verbal skills, teach him progressive relaxation techniques, tightening and releasing muscles starting at the toes, then the feet, and all the way up to the top of the head (I list tapes and books on relaxation in the back of the book). You can also try creative visualization, helping your child imagine that he is playing on the beach with his cousins or walking in the park as the leaves

change color, any image that will make him feel happy and calm. Children sometimes like to pretend they are a character in a favorite (non-scary) book or like making up stories where they are a prince or princess or magic fairy in a beautiful garden.

8. It is also wise to avoid high-dose vitamins close to bedtime; and if your child takes any medication, talk to your pediatrician about whether it might interfere with sleep and whether you can find an alternative or at least change the dosing times.

NIGHT TERRORS

Night terrors are not bad dreams, and although they are distressing to witness, they are not a sign of psychological problems. They are different from nightmares, although the first time your child experiences one you may not immediately recognize that it's a terror. A child experiencing a terror may scream, shout, sweat, have a racing heart, appear anxious, and seem inconsolable. His eyes may be wide open and he will look awake, but this is a partial-arousal disorder and he is actually still asleep and probably won't recognize you. He may even push you away, or flail at you, even while he is calling out for you. The terror usually lasts five to fifteen minutes and then subsides. It is often more upsetting for the parent to endure than for the child to experience, since the child usually won't remember it—and the parent will. Night terrors occur during non-REM sleep (when they are coming out of deep sleep) and usually within two hours of falling asleep. The single biggest risk factor is probably being overtired—terrors may stop when your child starts getting more sleep. Sleep apnea can be a factor, so discuss that possibility with your doctor. Stress that disturbs sleep, such as a major change in the child's sleep schedule or a new place to sleep, can also be a factor. A child who has an erratic sleep schedule is also at higher risk. Terrors may also occur during developmental milestones, or when a child is sick or running a fever. I know of one three-year-old who would experience terrors between 10:00 and 11:00 on the night before he got sick. His mother learned that if he had a terror, he'd be ill by morning.

Children are more likely to experience night terrors if either parent had them as a child, or if a parent had a partial-arousal sleep disorder such as sleepwalking. If your child gets up and walks around while having a terror, which can happen occasionally even with children who do not otherwise sleepwalk, make sure she is safe. Think about placing a gate at the top of any nearby stairs.

> *"My child didn't have too many bad dreams and I don't think he had any full-fledged monstery nightmares that I was aware of. Then one night when he was sick and had a slight fever, just before his third birthday, I heard this ear-splitting terrorized screech at about ten-thirty or eleven,"* the mother of that three-year-old said. *"He was screaming, 'MOMMY, MOMMY,' and when I ran to him and told him I was there, he kept alternating between screaming for me and hitting me, like he didn't recognize me and I was scaring him. I picked him up and held him, which I later realized I probably shouldn't have done, and he kept screaming for me, and I kept telling him I was there, and he seemed to go back and forth between recognition and terror. Then all of a sudden, it was over. The tension went out of his body and he went right back into a peaceful sleep, looking perfectly calm and content. I was so shaken that I slept in his room the rest of the night, but he was fine and never said a word about it in the morning. He didn't have any problems again, including the next time he had a cold and tummyache, but then a few months later it happened again when he was running a fever. It still took me a few minutes to realize what was going on, but at least I was a little better prepared. It still felt horrible to watch and I felt helpless, but at least I knew it was only the fever and that he would be okay in just a few minutes."*

When your child has a night terror, monitor him and make sure he is physically safe and not thrashing around in a dangerous way during the episode, but don't interfere, as this could intensify it. Try not to touch your child or pick him up since this can actually prolong the terror. Go to him, stay in his room, and calmly reassure him. Don't talk to him about the terror in the morning. Since sleep deprivation plays a major role in night terrors, put him to bed earlier, even if only by thirty minutes. Be extra vigilant about keeping him on a consistent sleep schedule.

If night terrors seem to be regular events, not an occasional side effect of a fever or temporary schedule disruption, keep a sleep log to monitor the timing and frequency. If they are occurring two to three times a week at set times (e.g., two hours after going to sleep), try waking him fifteen minutes before the typical onset of the terror. Don't get him completely wide awake, rouse him just enough for him to mumble, move, or roll over. Then let him fall asleep again and see if you can disrupt the sleep cycle that leads to the terrors.

Do this every night for seven to ten days. If the terrors return, do the waking again but this time do it for two full weeks to see if you can extinguish the problem.

Although this may not be a psychological problem nor an illness, you might want to discuss frequent, ongoing terrors with your pediatrician to make sure there is no underlying trauma, illness, or apnea that must be addressed. Check to see if any medications he is taking, including any over-the-counter drugs, could be interfering with his sleep and contributing to the terrors.

 SLEEPWALKING

Like night terrors, sleepwalking is a partial-arousal disorder that occurs during non-REM sleep, when the child is not dreaming. Episodes usually occur within two hours of falling asleep, and the child doesn't remember sleepwalking later. A sleepwalking child looks awake but usually appears confused, and may be clumsy and do strange things. He may not want comfort from a parent, although he probably won't scream and act afraid as he would if he were having a terror. Sleepwalking, as with terrors, often runs in families.

You may be surprised to find that sleepwalking is actually quite common, although chronic or frequent sleepwalking is relatively rare. In *A Clinical Guide to Pediatric Sleep: Diagnosis and Management of Sleep Problems*, Jodi Mindell and Judith Owens write that between 15 and 40 percent of children sleepwalk at least once, and 3 to 4 percent have frequent episodes. The peak ages for weekly or monthly episodes are from four to eight years of age, but about one-third of sleepwalkers will experience episodes over a five-year span, and about one in ten will sleepwalk for ten years.

The most important concern is of course safety. You don't want a sleep-walking child to fall down the stairs, climb anywhere he shouldn't be, stumble into the basement, or go outside. You should put gates on the stairs, and lock doors. If you hear him walking around, don't wake him but try to gently guide him back to bed. If you are afraid you won't hear him, think about installing an alarm, or even some kind of makeshift system like a bell that will ring if he opens his bedroom door. Sleep deprivation is a risk factor for sleepwalking, so make sure he gets plenty of sleep and is on a nice consistent schedule. With sleepwalking, I do recommend you contact your pediatrician. Depending on the frequency of the episodes and his risk of injury, she may want to prescribe a short-term sleep medication.

MEDICAL PROBLEMS

COUGHS, COLDS, EAR INFECTIONS, AND TUMMYACHES, those routine childhood illnesses, can temporarily disturb sleep and my next chapter, Routine Busters, will help you through those rough spots. Here I will talk about some of the more complex and persistent medical problems—including reflux, asthma, apnea, and allergies—that can create longer-term sleep disruptions. I'll also give you a few tips about helping kids with attention deficit disorder and attention deficit hyperactivity disorder (ADD, ADHD) sleep, although these are not usually diagnosed or treated until children get a little older. If you have consistently applied a behavioral modification program—whether it's my Sleep Lady approach or one of the crying-it-out alternatives—and your child is still not sleeping well, please consult your doctor to determine if her sleep problems have medical roots.

However, even children with medical components to sleep difficulties can benefit from behavioral modification techniques. For instance, your child might have health concerns that require night feedings past the age where most other infants are learning to sleep longer intervals. But you can still work on teaching good sleep habits at bedtime and nap time, even if you can't grapple with those night wakenings yet. Rare, serious illnesses are beyond the scope of this book, but I include Ayanna's story because it illustrates how sleep shaping can help even a seriously ill child. Ayanna has cystic fibrosis, and her wheezing and coughing created overwhelming sleep obstacles. While working with her team of physicians to bring her life-threatening symptoms under control, her parents also incorporated my Sleep Lady techniques to address the behavioral component inevitably created by her disease. It made a huge difference in all their lives.

As I'm not a medical doctor, I called on my own family pediatrician, Dr. Faith Hackett, to review this chapter. Please consult your own doctor, and if necessary ask him or her to refer you to a specialist, if you think your child needs a medical evaluation.

When you do talk to your pediatrician, including at routine checkups, make sure you mention your child's sleep patterns, even if the doctor doesn't bring it up herself. Provide her with enough information to evaluate the problem. Keep a sleep log, or at least jot down some notes, and be prepared to explain the behavioral approach you have adopted. If your child throws up regularly and you wonder if it may be a symptom of reflux, try to keep track of how often and when. For example, telling your doctor that your baby throws up five to seven times a day, ten minutes after eating, is more helpful than telling the doctor that the baby throws up "a lot." Similarly, if you think your child may have allergies, note the circumstances of the reactions. If you suspect apnea, make a five-minute tape of the snoring, snorts, or those other loud and strange nighttime noises so the doctor can hear for herself.

REFLUX AND COLIC

Spitting up is a normal part of infancy. It may create a laundry problem, but it's not a health problem. However, when babies spit up or throw up excessively, numerous times a day, they may have gastroesophageal reflux disease. Reflux is very common, affecting as many as one in ten babies. It can be caused by a host of factors, often related to the fact that in many babies the gastroesophageal valve (in layman's language, the valve at the top of the stomach) has not yet fully developed and needs more time to grow. In mild cases, it's akin to baby heartburn. In more severe cases, the stomach acid as well as food, breast milk, or formula get pushed back up out of the stomach, up the esophagus and out the mouth, or even sometimes the nose. In addition to the vomiting, many babies develop related respiratory symptoms and may face a risk of aspiration. Luckily, reflux can usually be managed and your doctor can suggest many techniques, possibly including medication. Most babies will outgrow the condition in six to ten months. Reflux babies can develop sleep problems that can persist even after the reflux symptoms are controlled. Perhaps as many as a third of the children I work with have, or have had, reflux past the age of three to four months. (If they get over it very early, you should be able to follow the sleep-shaping ideas in the age-by-age section of this book without having to worry too much about longer-term sleep disruption.) My own second child, Gretchen, had reflux and her first few weeks were not easy. But with our doctor's help, we were able to manage her condition with medication and have a happy, healthy baby who slept eight hours at a stretch pretty consistently by the time she was ten weeks old.

Parents often confuse reflux with colic, but they are not the same. Reflux is a structural, though not permanent, problem with the digestive system. Colic is a catchall term that basically means a baby cries a lot, mostly in the late afternoon and early evening. Up to one in four babies under age three months experience these crying jags. But it doesn't mean you are a bad or incompetent parent, or that your baby is in pain, or that he will be a fussy or unhappy child. Some people believe that colic may be a sign of overstimulation, and that your attempt to calm the baby will only add to the problem. Dr. Ferber, for instance, says that if the colicky baby doesn't respond to our soothing, then soothing isn't what he is seeking. He recommends that you let the colicky baby cry for fifteen to thirty minutes and see if he can calm himself down. My own preference is for you to review the soothing techniques, such as swaddling and swinging, that I outline in Chapter 3, The Right Start for Newborns and Infants. *Remember—don't get in the habit of nursing him every time he cries.* Since the crying might make it harder to read his sleep window cues, keep an eye on the clock so you know how long he's been awake. Try taking him into a quiet, dimly lit room where he may start showing signs of tiring.

How to Recognize Reflux

Reflux symptoms can emerge in very young infants. They can include:

- Frequent vomiting—sometimes and quite unpleasantly through the nose. (Some babies have *silent reflux*, meaning they have the pain and surges of acid without spitting up. Adam, whom you met as an eight-month-old, was one of them.)

- Slow weight gain or even weight loss. However, not all reflux babies are underweight.

- Reluctance to eat or signs of pain when eating, such as stiffening up, arching his back, or pushing away from the breast or bottle.

- Wanting to eat, but just a little at a time.

- Frequent coughs (this can have other causes; check with your doctor).

- Aspiration causing chronic nasal or sinus congestion.

- Choking or gagging.

- Sour breath.

- Excessive crying—more than a few hours a day.

- Baby wakes up frequently, often showing signs of pain in his stomach or chest.

Don't panic if your child displays a few of these signs once in a while. You are looking for a pattern, not a single episode. But if you do suspect a problem, call your pediatrician. It's important to get an accurate diagnosis. You might think the baby has reflux when he is lactose intolerant or just gassy. In severe or stubborn cases, your pediatrician may suggest you consult a specialist, a pediatric gastroenterologist, as well.

Managing Reflux

Sometimes we can control reflux with a few simple positioning and feeding tricks, which I'll address in a moment. But sometimes we face slightly more complicated choices, and the solutions you choose will be a blend of your values and parenting style, and your doctor's advice. For instance, if you are completely committed to breast milk and don't want formula, you may opt for medication and modify your own diet by reducing or eliminating dairy. Conversely, if you don't want to put your infant on medication, you might prefer to cut back on breast milk and try to find a formula that works for her instead of or in addition to nursing. Sometimes you won't have a choice. The child will clearly need medication and your doctor will explain why.

The following suggestions are widely accepted by pediatricians, but check with your own doctor anyway. Not every pediatrician agrees with every element on this list, and your doctor may feel that some aspect of reflux management is inappropriate, unwise, or even unsafe for your unique child. Keep in

mind too that some of these tools will tame the spitting up but will not necessarily stop all the surges of pain.

Gravity is your baby's friend. Keep your baby upright, but not slumped
over, for twenty to thirty minutes after all daytime and bedtime feedings to
help digestion. You can seat her in a bouncy chair or hold her in your arms—
but don't get into the habit of holding her until she falls asleep in your arms. Time
the feeding early enough so that you can feed her, hold or sit her down for a
half hour, and then put her to sleep drowsy but awake.

(Babies tend to like bouncy chairs even if they don't have reflux, and not
just after eating. Bouncy seats hold babies at an angle that "folds" them less
than a car seat. You don't need all the bells, whistles, and elaborate sound and
light effects; a simple seat is fine. They are available in all baby stores and
many discount and department stores.)

- Offer frequent, small meals.

- Burp your baby several times during a breast or bottle feed, not just
  once after feeding.

- Consider using a formula instead of/in addition to breast milk.
  Experiment with different formulas. Some babies do better with soy
  formula, or a hypoallergenic formula or with a relatively new formula on
  the market that is rice thickened, making it more viscous and easier for
  the baby to keep down. (Some doctors recommend that you thicken
  your own formula, adding one tablespoon of dry cereal to two ounces of
  formula, but ask your pediatrician before you try this on your own,
  particularly with very young infants.) You might even find that your
  baby does better with one brand formula than another, or that he still
  throws up the powdered version but does better with the thicker (and
  alas usually costlier) premixed canned variety.

- Elevate his crib or bassinet under the head. You can buy a simple,
  inexpensive wedge at a baby store that goes under the mattress (and is
  also helpful when he has a cold). You might be able to put a dictionary
  or telephone book under the legs of the bed to get the desired effect, as
  long as it's stable and won't fall over. One family I worked with,
  following their doctor's advice, rolled up a baby blanket in a U shape to
  make a nest in the elevated crib so the baby wouldn't roll down to the
  bottom of the crib. For safety's sake, they stuck the U-shaped blanket

under the fitted sheet, and placed the baby with his feet at the bottom curve of the U. The sides of the U shouldn't reach past his chest.

• Dress him in outfits that are loose at the waist.

• Try having him sleep on his left side, once he is old enough to do so safely. Talk to your physician and familiarize yourself with safety precautions to avoid SIDS ("crib death").

• Encourage him to sleep on his tummy, once he learns to roll over in both directions and the SIDS risk lessens (usually around six months; check with your doctor). Citing a few small studies showing that even younger infants with reflux do better on their tummies, some websites out there urge this sleeping position for reflux. However, the North American Society for Pediatric Gastroenterology and Nutrition does *not* endorse sleeping on the stomach for young infants, except in extremely rare cases where the reflux disease is so severe that the risk of death from reflux outweighs the risk of SIDS.

• It also helps to have a sense of humor and a mommy wardrobe that does not require dry cleaning! Carry around lots of spare clothes in your car, stroller, or diaper bag—for your baby and for you!

How to Help Reflux Babies Sleep

As parents, our natural instinct is to soothe a baby who hurts. That's exactly what we should do. But we need to pay attention to how we soothe a reflux baby. While a baby without tummy problems is learning to rock himself to sleep, a reflux baby dealing with projectile vomiting may miss out on the chance to learn how to self-soothe and fall asleep on his own! As we comfort our babies, we may inadvertently reinforce poor sleep habits. Then, even after the reflux (or colic) has passed or been controlled, our babies still don't sleep well. They must then learn, or relearn, how to put themselves to sleep without being walked, rocked, fed, put in the swing, the car seat, or ridden around the block—you know the drill.

I will give you two related sets of suggestions—one on how to deal with sleep while you and your child are still handling the worst of the reflux, and a second one on how to get him on a better sleep path once the medical part is under control or he has outgrown it. In both cases he'll do better if you tackle bedtime first, then naps. Before the nap piece falls into place, do whatever you need to do to get him some sleep during the day, even if it means breaking my usual rules of not using the car to get him to sleep. If you are feeding him at night for medical reasons, don't worry about changing that right away, although the night wakenings might diminish on their own as other aspects of his sleep improve. Work with the information here as well as the relevant age chapter earlier in this book.

As with a colicky baby, reading reflux babies' sleep cues can be difficult. I suspect this is because they don't learn to differentiate their cries because pain, vomiting, hunger, and tiredness all sort of blur together for them. We then have more trouble figuring out what they're crying about and may not respond as consistently to whatever it is they're trying to tell us. So you have to be more diligent about watching the clock, not just your baby. Keep track of when he ate. As he gets older, you'll want to stretch out the time between feedings as long as you can without provoking more vomiting, particularly overnight. Also pay attention to how long he has been awake. Make sure he naps on time. The last thing he needs is an overlay of exhaustion on top of his burning esophagus. Taking him into a quiet, dim room for a while before nap or bed often helps. He may show his sleepy signals more clearly in such a setting. Also, the quiet environment may cue him that it's time for bed.

As I mentioned, your doctor will probably recommend that you hold or seat your baby upright for about twenty to thirty minutes after he eats. Don't hold him until he falls asleep. You don't want him to develop an association between sleeping and being in your arms, otherwise you'll have to hold him to sleep all the time, including overnight, for months to come. Don't worry if he falls asleep in your arms occasionally. Just don't teach him that your arms are his bed. Allow enough time between feeding and bedtime for another activity in between. Feed him, hold him upright, and then read him a book, give him a bath, let him get some tummy time on a play mat. When it's time for him to sleep, put him down drowsy but awake. You can also try to arrange his daytime schedule so that you are feeding him when he wakes up in the morning and when he gets up from naps, instead of before he takes naps, to avoid that holding-sleeping association.

Some reflux babies fare better if they eat small, frequent meals. That might mean you will have to feed him overnight to an older age than you would a baby without reflux. At some point, the nighttime nursing (or bottle feeding) ceases to be a physical requirement and starts being a sleep-disrupting habit. When that happens, you need to stop those nighttime feedings. Please don't let this go on too long—address it before his first birthday. If not, you may well have a child who wakes you up demanding a drink every few hours well into his second or third year. Babies who feed at night also tend to get emotionally attached to the cup or bottle, as though it were a pacifier or a teddy bear. Some babies give up the night feeding much more easily than you would have guessed, in a night or two. Some resist longer. In each age chapter, I give detailed advice on nighttime weaning. For older babies who did not have reflux but still have a nighttime eating pattern, I usually recommend a pretty quick end—maybe not quite cold turkey but something close. However, with children who had reflux, you might want a more gradual and gentler approach. I give many suggestions in Chapter 5 (page 91), covering ages six to eight months.

I have found in my own sleep practice that post-reflux babies often remain very sensitive to their environments. They react more to such stimuli as bright lights, crowds, food, and textures. You then need to be sensitive to their sensitivities! (I talk a little more about sensory integration issues and give some resources in the section on ADD/ADHD later in this chapter.) Continue to be very careful about his schedule. Watch the clock, and keep using that quiet, dimly lit room to help him calm down.

> *Tracy and Drew's son, Lucas, had been diagnosed with reflux shortly after his birth. His pediatrician prescribed Zantac. It took a while to get the dosing and timing right for Lucas, but by four months, the medication and reflux management techniques had brought the problem under control. But they didn't do anything for his sleep. If anything, his sleep was getting worse. While other babies had been learning rudimentary self-soothing techniques, Lucas had his mind on his hurting tummy. Now he was getting up every three or four hours—more on a bad night. Naps were also problematic, and sometimes he woke well before dawn.*
>
> *Tracy started paying a lot more attention to his schedule and the timing of his meals. She shortened his feedings, sometimes letting him nurse only two or three minutes. "I shaved minutes off nursing to convince myself it was about soothing, not feeding. He was doing it for fun!" she said. "I knew he really didn't need to eat that often. And it wasn't the reflux cry anymore—it was the unhappy cry." At four months, his pediatrician said they should try to get Lucas to sleep, without food, for about seven hours a night. Seven hours seemed beyond comprehension to the sleep-deprived couple. They called me. Tracy still*

breastfed Lucas before he went to bed, at about 7:00 p.m. But for the next feeding, at about 10:00 or 11:00, I suggested they give him a bottle of formula (I talk a lot about these dream feeds in my chapters on infants). They also gave him his medicine then. Then they would not feed him again until at least 6:00 a.m., or even 6:30 if he slept that late. They would stay with him and comfort him if he cried and protested, but they did not feed him or lie down with him. (I gave them the option of picking him up briefly if they needed to calm him down, although they chose to soothe him without lifting him out of the crib, a decision that might have made their first few nights a little more teary than they had to be.)

"The first night, he cried for an hour and forty-five minutes. Then he collapsed. We soothed him, but we didn't pick him up. It took about two weeks before he wouldn't cry at all, but other nights he didn't cry as long," Tracy said. By the end of the two weeks, he was getting up once for ten minutes or less in the middle of the night but they wouldn't feed him and he woke up less and less. At about six months, they took the next step and gave up that dream feed. "It was pretty easy," she said. "He woke up and fussed and we went in and said, 'Sorry buddy!'" So then he went to bed at 7:00 at night and slept all the way through until 7:00 in the morning.

Although those first two weeks of transition were unpleasant, Tracy and Drew's wholehearted belief that Lucas needed to learn to sleep better made it a lot easier for them to be consistent. And with Tracy having to go back to her job at a social welfare program at five months, they knew they needed to deal with his sleep problems now. "We couldn't have done it if we had to leave him alone crying. Being in the room made it easier. But we really believed he would be better off if he could sleep. He had to learn how to do it." Tracy was also motivated by the secret confessions of her girlfriends that some of their kids were still waking multiple times at night at ages two and three. She also was clear-sighted enough about herself to know that she needed more sleep to be the mother she wanted to be. "I was so tired, I couldn't function and I wasn't enjoying him as much as I wanted to," she said. Those first few nights, she let Drew give Lucas a bottle and deal with his protests. That was partly to avoid getting Lucas even more upset by letting him see his mother but not letting him nurse. But it was also because by then Tracy really needed a break. She went downstairs, put in some earplugs, and slept for three nights. "I felt I'd been reborn."

ALLERGIES AND ASTHMA

Eczema, milk sensitivities, and environmental allergies can all hamper a baby's ability to learn how to sleep, and can disrupt sleep at any time from infancy through childhood.

Food and Milk Allergies

If you are nursing and suspect your child is allergic or intolerant to milk, you can try eliminating dairy products from your diet for three or four weeks. Make sure you get alternative sources of calcium for your sake and your baby's. Some mothers mistakenly expect to see a difference in a few days so they don't stick to it. Milk allergies can contribute to mild reflux, and may also cause nasal congestion that can contribute to apnea.

Talk to your pediatrician about giving your baby a milk test. You might also, with your doctor's guidance, try hypoallergenic, lactose-free, or soy formulas. Think about eliminating or cutting out caffeine and alcohol if you are nursing. Because peanut and other nut allergies are becoming more common and can be dangerous, some pediatricians advise nursing mothers to eliminate peanuts, peanut butter, or other nuts from their diet. Also, if you or your husband had childhood food allergies, tell your pediatrician. She may want you to delay introduction of certain solid foods—like wheat, eggs, citrus, shellfish, berries, chocolate, or corn—or modify the timetable. For instance, she might want you to introduce one food a week, instead of trying a new one every few days, so you can more easily monitor reactions.

Eczema and Dermatitis

Numerous allergies can cause hives, rashes, and itchy skin, which can disrupt sleep. According to the *Guide to Your Child's Sleep*, from the American Academy of Pediatrics, allergic children can have trouble sleeping even at those times when they are symptom free. Some research suggests that children with skin allergies may be at higher risk for developing asthma. There are lots of treatments, some over-the-counter, some by prescription, for eczema and related conditions, so you and your pediatrician should be able to get this problem under control with relative ease.

Stuffy Noses, Coughing, and Other Allergy Symptoms

Your child might have seasonal allergies, or a sensitivity to dust, pollutants, mold, or a household pet. You know how poorly you sleep when you have a cold. Children with these allergy symptoms feel like that all the time. Seasonal allergies can also inflame adenoids and tonsils, which in turn can cause sleep disturbances or sleep apnea.

Allergic or asthmatic children often have disrupted or poor-quality sleep. They may then struggle to stay awake during the day, and perform poorly in school. Sometimes they are judged to be hyperactive or to have behavior problems when in fact all that fidgeting is just their attempt to stay awake. Good diagnosis and treatment leads to better sleep—and to a better-behaved, higher-functioning daytime child.

Depending on your child's age and the severity of symptoms, your doctor may recommend a saline spray, a decongestant, a bedroom humidifier, or allergy medications. Some medications are available over the counter, but don't give them to a young child without consulting your doctor first, particularly before age two.

Unfortunately, some asthma medications themselves disrupt sleep, although this is less of a problem with the newer drugs. Watch out for changes in sleep patterns if your child takes asthma or allergy drugs. You might need to try a slightly different drug, or a different dose. Ask your doctor if the child can take the medication a little earlier in the day, rather than just before bed, to see if that helps.

SLEEP APNEA

A child with sleep apnea stops breathing briefly during sleep because of obstruction of the upper airways, in the back of the throat. Sometimes swollen or overly large tonsils or adenoids cause the obstruction. (But not all large tonsils or adenoids cause apnea—many kids will "grow into" them in time.) Lax neck muscles during a child's sleep can also contribute to apnea. Even mild cases of apnea can disrupt sleep, and severe cases might warrant surgical removal of the adenoids and/or tonsils. When the child can get some air despite the obstruction, you might hear loud snoring. When he can't get any air, his brain will tell him to get up and breathe ASAP! He will get up to move the muscles in the tongue and throat to open the air passage. But he won't necessarily be able to get himself back to sleep again without calling for you. Loud and persistent snorting and snoring is often a key symptom of apnea, and it's a good idea to make a five-minute tape of those strange night-time noises so your doctor can evaluate them. But don't get overly alarmed. Lots of kids snore, and they don't all have apnea. Also, while it's worth getting a good evaluation, first from your pediatrician and then from a pediatric ears, nose, and throat specialist, don't be in too much of a rush to get those tonsils or adenoids removed surgically. Sometimes it's necessary, but you don't want your child to go through unnecessary surgery if it's not. It's a myth that removing tonsils or adenoids will reduce the number of colds and sore throats he catches, or "cure" allergies. It doesn't even help recurrent ear infections except, according to Dr. Barton Schmitt's book *Your Child's Health*, in those children whose large adenoids are causing the nasal obstruction that leads to the ear problems.

How to Recognize Apnea

Apnea has one set of symptoms by day and another by night. Day symptoms include:

- breathing through the mouth

- nasal congestion

- nasally voice

- difficulty swallowing

- frequent infections (ears and sinuses)

- poor appetite

- morning headaches (if they are old enough to tell you)

- waking up tired and being very sleepy during the day

- behavioral problems

Nightime symtoms include:

- snoring—often loud ("grandpa" snoring, as one specialist puts it)

- pauses in breathing while sleeping

- frequent nighttime wakenings—particularly if they don't have any other sleep crutches

- very restless sleep

- sweating during sleep (body is working harder to breathe)

- unusual sleep positions such as sleeping on their knees, propping themselves up on pillows or stuffed animals, hyperextending their neck, sitting up, etc; these positions reflect an effort to keep the airways open

- bedwetting if the child is trained during the day and had been trained at night

- mouth breathing

- sleep fewer hours than the average

If you co-sleep and your toddler or preschooler wakes up frequently, you might want to think about apnea. This isn't true if she is nursing on demand and still wakes up to nurse frequently, but it is a possible indicator for a child who may wake up, sit up and reposition herself, and then go back to sleep. I worked with one two-year-old who slept with his parents and would sit up, cry out, and plop back down in the middle of the night. He didn't need them to do anything else for him to get back to sleep. We worked on bedtime, and nap time, and we did lots of sleep coaching to reduce night wakenings. But we didn't eliminate them completely. He didn't snore, but he was a mouth breather and he had milk allergies. His doctor finally ordered an X-ray of his adenoids and sure enough, they were quite enlarged. He had them removed, and started sleeping all night almost immediately.

How to Help a Child with Apnea Sleep Better

If your child has even mild sleep apnea, behavioral modification will only get you so far. You can teach him to get himself to bed at night and at nap time, but you will have a very hard time stopping the night wakenings since it is a physical condition that is getting him up. So you need a double-pronged approach. Get him evaluated, by a pediatrician and by an ears, nose, and throat specialist if necessary. You may need to take him to a special clinic for an overnight sleep study. Few clinics deal with pediatric behavioral sleep problems but many do evaluations for apnea or other breathing disorders. Your doctor can refer you, or check www.aasmnet.org, the website of the American Academy of Sleep Medicine. (Click on "Patient Resources.") Sometimes treatment, which can include surgery or allergy medication, solves all the sleep problems. In many cases, however, you will still have some behavioral problems to address. Follow the advice in this book for your child's age. You should find improvement comes quickly.

> *Amanda and Tony, whom you met in Chapter 9, went through my whole Sleep Lady Shuffle with Wes. He quickly learned to fall asleep on his own without protest and to go back to sleep with less parental intervention. But while Wes woke up a lot less frequently at night, no matter what behavioral approaches Amanda, Tony, and I tried, we never got him to stop waking up at least once or twice a night, often around the same time. Approaching his fourth birthday, he often seemed very tired during the day, as though he was fighting to stay awake. During one of our follow-up conversations, Amanda mentioned that Wes breathed very, very loudly at night. I urged them to call their pediatrician.*
>
> *It turned out that Wes had severe allergies. Not quite full-fledged asthma, but enough difficulties to keep some emergency medicines on hand if the wheezing got too bad. The doctor also suspected apnea. Amanda and Tony tried to get Wes a thorough overnight sleep study at an established clinic—but he got so distraught each time that they always had to give up and go home. But the ears, nose, and throat specialist, and the pediatrician agreed that his extremely large adenoids and tonsils should come out. Unfortunately, the operation took place on his fourth birthday, and he had a pretty miserable few days. When he began to feel better, his parents revived his old sticker chart and started talking to him again about the Sleep Lady and sleep manners. This time, lo and behold, Wes started to sleep all night.*
>
> *"He was always a happy and loving child but he's even happier now," his mom said. "He needed so many naps, he struggled so much, it has made such a difference for the whole family. I feel much more patient now. Then, I would look at myself in the mirror and I looked all fuzzy—I was so exhausted."*

ADD/ADHD—ATTENTION DEFICIT DISORDER (ADD) OR ATTENTION DEFICIT HYPERACTIVITY DISORDER (ADHD)

These conditions are not usually diagnosed in very young children but it sometimes does become an issue in preschool years. Children with other behavioral or attention problems, including sensory integration issues, may be mislabeled as ADD/ADHD, particularly in these early years. Whatever the cause, hyperactive children often have trouble falling asleep. These children, even more than others, need lots of consistency and a steady parental hand. Set bedtime rules, and make sure your child understands that they are rules, not suggestions! Give your child an extra long wind-down period before bed—maybe forty-five minutes will do the trick. Try to get homework and any other tension-producing, argument-inducing activities out of the way in the afternoon or early evening, leaving plenty of time for the child to switch into a calmer gear before bed. Stimulating games (including videos) should also be over and done with well before bedtime— and you may want to keep them out of his bedroom. Bedtime activities should be quiet, gentle, borderline boring. ADD/ADHD kids, even more than other children, may stall, engage, delay, provoke—they do whatever it takes to keep themselves up and you at their side before bed. Be patient but be firm.

If your child takes medication for ADD/ADHD, it may make it harder for him to fall asleep. Work closely with your doctor on timing and dosage. These drugs are short acting, meaning they wear off during the day. But you want to time the medication so it wears off late enough to get homework done (with older kids) but early enough that it does not interfere with bed. If you think medications are keeping your child up, or making him have trouble falling asleep, talk to your doctor about alternatives. There are several medications on the market now for ADD/ADHD, and if one is creating sleep difficulties it might be worth trying another.

There are many good books out on ADD/ADHD. My favorites include *Healing ADD* by Daniel Amen, and *Taking Charge of ADHD* by Russell Barkley. You may also want to explore whether your child has sensory integration (SI) difficulties, which I find often play a role in sleep problems. SI signals can include a lack of focus and an oversensitivity or an undersensitivity to stimuli such as light, food, textures, water temperatures, loud noises, and being touched. By far the best book on sensory integration is *The Out-of-Sync Child* by Carol Stock Kranowitz. It's a superb, easy-to-understand resource. You may also want to consult an occupational therapist certified in SI.

BEDWETTING

Most children are potty trained by day sometime between age two and three, some earlier, some later. Girls are usually, but not always, earlier than boys. Listen to your child's signals regarding potty training—if he isn't ready, it won't go smoothly. I don't see any problem in working on daytime potty training, with a receptive and enthusiastic child, at the same time that you are doing Sleep Lady coaching. But I would not make a big push on nighttime potty training in the midst of sleep coaching. Wait until he is going to bed and staying asleep consistently. Think of how confusing it would be for him to go through this behavioral modification program to learn to go to bed and stay in bed—and then be told he'd better get up and pee! It often takes until age four or five for a child's bladder to grow big enough to contain the night's urine production, or for his sleepy brain to learn how to respond when his bladder shouts "full." Do get in the habit of having him go to the bathroom before bed, but I personally don't see any problem in keeping him in a diaper or pull-up at night until age four or five. If he stays dry, fine; it will make night training that much easier later. Or you may notice that he's always dry, that he has basically trained himself at night, and then you can get rid of the diapers.

After age five, bedwetting still affects about one in ten children. It's twice as common in boys as girls. The reasons for bedwetting are not well understood, but there is often a family history. Many doctors now regard it as a *parasomnia*, a sleep disorder found in deep sleepers. Sometimes bedwetting—particularly if the child was trained at night but then starting wetting the bed again—can be a sign of sleep apnea, so discuss that possibility with your doctor.

Some families report success when they wake up the child an hour or two after he goes to bed, or right before the parents go to bed. But it isn't a sure-fire solution. I know of cases where that approach didn't work and the child eventually developed nighttime control on his own. Some families also find moisture alarms very useful. Alison Mack's *Dry All Night: The Picture Book Technique That Stops Bedwetting* is my favorite resource on bedwetting for children age five and above. She contends that many of the "sleep wetters," as she calls them, are simply deep sleepers who have trouble rousing themselves in order to go to the bathroom. My own pediatrician tells parents not to worry much about it until the child is seven or eight and starts sleeping over at friends' houses.

 RESTLESS LEG SYNDROME AND PERIODIC LIMB MOVEMENT

Both of these syndromes are quite rare in children, but we do see pediatric cases once in a while, so they are worth a brief mention.

Restless leg syndrome (RLS) is characterized by an uncomfortable feeling in the legs right before going to sleep that is temporarily relieved by movement. People who experience it describe it as a crawling, tingling, or itching sensation. The feeling seldom occurs during the day, except sometimes when the person has been sitting for a long time. At night, it interferes with the onset of sleep.

To diagnose RLS, your child should have an overnight sleep study at a qualified sleep center. Results are more accurate if you eliminate caffeine, antihistamines, or cold remedies. Then her sleep should be well regulated—consistent bedtimes, good schedules. Exercise also helps. Sometimes the syndrome is linked to anemia or deficiencies of folate or vitamin B12, so iron supplements and vitamins may help. Drugs are sometimes used on adult cases but I'm not aware of studies on medication for children with RLS.

Periodic limb movement (PLM) often occurs in people who also experience restless leg syndrome, although people can experience one without the other. Sometimes PLM accompanies narcolepsy or sleep apnea. PLM causes repetitive, rhythmic motions, often of the toe, leg, or ankle during sleep. People often wake up frequently when they have this disorder, and report that they don't feel rested and refreshed in the morning. Diagnosis requires a sleep study, and the treatment is quite similar to RLS.

NARCOLEPSY

This unusual neurological disorder makes a person extremely sleepy, and people who suffer from it often nod off every few hours for twenty- to thirty-minute naps. Symptoms may include *cataplexy*, a sudden, brief loss of muscle tone linked to strong emotion; *sleep paralysis*, which occurs when a person can't move for a few seconds or even minutes as they transition from sleep to waking—or from waking to sleep; and *hypnagogic hallucinations*, frightening and often vivid dreamlike images experienced just as a person is falling asleep. Narcolepsy often runs in families, though its appearance is quite rare under age fourteen.

If you think your child has narcolepsy, ask your doctor to refer you to a sleep specialist or a pediatric neurologist. Medication sometimes helps, and behavioral changes such as a very strict sleep-wake schedule, short naps, and increased exercise are often beneficial. If your child is nodding off a lot during the day, it probably is not narcolepsy; he is probably not getting enough sleep at night either because he is waking up for behavioral reasons or because he has allergies, apnea, or one of the other problems described in this chapter. If your doctor rules out all other causes and you are completely convinced that behavioral modification can't solve the problem, ask your pediatrician about narcolepsy but, as I said, it's extremely rare in young children.

A host of other serious diseases and syndromes can also disrupt children's sleep—autism spectrum disorders, rheumatoid arthritis, neuromuscular disorders, sickle cell disease, and brain injuries, to name a few. Those diseases are rare, and require medical expertise well beyond the scope of this book. However, even children coping with severe physical challenges and the accompanying emotional trauma can benefit if they learn to sleep better. These children usually make the most improvement when their physical symptoms are under control, or at least reasonably contained, and they can begin to shake off some of the bad sleep habits they developed while they were sick. Ayanna and her family had just such an experience.

Ayanna's Story

For the first ten months of her life, it seemed that Ayanna never slept. She coughed, choked, and gagged. She cried. Her frantic parents, Lakeisha and Al, never left her alone. They slept beside her, watching her breathe and hoping for the best. At ten months, she was diagnosed with cystic fibrosis (CF), a very serious lung disease. Although there is no cure yet for CF, Ayanna benefited from the recent advances in treating and controlling it. Within a month of her diagnosis, she was on medication that made her breathing less labored. Her overall health improved. She was happier. But she still didn't sleep.

"Once she got diagnosed and everything got better, we thought, 'Well, she'll sleep better.' But she didn't," her mother, Lakeisha, said. Although Ayanna was doing better physically, she was used to being near her parents at night. And since her health was better but still fragile, they were understandably reluctant to be very far from her, despite their doctor's reassurances that she could and should be in her own room. Lakeisha and Al did get her out of their bed, but she moved into a toddler bed, right

alongside theirs. "Too convenient," her mother laughed. "We spent all night putting her back in her bed." In addition, one of the medications she took often made it hard for her to fall asleep—and her parents aggravated that by letting her stay up too late, until 9:30 p.m., meaning she was both pumped up by the drugs and overstimulated by the late hour. It was often 10:00 or 10:30 before she would finally fall asleep, and then she'd be up many, many times, all night long, tossing, turning, screaming, and yelling.

This went on for a very long time, until one of Lakeisha's coworkers commented on how tired she seemed. That coworker happened to be my brother Glenn. He gave her my number and she waited about one whole minute before she called me. Ayanna by this time was two and a half and Lakeisha was beyond exhausted.

"I had wanted to get her into her own room; I knew it would be healthier for her. But I didn't know how. I didn't want to go through the whole crying-it-out thing," Lakeisha said. "My kid had gone through enough crying in her life. I just wasn't going to do that to her."

I knew that Lakeisha had very low expectations. She kept telling me that this case was going to be my first failure. I surprised her—or rather I helped Ayanna surprise her. Lakeisha and Al did my Sleep Lady Shuffle, and Ayanna responded immediately. In fact, they didn't even have to go through the whole program; within a week she was going to sleep on her own. "We had to remind her, 'No talking, lie quietly, sh-sh, night-night,' but that's all it took," her mother said. "In the morning, she would tell us she slept in her 'big girl' bed, she was so proud, she'd get her stickers."

Sleeping through the whole night took longer, about two or three weeks. It wasn't completely consistent. Some nights she slept, some nights she woke up and wanted her parents to sit by her. "We'd sit and she'd fall right back to sleep. It wasn't an hour, it was five, ten minutes and then she'd be out again. I'm still in awe."

Ayanna is lucky in that her CF is relatively mild, and the worse of it can be controlled. But she still gets sick a lot, which causes sleep disruption and a lot more anxiety than in other households where the worst thing is an occasional earache. When she's sick, Lakeisha and Al still stay with her, but they don't take her into their bed, and they try not to climb into hers too much either. Instead, they try to restrict themselves to sleeping on a mattress on the floor beside her. When the episodes are over, they quickly go back to their own room, and she can deal with the transitions. At age three, she was usually sleeping from 8:30 p.m. to 7:00 a.m. without interruption.

"I couldn't believe it," her mother said. "Oh, my goodness, I absolutely have a life back. I have time with my husband now. Our life does not revolve around getting our baby to sleep. We talk about things other than what an awful night it was."

They go out sometimes now and leave Ayanna with a babysitter. She goes to "cousin slumber parties" at her aunts' homes, and Lakeisha and Al get a night off, which is great for all couples and absolutely invaluable for a couple dealing with this kind of stress. When they gave away the crib, though, they had to blow the dust off it first. Ayanna had never spent a night in it.

14
ROUTINE BUSTERS

No matter how hard you try to keep your child on a pre-dictable and comforting routine, disruptions are inevitable. Some routine busters, like a vacation or a weekend visit to the grandparents, are planned and welcome. Others, like illnesses, strike without warning and can turn a child's sleep upside down. In this chapter, I explore ways to get through such common disruptions as travel, illness, teething, the birth of a sibling, and moving to a new home. I also offer some advice in the event of lifestyle changes, like Mom returning to work, or a divorce. I offer guidelines but not rigid rules. Some children are more adaptable than others, and get back into their normal routine without missing a beat. Parents also react differently. Some moms and dads strive to keep the schedule in place at all costs. Others consciously decide that the circumstances warrant breaking the sleep rules temporarily, knowing they may have to pay a price later. For instance, during the fall when Ilan turned three, Joanne's normal three-day workweek became a grueling marathon of fifteen-hour workdays—sometimes even longer—five or six days a week. Ilan didn't see her before bedtime, and woke up frequently wanting to see her at night. She was exhausted, he was miserable, and she decided to co-sleep temporarily. After the work crisis ended, she took several days off and spent lots of time with him, and explained he was going to sleep alone in his fire truck bed again. She cuddled him a lot right before bedtime and sat in the hallway while he fell asleep. He began sleeping through the night again within a week.

As a rule, if you have deviated, it's a good idea to return to your normal routine as soon as possible. Most kids adapt quickly, particularly if they have already developed fairly good sleep skills. Sometimes you'll have to do another round of sleep coaching (often accompanied by some crying), but it usually goes faster than the initial go-round because you are reminding them of a learned skill, not introducing it from scratch. I give some help on how to do a refresher version of training at the end of this chapter and, as always, you can comfort your child as you ease him back into his routine.

I like reminding children of sleep rules even while we're bending them. "You are sleeping in the same room as Mommy and Daddy while we are at the lake but as soon as we get home, you and Teddy Bear will be back in your princess bed and Mommy and Daddy will be in our bed but we'll come check on you every night." Or "I'm going to pick you up and hold you until you fall back asleep to make you feel better, but as soon as your tummy ache goes away, you won't need Mommy to do this. You are going to sleep great again and I'll give you so many stars and stickers because I will be so proud." Even very young toddlers understand some of this, and older ones get it quite well. It helps to make the rule-breaking less confusing to them, and makes the intermittent reinforcement less powerful. By understanding your expectations, they may have an easier time readapting to their old routine once the disruption has passed.

DEVELOPMENTAL MILESTONES

Cognitive, emotional, or motor developmental milestones often affect sleep. In fact, Dr. T. Berry Brazelton in his book *Touchpoints* reminds us that we may see regression or a period of disorganization not just in sleep, but in social, emotional, and feeding patterns as well. I find that the most pronounced, although temporary, sleep problems occur as a child is learning to walk. You may also see problems right before your child sits up, crawls, stands, and is potty trained. I address many of these leaps in the relevant age chapters but the key is remembering that these new skills excite children and change their view of their world, sometimes quite literally. For instance, when your child stands up in her crib for the first time, she may discover everything looks different from up here! Of course, it's hard to know that a child is about to reach a milestone. We see the disorganization, the regression, and we may think something is wrong. We might even rush to the pediatrician. Only in hindsight do we realize that she was about to take her first step. Be flexible, but stay consistent during these periods. When a child is sick, or when we travel, we do have to deviate from normal sleep rules, but with the developmental milestones, if you stay the course, the child will quickly adapt.

"I don't know if this is true for all babies, but for both of mine, sleep got worse before they reached a new milestone. Both kids would have two or three fussy nights—it usually didn't require any intervention from me, but I could hear their disrupted sleep," said Lisa, mother of Teddy and Brittany, and a champion keeper of sleep logs. "Then they would roll over, or stand up, or sit for the first time."

 TRAVEL

The better a child sleeps at home, the better the odds are that he will sleep well when you travel. Even if he does get out of kilter while you are away, if he's a good sleeper, he'll probably return to good patterns when he gets home. Conversely, if your child has only recently started sleeping through the night or going to bed without a great deal of fussing, try to postpone any discretionary travel for at least three weeks.

When you travel, your child will probably backslide a little bit, but try not to throw out all your gains and try not to rely on whatever sleep crutch you've just eliminated. For instance, if you stopped nursing during the night, don't start again. Go ahead and do lots more soothing and comforting on the road than you would at home, but find some way of soothing that won't lead you back to where you started, that won't let you get caught in the intermittent reinforcement trap. You don't want him thinking, "You got me up to nurse when we were in that strange place; maybe you will still get me up to nurse now that we are home!" You can't blame him for trying.

Always bring along the lovey and pack a night-light, and, since there's no such thing as traveling light with a small child anyway, go ahead and take along favorite books and toys. Many families bring crib sheets or blankets too. (Some hotels don't provide much in the way of bedding with a crib or portable crib, so check in advance or pack linens protectively.) You want the child to have items that feel and smell comforting and familiar. If you are one of those moms who always keeps a small bag stocked with first-aid supplies, travel-size medications, and baby toiletries, stick the spare night-light and bulb in there as well, so you don't have to worry about forgetting it. If you are staying at a relative's home or a rental condo, you may want to take your baby monitor with you, too, so you don't feel like you have to stay by his side in a dark room from 7:00 on!

"We go to my parents in Baltimore pretty frequently. I used to bring the whole sheet set—including the bumper and the mobile! But I don't do all that anymore," said Jayne, who worked with me when Cynthia was four months old. "She sleeps in a crib there, and although she usually doesn't sleep well the first night, she's okay the second night. I try to be consistent with her routine there, I don't skip naps and I put her down at her usual bedtime. She's fine as soon as she gets home."

One obvious drawback to staying in a hotel or motel is that young children go to bed early, and you may not want to sit in the dark all night. (Some couples take turns reading in the lobby or even in the hall. A balcony can be a good alternative, weather permitting. If you have older children, one of you might want to put the baby to bed in the hotel room while the other keeps the big kids occupied—ice cream, mini-golf, or something like that, but then try to have them tiptoe into the hotel room and get into bed as quietly as possible.) Think about how to position the child's crib or bed so that you may be able to turn on a small lamp later without having it shine in his eyes, or maybe take one of those little travel book-lights along. Some all-suite hotels oriented toward long-term business travelers have good deals for families on weekends and holidays. Even in a suite, you may have to turn off all or most of the lights for a few minutes when you put the baby to bed, but then you have some adult space to talk or read or watch a movie with the volume on low. (They also have kitchenettes that are convenient when traveling with children.) One creative mom I know packed an extra sheet and thumbtacks with her every time she stayed in a hotel with her child. She could make a curtained "wall" between the crib and the bed à la *It Happened One Night* so the child wouldn't think she was going to get to sleep in Mom and Dad's room from now on.

"Randy travels for work and since I'm not working right now, we try to travel together. I bring everything, the blanket, pillow, more than one teddy bear, toys, and food," said Suzanna's mother, Sheila. "We try to get a suite—if she's in our room, it doesn't work as well." Initially, Sheila would "do anything" to get Suzanna to sleep away from home, including co-sleeping, and that set up problems when they got home. Over time, Suzanna became more adaptable and Sheila got better at figuring out how to backslide on the road without creating longer-term disruptions at home.

Before you go, talk to the hotel about whether it has cribs, portable cribs, or Pack-'n-Plays. Or if you are visiting relatives, think about whether there will be enough grandchildren visiting over the years to make it worth investing in an inexpensive crib, even one of the smaller fold-up varieties. Some babies don't really like sleeping in those portable cribs with thin mattresses. You'll learn quickly what your child can adjust to, and you'll then be able to pack and plan accordingly on subsequent travel.

With older children who are no longer in a crib, you may request a roll-away bed, or if the child will be in a regular hotel bed in your room, you may see if you can move it closer to the wall for safety. Put an extra pillow on the floor in case he falls out, or place the bed or cot mattress on the floor so it doesn't matter if he rolls off. You may want to place the mattress next to your bed, or between your bed and another bed holding older siblings, so that the little one is reassured by being close to you. There's a good chance he will get out of his bed and sneak into yours. Some parents return the child to his own bed, others figure it's a losing battle in the hotel. If he does end up with you, carefully explain that he can sleep with you in the hotel (or at Granny's house or wherever) but will have to go right back into his own bed when you get back home. Ilan understood this immediately, and even if he didn't sleep through the night right after a schedule disruption, he did understand that he could sleep with Mommy in a hotel or at Granny and Grandpa's house, but at his own house he'd be in his fire truck bed with his stuffed animal friends, and Mommy would be in her room with Daddy.

If possible, try to have your child sleep in one place throughout the whole vacation. You may be better off with a week at the beach than on a road trip with a different motel (and possibly a different crib) every night. If you are visiting several relatives, it may be worth sleeping in one home for the entire trip, and visiting with other family members during the day or over early dinners. For instance, one couple with a nine-month-old originally planned a five-day vacation—two nights with one set of grandparents, two with the other, and one night at an aunt's. I gently suggested they might want to reconsider, so they chose one set of grandparents as a "base camp" and arranged to have relatives visit them there or to spend part of the day at other family members' homes. They carefully explained to all concerned why their baby needed this, and to avoid bruised feelings or rivalries they immediately let all concerned know that the other grandparents would be the "base" for the next visit.

Try very hard to make sure your children get enough rest on vacation. With all the change and stimulation, they may not nap while traveling. It's up to you how hard you press the nap; you may get a sense that if you insist and make the effort, he will nap. Alternatively, you may figure that you can spend the whole afternoon in your hotel room and he still won't sleep a wink so you might as well go out and enjoy yourself; maybe he'll doze in the stroller. It depends on how old the child is, and how long you are away. An infant absolutely still needs naps, a three-year-old can probably skip naps for a few days as long as you get him to bed at night earlier than usual. You might also want to plan some of your travel to overlap with nap time. As you know, I normally want children to sleep in their beds, not in cars, but on vacation, a car nap might be the best you can do. Plus if you are going to be in the car for a few hours anyway, it may be easier on everyone if he sleeps through it. Try to get back to your hotel (or relatives' home) on the early side, to have an early bedtime. A vacation isn't much of a vacation when the kids are melting down all day. "We had trouble with naps on vacation," said Lucas's mother, Tracy, whom you met in Chapter 4, Newborn to Five Months. "But we found that if we had to disrupt his day, we were better off disrupting it in the morning. He'd often fall asleep and catch up later."

When you get home, make it a top priority to return to your normal routine as quickly as possible. Some families keep their activities very light for a day or two when returning home, to really focus on getting napping and bedtime back in place.

If you are traveling across time zones, get your child up at his usual wake-up time, both when you start your vacation and when you get back home. In other words, if he wakes up at 7:00 a.m. at home in Miami, wake him up at 7:00 a.m. local time in Seattle and then when you get back home to Miami, wake him at 7:00 a.m. Eastern Time. Do this the day you arrive on vacation, or if you all need to recover from a long trip or a red-eye, do it the next day. Switch naps and sleep times to local time the first full day after your arrival. So if you got in late and everyone goes to bed later than usual and then sleeps in, naps will obviously be off that first day. But don't let him nap late. Wake him from his last nap (or his only nap) early enough so you can get him to bed at his regular bedtime. In other words, if you arrived in Seattle at midnight, everyone will sleep late in the morning (you hope!). Then instead of napping from 1:00 to 3:00 p.m., he might not begin his nap until 4:00. Don't let him nap too late, though, even if he's a little cranky when you rouse him, so you can get him to bed that night at his regular bedtime, at 7:00 or 8:00 (Seattle time). Don't fret if you can't follow this exactly. A few car or stroller naps aren't a big deal on a vacation; you'll get everyone back to normal when you get home.

"We went to Hawaii with two young kids, and we had to lie down with them. We knew it was a no-no, but we had to do it, they were getting up so early—one-thirty a.m.," said Kathleen. "Sean had an easier adjustment than Maude, although he did want dinner at midnight. But when we got home, they readjusted in four nights. They both cried a little on the third night, but just for a couple of minutes, that's all."

Enjoy Life!

Although I stress routines and consistency, I don't want you to take it to such an extreme that you can't enjoy your life! I'm not sure I would have been as courageous as Kathleen, flying to Hawaii with two children under the age of four. But don't let yourself get caught in the trap Linda and Miguel experienced either. Four months after they got Amy sleeping well, they were still too petrified even to visit out-of-town relatives for a weekend, never mind try a vacation.

"I'm afraid to get her out of her routine, I'm afraid she'd get out of whack. She would probably adapt better than I think, but I would dread going back to the way things were, it was just so awful," Linda told me when Amy was fifteen months old. Finally, after a few more months, they did venture away for a weekend with great trepidation. "She did great!" Linda said. "Nap time the first day was nearly nonexistent because of the strange environment and a new portable crib, but beyond that she did wonderfully!"

DAYLIGHT SAVING TIME CHANGES

When we change clocks in spring and fall, switch immediately to the new time. In other words, if her bedtime was 7:00 p.m. and you moved the clock to 8:00 p.m., keep putting her to bed at 7:00 p.m. according to the new time. She may wake up a little early or a little late for a few days but then she'll adjust. Stay consistent and don't let her start her day before 6:00 a.m. (new time). The adjustment seldom takes even a week.

If you think your child can't make a one-hour adaptation that easily, split the difference. Using the example above, put her to bed at 7:30 p.m. (new time) for a few days, and then shift it to 7:00 p.m.

ROUTINE CHILDHOOD ILLNESSES

You have some control over when your child travels, but you don't get to choose when he gets an ear infection, a tummy ache, or bronchitis. If he gets sick during a sleep-training program, pause until he's feeling better. Don't abandon the program. If you can, "freeze" or maintain your Shuffle position until he feels better. If you feel he absolutely needs you closer, go back to sitting near the crib as you did on the first three nights of the Shuffle, and then move halfway across the room when he feels better. Don't draw this out; you will just make it harder for him. If he gets sick shortly after you complete his "coaching," he'll probably backslide a bit and you may have to do an abbreviated version of training to get him sleeping all night again.

When your child is sick, respond immediately to his cries at night. Do whatever you need to do—give him medicine, aspirate his nose, clean him up after a tummy attack. Go ahead and hold him and comfort him as much as you think he needs, even if it sets back sleep training a few days. My advice about not picking up crying children during sleep shaping does not apply when they are sick. Don't totally overdo it. You want to take care of your child, you want to soothe your child, but there's a difference between a little backsliding and total regression. In other words, if you've recently ended co-sleeping, don't put your child back in your bed at the first sniffle. Sit by his side, hold his hand, stroke him, snuggle him but try not to take him back into your bed. I would even rather have you sleep on a makeshift bed in his room than have him back in your bed. But obviously, if you have been trying to get rid of his water bottle at night but he's now got a tummy ache, give him whatever fluid he needs to stay hydrated until his stomach calms down. Once you make a health-based decision to give him a drink, do it as soon as he needs it; don't make him cry for it. If age appropriate, feed him in a slightly different way during illness. In other words, if you just weaned him from nighttime nursing but he needs liquids because he's sick, try a cup or a bottle instead of nursing. If he was emotionally attached to a specific sippy cup, try letting him having a few sips out of a "big boy" cup.

Occasionally, we find a silver lining to an illness. I know one six-month-old who was very pacifier dependent, but he got so congested by a bad cold that he couldn't suck on it and breathe simultaneously. When he didn't use it for three nights, his parents seized the opportunity to make it disappear for good.

During and immediately after an illness, expect your child to wake up more at night and to take longer to get back to sleep. Don't assume over-the-counter cold, stomach, allergy, or pain relief medications will help your child sleep (and don't give them without checking with your pediatrician). These medicines do make some children sleepy but they stimulate others, and they can get so wired that they stay awake for hours. Some moms have found dye-free medicines reduce this problem, but it's not always a solution. And even if they do induce sleep, most medications wear off in a few hours.

Vaccinations throw some children off for a night or two. Ask your pediatrician whether you should give him Tylenol or a similar analgesic before the shot, and offer the baby more reassurance at bedtime and when he gets up at night because he might not be feeling completely himself. They usually feel better and are sleeping normally within a few days.

Ear infections are particularly brutal on sleep, because the pain intensifies when a child lies down. In fact, frequent and distraught awakenings may be one telltale sign that your child has an ear infection. If your child has chronic infections, talk to your pediatrician about consulting an ear, nose, and throat specialist on the wisdom of using a longer or different course of antibiotics, or whether he's a good candidate for surgery to insert tubes. If he gets an ear infection while you are doing the Sleep Lady Shuffle, pause where you are, and start moving ahead again after he's been on antibiotics for two or three days (faster if he feels better after only one day).

TEETHING

Teething can interfere with sleep, but far less than many parents anticipate or believe. Usually children who sleep well will experience minor disruptions when they begin to teethe (except for the molars, which come in between ages one and two and can cause more pain). But children who are overtired, or who don't know how to put themselves to sleep may have more trouble when teething. It's like she is saying, "I'm already tired, I'm not sure how to go to sleep and now I have this pain in my mouth. That's going to put me over the edge, so I'm going to stay up and yell."

To sort out how much of the sleep disruption stems from those new little teeth, compare day with night behavior. If she's her usual self all day but extra cranky or difficult at night, it is probably not the teeth. If a usually cheerful child is miserable around the clock, the trouble may well be a particularly painful tooth. The pain usually subsides as soon as the tooth comes through the gum. Ask your pediatrician about using infant Tylenol or a similar painkiller. I also found that letting my daughters chew on cold objects during the day, like a washcloth that I had put in the freezer for a few hours, was very soothing. They also liked chomping on a toothbrush. Occasionally I've worked with children who have a slew of symptoms—diaper rash, low-grade fever, disturbed sleep, excessive drooling, poor appetite, and crankiness—but they are a minority and it usually passes as soon as the tooth pops out. If teething problems crop up while you are in the middle of Sleep Lady behavior modification techniques, progress may slow down for a few days while the tooth comes through, but stick with it. You might want to be a little more soothing, do a little more holding or patting, but don't regress to all the patterns you are trying to change. If you are just about to embark on the Sleep Lady Shuffle or are introducing new sleep manners and you suspect a tooth is about to erupt, consider delaying any changes for a day or two.

MOVING TO A NEW HOME

Lots of families regard the move to a new home as a time to make sleep changes, but I'd be careful about this. Moving means change and stress, and you don't necessarily want to add to it if your child doesn't do well with change in the first place. Even though moving is hectic and tense for adults too, make sure you give your children lots of time and attention because it's an enormous change for them. Play in their new bedrooms, to promote comfort and familiarity. At night, babies, preschoolers, and even school-age children might want some extra reassurance as they acclimate to new surroundings, so sit in her room or by the door at bedtime. Don't forget a night-light, and a few practice runs at finding the bathroom! With older children, even around age three, you might want to let the child help arrange her room. Choosing colors or decorations will help her feel in control and make the move feel more fun. Be sure to let children talk out their concerns, including questions about their new routines, babysitters, preschools, or schools.

After Reid lost his job when the high-tech bubble burst, he and Julia traveled by car with three young children while they tried to figure out where they wanted to resettle. They spent lots of time in cars and hotels, and did a lot of backsliding regarding sleep. "We gave Todd back his pacifier," said Reid. "I'm not sure whether it helped him but I think it helped the real estate agents." Then when they finally did settle in a lovely southern coastal city and Reid opened his own business, the kids manifested pretty typical behavior. That's when the oldest daughter became a champion bedtime negotiator, earning that "Captain Loophole" sobriquet. The second daughter, who was moving to a new state and starting kindergarten simultaneously, started showing up in her parents' bed at night. And Todd needed that pacifier again—but he would get furious at bedtime, hurling it across the room. "It's an interesting ritual, if you stop to think about it," Reid said. "He was throwing the one thing he really needed to get himself to sleep." Naturally, as the parents gave their children reassurance and everyone adapted, life calmed down, or got as close to calm as any home with three children age seven and under can be.

With a very young baby, a move to a new house or apartment is a good time to move the crib out of your room and into her own room. If she's more than six months old, you might want to start the Sleep Lady Shuffle as you make this switch (although you may not want to tackle everything at once; for example, if you move her to her own room, you might not want to try to wean her off of her pacifier that same night). If she's less than six months old and too young for the Shuffle, sit in her room and give her some extra soothing and reassurance as she acclimates. However, a move is not usually a good time to switch from a crib to a bed. Let the child get accustomed to the new space first, or you will be inviting more bedtime conflict. If the room configuration allows it, I like putting the crib in the same place in relation to the door as it was in your old house or apartment.

As with all changes, the better your child sleeps, and the longer she's been sleeping well, the less disruptive a move is likely to be. If your child doesn't sleep well and you want to do some concerted sleep coaching, wait a few weeks after the move until she's adapted. You as a parent will also cope better with her sleep training if you've got the first wave of moving chaos under control.

When Bill and I moved into our home, Carleigh was two and half and Gretchen was minus three weeks (I was pregnant!). Being a little hyperfocused on sleep, I had the Realtor help me figure out which of the four bedrooms got the earliest sunlight. I then put the girls in the rooms with the least morning sun. Some people move into a new home and get the kitchen set up first, or maybe the big-screen TV. The first thing I did was put up room-darkening shades in the kids' rooms and get their furniture in place.

DAY CARE NAP OBSTACLES

Day care centers have their own approach to naps, and they aren't always the approaches that are right for your individual child, even if the overall care is excellent. For instance, many day care centers will not allow a baby to cry in the crib at nap time for fear of waking all those other babies. So the caretakers often rock or hold the babies to sleep. You should work on nighttime sleep and weekend naps, and when you are fairly confident of your child's ability to get herself to sleep, talk to the day care providers. Explain what you have accomplished, and ask them to work with you on getting her down drowsy but awake. Perhaps they can put your child in the sleep room or nap area a few minutes before they bring in the other babies, to give her a chance to get used to falling asleep on her own there. Maybe they can just rock or hold her for a shorter period of time and then pat and "sh-sh" her to sleep, instead of rocking her until she's totally out. Talk to them about meshing their nap schedule with your child's sleep windows. Share your knowledge of sleep science to see if you can get them to work with you. Talk to them about keeping a special lovey, blanket, or pillow at day care or preschool.

One family I worked with had a very active, alert six-month-old who had difficulty napping in a bright, somewhat noisy room with other children. Her day care center would not tolerate any nap-time crying, so the staff held her to sleep. That soon stopped working; as soon as they put her down in her crib, she would wake up and cry. The baby would end up taking several short half-hour naps, and be a wreck by the time her parents picked her up. They then had trouble with her at dinnertime and bedtime, and she started waking up more frequently at night because she was overtired. The day care center would not work with the family, so the parents withdrew her and hired a nanny. It was much more expensive but they felt they had no choice, given their daughter's temperament and sleep patterns. The day care center did agree to reserve a slot for the little girl so she could return at age two.

Some day care centers transfer babies on their first birthdays to a new care group where all children nap once a day. Unfortunately, this is premature; most children don't transition to one nap until about fifteen to eighteen months. Talk to the child care center about leaving your one-year-old in the baby room for a few more months until he's ready to give up his morning nap. In toddler classrooms, children usually nap on cots (not cribs) in a darkened room with lots of other children. If it works, leave it alone! You can work on bedtime and weekend naps, and many children can separate what happens at day care from home patterns. With a three-and-a-half- or four-year-old, your challenge might be convincing the day care staff that he no longer needs to nap, that he stays up way too late if he sleeps for two hours each afternoon. Most day care providers give sleep reports; if yours doesn't, ask them to fill you in.

FAMILY TRAUMA

Obviously going through a divorce, illness, or a death in the family is an upsetting time for everyone, and your goal should be to provide your child with maximum comfort and security. You will almost certainly see some sleep disruption—more clinginess at bedtime, more night wakenings, maybe more bad dreams. I wouldn't attempt to embark on any major new sleep training until the trauma (your child's and yours) has diminished and new routines have been established. You can, however, try to avoid creating any new sleep crutches during a time of stress. For instance, you might be tempted to start co-sleeping to comfort your child (or yourself), but I would recommend that you do lots of snuggling before bedtime and lots of comforting from a chair or the doorway, rather than getting into a new habit that may be difficult to break later.

Separation and Divorce

Here, as always, maintaining a routine will provide your child with a great deal of security and comfort. Children may adapt better than you expect to two different sets of sleep rules and expectations. They understand, for instance, that Mommy will lie down with them until they fall asleep at Mommy's house, but Daddy won't lie down with them at Daddy's house (or vice versa). What counts is consistency from each parent. In other words, if you lie down with her on Tuesday, she has every reason to expect you to lie down with her again on Friday, no matter what happened at the other parent's house on Wednesday and Thursday. Similarly, it's fine if your kids share a room at Dad's house but have separate rooms at Mom's. If you have to sleep coach them, you may have to separate them temporarily. It's generally better to move the one who sleeps better to a temporary bedroom, and leave the one being coached where he is. (Read Chapter 11, Twins and Siblings, for more advice on bedtimes and sleep training more than one child.)

A parent with shared custody can do the Sleep Lady Shuffle on his or her own, no matter what the other parent is doing. It may take longer and not be perfect, but you will see improvement. For instance, if you're a now-single father and don't want to co-sleep with your three-year-old daughter, you can start the Shuffle by having her sleep on a mattress on the floor of your room for a weekend or a week. Then, the next time she's at your house, you can sleep on the floor of her room while she gets into her bed. Continue the Shuffle, step by step, as best you can within the confines of your custody arrangement. Obviously the ideal is for both parents to work this out together but that's a tall order amid a divorce. Don't despair of sleep improvements even without cooperation from your ex-spouse.

Some parents have tremendous trouble setting any limits during the first year of divorce. They feel sad and guilty and don't want to "ruin" their time with their children by setting limits, enforcing rules, or risking arguments. Again, I must emphasize that children find routine, structure, and boundaries comforting, especially in times of stress.

Loss of a Family Member

In the sad event that your family experiences a death, follow the same advice mentioned above: be gentle and offer extra reassurance, ideally without creating new sleep crutches. Make sure you don't tell your child that Grandpa went to sleep and won't wake up again. That only exacerbates children's evening fears. Incorporate your own beliefs in explaining death to your child. If your spouse has died then you may want to seek grief counseling and discuss further strategies with the therapist on how to help your child. Some parents may decide to do whatever works and deal with the sleep fallout when they are feeling better themselves.

SCHOOL AND WORK CHANGES

All sorts of disruptions unsettle our children's lives—new day care providers, Mom going back to work, a parent traveling on business. Basically, you need to give extra reassurance and comfort without throwing your whole routine out the window. Keep bedtime and bedtime rules consistent, but make sure you are providing the sense of security your child needs. "When Vince travels, I stick to the plan, if I vary it for even one second, it's all over," said Beth, whose daughter, Madison, was then two and a half. Be extra diligent about making sure your child gets enough sleep because she will be able to handle stress and change better if she's well rested. Some parents who travel like to leave a tape recording of themselves singing a lullaby or reading a favorite bedtime book. Children sometimes like to mark off the days on a calendar until Mom or Dad comes home. It's very concrete and they can actually see that the parent's homecoming is approaching. It's nice to include the missing parent in bed-time songs or prayers. Be careful, though, about talking to Mom or Dad on the phone just before bedtime. This can be upsetting to a child who doesn't understand where his parent is. If your child reacts badly, try scheduling the phone calls earlier in the day.

BABY BROTHERS AND SISTERS

Most children experience some understandable regression when a new baby comes along. They may have temper tantrums, or ask for a thing they've outgrown, such as a diaper, bottle, or pacifier, or come up with some urgent, pressing need the minute you start to nurse the new baby. Sleep is also affected. If the older child starts waking up more frequently at night, just walk him quietly back to bed. If he's waking up because he hears the baby, explain that everything is okay, that new babies need to wake up and eat but that soon the baby is going to sleep all night just like his big brother or sister. Remind him during the daytime too, if he's old enough to understand. If he starts demanding more of your attention at bedtime, you might try starting bedtime earlier so he has longer to unwind with you (depending on everyone's nursing and sleeping schedules, this might only work if both parents are at home). Or you could involve him in the baby's bedtime, make him part of it. For instance, you could have him "help" you read the baby a simple story before reading an "older" story to him, or you could read to him while nursing the baby. (See Chapter 11, Twins and Siblings, for more advice on how to coordi-nate two bedtimes.) No matter how busy you get with the baby, it's essential that you spend special one-on-one time with the older child every day.

If the baby is sleeping in your room for the first few months, and your child knows that he used to be there, explain that the arrangement is tempo-rary, that the baby will go to her own room (or their shared room) as soon as she can go all night without eating. If your older child is co-sleeping with you, please don't kick him out of bed to make room for the new one! Keep the baby in a bassinet near the bed, or in a co-sleeper sidecar adjacent to the bed, but don't add to the older child's feelings of dislocation. Some parents temporarily have the father sleep with the older child in the child's room, while Mom sleeps with the baby in the parents' room.

As you know from Chapters 8 and 9, on toddlers and preschoolers, I believe in keeping children in cribs as long as you can! If you are going to transition a child to a bed before the birth of a sibling, do it at least two and as many as six months before the birth. If you wait until after the new baby is born, give it at least four months. Please don't rush this transition just because you need a crib, particularly if your older child is under two. If your older child is still happy in his crib, leave him there and buy or borrow another crib for the new baby, even a secondhand crib, or keep him in a bassinet for a few months. Occasionally an older child who is already in a bed will want his crib back. He may say it, if he has the words, or he may show you, for instance by climbing into his baby brother's crib at every opportunity. I would highlight all the advantages of having a "big boy" bed. Point out all the other things that he gets to do with you that the baby doesn't—like going to the playground or eating cookies! Crib envy is usually his way of voicing a fear that he is being replaced, so just keep giving him all the reassurance he needs. But if he's still pretty young, and hasn't been in a bed too long, don't rule out giving him the crib back (if you haven't already given it away).

As you know, the most important thing you can do for the older child is to reassure him of your love. Keep telling him how much you enjoy having a big boy or girl. Stress his "big kid" privileges. Tell him how lucky the baby is to have such a great big brother or sister, and how much the baby will adore him. Make sure your visitors make just as big a fuss about your big guy as your little one. Give the older child some jobs to do; let him fetch a diaper, or help wash the baby's toes. Remind him of the safety rules too—no touching the face, no throwing things or picking up the baby without Mommy or Daddy's help, and definitely no waking up the baby or going in when he's sleeping.

RETRAINING

When you do experience a sleep disruption, address it promptly. You need to be extra consistent at the first opportunity, both in terms of scheduling and in terms of scaling back your own comforting at bedtime and at night wakenings. Usually, the briefer and less extreme the disruption is, the easier it will be to overcome. For instance, a twenty-four-hour stomach bug is going to be a lot less difficult to cope with than a week in the hospital, and a napless weekend at a relative's house an hour's drive away will be a lot less disruptive than a two-week trip to London. But as long as the regression doesn't last months, it's usually less a matter of relearning a sleep skill than of remembering to use a skill they already know. A child who has lots of disruptions, irregular parental schedules combined with frequent illnesses, may have more trouble than a child who goes away for one week a year. You may have to go through the Sleep Lady Shuffle again, but you can probably do it quickly, just one or two nights in each position. Usually you don't even have to do the entire

Shuffle; it's enough to just do the last few nights, sitting in the hallway and then doing checks.

If the regression is significant and recurs soon after you've finished the Shuffle, say a week or two, you may have to go back to the beginning, to sitting beside the crib or bed. But then move very quickly; change positions every night instead of every three nights. Other families just go to the sitting-in-the-doorway stage, and progress from there. You may have to endure some crying because the break in the routine amounts to intermittent reinforcement, even if it wasn't intentional or avoidable. In general, the longer your child has been sleeping well, the longer he's been well rested, the quicker the transition to peaceful nights. I remember getting an email from an amazed parent who had worked with me six months earlier on both her children's sleep. They had just returned from a vacation, and for the first time ever, both kids slept all night while they were away, and didn't miss a beat when they came back home.

Some children conquer their sleep problems and just shake off later disruptions. Others remain highly sensitive to them—and often these are the children who were very alert as newborns and reached developmental milestones early. Babies who have reflux for more than three months often tend to have more long-term vulnerability to sleep disruption. Joanne, for instance, certainly knew all the ins and outs of my sleep system as we worked on this book, but Ilan remained one of those children whose sleep was easily thrown off by even a minor illness—and he had more than his share of minor illnesses. (Travel didn't disturb him quite as much; even if he co-slept in hotels, once home he returned to his usual routine easily.)

Ilan had been one of those very alert newborns, and he also had persistent reflux, with traces of it remaining well into his third year. His parents' uneven work schedules (Joanne works part-time but she's a reporter with unpredictable hours, and her husband's job also requires the family to be out a bit late every Friday evening) have also been problematic for Ilan. Sometimes Joanne gets him sleeping through the night in a couple of days, sometimes it takes weeks—but even then, he's usually just up once for a few minutes, not back to his old pattern of waking up three, four, or five times each and every night. The less tired she is, the easier it is to stay consistent in the middle of the night and get him back on track. One time, after he'd been running a high fever for a whole week, she kept toppling over, finding herself curled up sleeping like a kitten at the foot of his bed. He of course would want her to resume her kittylike pose at 3:00 a.m. the next night too. She has gone through countless variants of star and sticker charts, including special glow-in-the-dark star bonuses. Once, she noticed that he always wanted to sign himself in and out of preschool (only adults were allowed to do that) so she started having him "sign" himself into bed every night! Once he signed himself in, he knew he wasn't allowed to get up and go out again. You'd be surprised how well it worked. He loved that sign-in privilege.

15

PROBLEM SOLVING AND
TAKING CARE OF MOM AND DAD

AFTER WEEKS, MONTHS, OR EVEN YEARS of caring for a baby or child who does not sleep well, you may be more exhausted than you ever imagined possible. You may well be irritable and depressed—and feeling guilty about being irritable and depressed when you are supposed to be blissful about parenthood. You may feel that you can't be the parent you want to be. In this chapter, I want to help you minimize the stress and maximize the success of my Sleep Lady program. I want to help you get your own sleep back on track after months or years of disruptions that may date back to your pregnancy. As demanding and rewarding as it is to take care of your children, it is also important that you take care of yourself, your spouse, and your marriage.

 PROBLEM-SOLVING BASICS

Review the Information

After almost a decade of working with families with sleep problems, I know my system works for almost everyone who tries it *and* sticks with it for at least a couple of weeks. I also know from years of experience that parents want quick fixes, and, in their desperation, they don't even want to read a whole book; they just want a few key paragraphs. You don't have to read this entire book to implement my system, but if you tried to pick out a few pages that applied to your child and found that you didn't make much progress, please go back and read (or reread) the first three chapters (four if you have a newborn). It won't take long and you'll get a much better sense of how and why the Sleep Lady system works, and what it needs from you: patience, consistency, and faith in your own intuition as a parent. Then review the relevant age chapter.

Eliminate the Possibility of Medical Problems

If you have been utterly consistent in your response to your child's awakenings and you still see scant progress, read Chapter 13, Medical Problems, and consult your pediatrician. Summarize your sleep log for the doctor, and note if your child has any symptoms of reflux, sleep apnea, or allergies. Even if your child is healthy now, if she had colic or reflux past the age of three months, if she has multiple allergies, or she is unusually active or alert, it may take longer for you to see results. (Very alert children may need a little extra time during the bedtime and nap routines to prepare themselves for sleep.)

Keep a Food and Sleep Log

If you haven't kept a food and sleep log, start one. You don't need an elaborate log with flow charts and diagrams, just a pad of paper that you won't lose. The log gives you a more vivid picture of your child's patterns. It will help you identify the negative associations, the sleep crutches that you will have to help her eliminate, as well as the scheduling flaws that you will have to correct. The log will also help you detect her good patterns—what you are doing right—and that's a foundation upon which you can build. The log also helps boost morale because it helps you discern progress when you might be feeling tired and discouraged. Maybe your child is still waking up twice a night, but she now only stays up for three minutes of whimpering instead of twelve minutes of crying, or maybe she is waking up at 6:05 a.m. instead of 5:50, meeting that critical 6:00 a.m. threshold. Celebrate each little victory. Reward yourself and your child.

Use the Buddy System

Keep in mind my suggestion about finding a "buddy" to talk to each morning and review how the night went, what you did right, what was not so hot. Your buddy can be your spouse, but you may do better with a friend or a group of friends. The buddy system is like stepping on the scale at Weight Watchers; it's easier to stick to the program when you know you will be held accountable. Maybe your buddy will help you realize that you aren't being quite as consistent as you are telling yourself. Maybe you are breaking the rules just a wee bit at 3:00 a.m. when you are so tired it is really easier to give in and nurse her one more time, or hold her hand until she falls asleep, or let her crawl into your bed just this once. If you are doing everything right but still feel tired and discouraged, your buddy might be able to help you see that you really are making more progress than you realize. It's also nice just to know that you aren't alone.

As Julia, a mother of three whose youngest had sleep difficulties, put it, "When you are making decisions about sleep, you are already so tired. By eight o'clock I am exhausted and kids have been placing normal childhood demands on me all day long. My willingness to lay down the law is less evident than when I have more energy and more sleep." Knowing she had to report to someone in the morning helped Julia summon the energy she needed to follow the sleep path she charted for her children.

Respect Your Own Limits

You may also reach a point in my program where you have solved some, but not all of your child's sleep problems, and know that you have reached your own limits. For instance, you might have decided that you can't cope with nap training now, that it's taking you two hours a day to get your nine-month-old to nap in his crib for thirty minutes at a stretch. Grant yourself permission to give up for now, find a stopgap way of getting him the needed daytime sleep, and try again in a few months. Or you may have reduced your eighteen-month-old's awakenings from three times a night to three times a week; not perfect but tolerable. You may sense that getting her over that last hump, that last need to say "Hi, Mom" now and then, might be too hard on her, or maybe just too hard on you. Maybe you can take tears at bedtime now but you can't take too many of them at 4:00 a.m. You know her limits and you know your own. You'll come back to tackle those remaining awakenings when you feel ready, maybe when she's got more words and you know she can articulate what she needs from you in the middle of the night. You may decide that you really aren't ready to give up co-sleeping after all, that you'll do what you can to improve the quality of your shared sleep but that you like having your toddler in your bed, even if she does kick you in the head, sleep sideways, and hog the pillow. None of this means you are failing. Do what's right for you now, and know that you have the tools for change, whenever you are ready to use them. Indeed, even if you have achieved all your sleep goals, if your child has become, as Ellen said of James, "an Olympic sleeper," you may still find yourself reaching for this book now and then. Children go through so many different stages and their sleep, like any complex engine, needs periodic maintenance and an occasional tune-up.

Resolve Sleep Deprivation (Yours!)

Many parents complain to me that they become even more tired when they begin sleep training, and that can tempt them to give up. It's true that you might feel worse before you feel better. Remind yourself that it's short term, usually a matter of days until you start seeing results. That's because you have to give up all those little tricks you use to get your child back to sleep so that he can now learn to do it himself. So instead of being half awake for two minutes while you fetch a pacifier, or take him into your bed to nurse, you may be wide awake for twenty minutes helping and soothing a frustrated child, quite possibly a crying, frustrated child, who no longer has his sleep crutch but has not yet learned what to do instead. And once you've been up and around and experiencing the stress that we all feel when our child is in tears, it might be harder to get back to sleep yourself. Be kind to yourself if this early stage of sleep shaping is difficult. Take naps when you can. Hire a babysitter if that's an option, or arrange some co-op sitting with a friend. Accept all the help you can get from your partner, relatives, and friends; and if you are uncomfortable imposing even on people who care about you, then swap favors instead. Get to bed early yourself too, by 10:00 p.m. or earlier, even if you are normally a night owl. I know the temptation is to get the kids down and then run around and pick up the house and answer your email and do a load of laundry and pay the bills but, really, you are better off going to bed at the first available moment. You'll manage to get the essentials done during the day, and whatever isn't essential can and should wait a few more weeks (or, some would say, eighteen more years). When you're sitting in his hallway at 3:00 a.m., shushing him back to sleep, you may be really glad you had that extra hour or two of sleep.

Work Out a Schedule

Some parents express concern that if they commit to sleep training they will lose their freedom. To the contrary, I believe they gain freedom: the freedom for them and their children to enjoy themselves and each other without being exhausted, cross, or at their wit's end. You do lose a little flexibility, particularly for the first two or three weeks, maybe a little longer if your child's nap problems are especially stubborn. For those few weeks, until you get the nap schedule down, you (or your babysitter) will have to be somewhat housebound. And once your child adapts to a nap schedule, you need to respect it. She can't sleep on the run, or change her schedule every day to suit yours. But if you lose some flexibility, you will gain a great deal of predictability. You will be able to make plans and enjoy your outings because you'll know when she needs to sleep and when she'll be awake and sociable. I've often been amazed at how many baby and toddler activities, gym classes, music classes, even new moms' groups, are so poorly scheduled, smack in the middle of nap time. Don't take a class if it means skipping a nap, or gently persuade the school or teachers to consider rescheduling, so the eighteen-month-olds' class is not at 1:00 p.m., or the six-month-olds' class isn't at 9:30 a.m.—prime nap time for those age groups.

Once your child is well rested and sleeping well, she'll deal better with an occasional deviation from her schedule. But keep that a rarity, and ask yourself whether it's absolutely necessary, whether you can do what you want within the schedule. When I was a new mom I ignored the schedule a little too frequently and we all always paid a price. Later, Bill and I learned to adapt and work around my girls' sleep needs. For instance, instead of keeping your child up late for a family gathering, why not ask the family to gather a little earlier? I've found that my relatives are always accommodating if I make simple and sensible demands. We can have a holiday dinner at 5:30 or 6:00 instead of 8:00—particularly if it means a pleasant evening around the table with no meltdowns. Then we can either get our daughters back home to bed at a reasonable hour, or we can all eat together, put the kids to sleep at their grandparents', enjoy some adult family conversation, and then transfer the kids into the car and home to their own beds. The better they sleep, the more easily they adapt to sleeping in unfamiliar places, or getting themselves back to sleep after they've been moved.

Start the Sleep Lady Program at the Appropriate Time

When you start my program, make sure you choose a realistic timetable. If you work outside the home, do as much of the sleep shaping as you can while you are still on maternity leave and aren't trying to juggle work, family, and sleep training. But whether you are home or back at the office, make sure that you don't set yourself up for failure by creating a plan that you can't follow through on. For instance, you wouldn't start a strict diet on Thanksgiving Day or when you set sail on a cruise. Similarly, don't choose to start sleep training when you know you are going to have all kinds of disruptions and difficulties. If your husband is about to start a new job in a different city, and you are going to have a commuting marriage for the next eight weeks, and then you are going to have fifteen houseguests staying with you for your sister's wedding, and then you are going off for a month to visit both sets of grandparents, hold off until you get settled again. I worked with one mother who co-slept with her thirteen-month-old and nursed frequently through the night. The family was going to move to a new house in a month, so she decided it wasn't the right time to make any nighttime sleep changes. But she did begin working on improving naps and helping her baby go to sleep at bedtime without being nursed. She had a clear sense of what she could realistically do now, and what she needed to postpone. She set her goals, and she achieved them.

TROUBLESHOOTING EMOTIONAL FACTORS

If you are having trouble following my Sleep Lady program, take a step back and ask yourself whether some of your own emotional history may be getting in the way, involving either your own childhood or your marriage. And if you are working outside the home, remember that we all have moments when we second-guess ourselves, when we feel guilty, when we wonder if we should be spending more time with our babies. It's a tricky balancing act, not just when our children are infants, but throughout their lives. Know that we aren't helping our children if we try to compensate by letting them sit in our lap for an hour at 3:00 a.m. If you get your child sleeping through the night, you'll have more joy and fewer power struggles the rest of the time.

Separate Your Issues (if Any) from Those of Your Children

As parents, we have to be cognizant of our own fears, problems, and "stuck" points and how they play out in our children's lives. Our own unresolved issues from our childhood and the parenting we received may color our attitudes about sleep and make it harder for us to be consistent as we embark on a sleep program. Even if we had a relatively happy childhood, we may still react or overreact to our own experiences as we find our way as parents. For instance, an adult who recalls being afraid of the dark as a child may be overly concerned with shielding his own child from being alone in a dark room, and may project that fear onto his child. One mother I worked with felt her own mother had been cold and abandoning. When she had her own baby, she was not able to set any limits whatsoever, equating *no* with *no love*. Not surprisingly, the baby was not a good sleeper. The mother never set any limits around nursing, or any limits around bedtime. Her own unresolved feelings obstructed her child's healthy sleep. Another woman was so scarred by her girlhood separation fears that she was convinced her own baby couldn't be without her for more than the most fleeting of moments and wouldn't even let her husband form healthy bonds with their baby. Arriving home from work, the father would want to take part in his fifteen-month-old daughter's bedtime routine, both because he wanted to spend time with his baby and because he considerately wanted to give his wife a break after a long day of nonstop child care. But if the little girl cried for even a nanosecond, the mother rushed in, taking the baby from her father and nursing her to sleep.

Sometimes we need professional assistance or therapy to sort out these issues but usually we just need to be aware of them, to figure out which of our own burdens we are trying to rest on our children's slender shoulders.

Let Them Learn

It is essential to find the balance between "doing for" our children all the time in an attempt to shield and protect them, and not providing enough direction for them and leaving them vulnerable. That's why I urged you at the beginning of this book to think of sleep training as a form of coaching. Remember, you are giving your child sleep strategies but he's the one who has to play the sleep game. A coach doesn't "emotionally damage" his players by letting them go out on the field, even if they make mistakes once in a while. We as parents don't damage our children by helping them learn to sleep.

A lot of the parents I work with recognize that they struggle with sleep issues and are having a difficult time overcoming them. Many say they have tried everything but acknowledge they have not really given anything a chance to work. Some have not tried anything at all because they are so afraid of emotionally damaging their child. They are afraid of breaking their child's spirit if they impose any limits and structure around sleep. As my friend and colleague Peter Grube, a clinical social worker whose private psychotherapy practice focuses on play and talk therapy with children, notes, "Many parents carry around the fear of abandonment and the loss of their child's love. Parents with these insecurities tend to overrespond. They go out of their way to comfort, 'do for,' or overindulge their child, instead of setting clear rules and logical consequences and allowing the child to explore, learn, and sometimes make mistakes. For example, a child's tears at bedtime can be distressing for a family. But if the parents regularly rush in to put the child to sleep, the child will depend on the parents to do this each time he wakes. The development of the child's own self-control, his own ability to self-regulate, may be delayed."

This book gives you a framework for making changes gently and helping you understand why you have to make them. If you understand how and why you are helping your child, you will understand the difference between "crushing" him, harming him, or making him feel abandoned, and making him feel loved. Once you get it, your perspective changes. As you see your child thriving because he's not so sleep deprived all the time, it will become so much easier for you. "If I'm not comfortable with what I'm doing, then I can't live with the crying," said Sam's mom, Nora, a nurse. "But if it's something that will work for my kid, then I don't have trouble listening to him cry."

Resolve Marital Tensions

Marital tensions can also make sleep success elusive, and let's face it, sleep deprivation isn't exactly an aphrodisiac. It's hard to be a good parent or attentive partner when one is irritable, impatient, anxious, depressed, forgetful, unfocused, and just plain exhausted. "I was so tired and so nervous about going back to work when I was so tired," said Nina, Lydia's mother. "I got real snappy with my husband, I didn't care what I looked like, and I couldn't be bothered to brush my hair." Try to recognize that this is transitory, and that when you solve your child's sleep problems, many marital tensions may dissipate.

However, as we all know, some marital problems go much deeper than exhaustion. Indeed, I have found that couples with troubled marriages often have a lot more difficulty in solving their kids' sleep issues than those with basically solid marriages that are experiencing temporary exhaustion-induced stress. Although almost all the families I work with in my private practice do achieve their goals for sleep shaping, those who don't tend to be the couples with serious marital friction. If two people are constantly at loggerheads, it is difficult to give a child a consistent message, and larger marital power struggles might create a tug-of-war over the child's sleep. It's a vicious circle, because exhaustion, depression, and irritation aggravate marital tensions, and the marital tensions will then prolong the exhaustion, creating more depression and irritation. Seek counseling if you feel that there are longer-term issues that need to be resolved in your marriage.

Work as a Team

In my private practice, I always urge both parents to come in for the consultation, and I would hope that both of you acquaint yourself with my program. Ideally, both of you should read and discuss the first few chapters. But even if only one of you actually reads the book, you both need to talk about it and think about it. You may need to make some decisions as a couple, like how quickly to end co-sleeping, or whether you should dream feed, or what to do about the pacifier. You need to know how you are going to support each other when one of you feels too tired or too discouraged or too upset to stick it out. You need a plan for how you will respond to your child's wakening, a plan you are both comfortable with and will be able to carry out, whether it's 10:00 p.m. or 4:00 a.m. "We needed to bounce ideas off each other, how to tailor this program to Kerry," said Laurel, whom you met in Chapter 9. "We needed to figure out how to make it work with what Kerry's used to. And we needed the encouragement from each other. Richard was logical and I was emotional. I guess that's fairly typical but he helped me look at it more practically." Like Laurel and Richard, you should talk this through before you start working on sleep, not after, or else you may end up undermining or even sabotaging each other. If one of you is trying to teach the child to sleep longer between feedings, and the other one is jumping up with a bottle every two hours, the marital repercussions can get ugly.

In addition to talking through these big-picture issues, work out the nuts and bolts of the sleep logistics with your partner. Review who is responsible for which tasks, and at what times. You can take turns being on duty at night, and whoever is "off" can even go to a quiet room with ear plugs. Or you can take shifts, depending on who functions better at which times and who gets back to sleep more easily. For instance, one of you could take the 11:00 p.m. to 3:00 a.m. "get the baby back to sleep" shift, and the other can take 3:00 a.m. to 6:00 a.m. shift, if that's the best fit for your particular internal clocks. Divide up household errands on weekends, so one of you can stay home during naps (and maybe nap yourself) and one of you can do the running around. Alternate weekends, if it suits you. Remember this is a shared responsibility, and even if one of you is a stay-at-home parent and takes on a larger share of sleep-training responsibilities, you should not have to take on 100 percent of it. You can maximize your sleep and minimize your stress if you do this together. Remember that sleep learning is a partnership between you and your child, and between you and your spouse.

Spending time on the blame game will prolong your child's sleep problems and might do long-term damage to your marriage. Make sure that you are responding to your partner calmly and consistently, not fighting about what to do or whose fault it is that your child doesn't already know how to sleep. "This placed a lot of stress on our marriage. We're still recovering," one mom said. "He was blaming me that the baby didn't sleep. He said it was all my fault, that I was establishing patterns that the doctor told me not to. But he didn't help much. He didn't have any solutions. In fact, later when he did try to help some of the time, by then our daughter wouldn't even let him put her to bed."

Another couple, the parents of twins, recalled constant arguments in the middle of the night as they tried to figure out how to carry out my program, arguments that lessened as they grew more comfortable with sleep shaping and learned to discuss it at a more civilized time of day. "We were groggy and the next thing you know we were arguing," the wife said. "We weren't making good decisions. We were talking about divorce—even though divorce wasn't in the picture before or after that. It was just a scary time."

It helps to reward yourself for doing well, as a couple. Getting a good night's sleep in itself may make you feel like you've won the lottery, but beyond that, one of the benefits of a child that knows how to sleep is that you can leave her with a babysitter and take a night out, or maybe let Grandma take her for a slumber party. Four months after working with me, Adele and Geoff took a day off and left Alex, then nineteen months old, with friends who had a toddler of their own. "He stayed with them, he played with them, he even napped there. He went to bed, only fussing a little. Then we came, got him into the car, and drove him home, a half-hour drive. He had his eyes open the whole time, glassy-eyed. When we got home, we put him to bed and he went right to sleep," Adele said. "It was such a huge moment of triumph!"

Shape Your Own Sleep

After months of sleep disruption, parents may find their internal clocks are waking them up every few hours, even after the baby has learned to stay asleep. Some parents awake with jolts of anxiety when they don't hear that familiar sound of 2:00 a.m. tears and wonder if the baby has stopped breathing. (It's very common, so don't feel silly.) Jayne and Paul, whom you met in Chapter 10, Co-sleeping and the Family Bed, found their sleep problems, exacerbated perhaps by the extra layer of anxiety that accompanies having a premature baby, lasted far longer than their infant daughter's! "Cynthia still sometimes cries out in the middle of the night. She gets herself right back to sleep but it would wake us up; we wouldn't be able to get back to sleep," Jayne said. "Both of us have become bad sleepers. I used to sleep like a rock, now I'm always keeping one ear out for her. Both of us have a really hard time falling back to sleep. She can cry out once, and we're awake for hours."

Treat yourself and your spouse with the same tenderness you give your child, and take your own sleep needs just as seriously as you take those of your child. You've spent a lot of time creating an appropriate bedtime routine for your child; make sure you have one for yourself. Give yourself time to unwind and switch your own gears from wake to sleep, and learn to respect your own sleep windows. It can take one to three months for parents' sleep to get back on track, but if you follow the advice here on sleep regulation, it may go faster.

- Go to bed and wake up at around the same time (and while you have young children you might want to set your bedtime earlier than usual). Even on weekends, try not to modify it by more than an hour. Routines "condition" us for sleep, psychologically and physiologically, and the conditioned response then makes it easier to fall asleep and stay asleep.

- Give yourself plenty of time to wind down, letting your body and mind become more relaxed and ready for sleep. Listen to quiet music, take a bath, read a book. Some people find light stretches, meditation, creative visualization, or progressive relaxation helps. This is the adult equivalent of going to bed drowsy but awake!

- If you need to catch up, rather than tinker too much with your nightly sleep schedule, take naps. But either take a short twenty- to thirty-minute nap, or take a longer ninety- to one-hundred-minute nap so you don't wake up during a non-REM sleep cycle and feel groggy. Before I learned that, I used to set the alarm for one hour and wake up feeling lethargic and lousy, like I needed a major infusion of caffeine.

- Make sure your bed and your bedroom are sleep friendly. Your room should be quiet, dark, and secure, and your mattress, pillows, and sheets should be comfortable. Sort out any temperature-control issues with your spouse!

- Exercise at least twenty to thirty minutes three times a week, but try to do it in the morning or during the day, not in the evening. If possible, leave at least three to four hours between strenuous exercise and sleep, and you certainly don't want to work out right before you go to bed.

- Try to get some natural light in the afternoon. Go for a walk, sit in a sunny room; try to get out of the house or at least briefly escape your artificially-lit office cubicle.

- Eat dinner at least three hours before going to bed.

- Reduce your caffeine consumption, and don't have any caffeine for at least six to eight hours before bedtime because it stays in your bloodstream. Caffeine doesn't just mean coffee, it means tea, many sodas, chocolate, and some over-the-counter cold and headache remedies. We become more sensitive to caffeine as we approach our forties.

- Nicotine is a stimulant, so if you haven't stopped smoking, poor sleep is yet another incentive.

- Watch your alcohol consumption. Alcohol may help you fall asleep but more than three to five glasses, even less for some individuals, fragments our sleep. We wake up more often at night and earlier in the morning.

- To figure out how much sleep you need to function optimally, go to bed at the same time every night for three weeks and don't use an alarm clock in the morning. (Of course, this assumes your children are not human alarm clocks, but you can give it a try.) Even if you can't do this until your kids are older and sleeping better, keep it in the back of your mind and try it when you can; it's quite a useful exercise. I learned that I needed nine hours of sleep. No wonder I made a career out of this!

If these steps don't help you, I strongly recommend *The Promise of Sleep*, by Dr. William Dement, the Stanford doctor who more or less invented the modern field of sleep medicine. I have yet to come across a more useful volume on adult sleep.

Withdrawal from Sleep Medication

If you have been taking any sleep medication, either prescription or over the counter, you may experience withdrawal symptoms and a "rebound" effect when you stop taking them—meaning you may have more trouble going to sleep in the short-run before your sleep patterns level out again. This is normal, but give yourself a little extra TLC at bedtime. Talk to your doctor about any specific concerns.

Insomnia

If you suffer from insomnia, it's even more essential that you pay attention to sleep hygiene. If after fifteen minutes or so of trying to sleep, you are still wide awake, get up and go to another room. Read, relax, watch television, whatever soothes you. (Actually, it's a good idea to try to get yourself out of the habit of falling asleep with the TV on, but you can tackle that when your sleep is better regulated and you aren't having as much trouble with insomnia.) When you feel tired, go back to bed. Make sure you follow the general sleep rules above; the advice about getting some natural light in the afternoon is especially useful for insomnia.

Sleep Apnea

If one person snores, two people can suffer sleep interruption. Dr. Dement estimates that nearly 40 percent of the adult population has some sleep apnea, and about half the cases are clinically significant. In addition to snoring, signs of obstructive sleep apnea in adults include pauses in breathing, waking up with headaches, having difficulty concentrating, fighting sleep while driving, feeling tired after eight hours of sleep, and extreme fatigue. Consult your doctor and consider undergoing a sleep study. (Women who are persistently fatigued after pregnancy or as they get older might want to check with their doctors about thyroid hormone levels.)

TRUST YOURSELF AS A PARENT

For my system to work you need to have faith in yourself as a parent. This isn't a one-size-fits-all program so you must trust your intuition and respect your child's individuality. The schedules I give you are guidelines, not decrees, so don't get overly attached to numbers. Watch your child for her sleep cues, and adjust her schedule accordingly. Adapt the program to the realities of your family. Obviously, you can't feed your child dinner at 5:00 and have her in the bath by 6:00 if she is still at day care and you are stuck in traffic. Do the best you can and don't beat yourself up if you can't be perfect. But please try not to fall into the trap of convincing yourself that your child needs less sleep than average. Chances are that at least part of her sleep problem is that she isn't getting enough sleep as it is.

Many moms have told me that their friends or mothers or mothers-in-law have dismissed my advice, telling them that they are being too rigid or that children don't really need to nap, or that all eight-month-olds wake up at 5:00 a.m., or that it's normal for eighteen-month-olds to still wake up twice a night or that they read something in a magazine in the doctor's office that says you are doing everything wrong. Don't let them deter you. They aren't living your life, or parenting your child. "My friends told me it was normal, that kids wake up at night, that you have to lie with them, that all mothers are exhausted," said Amanda, who got her son, Wes, sleeping well at age four through a combination of Sleep Lady behavioral modification and medical treatment for his sleep apnea. "But now my son wakes up happy. He isn't tired, he doesn't struggle anymore. And my friends are still having sleep issues with their kids."

Similarly, you may be one of those parents who read a dozen different parenting books and then can't figure out whose advice to follow. Take a deep breath and listen to your own voice. You know what's right for your child, and you know what you need to do. I believe I give you enough flexibility to make my program fit your needs, your values, and your parenting style. If you like what you've read here, then follow my advice, and give it time. If you don't think it will work—well, I disagree, but go ahead and try something else. *Whatever you do, stick with it.* Don't do one system for two days, decide it won't work, do something else for another two days, and then complain that nothing works. You'd be surprised at how easily you can confuse even a very young child. Consistency counts.

Remember how Carol, Joshua's mom (in Chapter 7, Thirteen to Eighteen Months) thought of herself as a "major rescuer"? She held Joshua all the time, nursed him all the time—and still felt guilty all the time. "I still like some of the ideas about attachment parenting but it messed me up about setting limits; it messed up my boundaries and made me crazy. I was always soothing him but I wasn't always giving him what he needed. I wasn't doing him any favors by always rescuing him," she said. "Sleep is still where Joshua's issues come out; any transition or stress in our lives, any developmental change, we see sleep disturbances. But we can deal with it now. We have a foundation, and he understands it too. As I rescued him less, he became a more confident child and that's my mantra now. I say, 'Joshua, I know you can do this. I know it's hard but you can do it.' And he does it. Changing how I dealt with sleep led to changes in so many other things. It helped me have a lot more faith in myself as a parent."

Marcy too came to see herself as "a very different parent." Initially loath to let her baby cry, equating it with teaching a child to "give up" and suffer, she had gone into overdrive every time Ariella whimpered. But by the time she had a second daughter, Peg, she knew the difference between a cry and a crisis. "Every time Ariella cried, I thought, 'She needs me.' With Peg, I hear a cry and I think, 'She's clean, she's safe, she's warm, she's okay, she'll work it out.' " After three years of motherhood, Marcy trusts in her ability to know when something's wrong, when a child is sick, when a child is in need, and then of course she or Doyle goes in immediately. "I know when a cry means something's up, I know when something's hurting. I can tell the difference. With Ariella, I was the one who created the sleep problems. With Peg, I've set her up for sleep success."

Carol and Marcy have come to understand that sleep requires learning, and learning may require a few false starts, a few moments of frustration, and even a few tears. We can and should help our children, support our children, comfort our children, but we can't airbrush all sadness, anger, or frustration out of their emotional picture. Luckily, learning isn't only about frustration. It's about pride, achievement, a sense of self-worth—and a good night's sleep. When our babies are newborns, they need us to get them to sleep, they need us to make that magic. But then it's time to pass them the wand, to let them make their own magic. Go ahead and do it now. Good night, and sleep tight.

# RESOURCE DIRECTORY

BOOKS

ADD AND SENSORY INTEGRATION BOOKS

Amen, Daniel G. *Healing ADD: The Breakthrough Program That Allows You to See and Heal the 6 Types of ADD* (Berkley Publishing Group, 2002).

Barkley, Russell A., PhD. *Taking Charge of ADHD: The Complete, Authoritative Guide for Parents* (Revised Edition; Guilford Publications, 2000).

Kranowitz, Carol Stock, M.A. *The Out-of-Sync-Child: Recognizing and Coping with Sensory Integration Dysfunction* (Perigee Books, 1998).

ADULT SLEEP

Dement, William C., MD, PhD, and Christopher Vaughan. *The Promise of Sleep: A Pioneer in Sleep Medicine Explores the Vital Connection Between Health, Happiness, and a Good Night's Sleep* (Dell, 2000).

Hauri, Peter, PhD, and Shirley Linde, PhD. *No More Sleepless Nights: A Proven Program to Conquer Insomnia* (John Wiley and Sons, Inc., 1996).

BEDTIME

Bauer, Marion Dane. *Sleep, Little One, Sleep* (Simon & Schuster, 2002).

Bentley, Dawn. *Good Night, Sweet Butterflies* (Simon & Schuster, 2003).

Boynton, Sandra. *Snoozers: 7 Short Short Stories for Lively Little Kids* (Little Simon, 1997).

Brown, Margaret Wise. *A Child's Good Night Book* (HarperCollins, 2000).

————. *Goodnight Moon* (HarperFestival, 1991).

Dillard, Sarah (illustrator). *Ten Wishing Stars: A Countdown to Bedtime Book* (Intervisual Press, 2003).

Fox, Mem. *Time for Bed* (Red Wagon Books, 1997).

Good, Mike, and Steve Shott (photographers). *Good Night, Baby!* (DK Publishing, Inc., 1994).

Hague, Kathleen. *Good Night, Fairies* (Seastar Books, 2002).

Henkes, Kevin. *Owen* (Greenwillow Books, 1993).

Imperato, Teresa. *Good Morning, Good Night!: A Touch & Feel Bedtime Book* (Piggy Toes Press, 2004).

Inkpen, Mick. *It's Bedtime, Wibbly Pig* (Viking, 2004).

Krosocza, Jarrett J. *Good Night, Monkey Boy* (Knopf Books for Young Readers, 2001).

Lewis, Kim. *Good Night Harry* (Candlewick Press, 2004).

McBratney, Sam. *Guess How Much I Love You* (Candlewick Press, 1996).

McCue, Lisa. *Snuggle Bunnies* (Reader's Digest, 2003).

RESOURCE DIRECTORY · 337

McMullen, Nigel. *It's Too Soon!* (Simon & Schuster, 2004).

Meyer, Mercer. *Just Go to Bed* (Golden Books, 2001).

Munsch, Robert. *Love You Forever* (Firefly Books Ltd., 1986).

Paul, Ann Whitford. *Little Monkey Says Good Night* (Farrar, Straus and Giroux, 2003).

Penn, Audrey. *The Kissing Hand* (Child & Family Press, 1993).

Rathmann, Peggy. *Good Night, Gorilla* (G.P. Putnam's Sons, 2000).

———. *10 Minutes till Bedtime* (G.P. Putnam's Sons, 2001).

Santomero, Angela C. *Good Night, Blue: Blue's Clues* (Simon Spotlight/Nick Jr., 1999).

Showers, Paul. *Sleep is for everyone* (HarperTrophy, 1997).

Steinbrenner, Jessica. *My Sleepy Room* (Handprint Books, 2004).

Trapani, Iza. *Twinkle, Twinkle, Little Star* (Charlesbridge Publishing, 1998).

Yolen, Jane, and Mark Teague. *How Do Dinosaurs Say Good Night?* (Blue Sky Press, 2000).

BEDTIME FEARS

Emberley, Ed. *Go Away, Big Green Monster!* (Little, Brown, 1993).

Holabird, Katharine. *Alexander and the Dragon* (Random House Children's Books, 1988).

Leuck, Laura. *Goodnight, Baby Monster* (HarperCollins, 2002).

Meyer, Mercer. *There's an Alligator Under My Bed* (Dial Books, 1987).

Nadeau, Nicole. *Caillou: Bad Dreams* (Chouette, 2000).

Robbins, Beth. *It's OK! Tom's Afraid of the Dark* (DK Publishing, 2001).

Weinberg, Jennifer Liberts. *Slumberfairy Falls* (Random House Books for Young Readers, 2003).

BEDWETTING

Bennett, Howard J. *Waking Up Dry: A Guide to How Children Overcome Bedwetting* (American Academy of Pediatrics, 2005).

Mack, Alison. *Dry All Night: The Picture Book Technique That Stops Bedwetting* (Little, Brown, 1990).

MEDITATION AND GUIDED VISUALIZATION FOR CHILDREN

Garth, Maureen. *Moonbeam: A Book of Meditations for Children* (HarperSanFrancisco, 1993).

———. *Starbright: Meditations for Children* (HarperSanFrancisco, 1991).

NEW SIBLING

Ballard, Robin. *I Used To Be the Baby* (Greenwillow, 2002).

Bourgeois, Paulette, and Brenda Clark. *Franklin's Baby Sister* (Scholastic, 2000).

Brown, Marc. *Arthur's Baby* (Little, Brown, 1990).

Henkes, Kevin. *Julius, the Baby of the World* (HarperTrophy, 1995).

London, Jonathan. *Froggy's Baby Sister* (Viking, 2003).

Meyer, Mercer. *The New Baby* (Golden Books, 2001).

Scheidl, Gerda Marie. *Tommy's New Sister* (North-South Books, 1999).

PACIFIERS

Murphy, Jill. *The Last Noo-Noo* (Walker Books, 1997).

———. *The Story of Binkyland* (www.binkyland.com).

TRANSITIONING TO A BED

Beck, Sheryl. *Going to My Big Bed!: Barney's Little Lessons* (Lyrick Studios, 2002).

Bunting, Eve. *My Big Boy Bed* (Houghton Mifflin Co., 2003).

MUSIC FOR RELAXATION AND BEDTIME ROUTINE

Ackerman, William. *The Opening of Doors* (1992).

Baby's First: Lullabies & Sleepytime (2000).

Baby's First Lullabies (1999).

Disney Babies: Lullaby (1999).

Falkner, Jason. *Bedtime with the Beatles: Instrumental Versions of Classic Beatles Songs* (2001).

Golden Slumbers: A Father's Lullaby (2002).

Malia, Tina. *Lullaby Favorites: Music for Little People* (1997).

Music for Babies. *Sleepy Baby* (2003).

Parents: The Lullaby Album (1993).

Sleeplullabies.com (various titles).

Solnik, Tanja. *From Generation to Generation: A Legacy of Lullabies* (1993; in Yiddish, Ladino, and Hebrew).

Stroman, Paige. *Mother and Child* (2001).

WEBSITES

National Sleep Foundation
www.sleepfoundation.org
The website of this non-profit group addresses numerous sleep issues for children and adults and includes the group's new childhood sleep guidelines.
American Academy of Sleep Medicine (formerly the American Sleep Disorders Association)
www.aasmnet.org
The website of this membership group of doctors and other professionals contains links to sleep resources and research and also can direct patients to accredited sleep disorder centers (not all of which treat children). Click "Patient Resources" to see a list of sleep disorder clinics.

American Academy of Pediatrics
www.AAP.org

Consumer Product Safety Commission
www.cpsc.gov

Index